LOST TWIN CITIES

LOST TWIN CITIES

Larry Millett

Minnesota Historical Society Press · St. Paul

Published with funds provided to the Minnesota Historical Society by the Elmer L. and Eleanor Andersen Publications Endowment Fund, Leonard Parker & Associates, and the *Saint Paul Pioneer Press*.

Minnesota Historical Society Press
St. Paul 55102

This publication is printed on a coated paper manufactured on an acid-free base to ensure its long life.

Printed in Canada
10 9 8 7 6

International Standard Book Number
0-87351-273-1 Paper
0-87351-274-X Cloth

Library of Congress Cataloging-in-Publication Data

Millett, Larry, 1947-
    Lost Twin Cities / Larry Millett.
        p.   cm.
    Includes bibliographical references (p.   ) and index.
    ISBN 0-87351-274-X (cloth : acid-free paper).
    ISBN 0-87351-273-1 (paper : acid-free paper)
    1. Architecture—Minnesota—Minneapolis—Mutilation, defacement,
etc. 2. Architecture—Minnesota—Saint Paul—Mutilation, defacement,
etc. 3. Minneapolis (Minn.)—Buildings, structures, etc. 4. Saint Paul
(Minn.)—Buildings, structures, etc. I. Title.
    NA735.M5M55 1992
    720'.9776'579—dc20   92-10460
                                                                  CIP

CONTENTS

TO STACEY

ACKNOWLEDGMENTS

This book was five years in the making, and it is fair to say that had I known how much work it was going to be, I probably would have gone fishing instead. Fortunately, I had the help of many people to keep me going through the long years of research and writing. Some of the most valuable help came from James Roe, who provided expert research assistance at a critical stage of the project by examining building records in St. Paul and Minneapolis. John Mallander, who like me remembers what downtown Minneapolis was like before skyscrapers gobbled up everything, helped with newspaper research and always came ready with a roll of quarters to keep those insatiable library copy machines humming.

A number of local historians also provided crucial assistance. First and foremost is Paul Clifford Larson, now executive director of the Gardner Museum of Architecture & Design in Quincy, Illinois. It is fair to say this book owes more to him than anyone else. Paul, who recently completed (with Jeffrey Hess) a history of St. Paul architecture that will be a fine companion piece to this volume, provided help throughout my labors. He shared with me his vast knowledge of Twin Cities architects and architecture, helped me locate information and photographs, read the manuscript, and offered numerous valuable insights. He also saved me from several egregious errors, for which I am grateful. Of course, whatever mistakes still lurk in this book are mine alone.

Jim Sazevich, St. Paul historian extraordinaire, provided significant help during the early stages of my research and also read the completed manuscript, offering a number of helpful comments and corrections. Rosemary Palmer, John Wickre, and Nicholas Westbrook, among others in the local community of historians, also were on hand to assist at various stages of this project. To all go my thanks.

Anyone who sets sail on the vast sea of history can only do so with good librarians at the helm. Alan Lathrop, curator of the Northwest Architectural Archives, was, as usual, extremely helpful in answering obscure questions, of which my research produced an inexhaustible supply. I also wish to thank the staffs of St. Paul Public Library and Minneapolis Public Library (especially the patient and friendly people who care for the Minneapolis History Collection), the Hennepin County Historical Society, and the Ramsey County Historical Society. At the Minneapolis Institute of Arts, I received valuable assistance from Christian Peterson, associate curator in the department of photography.

At the Minnesota Historical Society, Jean A. Brookins, assistant director for publications and research, and Deborah L. Miller, research supervisor, were instrumental in awarding me a research grant funded by the state of Minnesota, and John McGuigan, former managing editor of the Minnesota Historical Society Press, offered me early encouragement. Bonnie Wilson, Robert Hoag, Jon Walstrom, Alan Woolworth, and many other members of the staff made my research work pleasurable. Also helpful at MHS were Alan Ominsky, who helped select photographers, Deborah Swanson, who handled all the photo orders, Kathy Mahoney, who willingly keyed numerous changes in the manuscript, and Phil Hutchens, Sarah Jordan, and Bill Johnson of the photo lab, who produced the best images possible from old prints.

I also received aid from more distant locales.

In Chicago, Tim Samuelson—master of all Windy City lore—answered numerous questions large and small about Chicago architects who worked in the Twin Cities. And at the New York Life Insurance Company, David Sanders kindly provided information about that company's splendid buildings in St. Paul and Minneapolis.

At the *St. Paul Pioneer Press*, where I have worked for twenty years, librarian Linda James allowed me unlimited access to the newspaper's excellent collection of historic St. Paul photographs, some of which appear in this book. Deborah Howell, the paper's executive editor during the time I was writing this book, granted leaves of absence and was supportive of my efforts, as was Walker Lundy, the current editor of the *Pioneer Press*. Some of my colleagues at the paper, particularly George Beran—a St. Paulite of the old school—shared their detailed knowledge of the city with me. A book needs an editor, of course, and at the Minnesota Historical Society Press I was fortunate enough to work (for the second time) with Sally Rubinstein, who as usual did her best to keep my wayward prose in check and insert commas where God intended them to be.

Finally, I owe a debt of gratitude to my wife, Stacey, who in a sense married this book when she married me in 1987. Now that this book is done, we can both rest more easily, especially since our beautiful new daughter, Alexandra, is sleeping through the night.

The Gateway District where Hennepin and Nicollet avenues converge, about 1930; all of the buildings facing the park have been lost

INTRODUCTION

On December 18, 1961, wrecking trucks rumbled through the streets of downtown Minneapolis toward a rendezvous with the past. Their destination was the corner of Third Street and Second Avenue South, where for seventy-one years the Metropolitan Building (originally known as the Northwestern Guaranty Loan Building) had towered above its neighbors like a "small red mountain." But with Minneapolis in the midst of the greatest urban renewal project in its history, the Metropolitan was about to come down, a victim of age, politics, and ideology.[1]

Once, it had been the pride of the city, the building that more than any other announced to the world that Minneapolis had come of age. "Here there has been erected . . . the most magnificent office building in the whole round world," gushed the *Minneapolis Journal* when the great sandstone structure opened on May 31, 1890. The inaugural was a glittering extravaganza that drew thousands of visitors. "As early as 7 o'clock [in the evening] the throngs began to converge toward the building," reported another newspaper. "Every street in the city seemed to lead to it, as all roads in ancient times are said to have led to Rome. Motors, electric cars, street cars, steam cars and hacks deposited their loads before the marble entrance." Amid the bright glow of arc lamps and the aroma of fresh cut flowers, visitors strolled along the building's glass floors (which occasioned some fright), toured its four hundred shops and offices, and fought off vertigo to gaze across the central light court—a twelve-story-high fantasy in glass and iron that was among the greatest spaces of its kind ever

built in America. Many members of the crowd eventually found their way to the rooftop garden, where they danced the night away beneath the stars, enjoying the "incomparably grand" view.[2]

By the early 1950s, however, the Metropolitan no longer seemed so grand a place, in part because of the company it kept. The building had the misfortune to stand at the edge of the Gateway District, which by midcentury was the city's most visible example of urban blight, a broken landscape of pawnshops, cheap hotels, brothels, nightclubs, and bars. Yet for all its squalor, the Gateway District was also a treasure trove of nineteenth-century commercial architecture, with the Metropolitan its crown jewel.[3]

Metropolitan Building, 1904, viewed from Fourth Street and Second Avenue South

1

Gateway District, about 1960

No one in Minneapolis city government saw this side of the Gateway, however. All they saw was a fetid slum that, unless cleared, could forever poison attempts to reinvigorate an aging, dormant downtown rapidly losing business and population to the suburbs. These concerns were genuine. The Gateway was in desperate need of redevelopment. But the solution chosen by the city was an extreme one—total destruction. This strategy of obliteration received final approval in 1957 when Minneapolis Mayor P. K. Peterson went to Washington, D.C., and convinced federal officials to help fund the ambitious project. Five years and many millions of dollars later, much of the Gateway District, including the Metropolitan Building, was gone. All told, nearly two hundred buildings spread over seventeen square blocks were demolished. This amounted to 40 percent of the city's historic central business district. The Metropolitan was among the last

buildings in the Gateway to fall, and it did not go down without a fight.[4]

A loose coalition of architects, historians, and people who simply loved the building did their best to keep it standing. Their efforts proved fruitless. Despite the building's architectural and historical significance, it had few friends in high places, and the temper of the times was against it. Several years earlier, a prominent academic historian, displaying the bias of the era, had written that "perhaps no single building by a Minneapolis architect is worthy of measurement or preservation." Such thinking was endemic in the 1950s and 1960s, when old buildings generally were viewed as aesthetic embarrassments, worthless relics cluttering the road to progress. An attorney for the Minneapolis Housing and Redevelopment Authority called the Metropolitan "a monstrosity in the eyes of most observers." The Minnesota Supreme Court, in an opinion permitting destruction of the building, was equally unsympathetic. Allowing the Metropolitan to stand, the court said, "would have an unfavorable effect upon the value of surrounding property." Other arguments against the building—that it was too old, too dangerous (because of the threat of fire spreading up through the light court), and too poorly designed for modern use—could all have been answered a decade later when historic renovation became commonplace.[5]

The day before the wrecking crews arrived, a newspaper reporter interviewed fifty-eight-year-old Wally Marotzke, who for twenty years had been the building's engineer. "I'm not gonna watch 'em rip it down," Marotzke told the reporter. "I don't think I could. But I'll tell you one thing: The future generations are gonna read about this building and they'll see some of the buildings they're putting up here and they'll damn us, they will, for tearing down the Met."[6]

THE METROPOLITAN BUILDING is perhaps the most famous inhabitant of Lost Twin Cities, a community of architectural ghosts that grows larger by the year. The size of this community is astonishing. Its dimensions appear most clearly on old panoramas, insurance maps, and real estate atlases. The panoramas—painted aerial views done mainly in the 1870s and 1880s by itinerant artists—are especially stunning. They show how dense the two cities once were at street level, how buildings of all shapes and sizes crowded along the downtown streets. But the panoramas also lie because their artists neatly excised from view the unbelievable mess that was part of urban life in nineteenth-century America.[7]

Atlases provide a more accurate picture. Among the best were those published by the G. M. Hopkins Company in 1884–85 when the Twin Cities were in the midst of an unprecedented building boom. Filled with carefully drawn maps intended to chart the progress of real estate speculation, these atlases show the precise location of streets, buildings, bridges, and parks throughout the two cities. The downtown maps

Metropolitan Building in the last stages of demolition; Sheraton-Ritz Hotel and parking ramp (right center) are under construction

Aerial panorama of Minneapolis, 1885, showing the city hall in the center (detail)

Aerial panorama of St. Paul, 1883; note the Capitol toward the top (detail)

are among the most intriguing. They depict hundreds of buildings, ranging from small wooden shanties to substantial brick office blocks to such recently completed giants as the Ryan Hotel in St. Paul and the Union Depot in Minneapolis. Virtually all of these buildings—the lavish as well as the lowly—are gone. Assumption School (1864) and Church (1874) and First Baptist Church (1875) are among the few buildings of consequence pictured in the Hopkins atlas that still survive in downtown St. Paul. In Minneapolis the survivors are limited to a few industrial buildings, now either vacant or adapted to new uses. The Hopkins atlases also show streets, parks, and entire neighborhoods that have vanished with hardly a trace.[8]

The pace of change in St. Paul and Minneapolis has been so rapid that it is not uncommon to find downtown lots that are already on their fourth or fifth generation of buildings. Significant pockets of old buildings remain, of course, especially in the warehouse districts of both cities. But even these "historic" warehouses are often third generation structures, built on the ruins of the past.

Many of the Twin Cities' lost buildings have been almost entirely forgotten, while others remain vividly etched in thousands of memories. A few—the Metropolitan, the Ryan Hotel, the two New York Life buildings, the Minnesota (later Radio City) Theater, the John Merriam and Samuel Gale mansions—were works of national importance. But most had a purely local significance, although their architectural quality was often considerably higher than what replaced them.

Lost Twin Cities is populated by all kinds of buildings, from every rank and station and every era, although many of its most distinguished citizens date from the boom time of the 1880s and early 1890s. It comes as no surprise that very little survives from the 1840s and 1850s, when the Twin Cities were founded and virtually every-

thing was built quickly and of wood. But it is surprising to find how many twentieth-century buildings are gone and how brief their life spans sometimes were. The Minnesota Theater, built in 1928, survived just thirty-one years despite, or perhaps because of, its costliness and grandeur. The record in this category appears to be held by a neoclassic building that the First National Bank of Minneapolis erected in 1906 and tore down only eight years later to make room for something bigger. James J. Hill's first house in St. Paul survived just thirteen years; Norman Kittson's, only twenty-four.

What follows is an effort to reconstruct, in words and illustrations, a lost urban world. It is not a formal architectural history of Minneapolis and St. Paul. Rather, it is a kind of mosaic, a narrative made up of bits and pieces retrieved from a largely forgotten past. Its theme is memory. Whatever else they may be, cities are structures in time, where past and present mingle and the future gapes out from empty holes awaiting yet another round of development. But time moves with a special and destructive speed in American cities, often erasing our monuments before we have a chance to appreciate them.

Buildings, as writers since antiquity have understood, occupy a prominent place in those landscapes of memory we all construct as a means of understanding the world. "The ambition of the old Babel builders was well directed for this world," John Ruskin once wrote. "There are but two strong conquerors of the forgetfulness of men, Poetry and Architecture."[9] Few of us, it seems, read poetry any more, but many of our memories, whether for good or ill, remain deeply colored by buildings we knew as children.

I particularly remember the first time my father took me to the top of the Metropolitan Building, how incomparably grand its atrium seemed, and how small the people looked in the lobby eleven stories below. I remember, too, the old church I attended in north Minneapolis, where I grew up. Although I later came to realize that this church was a copy of a hundred other copies of a French Gothic cathedral, I thought it in my youth to be a splendid and mysterious place, with its great altar of creamy white marble, its frescoed walls, and its high vaulted ceiling hidden in clouds of incense. I can also remember, with a precision that startles me forty years later, the houses on the block where I lived, from the big white duplex next door (there were Ionic columns, I think, on the front porch) to the Cape Cod bungalow down the street, where a man lived who did not at all like children wandering through his yard.

Yet even though this book is a celebration of memory, it is by no means a lament for some golden age now lost forever. Nostalgia is memory with its teeth out, which means it cannot bite, the way real memory often does. Although many buildings and places of great beauty and charm have been lost in the Twin Cities, so, too, has

The boxcar chapel in Swede Hollow, St. Paul, about 1950

much that was ugly, mean, and inhuman. And, of course, Lost Twin Cities also includes many ordinary buildings used by ordinary people in the course of their lives. Books about vanished architecture too often are written as thinly disguised histories of high society, presenting a numbing succession of grand hotels, palatial mansions, and elegant clubhouses inhabited by the rich and famous. To some extent this is unavoidable, since fancy buildings—like fancy people—tend to expire in well-documented fashion, thereby assuring themselves a place in the history books. But riverfront shanties, "blind pig" taverns, and freight cars doubling as churches are also part of the architectural history of the Twin Cities, and I have done my best to include at least a few such humble structures in this narrative.

In selecting buildings, structures, and places to include in this book, I have applied criteria similar to those used for nominations to the National Register of Historic Places. This means I have tried to select buildings that have architectural significance, that were known and used by large numbers of people, that were associated with prominent historical figures, that were typical of once-common building types, or that show, in some sense, how the other half lived. In a few cases, I have chosen one particular building over another simply because better photographs or drawings were available. Yet any selection process inevitably is subjective, based on personal tastes and prejudices, and there undoubtedly are deserving buildings that have been left out.

The scope of this book is limited to the downtowns of St. Paul and Minneapolis and their immediate residential environs. For St. Paul, my boundaries largely follow the ring of hills that surround downtown. Included within this area are Irvine Park, parts of West Seventh Street, lower Summit Avenue, Capitol Heights, portions of the Dayton's Bluff and Railroad Island neighborhoods, and the lower West Side. For Minneapolis, this book takes in an area roughly

Workman removing a stone head from the old Ramsey County jail, 1980

bounded by Plymouth Avenue on the north, Interstate 94 on the west and south, and Interstate 35W on the south and east. I have also included a few buildings on the east side of the Mississippi River opposite downtown. However, I have fudged these boundaries in places, extending them to take in the Lowry Hill area and some of the mansions along Park and Portland avenues as far south as Twenty-fourth Street.

I set these territorial limits partly as a matter of convenience, since trying to encompass all of Lost Twin Cities seemed to present a task beyond my reserves of time and energy. But it is also true that downtown is where most of the largest and best buildings in the Twin Cities have been constructed. Moreover, the rate of change has been more rapid in and around the two downtowns than elsewhere, accounting for a large number of lost buildings. Obviously many important lost buildings fall outside the artificial boundaries I have established, but they will have to be the subject of another book.

I have generally tried to locate lost buildings on the basis of street corners or blocks rather than by numerical address, since numbering systems in both St. Paul and Minneapolis have changed over the years. Locating buildings by corner generally poses no problem in downtown St. Paul. But it can be tricky in downtown Minneapolis because not all sources agree as to whether certain streets—Hennepin Avenue is the most notable example—run east-west or north-south. (In fact, Hennepin could fairly be assigned either direction, since it is oriented almost at a perfect diagonal to the compass points.) Uncertainty over street orientation can cause confusion as to what constitutes, say, the northwest corner of Fourth and Hennepin. Let there be no such confusion. I consider Hennepin, Nicollet, and other major downtown avenues (except Washington) to have a north-south orientation, while numbered street such as Seventh are considered to be east-west. All downtown corners are identified on this basis.

Finally, a note on dates: The completion date for all buildings in this book refers to the year in which the structure was first occupied, as far as that can be determined.

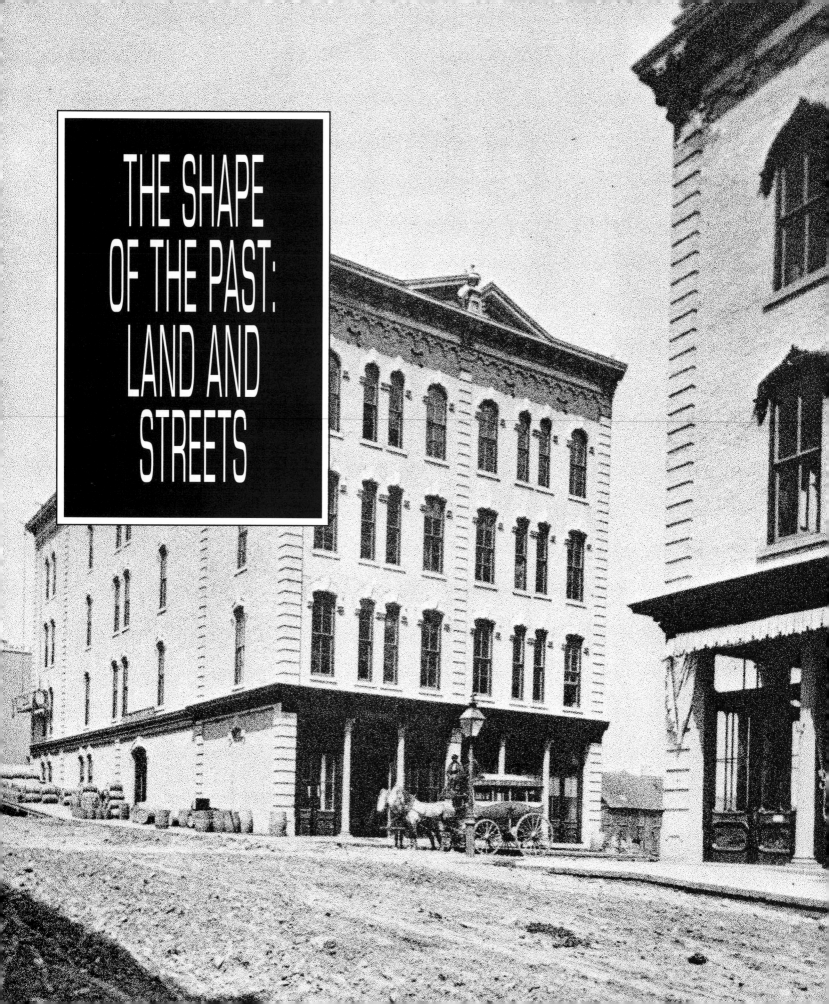

THE SHAPE OF THE PAST: LAND AND STREETS

On a clear October day in 1883 an enterprising newspaper reporter climbed the 250 steps to the top of the new Minnesota State Capitol at Tenth and Wabasha streets in St. Paul. After assuring his readers that the stairs offered numerous "breathing places for the fat or short-winded," the reporter went on to describe the view from the Capitol's two-hundred-foot-high tower. St. Paul, he said, was "a city of nooks and dells and hidden crannies; of mounds where foliage hides the handiwork of man; of bluffs which wind in graceful steeps and slopes."[1]

St. Paul was, in fact, unusually hilly by midwestern standards, so much so that the city at one time maintained eighty-eight public stairways to help its citizens move up and down. The site chosen for the city's downtown was especially troublesome because of its irregular and constricting terrain. Not surprisingly, the site seems to have been selected for no particular reason other than convenience. St. Paul's founders were, for the most part, people who had been evicted from the nearby Fort Snelling military reservation. Beginning in the late 1830s, this mixed lot of outcasts—among them French-Canadian traders and trappers, several Irish-born soldiers, and Scottish and Swiss refugees from the failed Selkirk colony in Manitoba—began staking claims to what is now the site of downtown St. Paul. There was not a city planner among them, but the group included a notorious whiskey dealer, Pierre (Pig's Eye) Parrant; a murderous former soldier, Edward Phelan; and a sufficient number of other disreputable characters to assure St. Paul a colorful history.[2]

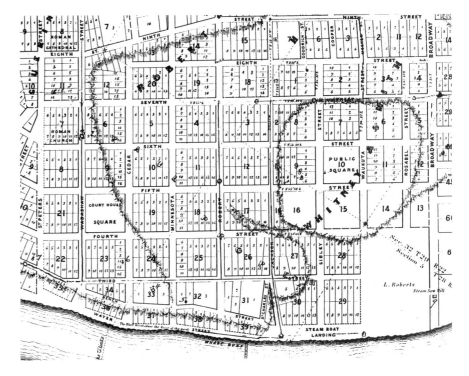

George Nichols's 1851 map of St. Paul, showing the topography of the downtown area; the large circle represents Baptist Hill

What this unlikely crew of city builders found was a landscape shaped by complex geological forces. Underlying the downtown area were layers of soft, white St. Peter sandstone, gray Platteville limestone, and dark Decorah shale. Most of this sedimentary rock, deposited by ancient seas, was buried under glacial drift, which formed high, gravel hills, such as Baptist Hill (gone) in Lowertown and Williams Hill (also gone) in the area known as Railroad Island. The wild card in this highly irregular landscape was the Mississippi River, which cut a series of deep valleys through the area before finally settling on its present course. Among these "buried valleys," as the geologists call them, were those of Trout Brook and Phalen Creek (site of Swede Hollow).[3]

This interplay of geological forces over millions of years gave downtown St. Paul the shape of a large, slightly tilted bowl. The edges were formed by steep bluffs on the west (now the site of Summit Avenue), sweeping hills to the north (where the State Capitol now stands), Trout Brook–Phalen Creek valley to the east (later filled in by railroad tracks and highways), and the Mississippi River, flowing beneath high cliffs to the south. There were two easy points of access from the river. One was the Lower Landing at the foot of present-day Jackson Street and the other was about half a mile upstream near the foot of Chestnut Street. These entry points shaped the early character of the city, producing two distinct communities—Lowertown and Upper Town—which initially maintained such strongly separate identities that they even kept different time.[4]

The sloping plateau that forms most of downtown St. Paul was originally drained by a series of small streams, including one that tumbled over a waterfall near what is now Tenth and Cedar streets, flowed through a lake at Eighth and Robert, and then entered a steep ravine before joining the Mississippi. A mixture of hardwood and evergreen forest and open prairie covered the plateau. The native forest included a magnificent stand of elms and other trees around the Upper Landing. Some must have been gigantic, given their great age. A tamarack cut down in 1854 near the Upper Landing was six hundred years old, according to an early settler who counted the rings. It is barely possible now to imagine what this world was like, so completely has it been altered. One thing is certain: St. Paul was quiet, since early residents could, on certain spring days, hear the roar of the Falls of St. Anthony eight miles away.[5]

St. Paul's rugged topography was to prove both a blessing and a curse. The city's setting, high above one of the most dramatic bends on the entire course of the Mississippi River, was indeed impressive. Boosters of the city never tired of extolling its natural beauty, in prose not always notable for its understatement. "Enthroned upon an amphitheater of circling terraces, calmly presiding over the Father of Waters, St. Paul deserves the meter of a majestic ode," wrote one chronicler of the city's history. What these apologists inevitably failed to mention was that much of downtown St. Paul's natural beauty disappeared soon after civilization arrived. To make room for the growing city, ravines and bottomlands were filled, hills leveled, lakes drained, streams diverted, and bluffs shaved away, with no environmental impact statements required. In fact, despite its romantic appeal, the city's up-and-down terrain inspired more complaints than paeans. "The drawbacks to building operations in St. Paul . . . are perhaps greater than in any other city in the United States," claimed a newspaper in 1881. "In some places great hills have had to be leveled to make way for the proposed building, while in other areas heavy piling has had to be done to secure a firm foundation."[6]

Wholesale alteration of downtown St. Paul's landscape required only about forty years. By 1880 the forests were gone, as was the waterfall at Tenth and Cedar, the lake at Eighth and Robert, and the deep ravine leading to the Mississippi. Gone, too, was Baptist Hill, where pioneer residents had watched for arriving steamboats and fired cannons to celebrate Union victories in the Civil War. The hill, roughly fifty feet above the present level of Mears Park, was sliced into pieces by deep road cuts in the 1870s, and then slowly hauled away, mostly as fill for the railroads coming through Trout Brook valley. "It [the hill] was just what was needed in other places near by, but not there," explained one historian in 1908, neatly summing up the strategy of cut and fill that so completely transformed the downtown landscape.[7]

Road and railway construction was behind much of this transformation. The city's topography made transportation difficult, and getting people in and out of downtown was to be a perpetual headache. Road building was a problem from the start because of steep grades—up to 20 percent in extreme cases. As the city grew, costly regrading projects were undertaken on East Seventh Street, St. Anthony Hill (also called Cathedral or Summit Hill), and the West Side in order to make ascent by streetcar possible. The problem of moving streetcars up the 16 percent grade of the Selby Avenue Hill was not completely solved until 1907, when a new tunnel reduced the grade.[8]

But it was the railroads, above all else, that reshaped the look of St. Paul. This was especially true along the downtown riverfront, which the city treated as a handy corridor for railroads and little else. A correspondent for *Harper's Weekly* summed up the city's attitude this way: "St. Paul cares about as much for the picturesque and poetic side of the river traffic as she does for the riparian laws of the Hottentots . . . her interest is the one interest of business." In order to squeeze more tracks along the Mississippi valley, which offered the easiest grades through St. Paul, the railroads cut back bluffs where possible and resorted to filling in the river channel elsewhere, destroying seven small islands in the process. By 1900 this extensive filling had narrowed the river by as much as one thousand feet in parts of the downtown area.[9]

Railroad development had an equally dramatic impact on Trout Brook, once a clear, fast stream that flowed past wooded hills and into a wide valley, often called "the bottomless bog," before emptying into the Mississippi east of downtown. In 1862 Edmund Rice, one of St. Paul's prominent pioneers, built a large house on a hill overlooking the brook, which he dammed to create a small lake. Descriptions of his estate, located near what is now Mississippi and York streets, suggest how lovely this part of St. Paul must have been. "There was much natural beauty to the land," Rice's last surviving daughter wrote in 1953, "and

A somewhat shortened Baptist Hill is visible at far left, up the street from McQuillan's store at Third and Sibley in the early 1870s.

Road grading on Wacouta Street near Baptist Hill, about 1905

Trout Brook estate of Edmund Rice, about 1875

Father had a German gardner [*sic*] who added to this beauty by his landscaping and making many gravel walks and rustic bridges. A plum orchard near the brook was a perfect fairy land in the spring when in blossom."[10]

By 1883 the estate was gone, sold to the railroads. The valley provided the only easy route through the bluffs into downtown, and within six years the Northern Pacific and the St. Paul, Minneapolis & Manitoba (later Great Northern) railroads had built so many tracks that the brook itself could barely be seen. "Every inch of ground [in the valley] is utilized," reported a newspaper in 1889. "At many points the bluffs have been so cut down that retaining walls of massive masonry were needed to keep the surrounding country from sliding into the abyss." As the railroads expanded into Lowertown, they also claimed much of a historic neighborhood that in the 1860s and 1870s had been the city's most exclusive residential enclave.[11]

Railroad and highway building also destroyed two of St. Paul's most distinctive natural landmarks—Carver's Cave and Fountain Cave—both along the Mississippi River. Carver's Cave was at the base of a sandstone cliff in the Dayton's Bluff district just below present-day Short Street. Known and used for centuries by Native Americans, the cavern was named for the English explorer Jonathan Carver, who visited the site in May 1767. Carver, never famous for his devotion to veracity, described the cave as having "amazing depth" and containing a lake "which is transparent, and extends an unsearchable distance." The cave was sufficiently impressive to attract other explorers, including Lieutenant Zebulon M. Pike in 1806, Major Stephen H. Long in 1817, and Lieutenant John C. Frémont in 1838. By the time of Long's visit, however, sand slides had already begun to obstruct the cave's entrance, which soon closed up entirely.[12]

But the most significant damage to the cave

occurred in 1885 when the Chicago, Burlington and Quincy Railroad, in need of more tracks, sliced seventy-five feet off the cliffs at Dayton's Bluff. This action destroyed the front part of the cave, obliterating its historic entrance. What remained of the cave was reopened briefly in 1913 and found to contain at least two large chambers, one occupied by a lake more than 150 feet long. Plans were soon announced to turn the cave into a public park, but they never materialized. Although there have been periodic revivals of interest, the cave remains inaccessible today.[13]

Fountain Cave was at the other end of downtown St. Paul, along the Mississippi River near the foot of Randolph Street. Major Long in 1817 found this winding cavern, with its "fine chrystal [sic] stream," to be "far more curious & interesting" than Carver's Cave. It was at Fountain Cave that Pig's Eye Parrant, the one-eyed whiskey dealer, set up shop in 1838. But he was evicted two years later by the military authorities at Fort Snelling, who did not appreciate his liberal sales policies. After Parrant's departure, the cave— sometimes referred to as Spring Cave—was used as a storehouse for many years. It also became something of a tourist attraction, cited in early guidebooks and often pictured in stereographic views.[14]

Carved out of sandstone, the cave was reached via a winding ravine where the spring-fed stream noted by Long tumbled over a small cascade before emptying into the Mississippi. The cave itself was more than a thousand feet long, with an entrance twenty-five feet wide and twenty feet high. By the 1890s industrial pollution had already fouled the cave and its once pristine waters, while railroad tracks made access difficult. Even so, the cave survived until about 1960 when it was destroyed for construction of Shepard Road.[15]

The Native Americans who had first explored these great caves, and all the land that later became St. Paul and Minneapolis, were also swift victims of progress. They have left nothing of their built world behind, except for the burial mounds that still crown a high bluff on St. Paul's East Side. The first humans to visit the site of the Twin Cities may have arrived as early as 6000 B.C. Later, beginning in about 1000 B.C., the Woodland and Mississippian peoples established themselves in parts of Minnesota and may have been the ancestors of the two tribal groups—the Dakota and Ojibway—that dominated the region when whites first appeared on the scene. By 1800 what is now southern Minnesota was occupied by the Mdewakanton and Wahpekute bands of the Dakota, who had gradually been pushed south in wars with the Ojibway. An 1834 census showed about two thousand members of the Mdewakan-

Carver's Cave, about 1875

Fountain Cave, about 1875

only be called geographic destiny. The singular feature that drew settlers was the Falls of St. Anthony, the only major cataract on the Mississippi River and the largest source of water power in mid-America. Like so many other prominent natural features in the Twin Cities, the falls were quickly transformed by civilization and today retain little of their original beauty.[18]

At first, it looked as though the center of a new metropolis might be on the east side of the falls in the village of St. Anthony, which was platted in 1849, about a decade after its first settlers arrived and two years after Franklin Steele had opened the first privately owned sawmill to exploit the power of the falls. Steele, like most of the early settlers of the Minneapolis area, was a transplanted New Englander with an eye for the main chance. But he picked the wrong side of the river, because the west bank was where the greatest growth would occur.

Development along the west bank had begun as early as 1821 when saw and grist mills were built to supply the garrison at Fort Snelling. This side of the river had been part of the fort's military reservation since being acquired by Pike in 1805. Private development technically was forbidden, as was establishing a residence on military land. But by 1850 John Stevens had talked the government into allowing him to obtain 160 acres near the falls (on what is now the site of downtown Minneapolis) in exchange for operating a ferry. Soon, other land-hungry pioneers filtered into the area and made claims, even though this remained illegal. Eventually the rights of these squatters—at least three hundred by 1854—were recognized, and in 1855 the whole west bank was officially opened for settlement. By this time, Stevens and others had already platted the new town of Minneapolis, which was incorporated in 1856.[19]

The site was quite flat, with a mixture of forest and prairie typical of the region, and it proved far easier to develop than St. Paul. "The land sloped

ton band, who by that time had already lost a small chunk of their homeland and were soon to lose it all.[16]

The taking of land began in 1805 when Zebulon Pike acquired the future site of Fort Snelling at the confluence of the Mississippi and Minnesota rivers. As part of their treaty with Pike, the Dakota also ceded the land around St. Anthony Falls, including much of what is now Minneapolis. A far bigger land grab came in 1837 when a treaty was negotiated with the Dakota and Ojibway for a large section of what is now east-central Minnesota and western Wisconsin. The future site of St. Paul was included in this treaty. The next major treaty, signed in 1851 at Mendota, removed another huge piece of the Dakota world, including the rest of what would later become Minneapolis.[17]

IF ST. PAUL'S site was determined more or less by accident, Minneapolis was the result of what can

*The Falls of
St. Anthony, 1875*

back gently from the bluff below the falls and from the low banks above and the site was an admirable one for the economical development of a large city," a magazine reporter wrote years later. Stevens, who in 1850 had built the first house on the present site of downtown Minneapolis, left behind a good description of the land around the Falls of St. Anthony before it was transformed by the hand of progress. "The scenery was picturesque," he wrote, "with woodland, prairie, and oak-openings. Cold springs, silvery lakes, and clear streams abounded. . . . The banks of the river above the Falls were skirted with a few pines, some white birch, many hard maples, and several elms, with many native grape-vines climbing over them, which formed fine bowers up to the first creek above the Falls." Farther back from the river, Stevens recalled, the land was covered with oak, "thickets of hazel and prickly pear," rolling prairies, and "a dense growth of poplar that had escaped the annual

prairie fires." Another pioneer, expressing a regret that always seemed to accompany settlement, wrote of the site of Minneapolis: "Only those who saw it, in its pristine grace and loveliness before [white] man had laid his defacing hand upon it, can have any conception of its surpassing charm."[20]

This unblemished landscape was to change rapidly over the next few decades, and nowhere was the transformation greater than at the falls themselves. The falls had been formed ten thousand years earlier, by a certain irony, in the heart of what later became downtown St. Paul. There, the vast torrent known as the Glacial River Warren (ancestor of the much smaller Minnesota River) encountered an old, deep valley and plunged into it, creating what must have been one of the most stupendous waterfalls in history. This falls—estimated to have been twice as high and wide as Niagara—immediately began receding upstream, a process caused by the steady erosion of soft sandstone under the falls' harder limestone cap. The falls eventually split at Fort Snelling, where the Minnesota and Mississippi join. The Mississippi segment of the falls kept right on moving upstream, at a rate of about four feet per year, gradually losing height but leaving in its wake a low, fast channel strewn with massive slabs of limestone, thereby assuring St. Paul its position as the head of river navigation.[21]

By the time Father Louis Hennepin saw and named the falls (then a mile below their present location) in 1680, they were probably no higher than twenty feet. Even so, they must have been quite spectacular. Major Stephen Long, who led an expedition that visited the falls in 1817, wrote in his diary on July 17 of that year: "The murmuring of the Cascade, the roaring of the river, and the thunder of the cataract, all contributed to render the scene the most interesting and magnificent of any I ever before witnessed." The Dakota had perhaps the most evocative name for the great cataract. They called it *Miniara,* usually translated as "curling water."[22]

Like a number of later explorers, Hennepin ventured into the realm of hyperbole when describing the height of the falls, putting it at fifty or sixty feet. Jonathan Carver, who dropped by for a look in 1766, estimated the height at thirty feet, not a bad guess by his loose standards. Pike in 1805 provided the first accurate measurement—sixteen and a half feet. The total drop of the river in and around the falls was closer to fifty feet, however, and it was this "head," as the millers called it, that made it such a desirable waterpower site, with an estimated potential of thirty-five thousand horsepower.[23]

The falls in their natural state did not last long once civilization arrived. The earliest photographs of the falls, taken in the 1850s, show a maze of stone and wooden mill structures already in place, the rude beginnings of what was to become probably the greatest direct-drive, waterpowered industrial complex in the history of the

world. Harnessing the falls inevitably destroyed their natural beauty. "The falls themselves have lost nearly all their scenic charm," E. V. Smalley, editor of *Northwest Magazine,* observed in 1895. "The apron of plank covering the rocky precipice and the booms above for sorting logs give to the cataract such a prosaic and business-like appearance that many travellers . . . look out on what they think is only a big mill dam and learn afterwards that they have passed with small notice one of the old historic, scenic spots of the continent."[24]

The apron had been installed to preserve the falls, which for a period were in danger of disappearing altogether. Nature and human stupidity were the culprits. By the 1860s the falls were within twelve hundred feet of the end of the limestone layer upon which their drop depended. Had nature been allowed to take its course, the falls eventually would have crumbled into a long run of rapids somewhere around Nicollet Island. But intense development had already imprisoned the historic cataract in a web of dams, tunnels, canals, and tail races. This work had weakened the limestone beneath the falls and increased the pace of movement upstream, which by the late 1860s had reached the alarming rate of one hundred feet a year. Then, in 1869, the end nearly came when a tail race under construction beneath the falls collapsed, taking huge chunks of the precious limestone cap with it. Frantic work saved the falls, but they would never be the same again. The first wooden apron went on in 1870, and over the next decade additional stabilizing measures so altered the falls' appearance that virtually all of their natural qualities were lost.[25]

Other natural features along the Minneapolis riverfront also disappeared with development. A series of small waterfalls—with romantic names such as Silver Cascade and Fawn's Leap— once tumbled into the river gorge beneath St. Anthony Falls. Most of these were either destroyed or significantly altered by development in the 1880s. Minneapolis also had its share of caves, most now either gone or inaccessible. Perhaps the most interesting of these was Chute's Cave near the Falls of St. Anthony on the east bank of the river. Also known as Nesmith Cave, this was actually a 250-foot-long mill tunnel dug in the 1860s but then abandoned because of objections from nearby property owners. A local accountant named Edward L. Wells, who obviously had time to spare, then concocted an elaborate hoax in which he depicted the sandstone tunnel as a mile-long, stalactite-filled cavern harboring the skeletons of ancient animals and an eight-foot-tall prehistoric man. Later, in the 1880s, the great American tradition of speleological kitsch asserted itself, and the tunnel was transformed into a tourist attraction. For a dime, visitors could climb aboard "a rude scow of a boat" and glide along a small stream that flowed through the cave. A "grim, Charon-like individual," it was said, served as guide. Chute's Cave was closed by 1889, leaving Charon unemployed.[26]

With only a few hills to worry about, there was more filling than cutting done in the area that eventually became downtown Minneapolis. Much of the filling involved small lakes, swamps, and streams. Bassett's Creek, which once meandered through the northern part of downtown, was straightened and eventually covered in the mid-1880s in response to railroad and industrial development. Other streams, such as a brook that once connected what is now Loring Park pond to Bassett's Creek, have disappeared altogether. Several lakes have also vanished, including Hoag's Lake (near Fifth Street and Sixth Avenue North), Oak Lake (near Sixth and Lyndale), and a pond in the vicinity of Franklin and Lyndale. There was also a large, treacherous swamp in the area occupied today by Parade Stadium and the Minneapolis Sculpture Garden. Filling here did not always prove successful, as the builders of the old Minneapolis Armory learned to their regret.

Completed in 1907 on a site near Kenwood Parkway and Lyndale Avenue, the armory settled so badly that it had to be condemned just twenty-two years later.[27]

The one part of downtown Minneapolis where extensive cutting occurred was in and around Lowry Hill, originally known as the "Devil's Backbone." A pair of distinctive, sharply crested glacial ridges once dominated the landscape here. The top of the northerly ridge "was only a few feet wide," an early Minneapolis resident recalled. Between these two steep hills, near present-day Groveland Avenue, was a deep gorge filled with "a thicket of brambles." Both of these hills were eventually lowered and the gorge filled in for residential development in the 1880s. Eighty years later, this area was further transformed by the construction of Interstate 94.[28]

IF LAND IS the clay from which cities are formed, streets are their lifeblood. A city's street plan is also its signature, as vital as landscape and architecture in creating a sense of place. The grand boulevards of Paris, the relentless grid of Manhattan, the unfathomable sprawl of Los Angeles are fundamental marks of character. Neither St. Paul nor Minneapolis produced anything quite so distinctive. But even though the two cities grew up just ten miles apart, their streets developed quite differently. St. Paul's early streets were narrow and crooked, named in no particular order, and numbered in a way that ignored block divisions. Minneapolis, by contrast, offered wide and generally straight streets, which were logically ordered by name or number (after 1872) and came with building addresses that changed with each block. Some of these differences are not so evident now as they once were. Yet it remains true that Minneapolis is a city whose plan can, with some effort, be logically comprehended, whereas St. Paul has to be memorized. Unfortunately the transforming power of the automobile has been especially destructive of St. Paul's old tangled

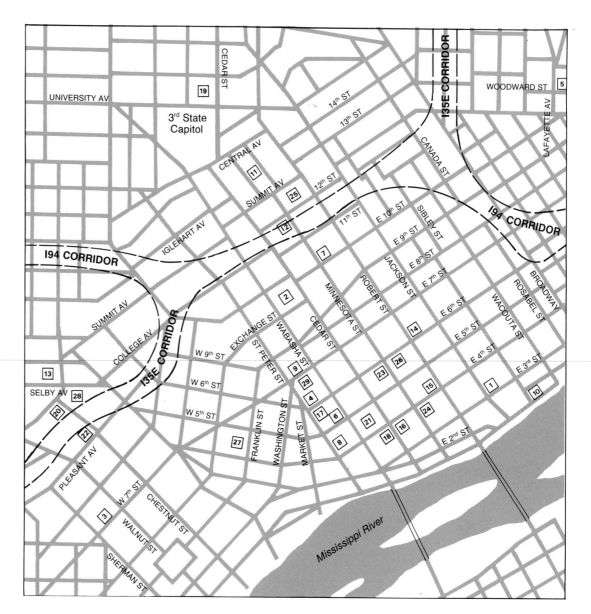

ST. PAUL

1. St. Paul House-Merchants Hotel
2. State Capitol (first and second)
3. Fuller (Emmett) house
4. St. Paul Cathedral (third)
5. Thompson house
6. U.S. Customs House
7. Central High School
8. St. Paul City Railway Co.-Dickinson's store
9. Market Hall
10. Union Depot
11. Central Park
12. Central Park M.E. Church
13. Kittson house
14. Ryan Hotel
15. National German-American Bank
16. Minnesota Club
17. Capital City Panorama
18. Globe Building
19. Merriam house
20. Wilder house
21. St. Paul City Hall-Ramsey County Courthouse
22. People's Church
23. New York Life Insurance Building
24. Germania Life Insurance (Guardian) Building
25. Baseball Park
26. Metropolitan Opera House
27. St. Paul Auditorium
28. Streetcar tunnel
29. Capitol (Paramount) Theatre

streetscape, which was both delightful and maddening and is now largely lost.

Few of St. Paul's early promoters found cause for such delight, however. In fact, the city's convoluted streets were a frequent object of denunciation and scorn. One of the loudest and most opinionated critics was James M. Goodhue, founder and editor of St. Paul's (and the state's) first newspaper, the *Minnesota Pioneer*. Goodhue, who wrote wonderfully colorful prose and died far too young, was a man with definite ideas about everything, including the proper way to make a city. And the surveyors of St. Paul, he wrote in the *Pioneer* in 1852, had made a fine mess:

> The projectors of this town, appear to have had but the smallest possible ideas of the growth and importance that awaited St. Paul. . . . The original plat, was laid off, in very good imitation of the old French part of St. Louis, with crooked lanes for streets, irregular blocks, and little skewdangular lots, about as large as a stingy card of gingerbread, broke in two diagonally; without a reservation, fit to be called a public square—without a margin between the town and the river, without preserving a tree for shade. . . . In fact, it was a survey without measurement, a plan without method. . . . Then came in Rice & Irving's [Irvine's] Addition [the area west of St. Peter street]. . . . This is laid out but little if any better. In fact the two plats appear to have taken a running jump at each other. . . . It would save immense cost and prove an eternal blessing to St. Paul, if the whole site of the town could be now thrown into one common field, and platted as it ought to be, with large reservations of public ground, with straight, wide, regular streets, and blocks and lots of uniform size.[29]

Goodhue's condemnation was echoed time and again through the years until it became a kind of municipal threnody. "Never was a city laid out so badly as St. Paul," grumbled the editor of the *Minnesota Democrat* in 1853. J. Fletcher Williams, writing in 1875, called the downtown street plan "a perpetual misery inflicted on posterity." A few years later, the *St. Paul and Minneapolis Pioneer Press* complained: "Just see what a maze of confusion—what a labyrinth, in fact, some portions of our goodly city exhibit; streets beginning anywhere and ending anywhere—running into and out of each other at every conceivable angle, but oftener not connecting with other streets at all." Another journalist alleged that the city "was laid out . . . with the same carelessness and destitution of purpose as the buffalo exhibits when he grazes along through thickets and obstacles."[30]

In fact St. Paul was a model of clarity compared to most European cities or to old eastern cities such as Boston. But downtown St. Paul, especially on its western and northern sides, offered a fair amount of confusion, largely because of what happened after the first plat, known as St. Paul Proper, was surveyed in 1847 by Ira and Benjamin Brunson. Contrary to Goodhue's diatribe, St. Paul Proper—which takes in the area bounded today by St. Peter, Wacouta, and Seventh streets north of the Mississippi River—is a straightforward grid in the conventional manner of midwestern American cities. The plat, with blocks about three hundred feet square, is also typical in that the east-west streets parallel the river, rather than following the cardinal points.[31]

City planning, like indoor plumbing and central heating, was unknown in those rude pioneer days, and the plat was designed not to accommodate any great civic end but to make it as easy as possible to sell real estate. Given this commercial motive, it is hardly surprising that the plat made no provision for public space, ignored the potential for river views along Third Street, and eschewed such land-consuming luxuries as alleys.

The names assigned to streets in St. Paul Proper did not follow any particular pattern; for all that several were named after prominent settlers, such as Henry H. Sibley, Henry Jackson, and Louis Robert. Others—such as Wabasha (originally spelled "Wabashaw") and Wacouta (originally "Wakouta")—were inspired by Native American names. East-west streets were numbered but in typically casual St. Paul fashion started at Third, there being no First or Second (although Bench Street was later renamed Second). In general numbered streets were never popular in St. Paul, reaching only to Fifteenth before the idea lost its appeal.[32]

All in all, St. Paul Proper was a reasonably orderly beginning. In the plats that followed, however, a certain sweet chaos prevailed. The biggest monkey wrench thrown into the civic works was the 1849 plat of Rice & Irvine's Addition west of St. Peter Street, around what is now Rice Park. Here, the streets were turned at a forty-five-degree angle from those of St. Paul Proper and also given new names—Fifth, for example, became Pearl and Sixth became State. It is not clear why the developers of this plat, John Irvine and Henry Rice, laid out the streets as they did. Perhaps the plat's sharp turn was simply a declaration of independence from Lowertown, since both men were promoters of Upper Town. A more likely explanation is that they simply followed the line of the Mississippi River bluff, which begins to curve inland west of St. Peter.[33]

Whatever made Rice and Irvine do it, this wrenching twist in the grid created endearing anomalies unique to St. Paul. Among other things, it produced a stretch where Sixth and Ninth streets ran parallel only one block apart, with cross streets bearing a 400 address number so as to confuse matters further. The bewilderment intensified when West Seventh Street had to be angled between Fourth and Sixth to connect with an old military road to Fort Snelling. All of this confusion came to a head at Seven Corners (later greatly altered), where Third,

Fourth, Seventh, and Eagle streets collided in a big whirling knot of traffic and befuddlement.[34]

Later plats to the west and north continued to go their own way. In keeping with the buccaneer spirit of the age, some developers even created deliberate street jogs in order to make neighboring plats less accessible. By the 1860s, no fewer than five grids, each at least slightly askew from the others, swirled around St. Paul Proper like a disjointed pinwheel. Eventually the city sought salvation in the cardinal points, and later residential grids were for the most part laid out on straight east-west and north-south lines.[35]

Despite its inconvenience, St. Paul's tangled web of streets had some distinct benefits. For one thing, it gave downtown St. Paul a powerful, almost European sense of containment. In many American cities, downtown streets follow an endless course to the horizon. But St. Paul's amiable jumble of colliding grids created the opportunity for strong visual end games because major buildings could terminate street views. As one observer noted in 1884: "The numerous curves, corners, angles and *culs-de-sac* of this irregular street system give fine opportunities for architectural effects which are beginning to be appreciated." Such comments not withstanding, the builders of St. Paul, who seem to have been gleefully ad hoc about almost everything, paid little attention to the urban design possibilities inherent in the city's fractured streetscape. Even so, wonderful accidents happened. Fourth Street, for example, once ended on the east with a fine view of the old Northern Pacific Building. And where Sixth Street turned at St. Peter, the Ford Music Hall, also gone, for many years provided a fine visual terminus, similar to that of the Saint Paul Hotel on Fifth. But it was not until Cass Gilbert began planning the present State Capitol in the 1890s that the potential for views in downtown St. Paul was exploited with any real sophistication.[36]

Besides being arranged in a most disorderly way, downtown St. Paul's streets were narrow.

The Northern Pacific Building terminated the view east on Fourth Street in St. Paul in the 1880s.

The standard street width in St. Paul Proper and most later downtown plats was set at sixty feet, including sidewalks, which were a measly ten feet. That is quite tight compared to most other midwestern cities. Both Chicago and Minneapolis, for example, were platted with eighty to one-hundred-foot-wide streets downtown and fifteen-foot-wide sidewalks. Omaha's founders provided for streets up to 120 feet wide, with one hundred the average. By contrast, planners in 1922 found only 30 percent of the land in downtown St. Paul devoted to streets, an "exceptionally low ratio." Why the men who platted St. Paul opted for such narrow streets and sidewalks is not known, but it may be that they recognized the constricted nature of the city's site and acted accordingly. Or it may be that they were reluctant to devote any more land than absolutely necessary to streets, which suffered from the disadvantage that they could not be sold for a profit.[37]

Yet even the minimal sixty-foot standard for streets was not always achieved in St. Paul. Jackson Street was only thirty-nine feet wide in places, Bench was forty feet, and Third Street (later Kellogg Boulevard) was just forty-five feet, despite being the city's principal thoroughfare. In other places, builders simply ignored the platted street width. J. S. Sewall, an early city engineer, found in 1878 that some buildings encroached ten feet onto the legal line of Robert Street, narrowing it to only fifty feet.[38]

As time went on, the narrowness and irregularity of St. Paul's street system was perceived as a problem threatening the very vitality of the city, and corrective measures were taken. Over a period of many years, the city widened, straightened, moved, or eliminated numerous streets. They were also frequently renamed. As a result, the street system in much of downtown St. Paul is completely different now from what it was at the turn of the century.

Third Street, for many years the city's main commercial artery, was apparently the first to be

Third Street looking west from Sibley Street, about 1870

widened. In 1872 porches were removed from all buildings on the street, which allowed its width to be increased from about forty-five to up to fifty-seven feet. The city undertook the same sort of thing, but on a much larger scale, along an eleven-block stretch of Robert Street in 1913. At a cost of $1 million, the city lopped off building fronts on the west side of the street to increase its width by twenty feet. Jackson, Sibley, Fourth, Seventh, Eighth, and Ninth were among other streets substantially widened at one time or another.[39]

Perhaps the single most massive street-widening project, and the first example of knock-it-all-down urban renewal in St. Paul, was the creation of Kellogg Boulevard and Mall beginning in 1928. Here, along Third Street and its seedy alter ego Bench, was the historic heart of the city—where Father Lucien Galtier in 1841 built the log chapel after which St. Paul was named, where James J. Hill began his climb to wealth and power, and where in steamboat days "low river dives and dance halls" flourished and "no respectable man, much less a woman, dared enter the neighborhood after dark."[40]

From the earliest days of the city, however, there had been complaints that Third Street, despite its location atop a high bluff, offered no public ground for viewing the great sweep of the river below. E. S. Seymour, a visitor to St. Paul in 1849, wrote that Third "would have made a pleasant place for promenading, affording a fine view of the river, which is now liable to be intercepted by buildings erected on those lots." Seymour proved prophetic. By 1870 a solid phalanx of buildings lined Third, blocking views of the river. The Kellogg Boulevard project was designed to correct this historic mistake, and it did so by creating a new bluff-top mall between Wabasha and Robert streets while more than doubling the width of Third. Progress, however, carried a price. Forty-three buildings, including many of the city's most important early commer-

cial structures, were demolished to make way for the new boulevard and mall.[41]

The Kellogg Boulevard project was one of the fruits of a city planning process that can fairly said to have begun with Horace W. S. Cleveland in 1872. That year, the city's common council invited Cleveland to "make a general outline report upon the proper location of parks, wide avenues, public squares and other improvements, on a scale suitable to the wants of a crowded city." Cleveland, a well-known Chicago landscape architect who was later to design some of the Twin Cities' important parks, responded to the assignment with an impassioned plea for intelligent long-range planning and civic-mindedness in a city then not known for either quality.[42]

Speaking to the common council on June 24, 1872, Cleveland first buttered up his audience with the usual superlatives, proclaiming that the view from Summit Avenue "certainly may be considered one of the most superb . . . in the world." But he was quick to note that this splendid vista was entirely in private hands, since no one had thought to preserve park land atop the bluff. "I have rarely experienced a more tantalizing sense of disappointment," Cleveland said, "than I felt as I followed it [Summit Avenue] along and tried in vain to get more than an occasional glimpse of the magnificent prospect that would have been open to the public forever, if the avenue had only been carried near the edge of the bluff, and no buildings allowed except on the opposite side."[43]

During the long speech that followed, Cleveland urged St. Paul's city government quite literally to seize the high ground for parks, not only on Summit Hill but also on Wabasha Hill (later Capitol Hill when the State Capitol was built there), Dayton's Bluff, and overlooking Trout Brook. He also recommended that the land around Lake Como and Lake Phalen and along the Mississippi River between Minneapolis and St. Paul be set aside for parks. On a more grandly

Kellogg Mall under construction in 1931

impractical note, Cleveland exhorted St. Paul to construct a system of wide radiating boulevards, à la Paris, to speed the flow of traffic. Other specific recommendations followed, after which Cleveland concluded, amid the standard rhetorical fireworks, with an either-or vision of the city's future. "It depends in great measure on the population of today," he told the council, "to determine whether the future character of the great city shall . . . make her known the world over as a centre of attractive interest . . . or merely as a great temple of Mammon, whose worshipers have irreverently desecrated and trampled upon the nobler altars of a higher faith."

Mammon, alas, proved hard to resist. Although many of Cleveland's recommendations were eventually carried out, his message had little immediate effect other than the purchase of land for Como Park. Here and there, however, private citizens took urban planning into their own hands, sometimes with splendid results. In the late 1880s, for example, wealthy residents living near what is now the State Capitol area helped finance a magnificent overlook that became one of the city's most visited places. Known as Merriam's Overlook (John Merriam and his son, William, both owned mansions nearby), this beautiful spot on Sherburne Avenue included a small fountain, exceptionally handsome iron railings, and a winding stone staircase that led down to Robert Street. But such well-planned places were a rarity in nineteenth-century St. Paul, despite the best efforts of Cleveland and other reformers.[44]

If Cleveland was the benign godfather of city planning in St. Paul, Cass Gilbert was his most brilliant pupil. Raised in St. Paul but with a decidedly continental sensibility, Gilbert brought the city its first real taste of classical grandeur with his winning design for the State Capitol in 1895. By the time the building was completed in 1904, Gilbert had also drawn the first of several plans for a suitable approach to his magnificent monument. In November 1902, Gilbert presented his initial approach plan to the Women's Civic League of St. Paul, illustrating his lecture with lantern slides of great European civic spaces. He offered a variation on this scheme in 1903.[45]

Both proposals envisioned a fan-shaped mall in front of the Capitol. This in turn would connect to another mall along Cedar Street and to a vast Parisian-style boulevard extending due south to the Seven Corners area. Public buildings were to be arranged around these spaces, and there was also to be a large veterans' memorial midway along the boulevard (near a little cul-de-sac off St. Peter Street known as Park Place). Unfortu-

Merriam's Overlook was a popular place to view the city in 1895. The twin towers of Assumption Church appear at right.

nately, Gilbert's airy visions of urban grandeur smashed head on into a stone wall of governmental inertia, causing the frustrated architect to complain at one point that St. Paul was a "dead" city. But after much public scolding by Gilbert, the Minnesota legislature in 1907 finally authorized $1 million in bonding authority for a new Capitol approach. The city of St. Paul, however, never got around to issuing the bonds. Undeterred, Gilbert kept on dreaming his Capitol dreams, preparing new plans in 1907, 1909, and 1931. But like his earlier schemes, these proposals never got beyond the drawing board.[46]

Gilbert had begun his capitol planning adventures at a time when the so-called City Beautiful Movement was nearing full bloom in the United States. Inspired by the success of the famous White City at the World's Columbian Exposition of 1893 in Chicago, the movement eventually spread to almost every major American city, with mixed results. St. Paul, despite its notorious reputation for civic sloth, was not immune from this high-minded effort to create classical order out of Victorian chaos. After Gilbert had whetted the city's appetite for grand urban gestures, a civic group in 1911 hired John Nolen and Arthur Comer to prepare a plan of St. Paul's central business district. Nolen and Comer followed many of Gilbert's ideas but also called for such improvements as the clearing of the river bluff along Third, the widening of Robert, and the development of riverfront parks. The Nolen-Comer plan, however, like so many of its successors, was largely ignored.[47]

The most thoroughgoing attempt to impose Beaux-Arts discipline on St. Paul's rather crabbed, disheveled downtown came in 1922, the same year the city adopted its first zoning ordinance. The plan was prepared by William E. Parsons and Edward H. Bennett, the latter a protégé and longtime colleague of Daniel Burnham, who in 1909 had produced for Chicago the most influential of all City Beautiful plans. Much of the

Bennett-Parsons plan devoted itself, with commendable optimism, to proposals for improving the flow of downtown traffic by widening or straightening existing streets and adding new ones. Bennett and Parsons also proposed a new city hall along Third Street (on what is today the site of the Civic Center parking ramp), a new grand approach to the recently completed Union Depot on Fourth Street, and a modified version of Gilbert's Capitol approach scheme. But aside from a handsome volume of drawings, this plan produced nothing tangible.[48]

Gilbert's dream of a suitable foreground for the Capitol was finally realized, albeit in much-revised fashion, in 1954 with the creation of the Capitol Mall. The new mall completely reordered the historic streetscape in front of the Capitol, but its impact was not nearly so profound as the highway work that followed. The construction of

Interstate 94, opened in 1967, did to the Capitol area what railroad building had done to much of Lowertown in the 1880s and 1890s, which is to say it destroyed an entire neighborhood, including the heart of St. Paul's historic black community along Rondo Avenue. Moreover, the decision to place the freeway between downtown and the Capitol was a disastrous mistake in urban planning that continues to haunt St. Paul.

Planners had envisioned a major new highway along what is now the Interstate 94 corridor in St. Paul as early as 1920. But it was not until 1944, when Congress authorized planning for the interstate system that the Minnesota Highway Department began selecting a route. This process—undertaken in an era in which highway engineers seemed to have the power of gods—was remarkably swift. It was nearly finished by November 1945 when the *St. Paul Pioneer Press*

Cass Gilbert's Capitol Mall plan, 1907

published an aerial photograph of the Capitol area with the proposed new highway drawn in. The route shown on the drawing proved to be almost identical to the actual path of the freeway completed twenty-two years later.[49]

Despite the road's enormous potential for disruption to the historic fabric of the city, its route was approved with minimal public discussion and little opposition. St. Paul's black community, which ultimately saw one-seventh of its residents displaced by Interstate 94, fought the freeway, as did a few other neighborhood groups. But there was only one lonely critic in city government— George Herrold, St. Paul's longtime planning engineer. Herrold, who battled the proposed freeway for more than a decade, predicted in 1956 that the road would "bring about many legal entanglements and disturbances to gracious living" and called the proposed route in front of the Capitol Mall "a mistake." He also argued that the best course for the freeway, if it had to be built, would be through the old railroad corridor north of University Avenue. Noting that the railroad lines had already divided St. Paul into islands, Herrold asked: "Why subdivide these islands into smaller ones by these depressed highways with all the disturbances that necessarily follow?"[50]

Herrold's protests—and those of the black community—proved to no avail. Besides severing the Capitol from its traditional connection to downtown, Interstate 94 (and the long-delayed Interstate 35E) dismembered the historic College Hill area and much of its quirky streetscape. Old streets such as Tilton and Central Terrace simply disappeared from the map, while others—most notably Summit Avenue—were amputated from the downtown torso. Scores of historic buildings were also lost to the freeway, as was one of the downtown's most unusual urban spaces, Park Place.

The Interstate 94 project, for all its destructiveness, was characteristic of St. Paul, which since its founding has struggled to reorder and rationalize its downtown streets, often without regard for the urbanistic consequences. By 1991 St. Paul's street wars were still continuing, especially on the western edge of downtown, with the usual casualties along the way.[51]

WHILE ST. PAULITES groused about their mixed-up street system, Minneapolis' more orderly downtown plan generally inspired praise. "A stranger sees at once that here is a city that was scientifically platted by men who believed that population would surely come to fill in their framework of regular streets and avenues," wrote E. V. Smalley in 1895. "No cart-tracks or cow-paths were followed in the building of the first streets, and as there were no hills to level or gorges to fill, the engineers ran their lines straight across the prairies and gave ample space from curb to curb for the traffic of the future."[52]

Even so, the man who in 1854 laid out what is now the heart of Minneapolis came to regret his work as a "great error." That man was John H. Stevens, who left an account of this first plat, known as the Town of Minneapolis, in his *Personal Recollections:*

I determined at first to make the streets eighty feet wide, the avenues one hundred feet wide. . . . As no one expected at that time that much of the land back of the first plateau [from the Mississippi River] would ever be used for any other than agricultural purposes . . . we concluded there should be one avenue laid out running parallel with the river, which should be the basis for laying out the town; that the name of this avenue should be Washington. This decision with regard to laying out the principal avenue in such a manner as to run parallel with the river as the foundation for laying out all the other land . . . was a great error that, had my foresight been as good as my present sight, would never have occurred. What I should have done, was to have

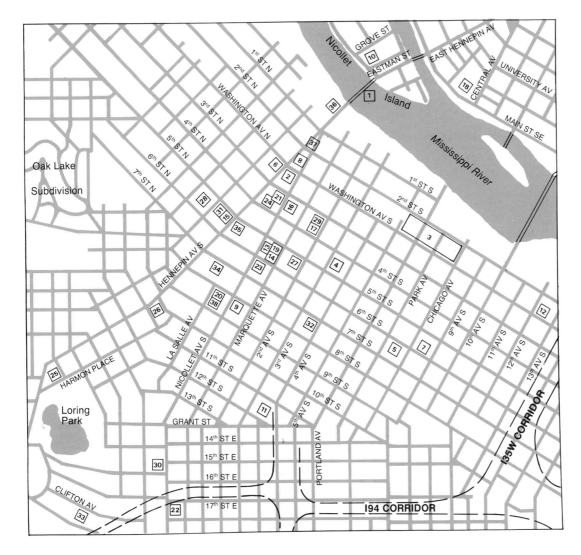

MINNEAPOLIS

1. Suspension Bridges
2. Nicollet House
3. West Side Milling District
4. Washington School (first)
5. Washington School (second)
6. Academy of Music
7. Judd house
8. Minneapolis City Hall
9. Plymouth Congregational Church
10. Eastman Flats
11. Central High School
12. Beard's Block
13. Syndicate Block
14. Grand Opera House
15. West Hotel
16. Minnesota Loan and Trust Building
17. Tribune Building
18. Industrial Exposition Building
19. Panorama Building
20. First Unitarian Church
21. Bank of Minneapolis
22. La Veta Terrace
23. Donaldson's Glass Block
24. Globe Building
25. Gale house
26. Minneapolis Public Library
27. New York Life Insurance Building
28. Athletic Park
29. Northwestern Guaranty Loan (Metropolitan) Building
30. First Free Baptist Church
31. Cream of Wheat Building
32. Bradstreet crafthouse
33. Clifford house
34. Radisson Hotel
35. Loeb Arcade
36. Great Northern Station
37. Gateway Park
38. Minnesota (Radio City) Theater

paid no attention to the windings of the river, but ran [*sic*] the streets directly east and west, and the avenues directly north and south. . . . No one ever supposed at that time that Minneapolis would expand into a city of more than fifty or sixty thousand inhabitants, and many looked upon my platting the streets and avenues so wide as a great waste of land; and on some accounts I am rather inclined to think it would have been preferable to have reduced the width of the avenues and streets about twenty feet [which would have made them the same width as St. Paul's streets]; especially when we take into account the great cost of paving.[53]

Stevens was being too hard on himself. His decision to follow the line of the river was more or less standard practice at the time, mainly because early town builders were afraid to move the center of things too far from the steamboat landing. Stevens's plat, which extended back from the Mississippi in irregular fashion from about Seventh Avenue on the north to Seventh Street on the south and west, also lined up nicely with the river-hugging plat of St. Anthony, laid out in 1849. Although most of the Town of Minneapolis was virgin land, Stevens had to adapt his plat to existing circumstances in the case of Hennepin Avenue, which followed the line of a territorial road. Hennepin also acts as a hinge for the north-south streets in Stevens's plat as they bend slightly to follow the river.[54]

Stevens's decision to make Minneapolis' streets quite wide—Hennepin and Washington avenues were platted at one hundred feet, most others at eighty—hardly seems unwise in retrospect. The downtown occupied a large, generally flat and quite open site, and wide, straight streets arranged in gridiron fashion were a natural response to this environment. Stevens also made provision for alleys, which proved most useful. Where Stevens erred was in his failure to set

aside any land for public use, although this, too, was typical of the age. About the only public space in the plat was Bridge Square, a small wedge of land where Hennepin and Nicollet avenues converged at a dramatic angle near the river. For many years, especially after the first city hall was built there in 1874, Bridge Square served as a de facto civic center. In 1914–15, after demolition of the city hall building, Bridge Square was enlarged into a superb public space, Gateway Park. Unfortunately the park was foolishly destroyed in the 1960s and replaced by high-rise apartments.[55]

One of Stevens's happier decisions was in the choice of names for east-west streets. He seems to have done it by a kind of free association, mixing names of friends, relatives, explorers, and places in no special order. Most of these street names are gone. Marquette Avenue, for instance, began life under Stevens as Minnetonka Street. It was later changed to Marquette, then to First Avenue South, then back again to Marquette. Second Avenue South originally was Helen Street (named after Stevens's wife). Third Avenue South was Oregon, Fourth Avenue South was California, Fifth Avenue South was Marshall, and Portland Avenue was Cataract Street (an appropriate name, since the street ends at the Falls of St. Anthony). But after Minneapolis merged with St. Anthony in 1872, almost all of these named streets were changed to numbered avenues. The triumph of the numeral in Minneapolis street nomenclature drew a protest from one local editor, who complained: "It is carried too far. . . . there is neither poetry, history nor local color in it. You turn for relief to the few streets . . . that have not been forced to take titles from the arithmetic."[56]

As was the case in St. Paul, the skewed downtown grid of Minneapolis eventually had to align with later residential plats that followed the compass. Where this adjustment occurred, there were areas of confusion, most notably at Seven Corners (where Washington and Cedar avenues, among others, intersect) and in the Loring Park area. A few Victorian-era developers also tried to inject variety into the street grid by laying out curving residential streets in subdivisions such as Oak Lake, which was located near Sixth and Lyndale avenues north and is now long gone. It is no coincidence that the area around Loring Park, where the grid gives way to a picturesque arrangement of rather narrow streets, continues to be one of the city's most urbane locales. Because the downtown grid in Minneapolis was much larger than in St. Paul, it afforded fewer opportunities for closed views or axial effects. To this day, a sense of spaciousness prevails in downtown Minneapolis that allies it visually with other large gridiron cities of the Midwest and West.

With one great exception, Minneapolis had little time for urban planning in the nineteenth century. The exception was the Minneapolis Park Board, an independent agency created in 1883 and destined to have a profound impact on the character of the city. Here again, Horace Cleveland played a key role by providing vision at a crucial time. Addressing the park board in June 1883, Cleveland outlined the system of parks and connecting boulevards that was to become Minneapolis' most distinctive urban feature.[57]

But Cleveland's comments barely touched on downtown Minneapolis, which continued to

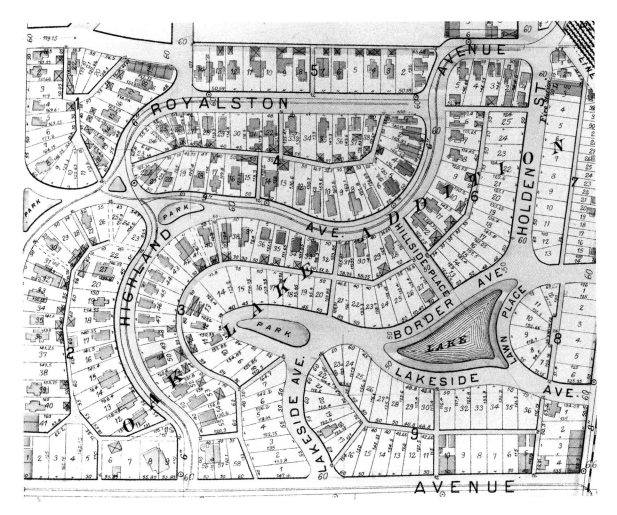

Oak Lake subdivision south of Sixth Avenue North

grow in helter-skelter fashion throughout the 1880s and 1890s. In this free-for-all atmosphere, real estate speculation more than anything else shaped the downtown, and nobody worried much about larger civic considerations such as the creation of public spaces or the grouping of public buildings. "Additions were laid out and joined to the city . . . with no consideration of the public interest or the future of the city," one historian noted in 1908. He further complained that a "great opportunity" was lost in the 1880s, "when a large number of public buildings being under consideration, the city failed to group them around a common civic center, or, at the very least, to provide some suitable setting for each."[58]

Like St. Paul, Minneapolis made its initial effort to correct these deficiencies during the City Beautiful Era. In 1906 a team of four architects led by John Jager, who had studied in Vienna, drew what may have been the first really grandiose plan for Minneapolis. Proceeding on the dubious assumption that "the modern city is a business corporation" and should be managed as such, Jager and company laid out a plan that was eminently rational yet also utterly unattainable within the social, political, and economic context of the time.[59] Based on European models, the plan called for new diagonal streets, a cluster of civic buildings at either end of a blockwide concourse along Third and Fourth streets south, a new riverfront boulevard, a new Union Depot near Second Street and Second Avenue South, and the creation of a large exposition center with public baths on Nicollet Island. Although the plan received wide publicity in the *Minneapolis Journal,* its only real impact seems to have been as a stimulus for further planning.

Much of this attention concentrated on the city's historic Gateway District, which was the subject of ambitious plans submitted by local architects, including Harry Jones, Lowell Lamoreaux, and Edwin Hewitt. Their proposals appeared in 1908 in *Western Architect* magazine,

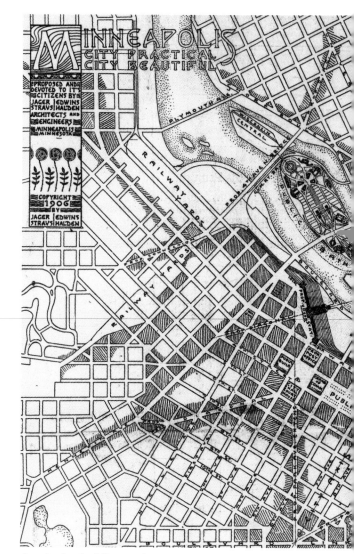

Jager's plan for Minneapolis

which along with the *Journal* strongly supported the ideals of the City Beautiful. The magazine saw large-scale renewal as a way to bring health and cleanliness to the dense disorder of the Gateway District, which was viewed as a breeder of both moral and physical decay. "As it has been said that the first advance toward civilizing the barbarian is to give him a clean shirt, so the greatest force toward civic advancement is cleanliness," opined the magazine in December 1908. "Minneapolis, particularly the down town district, needs a clean shirt, and needs it worse than

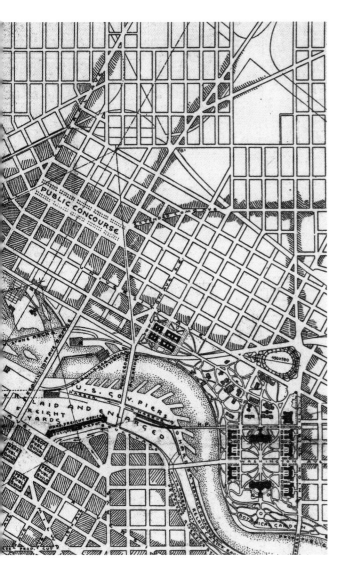

applied. The commission then hired Edward Bennett (with Burnham as adviser) to prepare a city plan, which was ready by May 1912 but was not published until 1917.[61]

The authors of the plan tried to assure everyone that they were not pie-in-the-sky idealists. They wrote: "This is not a report on that misleading idea called 'the City Beautiful,'—that millstone around the neck of city-planners. If a phrase were wanted it might be called a report on the city-economic, the city-scientific, the city-efficient, the city-prepared." True to their word, Bennett and company did have much of practical value to offer, suggesting improvements in traffic control, zoning, parks, and other areas of municipal concern.[62]

But the bulk of the plan turned out to be a grand and seductive hallucination. It envisioned Minneapolis as the Paris of the Prairies, organized around a new system of diagonal boulevards lined with look-alike neoclassic buildings. Wide enough for conquering armies, these great urban pathways, it was promised, would not only increase property values but also "send the life blood coursing through the decayed tissue of the city." Other features of the plan included new bridges across the Mississippi, a multilevel riverfront parkway, a transportation complex in the Gateway District, and a vast civic center plaza at Portland Avenue and Eighth Street. Bennett and his designers depicted this Beaux-Arts Eden in gorgeous, dreamlike renderings, many done from a bird's-eye perspective. These show a brave new urban world, imperial in scale, remorselessly monumental, and purged of all that is old, irregular, or unusual.[63]

The plan's grandiosity, at times approaching megalomania, turned out to be its undoing. Newspaper editorialists began to complain that Bennett was preoccupied with beautification while devoting too little attention to traffic and other more mundane problems. Others raised concerns about the staggering cost of the scheme.

any city of its size and possibilities that we know of."[60]

Such talk had results. In 1910 Minneapolis civic leaders formed an eleven-member commission to plan for the city's future. With the exception of a token laborer, the commission consisted entirely of wealthy businessmen, led by flour-milling magnate William H. Dunwoody. These august gentlemen concluded that the city's pioneers, like a roomful of naughty children, had made a terrible mess of things and that some stern Beaux-Arts discipline would have to be

The plan of Minneapolis envisioned huge plazas and grand boulevards. Top center is Minneapolis City Hall.

In the end, the plan—like its counterpart in St. Paul—proved to be of limited practical consequence. A few of the plan's recommendations for locating buildings, such as the Minneapolis Institute of Arts and the Great Northern Station, were carried out. But none of the major new streets it called for was ever built. Perhaps the plan's most positive influence was the creation of Gateway Park. Because it required the demolition of two blocks full of historic buildings, the Gateway project was in many respects a foretaste of things to come in the 1950s and 1960s. Unlike many of its ill-advised descendants, however, the project did give the city something truly worthwhile in return—an elegant public space in the heart of downtown.[64]

Although downtown Minneapolis has not undergone nearly as much street widening or straightening as St. Paul has, there have been changes over the years. Nicollet, for example, no longer joins Hennepin at the river and in 1967 was turned into a serpentine mall. Roads have also been significantly altered around the new Convention Center (1989), new freeway distributors have changed the grid north of Hennepin, and a new riverfront parkway has been built. But the freeways that so dramatically altered St. Paul were generally kept to the periphery of downtown Minneapolis, although they still managed to wreak great urban havoc, especially in the Lowry Hill area. Here, the construction of Interstate 94 in the 1960s severed Loring Park from the Parade area and destroyed the historic "Bottleneck," where Hennepin and Lyndale avenues had once crossed at a spectacularly acute angle. Yet what is perhaps most striking about downtown Minneapolis is how intact its street system remains compared to St. Paul's.

CURIOSITIES AND EXOTICA

A NUMBER OF strikingly unusual buildings could once be found in and around downtown St. Paul and Minneapolis. All of these architectural follies and oddities are long since gone.

SH'ARE TOF SYNAGOGUE (TEMPLE ISRAEL)
Fifth Street between Marquette and Second avenues south, Minneapolis, LeRoy Buffington, 1880–1903.

Minarets were not an everyday sight on the streets of Minneapolis in the 1880s, but this early synagogue offered a pair of them along with a small dome, Islamic arches, and other motifs right out of the *Arabian Nights*. Built almost entirely of wood, the building's willfully exotic look was typical of nineteenth-century synagogues in the Twin Cities. In about 1886 the structure was moved to a new location at Tenth Street and Fifth Avenue South and remained there for seventeen years until fire destroyed its Oriental charms.

TEMPERANCE HOUSE HOTEL (MOFFET'S CASTLE)
West side of Jackson Street just north of Fourth Street, St. Paul, Lott Moffet, 1852–82.

This boulder-walled hotel was built at the bottom of a forty-foot-deep ravine by an eccentric teetotaler named Lott Moffet. The hotel's below-grade location meant that its entrance, which could only be reached via a footbridge off Jackson, was on the top floor. Another oddity was that the hotel literally encased a wooden house Moffet had built in 1847. The ravine was filled in by 1855, forcing Moffet to build above grade to make up for space lost below. By the time Moffet died in 1870, the hotel was actually four stories above the street.

ISIDOR ROSE HOUSE
220 East Ninth Street (at Sibley Street), St. Paul, ca. 1860–ca. 1930.

Built for a St. Paul fur merchant, this mixed Greek Revival-Italianate house in Lowertown featured some truly idiosyncratic details. Its two-story portico was especially peculiar, with multi-

ple-shaft columns that seem to have been pure invention, although they hinted at the Egyptian Revival style. Rectangular ornamental panels inserted beneath some windows added to the house's strange appearance. Rose himself eventually moved to Summit Avenue, and other families occupied the house until it was razed about 1930.

FIRST SWEDISH METHODIST EPISCOPAL CHURCH
Northeast corner of Tenth and Temperance streets, St. Paul, George Wirth, 1887–ca. 1920.

Serving God and Mammon in the same building was unheard of in the Twin Cities until this brick church appeared in 1887. The ground floor consisted of small shops intended to provide a source of rental income for the congregation. Above there was a commodious church hall for the conduct of less worldly affairs. It is not clear how well this mixture of religion and retailing functioned, but the idea was used for at least one other Protestant church in St. Paul in the late 1880s.

SPECTATOR TERRACE
15 Fourth Street North (south side between Hennepin Avenue and First Avenue North), Minneapolis, Alexander Murrie, 1889–ca. 1920.

Built for C. H. Du Bois, eccentric publisher of the short-lived *Saturday Evening Spectator*, this improbable Oriental fantasy included horseshoe-shaped windows, a Moorish dome, and a tower topped by a Chinese pagoda. After the *Spectator* folded about 1895, an insurance company moved in and tamed all this delightfully tasteless visual mayhem by removing the dome and replacing many windows. The pagoda, however, remained to the very end as a distinctive feature of the Minneapolis skyline.

ADDITION TO FRANKLIN LONG HOUSE
41 Groveland Terrace, Minneapolis, Long and Kees, 1893–ca. 1930.

Architects can usually be counted on to live in peculiar houses, and Franklin Long was no exception. In 1893 Long (undoubtedly with help from his partner Frederick Kees) expanded his twenty-year-old house by means of a large addition that included oval windows, bands of horizontal ornament, and a sweeping corner curve. The addition was unlike anything else of its time in the Twin Cities and in many respects seems to have anticipated the sleek Moderne style that was to become popular forty years later.

ELKS HALL
West side of Washington Street between Fourth and Fifth streets, St. Paul, Mark Fitzpatrick, 1908–ca.12.

Although the gabled exterior of this short-lived building was quite impressive, the interior was—in every sense of the word—overwhelming. Some of the rooms were decorated in a style (supposedly of Austrian descent) that can only be described as Elkhorn Eclectic with antlerlike ornamental flourishes sprouting up around doorways and even over fireplaces. It must have made one proud to be an Elk. Alas, the ever-dangerous forces of good taste intervened after a fire about 1912, and a new Elks Hall built on the site proved to be far more staid.

DUTCH MILL SERVICE STATION
Southeast corner of Third and Robert streets, St. Paul, Myrtus Wright, ca. 1920–ca. 28.

Before the giant oil firms standardized designs, service stations came in a bewildering variety of styles, including everything from neoclassic temples to mock English cottages. For reasons that defy logic, a small oil company in St. Paul even went so far as to mount windmills on its four stations, one of which was downtown. The windmills failed to blow in a steady stream of business, however, and they are long since gone, as are most early examples of roadside architecture in the Twin Cities.

URBAN BEGINNINGS, 1840-1880

I n the summer of 1857, three years after St. Paul's incorporation, pioneer photographer B. F. Upton hauled his equipment to the top of the Ramsey County Courthouse, then located at the southeast corner of Fifth and Wabasha, and took nine views—comprising a panorama—of the young city. It was not a pretty sight. Upton's unsparing camera showed a raw, unkempt, and treeless place, an embryonic sprawl of small square buildings, rough dirt streets, and ragged backyards littered with piles of lumber, limestone, and miscellaneous debris. Later, Upton climbed to the roof of the Winslow House hotel in what is now southeast Minneapolis and recorded a similar panorama of St. Paul's fast-growing rival.[1]

Upton's remarkable series of photographs came at a time when the two cities were concluding their first great period of building. Although this pioneer age lasted through the Civil War, it reached its zenith in 1857—a year of fabulous growth and frenetic speculation that climaxed in disaster. A boom-town atmosphere pervaded that memorable summer, but the times were especially flush in St. Paul, where as many as five hundred immigrants a day arrived at the steamboat levees. Describing this period, J. Fletcher Williams wrote:

> St. Paul was said by travelers, to be the fastest and liveliest town on the Mississippi River. . . . The hotels and boarding houses were crowded to overflowing. The principal business streets fairly hummed with the rush of busy life. Building was never so brisk. . . . Saloons, of course, throve as they always do, be times flush or hard. That season they coined money; so,

also, did the livery stables. The city was continually full of tourists, speculators, sporting men, and even worse characters, all spending gold as though it was dross.

Everyone in St. Paul, it seemed, had caught the speculative fever, and land prices soared on the wings of hope and greed. A sixty-foot lot on Third Street that had sold for two hundred dollars in 1847 was worth six thousand dollars by 1857, and there seemed no end to the upward spiral. "City lots jumped so high over night that the tallest ladder could not reach them in the morning," wrote Thomas Newson, with perhaps a touch of hyperbole, in his 1886 history of St. Paul. "It was land for breakfast, land for dinner and land for supper!"[2]

But when a New York insurance company failed in August, setting off panic in the financial markets, the bubble burst. Out of it spilled a cargo of economic woe that hit frontier cities especially hard. Williams recalled:

> Everything had been so inflated and unreal—values purely fictitious, all classes in debt, with but little real wealth, honest industry neglected, and everything speculative and feverish—that the blow fell with ruinous force. Business was paralyzed, real estate actually valueless and unsaleable at any price, and but little good money in circulation. Ruin stared all classes in the face . . . general gloom and despondency settled down on the community. In a few days, from the top wave of prosperity, it was plunged into the slough of despond.[3]

Despite the year's lugubrious ending, both cities—but especially St. Paul—had already come

B. F. Upton's panorama of Minneapolis showed Washington Avenue (left), Second Avenue South (middle), and Washington Avenue (right) extending past the foundations for the Nicollet House (upper right) toward First Avenue North.

B. F. Upton's panorama of St. Paul showed Minnesota Street (left, horizontally through middle) and Fourth Street (middle and right) where the road-grading crews were at work.

a long way. Only fourteen years earlier, according to Newson, "St. Paul had but three or four log houses, with a population not to exceed twelve white people, and was a mixture of forest, hills, running brooks, ravines, bog mires, lakes, whisky, mosquitoes, snakes and Indians." By 1857, however, St. Paul's population was nearly ten thousand. Minneapolis, meanwhile, had grown from a few hundred residents in 1854 to a population of thirty-four hundred, but it was still smaller than St. Anthony, which had almost forty-seven hundred people in 1857. St. Anthony, however, soon began to lose population and was absorbed by Minneapolis in 1872.[4]

Physically, St. Paul and Minneapolis were quite small at this time, each covering about five square miles. With mass transportation unavailable and horses expensive, most people traveled on foot. As a result, the vast majority of buildings in both cities were clustered around the downtown cores. An 1857 map of Minneapolis shows that all but about fifty of the city's 422 buildings were within a mile of Bridge Square. As late as 1875, half of Minneapolis' population continued to live no more than a mile from the downtown center.[5]

For a time, it had looked as though Bridge Square might not be the center of Minneapolis. Two other areas—a so-called "Lowertown" near St. Anthony Falls and a small commercial node near Washington and Second Avenue South—had emerged in the early 1850s as competitors. But the completion of a suspension bridge across the river at Hennepin Avenue in 1855 assured Bridge Square's predominance. There had been a similar competition in St. Paul, between the

Lowertown and Upper Town districts. Lowertown's superior levee and, later, railroad facilities proved decisive, and East Third Street soon developed into the city's main thoroughfare.[6]

The organization of the cities was extremely casual. Zoning did not exist, which meant that buildings of all kinds—residential and commercial, sacred and profane, costly and cheap—were jumbled together without much regard for the niceties of urban planning. The cities also lacked such modern amenities as sewers, piped water, and paved streets. The only public utilities available in either city before the Civil War were the telegraph, which arrived in 1860, and gas, used primarily for lighting. Henry Sibley formed St. Paul's first gas company in 1856, providing service to a limited number of customers.[7]

Despite the lack of zoning, both cities managed to sort themselves out by class at an early stage. With its steep bluffs overlooking downtown, St. Paul was a city made by nature for the display of social order, and the rich wasted no time in staking out the high ground—St. Anthony (Summit) Hill on the west, Wabasha (Capitol) Hill on the north, Dayton's Bluff on the east, and Prospect Terrace to the south. Summit Avenue could boast of eleven houses by 1865, while a scattering of stately villas had arisen on the terraced hills of Dayton's Bluff.[8]

But these hilly areas were still too remote to attract large numbers of residents. Instead, most of St. Paul's wealthier citizens lived in either Irvine Park or the northeastern part of Lowertown, where a fashionable neighborhood developed in the 1860s after banker Horace Thompson built a handsome Italian-villa style house

(long gone) at 33 Woodward Avenue. For a time, Woodward was the "Summit Avenue of Lowertown," but it eventually vanished, along with its mansions. The middle classes, meanwhile, filled in the first terrace above the river. St. Paul's poorest residents, including many squatters, had to make do with less attractive sites, such as the Mississippi floodplain or the narrow, polluted ravine known as Swede Hollow.[9]

In Minneapolis, where the topography was less conducive to the flaunting of wealth, the well-to-do tended to concentrate around the southern rim of downtown. In 1864, Samuel Gale built one of the city's most splendid early mansions near what is now Marquette and Fourth Street South. Later, Lowry Hill and the open countryside to the south along Park Avenue became the

First Samuel Gale house, about 1890

precinct of choice for the city's elite. The poor, of course, settled in the least desirable areas, such as Bohemian Flats along the river or the crowded tenement districts that eventually developed on the near North Side and in the Cedar-Riverside area. It was also common in both cities throughout the nineteenth and early twentieth centuries to find inexpensive houses being built next to, or even amid, heavily industrialized areas.[10]

The numerous buildings shown in Upton's photographs had certain features in common. They tended to be small, plain, inexpensive, and, above all else, combustible. This sort of provincial frontier architecture was to dominate the built environment of the Twin Cities until the 1880s. For the most part, these early structures were not built to last, and few have. A survey in 1983 found only about fifteen pre-Civil War buildings—mostly houses—in St. Paul, although the actual figure probably is closer to one hundred. In Minneapolis the number is roughly the same.[11]

Most of these early buildings were constructed of wood supplied by local sawmills. The carpenters who built them used the "balloon frame" method developed in Chicago in the 1830s. This method, still in use in the 1990s with some variations, eliminated the need for complicated joinery by allowing structures to be built quickly with standardized pieces of wood and machine-made nails. The balloon frame was also a boon to frontier builders because it did not require great expertise, as was true of older building methods.[12]

With so much wood construction and with buildings heated by wood or kerosene stoves, it is hardly surprising that fire was a constant threat. Although the Twin Cities never experienced anything like the conflagrations that ravaged New York in 1835, Chicago in 1871, and Boston in 1872, large and dangerous fires were common. In St. Paul alone, fifteen hotels burned down in the 1850s and 1860s, including the city's largest, the International House, in 1869.[13]

St. Paul's biggest fire, in March 1860, destroyed thirty-four wooden buildings along Third Street between Robert and Jackson. These buildings, a historian wrote, "represented the very beginnings of the town. . . . There [Louis] Robert had made his start; in one of the stores A. L. Larpenteur had been a clerk; in one of the buildings Governor [Alexander] Ramsey lived when he first came to town." The historian went on to note that "the antiquity of the buildings"—some were all of twenty years old—"made them food for the flames."[14]

Fire, in fact, seems to have been the first agent of urban renewal in both cities. Minneapolis' biggest bout with the "red demon," as newspapers liked to call it, also occurred in 1860 when a fire destroyed eighteen businesses in the Bridge Square district. It was finally put out with the aid of several women, who, in the words of one admiring if somewhat stunned historian, "did royal service that night." These fires occurred even though both cities had already established so-called "fire limits," which prescribed that only brick, stone, or iron buildings could be constructed within certain downtown areas. Existing structures were allowed to remain under "grandfather" clauses, however, and it was well into the twentieth century before wooden buildings disappeared entirely from the two downtowns.[15]

Even so, by the 1860s brick or stone had replaced wood as the favored building material for commercial, industrial, and institutional buildings and for many larger houses. Brick was manufactured in St. Paul as early as 1849 and in Minneapolis by 1854. This early local brick, often of poor quality, was grayish yellow to brown, although other colors developed as new clay pits opened. Henry Mower Rice is reputed to have built the first brick house in St. Paul, near the corner of Third and Washington streets, in 1849. The first brick structure in Minneapolis apparently was a hotel built in 1853.[16]

Terra cotta, another material made from clay,

was manufactured in Red Wing, just down river from St. Paul, as early as 1868 and began appearing on buildings in the Twin Cities by 1870. At first terra cotta was employed primarily for ornament, but later it came into widespread use as a fireproofing material.[17]

Iron also came into use at an early date. Minneapolis, for instance, had an iron foundry by 1859. Initially local builders used iron primarily for fences, cresting, and ornament. As time went on, it also was used extensively for structural beams and columns and storefronts. But prefabricated cast-iron building fronts—of the kind developed in New York in the 1840s—were never especially popular in the Twin Cities, although they were manufactured in St. Paul as early as 1868 by the North Star Iron Works. One of the best was on a three-story building (gone) at 48–50 East Third Street in St. Paul. Smaller limestone buildings with cast-iron fronts were more common, as in the Ingersoll Block

International House next to the St. Paul Pleasure Park (curved roof), a place that featured musical entertainment and a shooting gallery, 1867

Building with cast-iron front on East Third Street, about 1924

The Ingersoll Block, about 1885, when the St. Paul Public Library occupied the third floor

(1860–1928) just down the street at the corner of Third and Wabasha.[18]

The other major building material in this early age was the local Platteville limestone. It was first quarried commercially in St. Paul in 1856 and in Minneapolis in 1864. This stone—generally blue to gray in color—underlay much of the two downtowns, and builders often simply quarried it on or near the construction site. The casual removal of stone eventually became such a problem that the city of St. Paul passed an ordinance forbidding people from quarrying in the streets. Although prized for its easy availability, Platteville limestone—with the exception of blocks taken from a few select quarries—left much to be desired as a building material. It tended to come in rough laminated beds, was seldom of uniform quality, and had a crumbly texture that made it "extremely difficult to dress and virtually impossible to detail in any but the crudest way."[19]

Still, it was about the only stone readily available in the cities until the early 1870s. It was used for early public buildings, such as the U.S. Customs House (1873) in St. Paul and the first Minneapolis City Hall (1873), for large commercial and industrial structures, for schools and churches, and for many houses. Now found mainly in foundations and retaining walls, Platteville limestone—for better or for worse—lent a distinctive look to Twin Cities architecture. Among the best remaining buildings constructed of this stone are Assumption Church and School and the Alexander Ramsey House in St. Paul and the F. C. Hayer Company Building and the Nicollet Island Inn in Minneapolis.

Building types during this early period were limited to the basics: commercial buildings (usually long and narrow, with shops at ground level, working or living space above, and perhaps a large rental hall on the top floor), industrial buildings (mainly warehouses and mills), churches and schools, small government buildings, hotels and rooming houses, residences, livery stables, theaters, and a tumbledown array of wooden sheds and shanties used for every conceivable purpose. Although multiple dwelling units (usually duplexes) were built as early as 1859, it was not until the 1870s that larger "tenements," as they were called, began to appear, and it would be another decade before modern-style apartment buildings arrived. The large central railroad station, the department store, and the high-rise office building were also unknown in the Twin Cities until the 1880s.[20]

Perhaps the most imposing pioneer building was the Winslow House hotel, a huge hunk of limestone constructed in 1856–57 in what was then St. Anthony. Five stories high with a distinctive cupola, the Winslow House may also have been the tallest building of its day in the Twin Cities. Certainly no public building in either city was as large or impressive. The first

Platteville limestone buildings on the east side of Jackson Street, just south of Third, 1929

Winslow House, about 1870, after it had been converted to a hospital

First Hennepin County Courthouse, about 1860, and the jail at far right

State Capitol, completed in 1853 at Tenth and Wabasha streets in St. Paul, was a small Greek Revival-style structure topped by an uninspiring wooden dome. The first Ramsey and Hennepin County courthouses, and the first St. Paul City Hall, all dating from the 1850s, were equally small and provincial in character. These cheaply built structures were clearly viewed as temporary works, to be replaced by grander public edifices as time went on. Only one of these early public buildings—the Hennepin County Courthouse—survived more than thirty-five years. More impressive were early engineering works, especially the first two Mississippi River bridges in the Twin Cities. The Hennepin Avenue Suspension Bridge of 1855 in Minneapolis was the first span anywhere across the Mississippi. The first Wabasha Street Bridge (1856–59) in St. Paul was a peculiar steplike structure that, according to one traveler, resembled "a great clumsy fire-escape propped up against a high wall."[21]

With their tall steeples, churches were especially prominent at this time. The largest religious structure built in the Twin Cities before 1865 was the third St. Paul Cathedral. This great limestone barn, vaguely Romanesque in style, was completed in 1858 at Sixth and St. Peter streets. A few other early churches were built of brick with wooden spires. First Presbyterian Church (1850–1930) at Third and St. Peter streets was a Greek Revival brick structure. Its two-stage wooden tower, topped by a tall steeple, reputedly had the state's first church bell. But most pioneer churches were built of wood in simple versions of Gothic or Colonial styles. Examples include the First Christ Episcopal Church (1851) in St. Paul and the First Baptist Church (1857) in Minneapolis. All of these early churches are long since gone.

Because trained architects were in short supply, carpenters and masons—often working from pattern books—designed most buildings of this

First St. Paul City Hall, about 1890; Market Hall is at far left

period. A. C. Prentiss, a carpenter, drew plans for the first State Capitol and received fifty dollars for his efforts. The first Ramsey County Courthouse had an even more modest pedigree. Its designer, David Day, was a St. Paul physician who dabbled in architecture. Day reportedly received ten dollars for his courthouse design.[22]

The architects who practiced in the Twin Cities before the 1870s were almost all master builders, men who had learned the construction trade from the ground up and generally had no formal academic training in architecture. This group of early architects included Abraham M. Radcliffe, Augustus F. Knight, Romaine and Monroe Sheire, Robert F. Grimshaw, and Robert S. Alden. Alden arrived from Indiana in 1856 to design and build the Winslow House and was perhaps the first full-time architect-builder in

First Wabasha Street Bridge, 1859

the Twin Cities. Radcliffe, whose office was to serve as a training ground for some of the Twin Cities' most notable architects, also emigrated from Indiana. He opened a Minneapolis office in 1857 and an office in St. Paul the next year. By 1868, however, his practice was limited to St. Paul. Knight began practicing in St. Paul in 1857 and won a number of important early commissions, including the first St. Paul Opera House in 1867.[23]

These early architects and builders tended to employ styles that were already popular in the East. In the 1840s and 1850s, the local style of choice was Greek Revival, usually in simplified form. A few truly splendid Greek Revival houses, complete with overscaled Doric or Ionic porticos, were built in St. Paul in the 1850s. Among the best were the Daniel Robertson and Alpheus Fuller houses on West Seventh Street and the Bartlett Presley house at 229 East Eighth Street. Only a smattering of this Greek Revival legacy remained in the 1990s, largely in the restored

LEFT:
First Baptist Church, 1868

BELOW:
Daniel Robertson house and its spacious grounds, about 1880

Typical Gothic decoration, including small battlements, adorned the Asa B. Barton house in the Loring Park neighborhood, about 1862.

Irvine Park neighborhood.

Greek Revival gave way by about 1860 to the various "picturesque styles," including Gothic Revival, Italianate, and French Second Empire. The New York landscape designer Andrew Jackson Downing popularized these styles in such influential plan books as *Cottage Residences* (1842) and *The Architecture of Country Houses* (1850). A St. Paul newspaper noted the local influence of Downing and another plan-book writer, Calvert Vaux, in 1860: "Private dwellings are no longer constructed without any other plan than to get a certain number of rooms attached together under one roof, or a series of roofs, with-

out regard to convenience or architectural appearance. Downing and Vaux are consulted, and competent architects employed to make the plans, and good workmen to carry them into execution."[24]

These "competent architects" seldom ventured far from the safe haven of imitation. Dazzlingly original design was not their forte, and their early buildings tended to be conservative and provincial. Nor did early Twin Cities architects make any concerted attempt to respond to local conditions, particularly the climate, which was the most extreme of any metropolitan area in the nation, if not the world. Instead, they built pretty much what everyone else was building, content to take their stylistic cues from the East Coast and the pattern books.

Although a few early architects—Radcliffe, for example—found work in both St. Paul and Minneapolis, the two cities from the start developed as distinct architectural communities. St. Paul architects rarely worked in Minneapolis and vice versa. This situation changed little over the years. As late as 1891, the distinguished architectural critic Montgomery Schuyler noted: "It is very unusual, if not unexampled, that an architect of either [St. Paul or Minneapolis] is employed in the other." The rivalry between the two cities, which peaked about 1890 with a bitter census battle, seems to have discouraged architectural mingling. Nonetheless, a small number of architects—most notably LeRoy Buffington—were able to obtain significant commissions in both cities, although even Buffington was more or less limited to Minneapolis after 1885.[25]

THE PERIOD FROM 1865 to 1880 was the early adolescence of the Twin Cities, an era that left them poised for the great adventure of the 1880s, when almost overnight they blossomed into full-fledged cities. Both cities grew rapidly in the post-Civil War years, but Minneapolis, with its manufacturing might, led the way. By 1880 Minneapolis' manufacturing output was two and a half times that of St. Paul, and this spurred tremendous growth. The city's population increased tenfold between 1865 and 1880, to forty-seven thousand, moving it ahead of St. Paul for the first time. Minneapolis also grew in physical size, to about twelve and a half square miles, due largely to the absorption of St. Anthony in 1872. St. Paul was no slouch during this time, either, its population tripling from thirteen thousand in 1865 to more than forty-one thousand by 1880, while its territory quadrupled to twenty square miles.[26]

To keep up with their booming populations, both cities struggled to develop and expand their infrastructures. St. Paul began installing gas streetlights in 1867 (thereby lifting the city out of "cimmerian obscurity," according to one newspaper), established a city water system in 1869, started constructing sewers four years later (amid much public controversy over the quality of the work), and in 1873 also paved its first street—a short section of Third—with pine blocks.[27]

Minneapolis began a municipal water system in 1867 (the same year it was officially incorporated as a city), obtained gas service in 1870, and built its first sewers in 1871. But paved sidewalks, rather than the usual wooden variety, did not arrive in Minneapolis until the 1880s, nor did paved streets. Before the advent of paving, streets in wet weather were reduced to great troughs of mud, a foot or more deep in places and laced with a fragrant mix of horse dung and miscellaneous offal. The state of the streets may explain why both cities were among the first in the nation to establish telephone service in 1877. It was another two years before a phone line connected St. Paul and Minneapolis.[28]

Another major advance of the 1870s was mass transportation in the form of horsecar lines. St. Paul saw its first horsecars in 1872. The first line in Minneapolis opened in 1875, extending for six blocks along Third Street. However, a truly efficient mass transportation system was not put in place until the introduction of electric streetcars in 1889.[29]

It was also during this period that the different social and economic characters of the two cities came into sharp focus. St. Paul was, above all else, an entrepôt city. By 1861 there were nearly a thousand dockings a year at its levees, but steamboat traffic began to decline during the Civil War, and railroads emerged as the dominant mode of transportation. With so many transients arriving daily, especially during the summer months, St. Paul had all the rambunctious qualities of a seaport. A tenderloin district developed along Bench Street, where, according to one

Theatre Comique, about 1890

morally offended historian, there were "low river dives and dance halls, and groggeries flourishing" and prostitutes waiting "to murder the souls of men." Street toughs also flourished here, but several met their match one February night in 1858 when they accosted James J. Hill and a friend. The future Empire Builder reacted with characteristic forcefulness. "We attempted to go on," he later wrote, "but they tried to have us go back so I hauled off and planted one two in Paddy's grub grinder and knocked him off the sidewalk about 8 feet. . . . The city police came to the noise and arrest[ed] three of them on the spot and the others next day and they turned out to be Chicago Star Cleaners, a name given to midnight ruffians."[30]

During this rugged era, St. Paul attracted all manner of wandering humankind, the male portion of which appears to have been largely preoccupied with securing liquor and sex. Both com-

modities were readily available. St. Paul had a whopping total of 242 saloons by 1880, along with seven officially recognized brothels. There must have been many others, however, judging by the number of "female boarding houses," as they were euphemistically called, that appear on insurance maps from the period. So profitable was the business of prostitution, in fact, that the costliest private house (gone) built in St. Paul in 1870 belonged to a celebrated madam, Mary E. Robinson. Risque dance troupes and other forms of prurient entertainment also appear to have been more acceptable in St. Paul than in Minneapolis. In 1875 the Minneapolis chief of police traveled to St. Paul to view a "can-can" show said to be quite daring. After a close personal inspection, the chief determined that the show was indeed indecent, and it was banned from Minneapolis.[31]

Although Minneapolis—perhaps reflecting the prim morality of its New England founders—was less tolerant of vice than its free-wheeling rival across the river, the city was by no means sin free. By 1880 Minneapolis had four brothels and 176 saloons, not a bad total, but still markedly lower than the numbers for St. Paul, even though Minneapolis was a larger city. Minneapolis, however, could by 1879 boast of the single most notorious entertainment establishment in either city—the infamous Theatre Comique, which offered its exclusively male clientele the choice of several back doors, the attention of extremely solicitous hostesses, and the opportunity to observe female dancers who did not always adhere to Victorian standards of decency.[32]

The economic characters of Minneapolis and St. Paul were also different. Minneapolis drew its economic lifeblood from the industry around the Falls of St. Anthony, which powered the largest flour milling complex in the United States. Before 1865 only about ten mills clustered around the falls. By the mid-1880s there were twenty-five, the majority concentrated on the West Side

Washburn A Mill just before the explosion in 1878

along a three-hundred-foot-long power canal blasted out of solid rock along First Street South in 1857–58 and extended to nine hundred feet in 1865. In 1859 the first privately owned flour mill along the canal, the Cataract, was constructed near what is now Portland Avenue and First Street South. Originally, this was a diversified industrial district with flour, lumber, woolen, and paper mills, although the first two predominated. But technological advances such as the middlings purifier and the iron roller eventually propelled the flour milling industry to the forefront. Sawmills then began to leave the falls area, relocating upriver on the city's north side. This trend was already well established by the 1870s when all but three of the eighteen industrial structures built along the west side of the falls were flour mills.[33]

Built of brick or stone with heavy timber construction inside, these massive mills were among the largest and tallest buildings of their time in the Twin Cities. They were also among the most dangerous, exploding and burning with disturbing frequency. Early mills, such as the three-story-high Cataract, had been quite small, but in the 1870s some real giants began going up along the canal. Packed tightly together to gain access to precious waterpower, these mills by 1880 formed an almost unbroken masonry wall along either side of the canal, creating a dense, brooding architectural environment unlike any other in the Twin Cities.

The largest of the early Minneapolis mills was the Washburn A, erected in 1874 by Cadwallader

Pacific Elevator, 1874

Washburn. Six stories high and seemingly hewn out of solid rock, it had a run of forty-one millstones, Austrian-made machinery, and workers trained in the latest European operating techniques. It also had a short life, as did many of its workers. On May 2, 1878, the Washburn A exploded, killing eighteen men instantly and devastating much of the West Side milling district. Washburn quickly rebuilt, but by 1880 the great age of flour mill construction in Minneapolis was nearing its end.[34]

The mills brought with them auxiliary structures, most notably grain elevators, which in their later concrete form were the only major building type ever invented in Minnesota. The elevators built in the 1860s and 1870s—including the city's first large terminal elevator, dating from 1867—were all of wood, however. Typical of these early wooden elevators was the Pacific, built in 1868 near Washington and Third ave-

nues north.[35]

Minneapolis acquired its sobriquet—the "Mill City"—from the milling industry, which also spread the city's name worldwide on bags of flour. St. Paul, however, had no such instantly recognizable claim to fame. A few early boosters tried to remedy this deficiency by proposing that St. Paul be called the "Terrace City," a name not exactly redolent with romance. It did not stick, nor did other suggested nicknames. But if St. Paul had no distinctive product, it did have two primary engines—railroading and wholesaling—that drove its economic development after the Civil War.[36]

The first railroad came to Minnesota in 1862, linking downtown St. Paul and Minneapolis. After that, the rush was on. The cities were connected by rail to Chicago around 1867, and over the next decade more than three thousand miles of additional track spread across Minnesota. By 1880 St. Paul—largely because of James J. Hill's efforts—was the railroad hub of the Northwest. The city's excellent steamboat and railroad connections also helped to make it a wholesaling center, so much so that detailed if not always enthralling statistical summaries of the business done by local "jobbing houses" became a staple of St. Paul journalism. By 1869 the St. Paul Chamber of Commerce reported sixty-two wholesaling firms in the city.[37]

The Lowertown wholesale district along East Third and Fourth streets was the heart of St. Paul in the 1860s and 1870s. Here was another dense urban environment, where three- and four-story brick buildings crowded up to the sidewalk, forming a powerful street wall. Because the streets in Lowertown were so narrow, the wholesale district had a sense of bustling containment unlike anything in Minneapolis. Typical of the warehouse buildings of this period in St. Paul was the Beaupre and Kelly Wholesale Grocery Store, completed in 1873 at the southeast corner of Sibley and Third streets. Designed by Abraham Radcliffe, the store was basically a plain brick box, ornamented with a standard French Second Empire-style mansard roof and heavy Italianate window hoods. Like many of the Minneapolis mills, it did not last long, burning down in 1880.[38]

The architectural character of the Twin Cities remained quite modest through the 1870s, and wood, local brick, and Platteville limestone continued to serve as the predominant building materials. Improved transportation gradually brought new materials to the area, however. Kasota stone—a handsome gray, buff, to yellow dolomitic limestone quarried from the Minnesota River valley near Mankato—was in use in the Twin Cities by the early 1870s, as was St. Cloud granite. In addition, pressed red brick from Milwaukee and St. Louis was available by 1875. But it was not until the 1880s that the architectural palette of the Twin Cities significantly broadened with the introduction of a host of new materials.[39]

Nor was there any great enlargement in architectural scale until the 1880s. The Andreas atlas of Minnesota, published in 1874, shows that buildings in Minneapolis and St. Paul were not yet significantly larger or higher than those in other growing cities in the state, such as Winona, Red Wing, and Mankato. But the number of buildings in the Twin Cities was increasing rapidly. In 1872 alone 932 new structures went up in St. Paul.[40]

Warehouses were not the only large commercial buildings that clustered along Third and Fourth streets. In 1869 the St. Paul Press built what may have been the first four-story office block in the city at Third and Minnesota streets. A year later the St. Paul Fire & Marine Insurance Company erected a comparable building two blocks away at Third and Jackson. Other four-story blocks, of either stone or brick, sprang up nearby over the next few years, although the financial panic of 1873 put a damper on new construction. The four-story height limit was a

LEFT:
Fourth Street looking west from Sibley, about 1886

BELOW:
St. Paul Fire & Marine Insurance building, about 1875

restriction imposed more by human reluctance to walk up stairs than by structural or economic necessity. But in 1876 the beginning of the end came for the walk-up age in St. Paul. That year William Davidson built a four-story brick block at Fourth and Jackson streets that came equipped with a steam passenger elevator—possibly the first ever for a commercial building in the Twin Cities.[41]

In Minneapolis the Bridge Square area continued to be the center of downtown development. As in St. Paul, four stories seems to have been the de facto height limit for Minneapolis commercial buildings during the 1860s and 1870s. The most impressive commercial structure of this era in the Bridge Square district was the Brackett Block, a massive limestone pile constructed in 1871 at the corner of First Avenue South (now Marquette) and Second Street. Yet most build-

ings around Bridge Square remained small and narrow, and in some cases there were twenty or more to a block.[42]

Residential development followed trends established before the Civil War. In St. Paul the northeastern part of Lowertown solidified its fashionable reputation. Many of the city's wealthiest families—including those of Henry Sibley, Amherst Wilder, Conrad Gotzian, and James J. Hill—built homes here. Hill's house, completed in 1878 at Ninth and Canada streets, was among the largest in Lowertown. It was also one of the last, since railroad encroachment soon radically altered the neighborhood's character. Other upper-class residential districts included Irvine Park, which saw a spurt of homebuilding in the 1870s, and the College (Capitol) Hill district just north of downtown. Summit Avenue's primacy was still a decade away.[43]

Brackett Block, featuring one of the first mansard roofs on a commercial building in the Twin Cities, about 1875

In Minneapolis the southern and western fringes of downtown were the prime residential territory. Among the princely houses of this era were those of William S. Judd (1873) at Fifth Street and Portland Avenue South, Alonzo Rand (1874) at Seventh Street and Park Avenue South, and Thomas Lowry (1874) at Hennepin and Groveland avenues. All are gone. The Lowry Hill area, as it later came to be called, was platted as early as 1872, and in time became the city's most exclusive residential enclave. A scattering of mansions could also be found in the 1870s along Hawthorne Avenue and near what is now Loring Park.[44]

Those who lacked great wealth lived wherever they could in and around downtown. Working-class housing in St. Paul was concentrated to the north and east of the main commercial district, while the very poor continued to populate undesirable locales such as Swede Hollow and the flats

First James J. Hill house, 1884

Thomas Lowry house, 1925, shortly before its destruction in 1932

Swede Hollow in the 1930s

on both sides of the river. In Minneapolis, the near North Side and Seven Corners expanded as centers of working-class housing, while the indigent, as usual, had to settle for the leftover land no one else wanted.

True multiple-dwelling units (other than rooming houses) began appearing with some frequency in St. Paul by 1870 in response to a chronic housing shortage. Tenements and row houses came to Minneapolis about the same time. The largest was Eastman Flats, a block-long row house built between 1876 and 1878 on Nicollet Island.[45]

A number of significant public buildings (all gone) were constructed in the Twin Cities between 1865 and 1880. In St. Paul the major public work of this era was the U.S. Customs House at Fifth and Wabasha streets, opened in 1873. Another significant project was the enlargement

of the first State Capitol, which received three new wings and a new cupola in 1872 and a new mansard roof in 1878. Sizable new school buildings included Franklin School (1865) at Tenth and Broadway streets, the second Jefferson School (1870) at 395 Sherman Street, and Madison School near Park Avenue and Wabasha Street, on what is now the site of the State Capitol Mall.

Notable Minneapolis public buildings included the city hall (1873) at Bridge Square, Jefferson School (1877) at Seventh Street and First Avenue North, Central High School (1878) at Eleventh Street and Fourth Avenue South, and the City Market House (1876), a weird, one-of-a-kind Spanish neo-Baroque concoction (with Gothic flavoring) designed by LeRoy Buffington and located at Hennepin Avenue and First Street. A large and controversial engineering

City Market House, about 1885

LeRoy Buffington

work—the second Hennepin Avenue Suspension Bridge—was also completed during this period. The bridge opened in 1877 but lasted only twelve years amid continual complaints that it was too narrow and badly built.[46]

Entertainment also took a giant step forward during this time. Two large theaters opened in Minneapolis—the Pence Opera House in 1867 and the Academy of Music in 1872. Located a block apart on lower Hennepin Avenue, both were "upstairs" theaters, their auditoriums built above ground-level shops. This arrangement was dictated by economics (rental space helped to offset theater costs) and by structural necessity (the trusses used at this time for large spans such as theater roofs were usually made of wood and could not support heavy loads above). St. Paul, meanwhile, acquired its first large opera house, the St. Paul Opera House on Wabasha between Third and Fourth streets, in 1867. This was also an upstairs hall, and like its two rivals in Minnea-

polis it seated about one thousand people.[47]

A number of important architects arrived in the Twin Cities in the late 1860s and 1870s. Perhaps the most influential was LeRoy S. Buffington, a Cincinnati native who in 1871 moved to St. Paul to help superintend construction of the Customs House. Buffington went into partnership with Radcliffe for a time, and in 1873 also established an office in Minneapolis, where his practice eventually settled.[48]

The 1870s brought an influx of fresh architectural talent to Minneapolis. Some of these newcomers built notable careers, while others appear to have passed through virtually without notice. The quality of the talent was by no means uniform, as an anonymous Minneapolis correspondent for *American Architect and Building News* noted in 1878:

The condition of the profession here is not exceptionally desirable. All manner of quack-

Pence Opera House,
about 1870

St. Paul (Grand)
Opera House, about 1870

59

Franklin Long

ery has a rank growth in new soil. . . . New men (in more senses than one) are constantly swarming "from the East" or "from Europe." The architect lives his day and passes on, nor are those who live longer always cases of the "survival of the fittest."[49]

Even so, there were important arrivals during this time. Among them were Franklin B. Long, who formed a busy and productive partnership with Frederick Kees in the 1880s; Charles F. Haglin, a builder and engineer who, with Long, designed the first Minneapolis City Hall; Joseph Haley, architect for a number of early public buildings and houses, including the Judd family house; Edward Stebbins, who specialized in schools and other institutional buildings; Frederick G. Corser, a prominent voice in the local design community and later editor of *Western Architect* magazine; William Channing Whitney,

who eventually became the city's premier establishment architect; and William H. Dennis, best known for his work in the 1880s when he designed a series of distinctive French-influenced office buildings and houses.[50]

St. Paul did not attract as much new talent until the early 1880s when Cass Gilbert and a host of outstanding designers arrived on the scene. But a number of important architects, chief among them Edward P. Bassford, settled in St. Paul between 1865 and 1880. Bassford, born in Maine, arrived in St. Paul in 1866, worked in Radcliffe's office for several years, then struck out on his own. By the mid-1870s he was the city's busiest architect, designing houses, schools, and scores of commercial buildings. Two other prominent arrivals in the 1870s were Augustus F. Gauger, who opened a St. Paul office in 1878, and George Wirth, who moved to St. Paul in 1879.[51]

Local architects or builders appear to have designed every important building in the Twin Cities during this period, with the exception of a few churches and houses. In Minneapolis, St. Mark's Church (1870) by Peter Dudley of New York and Plymouth Congregational Church (1875) by Russell Sturgis, also of New York, bucked the general trend. At least two major St. Paul buildings of the 1870s—Assumption Church and First Baptist Church—were also the work of outside architects. Assumption was something of an anomaly, designed by a Bavarian architect, Eduard Reidel, brought in by the church's German congregation. But First Baptist was the work of a prominent Chicago architect, William Boyington, who a few years later designed one of St. Paul's most splendid commercial buildings, the Auerbach, Finch and Van Slyck Building (1882, gone) on Sibley Street. Chicago architects, as it turned out, were to play a significant role in St. Paul through the 1930s, designing many prominent buildings.[52]

William Whitney

The preferred architectural styles in the Twin Cities from 1865 to 1880 were the closely related Italianate and French Second Empire, used for almost all building types except churches; Gothic Revival, reserved mainly for houses and churches; and Romanesque Revival, which appeared rarely but was employed for two of St. Paul's largest buildings of the 1870s—Assumption Church and the U.S. Customs House. This period produced much delightful architecture, including some of the most romantic houses ever built in the Twin Cities. Yet workmanship was often crude ("there are few workmen here who are not executioners," sniffed the anonymous critic for *American Architect and Building News*), and few buildings displayed a truly distinctive architectural vision. As a result, with the exception of Assumption Church, and perhaps a few houses, no Twin Cities building of this period was a nationally significant work. Despite their rapid growth Minneapolis and St. Paul remained relatively small— and distinctly provincial—cities in 1880, with architecture to match. But this was soon to change.[53]

LEFT: *The French Second Empire influence is apparent in the John Prince house on Eighth Street in Lowertown, about 1880.*

ST. PAUL HOUSE-MERCHANTS HOTEL

Northeast corner of Third (now Kellogg Boulevard) and Jackson streets, St. Paul. Augustus F. Knight (1860s–80s). 1847, 1856, 1860, 1870, 1877, 1881, 1883–1923.

Merchants Hotel, 1867

The St. Paul House, opened by Jacob W. Bass in 1847, was the city's first hotel. Built of tamarack logs, it measured only twenty-eight by twenty feet and was a story and a half high. Despite these modest dimensions, the hotel (which doubled as a tavern) was a favorite meeting place in the late 1840s. At one such meeting, on June 1, 1849, Alexander Ramsey and others organized the Minnesota Territory. In 1856, the hotel changed its name to the Merchants, had its rough tamarack logs covered with clapboard siding, and began to expand. There were a few accidents along the way, one of which occurred in 1856 when a table of startled hotel diners went plummeting into a newly excavated basement after part of an old floor gave way. No one was seriously hurt, but appetites must have been ruined.

The hotel's most notable era of growth began in 1862 after John J. Shaw became sole proprietor. Shaw and his successor, Colonel Alvaren Allen, kept architect Augustus Knight busy with a building program that was to continue off and on for more than twenty years. By the time it was over, the hotel was a maze of stone, brick, and wooden structures cobbled together around a small central courtyard. The first big expansion came in the 1860s, when four-story additions were built north and east of the original log portion of the building, raising the hotel's capacity to more than one hundred rooms. But it was not until 1870 that the old log structure itself was demolished and replaced by a four-story stone building.

The Merchants enjoyed its greatest success in the 1870s and 1880s under the direction of Allen, described as "the ideal entertainer." The hotel was also popular with travelers because of its proximity to river and rail transportation, especially after the new Union Depot opened only a block away on Sibley Street in 1881. Even before then, however, the hotel had been once again enlarged, this time with the construction of a four-story brick addition along Third Street in

1877. A year later the hotel acquired its first elevator, and in 1881 a fifth floor was added to the entire complex. Despite these improvements, the hotel was "always overcrowded," and so yet another addition was built in 1883. By this time, the Merchants had 275 rooms—at a standard rate of $2.50 a day—and was "altogether the most famous and popular hotel in the Northwest."

Like its Minneapolis counterpart, the Nicollet House, the Merchants did not rely on architectural grandeur to achieve its popularity. The hotel, in fact, looks dowdy in old photographs. Its frequently revamped exterior was more or less Italianate in character but conveyed no strong sense of style. Inside, however, the hotel appears to have been a comfortable, homey place. Besides the usual parlors, ladies' rooms, and lounges, the hotel offered "elegantly equipped and spacious dining rooms," a bar, and the city's largest billiard hall. It also offered "the marble palace," an elaborately decorated basement barber shop operated by Professor R. J. Stockton. This "superb tonsorial establishment," as one newspaper called it, had eight full-time "artists" (barbers) and catered to women as well as men.

Guest rooms (some arranged as suites) were said to be "fitted and furnished in most elegant style with modern patterns of furniture, richly carpeted, and with wall ornaments and decorations unsurpassed by any hotel in America." The Merchants lacked one modern amenity: individual bathrooms. Instead guests made do with several shared water closets on each floor.

The hotel's big lobby, equipped with wooden benches and seats and a broad winding staircase to the second floor, was a favorite haunt for politicians, railroad men, and other movers and shakers of the community. "It is never dull around the Merchants," reported one magazine in 1886. "The spacious lobby is a never-ending scene of animation, enlivened by guests and their visitors from every part of the globe."

The Merchants's reign as St. Paul's great hotel was over by the turn of the century. The larger, better equipped Ryan, which opened in 1885, gradually pulled away first-class customers, while after 1900 new hotels such as the Frederic and Saint Paul drew travelers. The Merchants finally fell into bankruptcy in 1921 and was razed two years later. By 1990 the Minnesota Telecenter occupied the site.

LEFT:
Guest room, nicknamed the "Teddy Roosevelt Room," about 1900

BELOW:
Merchants Hotel, 1918

FIRST AND SECOND STATE CAPITOLS

Block bounded by Wabasha, Cedar, Exchange, and Tenth streets, St. Paul. N. C. Prentiss, Abraham Radcliffe, LeRoy Buffington. 1853–81, 1883–1938.

First Capitol in 1879

When the Territory of Minnesota was organized in 1849, Congress included a twenty thousand dollar appropriation for "suitable public buildings." But it was not until 1851 that the territorial legislature, meeting in rented quarters in St. Paul, established a building commission to begin site selection for a Capitol. Ignoring urban design considerations such as visual prominence, the commission concentrated on finding a free piece of property. The commission considered several sites before choosing a square block of land donated by Charles Bazille, a Canadian-born carpenter and brickmaker who had acquired large land holdings in St. Paul after arriving in 1843.

"Well-situated in the rear of the business portion of the city," as one publication described it,

Upton's panorama shows the first Capitol (center), 1857

First Capitol after 1872 remodeling

the site selected was by no means conspicuous. The first Capitol itself was equally unassuming. After reviewing three other designs, the commission in 1851 accepted a proposal from N. C. Prentiss, paying him fifty dollars for his efforts. Little is known about Prentiss other than that he was a Connecticut native who had been a "carpenter and joiner" for many years.

Completed in 1853, the first Capitol employed the familiar architectural imagery of the Greek Revival style. Its gabled two-story wings flanked a tin-covered wooden dome, which rose above a slender Doric portico facing Exchange Street. The walls were brick with stone trim. Although the first Capitol was hardly a thing of beauty (one critic likened the dome to "an inverted wash basin"), it was a good provincial building, solidly constructed and perfectly attuned to its time and place.

Government offices and a law library occupied the first floor, with legislative chambers upstairs. These plainly furnished, candlelit rooms offered few creature comforts. Wood-burning stoves were supposed to provide adequate heat, but in the dead of winter the temperature in the legislative chambers was sometimes said to hover near zero. Central steam heating was finally installed in 1871, an improvement that did not deter the legislature from its time-honored practice of appointing "firemen," who wandered the building in search of phantom stoves, receiving a tidy per diem for their presumably exhausting endeavors.

The building grew with the state in the 1870s. The first big change came in 1872–73, when a new Senate wing was built to the south toward Exchange Street. At the same time the exterior received a facelift in the fashionable Italianate style. This work, done by Abraham Radcliffe, also included construction of a new (and badly undersized) dome. In 1878 the building was extended to the west, toward Wabasha Street, to create a new main entrance and provide more room for the House of Representatives.

On the night of March 1, 1881, with both houses of the legislature in session, the building caught fire. For a time it appeared as though the entire Senate might be trapped. But someone found a small cloakroom window that provided an escape route, and the last senator crawled unceremoniously to safety moments before the roof of the chamber collapsed. Everyone else inside also managed to escape, but the building burned to the ground.

After the fire the legislature moved to the St. Paul Market Hall two blocks away, while Governor John S. Pillsbury sought bids for a new Capitol. A competition for the new building design attracted such prominent St. Paul architects as Edward Bassford, Abraham Radcliffe, and Augustus Knight, but the winner turned out to be LeRoy Buffington of Minneapolis. Buffington's victory cannot have been based on the quality of his design, which was nothing more than a retread of a proposal he and his former partner Radcliffe had submitted for a new St. Paul City Hall–Ramsey County Courthouse in the early 1870s.

Laid out in the form of a Greek cross, the four-story building (including the basement) was dominated by a two-hundred-foot-high tower with an open-air lookout. The building's walls of red Minnesota brick were offset by bands of white sandstone molding, creating polychromatic effects in the Victorian Gothic manner. The main entrance, reached via a grand staircase off Wabasha, was set within a tall arched opening. Overall

Second Capitol, about 1890

the design was quite eclectic, exhibiting traces of the dying French Second Empire style as well as Gothic and Romanesque elements.

Broad hallways on the ground floor divided the interior into four distinct sections, each containing a rabbit warren of small offices. These hallways intersected at a central rotunda (actually square in shape), near which staircases led to the second floor. Here were the Senate and House chambers as well as the Supreme Court room. The fifty-eight-by-forty-one-foot Senate chamber was especially opulent, with yellow birch and bird's-eye maple woodwork, a large stained-glass skylight, nine stained-glass windows, and a seventy-five-jet gas chandelier. Other public rooms were finished in similarly elaborate fashion.

Unfortunately the building proved to be far too small. By 1890 some state officials were working out of closets and in converted air shafts because no other space was available, while legislative committees sometimes met in corridors or even lavatories. The building was also badly ventilated, its air at one point declared "utterly unfit for human beings to breathe." Such blatant deficiencies did not enhance the second Capitol's reputation. A local magazine writer said that the building was "not much to brag of," while the *St. Paul Dispatch* in 1893 reported that its shortcomings "reveal its entire inadequacy to the demands of actual use." The *Saturday Spectator* of Minneapolis went farther, describing the building as a "useless, miserable and rotten pile." The legislature finally responded to the mounting criticism in 1893 by approving funds for a building to replace Buffington's lemon. When Cass Gilbert's magnificent new edifice finally opened, the old Capitol was turned into a storage facility. It was razed in 1937–38, and the Arts and Science Center later built on the site.

The Senate chamber in the second Capitol, about 1885

ALPHEUS G. FULLER (LATER LAFAYETTE EMMETT) HOUSE

North side of Seventh Street between Walnut and
Sherman streets, St. Paul. Architect unknown.
1854–1942.

Lafayette Emmett

Greek Revival was a national style between 1820
and 1850. It rose to prominence not only as a
reaction against British-influenced styles following the War of 1812 but also because of its association with Greece's struggle for independence in
the 1820s. Viewed by Americans as the true style
of democracy, Greek Revival was used for all
types of buildings but was especially favored for
houses. The style was still popular in the East
when it reached Minnesota in the 1840s. Most
Greek Revival houses in the Twin Cities were
small and plain, but a few elaborate examples
appeared in the early 1850s. Among them was
this splendid brick house built at 279–81 West
Seventh Street by Alpheus G. Fuller.

Fuller was a Connecticut-born entrepreneur
who arrived in Minnesota in 1848. He worked in
the fur trade, was active in St. Paul politics (serving on the city council in 1855), but was best
remembered as the builder of the Fuller House
hotel, which opened in 1856 and was the largest
in the city until it burned down thirteen years
later.

His own house, described by the *Minnesota
Pioneer* as "a large and handsome brick edifice,"
was one of the most monumental of its day in
St. Paul, with a full-height Doric porch supported
by four colossal wooden columns. The two middle columns were pinched together to frame the
front entrance, creating a rather unsettling appearance. Above the porch was an attic frieze
band complete with "belly" windows, so called
because about the only way anyone could peer
through them would be in a prone position.
Unfortunately little is known about the interior,
which must have been elegant and spacious since
Fuller and his wife entertained frequently. The
architect is also unknown, but Greek Revival
pattern books abounded, and any one of a number of local master builders could have constructed the house.

Fuller lived in his house for only three years,
then moved to South Dakota. The house was

The Fuller-Emmett house, about 1880

purchased in 1858 by Lafayette Emmett, first justice of the Minnesota Supreme Court. Legend has it that Emmett's brother Daniel wrote the song "Dixie" while staying at the house in 1859. The story has the tinny ring of apocrypha but could be true.

As St. Paul grew, the house and others like it nearby (including the Daniel Robertson house of 1856) were surrounded by commercial development along Seventh Street. The Fuller-Emmett house was eventually converted to commercial use and by the 1930s had become a funeral home. In 1941 the owners decided to tear the building down, prompting a brief preservation battle. The Junior Pioneers of St. Paul tried to raise two thousand dollars to buy and restore the old house. But the effort failed, and the house was demolished in 1942.

FIRST AND SECOND SUSPENSION BRIDGES

Hennepin Avenue at Mississippi River, Minneapolis.
Thomas M. Griffith. 1855–76, 1876–89.

The two suspension bridges that carried Hennepin Avenue across the main channel of the Mississippi River to Nicollet Island were prominent landmarks in early Minneapolis. Both were designed by Thomas M. Griffith, a New York engineer who apprenticed under the greatest American bridge builder of the nineteenth century, John Roebling. Although suspension spans had appeared in the United States as early as 1801, it was Roebling who first built such structures on a truly heroic scale. Among Roebling's triumphs was an 821-foot-long, double-deck suspension bridge built across the Niagara River gorge between 1851 and 1855. Griffith apparently worked on this project before being hired to build the bridge in Minneapolis.

Griffith's Minneapolis bridge, completed in 1855, was the first permanent span across the Mississippi River. Like most early bridges, it was built—for thirty-six thousand dollars—by a pri-

First suspension bridge photographed from St. Anthony, about 1869; Nicollet Island and the Pacific Lumber Mills are in the foreground

First bridge, looking toward Minneapolis

vate company that intended to recoup its investment through tolls. Despite its rustic appearance, the bridge was a sophisticated work of engineering for its time and place. It featured two forty-seven-foot-high towers over which cables were suspended to support a river span of 620 feet. The H-shaped, tapering towers were built of wood above stone foundations and had palelike vertical siding with a Gothic Revival flavor. Each of the two cables, secured by heavy cast-iron anchorages set back from the towers, consisted of more than four hundred strands of wire. The bridge deck, supported by wire suspenders hung from the cables, was barely seventeen feet wide and only a few feet above the river.

The bridge opened on January 23, 1855. Despite the cold, a mile-long procession, equipped with sixty-one sleighs, crossed the new structure, after which the celebrants repaired to a Minneapolis hotel for food and drink. Unfortunately the new bridge soon encountered difficulties. In March a high wind (ever the enemy of suspension spans) caused the bridge to sway so violently that it almost tore itself apart. Repairs were quickly made, however, and the bridge reopened by the Fourth of July.

Much of the early bridge traffic must have been four-legged in nature, judging by the toll schedule, which set varying rates (based on weight) for members of the animal kingdom. This system meant a horse (fifteen cents) or a cow (ten cents) faced a stiffer charge than a human being (three cents one way, five cents for a round trip). Sheep got by cheaply (two cents).

While the new bridge was under construction, traffic continued on the old bridge; note the anchorages for each bridge.

The toll taker was Captain John Tapper, who had once operated a rope ferry on the site. In 1868 Hennepin County bought the bridge, described by one newspaper as "rotten" and "unsafe," for $37,500 and removed the toll. The bridge was later turned over to the city of Minneapolis.

The bridge appears to have been rather unstable from the start, since signs warned of a ten dollar fine for crossing at faster than a walking pace. Heavily loaded wagons were also cautioned to stay at least one hundred feet apart. The bridge's instability and narrowness rapidly made it obsolete, and in November 1874 Griffith was called back to Minneapolis to design a replacement.

Controversy erupted a few months later when James J. Eads, another of the era's great bridge engineers, sent a letter to the Minneapolis City Council. Eads, who had just built an unprecedented steel-arch railroad bridge (extant) across the Mississippi at St. Louis, urged the council not to approve a suspension span. He said a steel-arch bridge would be stronger, stiffer, and more durable than a suspension span (all of which was true) and that "no sensible engineer would construct a suspension bridge where an arch or truss bridge can be built at the same cost." Griffith's reaction to this assault on his probity (not to mention his pocketbook) is not recorded, but he must have been furious. The letter came just as the city was preparing to take bids for construction of the new suspension bridge, and it threw the whole process into an uproar for more than a month. Griffith's supporters finally prevailed, however, and the project went ahead.

The new suspension bridge, completed in 1876, was built directly north of the old bridge, which was then torn down. The second bridge eclipsed its predecessor in every respect, with a central span of 630 feet, 80-foot-high stone towers, and a 32-foot-wide roadway (the total width, counting sidewalks, was 57 feet). It was also much higher above water than the first bridge and much costlier, with a price tag of $221,000 (double the original estimate). Although Griffith chose to echo medieval forms in the bridge's towers—which were decked out with embattled parapets, turrets, and other romantic flourishes—his structural system was state-of-the-art. This style was especially evident in the bridge's distinctive diagonal stays, a device Roebling used on almost all of his bridges (including his great Brooklyn Bridge of 1869–83) to increase their stability.

But the second suspension bridge, like the first, quickly proved to be inadequate to meet the city's needs. By 1877 one newspaper had already labeled it the "Bridge of Sighs" because of cost overruns and disputes over Griffith's fee. Maintenance also proved to be costly. The bridge, wrote a city engineer, constantly seemed to have "something wrong: an eye breaking here and a bolt there, and the trusses always loose and rickety." The *St. Paul and Minneapolis Pioneer Press* observed in 1882 that the bridge "was long ago voted an abortion and a nuisance" and would have to be replaced. It was, seven years later, by a new steel-arch bridge much like the one Eads had proposed. About the only mourner on this occasion was the prominent New York architectural critic, Montgomery Schuyler, who lamented that Griffith's suspension bridge had been "sacrificed quite ruthlessly to the need of greater accommodation."

Not every trace of the bridge is gone, however. In 1988, as Hennepin County prepared to replace the steel-arch bridge with a new suspension span (completed in 1990), archaeologists for the Minnesota Historical Society made an interesting find on Nicollet Island. There, buried under a century's worth of rubble, lay the stone foundation from the east tower of the old bridge, looking as massive and imposing as the day it was built.

Second suspension bridge, reaching from Minneapolis to Nicollet Island

NICOLLET HOUSE

South side of Washington Avenue between Hennepin and Nicollet avenues, Minneapolis. Architect unknown. 1858, 1871–1923.

This hotel was for many years the most popular one in Minneapolis, benefiting from its prime location and reputation for good food and service. Like other pioneer hotels that survived into the twentieth century (such as the Merchants in St. Paul), the Nicollet House was built in stages and frequently modernized to keep pace with customer demand.

The hotel's original section, five stories high, was completed in 1858 on a donated lot. Local citizens also chipped in another ten thousand dollars for construction. These sorts of subsidies were common practice at the time, since good hotels were considered vital to frontier communities. Two young Boston men, James M. Eustis and

Nicollet House, about 1865

W. H. Judd, were the main investors in the hotel and operated it for its first two years.

Built of local cream-colored brick above a limestone base, the 1858 section of the hotel looks primitive to modern eyes but was elaborately finished by the standards of the day in Minneapolis. The architect is unknown but was someone who knew just enough from pattern books to give the otherwise plain building a bracketed cornice in the manner of the soon-to-be-popular Italianate style. An observation cupola atop the low-pitched roof also provided a picturesque touch to the design.

The building's plan was as straightforward as its facades. The first floor contained storefront rental space as well as a saloon, a billiard room, and the main lobby. A large dining hall, parlors, and other public rooms occupied the second floor. These public spaces were furnished with Brussels carpets, lace curtains, tapestries, and other elegant accoutrements rare in Minneapolis at the time. The three upper floors contained about a hundred guest rooms, said to be large and "well ventilated." Guests remarked on the hotel's fine food (the owners at one point even maintained their own farm to provide fresh dairy products and produce). This culinary reputation was established at the hotel's opening banquet on May 26, 1858, an event that attracted two hundred guests.

For a brief time, the Nicollet House faced stiff competition from the other great Minneapolis (actually St. Anthony) hotel of the period—the Winslow House. Both hotels vied for the trade of southern planters, who came north in the summer to escape the heat. But the Civil War ended such voyages of relief, and in 1861 the Winslow House closed for good. The Nicollet House was also hit hard by the disruption of Mississippi steamboat traffic and shut down briefly in 1862–63.

Business picked up after the war, however, and in 1871 the hotel opened a large addition along

Lobby, about 1913

Nicollet. Although as high as the old part of the hotel, the addition had only four stories, creating awkward connections between the old and new sections. The addition, more strongly Italianate in style than the original portion of the hotel, gave the Nicollet House a total of 235 rooms. It also provided a second cupola, which appears to have been installed solely for reasons of symmetry, since the view cannot have been especially spectacular. With the addition, the hotel became U-shaped, sheltering a large open courtyard that offered plenty of greenery, a fountain, and even some tame deer.

In 1881 more renovation work was undertaken, and the hotel acquired an elevator, electric bells, and other improvements. Despite increased competition from new hotels (beginning with the West in 1884), the Nicollet House retained its popularity well into the twentieth century. During its long life, the hotel attracted plenty of famous visitors, including presidents (Ulysses S. Grant, James Garfield, William McKinley, and Teddy Roosevelt), generals (William Sherman and Philip Sheridan), and even one wandering poet from across the seas—Oscar Wilde.

Old age finally took its toll on the hotel in 1922 when city fire inspectors (echoing fears first voiced in the 1880s) declared the building unsafe and ordered installation of a sprinkler system. That cost was too high for the owners to bear, and later that year a public subscription campaign began to raise money for a new hotel on the site. The drive raised about $3 million, and in 1923 the old hotel came down. Its replacement was a twelve-story, 637-room hotel designed in vaguely neoclassic style by the well-known Chicago firm of Holabird and Roche. The second Nicollet (known after 1957 as the Pick-Nicollet) survived as a hotel until 1973, when the building was sold to Souls Harbor Church. In 1984 the church moved out, and the vacant building was finally demolished in 1991 after a plan to convert it into luxury apartments failed. The site became a parking lot.

Hotel Nicollet, about 1916

THIRD ST. PAUL CATHEDRAL AND BISHOP'S RESIDENCE

Northeast corner of Sixth and St. Peter streets, St. Paul.
Joseph W. Smyth (residence). 1858, 1860–1914.

Third St. Paul Cathedral (left), bishop's residence (center), and second cathedral (right, behind residence), about 1860

The log chapel built by Father Lucien Galtier in 1841 is generally accounted as the first St. Paul Cathedral, in name if not in grandeur. It was replaced in 1851 by a modest brick structure near the northwest corner of Sixth and Wabasha streets on a square block of land owned by the Catholic church. But the second Cathedral—which combined a school, church, and rectory in one building—was hardly satisfactory (smoke and fumes from the rectory kitchen often wafted through the sanctuary), and in 1853 Bishop Joseph Cretin began planning for a larger cathedral on the same block. Work began in 1854, but Cretin's death in 1857, along with the financial panic that year, slowed construction, and it was not until June 13, 1858, that mass was first celebrated in the new church.

The third Cathedral was a very plain affair. Buttresses, a tall steeple, and virtually all ornamentation were eliminated from the design to save money, so that the final product was basically a big limestone barn with a gabled roof. Even so, it was the largest church of its time in the Twin Cities, deriving a certain grim power from its great expanses of rugged masonry. In style, the church was a crude brand of Romanesque, with round-arched openings, a front wheel window, and three heavy staircases (perhaps the most striking feature of the design) ascending to doorways on Sixth Street. As built the church was basically an oblong box, but two small transepts were added at the rear, creating a Latin-cross plan. The architect is unknown.

Inside, the church was equally unadorned, although it acquired some decorative touches over the years. A low barrel vault covered the long nave, which had one unusual feature—side galleries that extended all the way to the transepts. Servants and other lesser mortals were consigned to these galleries, which helped to increase seating in the always crowded church.

Next door on Sixth was a more ostentatious structure—a bishop's residence completed in

1860 to the designs of an obscure master builder named Joseph Smyth. Built for Bishop Thomas L. Grace, who succeeded Cretin, the house was said to "compare favorably with the palatial residences of our Merchant Princes in the Atlantic Cities." A stately essay in the Italian Villa style, the three-story house had flanking two-story wings, a cupola, and an elegant Palladian entry with a balcony above. The house cost fifteen thousand dollars, nearly half as much as the Cathedral, suggesting that Bishop Grace enjoyed a comfortable life-style.

In 1904 Archbishop John Ireland began laying plans for a new Cathedral on St. Anthony Hill. Ten years later, on August 30, 1914, as the new Cathedral was about to open, Ireland spoke at a solemn farewell mass at the old church. "Look well around," he told the faithful. "For the last time see what so long you have loved to see." A few weeks later, both the third Cathedral and the old bishop's residence were demolished. The Hamm Building has occupied the site since 1920.

Third Cathedral, 1901

Interior of the third Cathedral decorated for the consecration of Bishops John Shanley, Joseph Cotter, and James McGolrick, December 27, 1889

WEST SIDE FLOUR MILLING DISTRICT

First and Second streets between Fifth and Chicago
avenues south, Minneapolis. Various architects and
millwrights. 1850s–1960s.

Although the first commercial flour mill was
built on the west side of the Falls of St. Anthony
in 1859, it was not until the 1870s that the
industry achieved a truly spectacular degree of
concentration. Spurred by new technologies that
made it possible to make better flour from spring
wheat, annual flour production in Minneapolis
increased tenfold between 1870 and 1880, then
tripled over the next decade. By 1880, when
Minneapolis had supplanted St. Louis as the flour
milling center of America, twenty-two mills were
lined up in tight formation along a four-block
stretch of First Street. The result was a landscape
of wonder and peril, where streets became canals,
trains ran by waterpower, the ground was as hollow as a honeycomb, and sudden explosions
could hurl huge chunks of stone a mile through
the air, sending men to instant oblivion.

Strictly utilitarian in character, the mill buildings nonetheless had tremendous architectural
presence by virtue of their size and blunt massing.

West side milling district, about 1880

They were three to eight stories high, often had
narrow rooftop monitors housing power shafts,
and generally were built of limestone or brick
with timber framing inside. Most had small windows and little ornamentation. Auxiliary buildings—such as machine shops, warehouses, and
storage elevators—clustered around the mills.
The mills themselves were usually designed by
engineers such as William de la Barre, although
an architect would sometimes be called in to
dress up the facades.

The First Street power canal was at the heart
of this one-of-a-kind industrial complex. As originally built in 1857, the canal was three hundred
feet long, seventy feet wide, and fourteen feet
deep. It was extended to nine hundred feet in
1865 and deepened by four feet in 1885. The
canal, which took up all of First Street, doubled
as a railroad corridor. A wooden trestle was built
over the canal in 1878 and rebuilt in iron in
1885. The trestle could not support heavy engines, so rail cars were pulled along by a rope tow,
which like everything else in the vicinity, was
waterpowered.

All along the canal, water thundered down
into wheel pits, some fifty feet below grade, turn-
ing turbines that ran the milling machinery. The

*West side milling district,
with lumber and paper mills
of Nicollet Island in the
foreground, 1870*

second Washburn A Mill (the largest in the city when it was completed in 1880) had two iron turbines, each capable of generating five hundred horsepower. Connected to the work floors by 235 feet of shafting, these wheels powered 120 porcelain-iron rollers and twenty French-made millstones that could turn out three thousand barrels of flour a day. A network of brick-lined tail race tunnels bored through the soft sandstone beneath the mills, carrying water back to the river below the falls.

The mills cannot have been healthy places to work. Not only were they filled with fast-moving machinery (belts in some mills sped along at close to fifty miles an hour), but they also produced enormous amounts of flour dust, which in certain concentrations could be lethally explosive. One mill visitor in 1883 remarked on seeing a worker "so white from head to foot that, as he stood motionless among the machinery, we mistook him for an elevator shaft."

Fire and explosion claimed a dozen mills by 1900. The greatest disaster was the explosion on May 2, 1878, of the first Washburn A Mill, built just four years earlier. Seven stories high with walls of solid stone, the mill had the look of a building that might last forever. But the explosion, later attributed to a buildup of flour dust, leveled the mill in an instant, entombing eighteen men, scattering blocks of stone in an eight-block radius, and breaking windows as far away as Summit Avenue in St. Paul. Two nearby mills were destroyed and three others damaged in the explosion, which one newspaper called "the most terrible calamity which has ever befallen Minneapolis." In the end, though, it was not the explosive quality of flour dust but a new economic order that doomed the milling district. Changes in tariff and freight rates, along with shifts in wheat growing patterns and the opening of the Panama Canal in 1914, all worked against Minneapolis. By 1930 Buffalo was making more flour than was the fabled Mill City. Meanwhile, the mills vanished one by one. An especially large number were torn down in the 1920s and 1930s. In 1960 the power canal was filled in. Five years later the west side's last working flour mill—the second Washburn A—closed forever, standing vacant until February 1991 when fire destroyed much of the structure.

LEFT: *The mill canal under construction, about 1885*

RIGHT: *Interior of the Washburn A Mill, about 1875*

HORACE THOMPSON HOUSE

33 Woodward Avenue (at Lafayette Avenue), St. Paul.
J. D. Pollock. 1860–1904.

Horace Thompson

Horace Thompson was one of St. Paul's prominent pioneer bankers. Born in Vermont in 1827, he began his career at age eighteen by joining his two older brothers—Norman and James—in a mercantile business in Georgia. James decided in 1859 to move to St. Paul, where he went into partnership with banker Parker Paine. Horace joined his brother a year later, and in 1861 they set up their own bank. Within two years, this institution evolved into the First National Bank of St. Paul, with James as president and Horace as cashier.

The house Horace Thompson built for himself as soon as he arrived in St. Paul suggests that he was already a wealthy man. Located near a bluff overlooking Trout Brook, Thompson's house cost ten thousand dollars—a princely sum in those days. It was among the first large houses in the Lafayette Park area, an exclusive Lowertown enclave that also attracted the likes of Henry Sibley and Amherst Wilder, who were Thompson's neighbors. The house also appears to have been one of the Twin Cities' first residences in the Italian Villa style popularized by Andrew Jackson Downing.

Built chiefly of Platteville limestone, the Thompson house sat amid a grove of oaks on a big corner lot bordered by a stone wall with an elegant iron railing. The design is attributed to J. D. Pollock, a local master builder whose inspiration may have been a country villa depicted in Downing's *Cottage Residences* (1842). Pollock's design displayed all the standard elements of the Italian Villa style—a graceful tower (said to offer a wonderful view of the city), bracketed eaves, tall arched windows with stone hoods, corner quoins, and asymmetric massing. The most ex-

ceptional feature, however, was a lovely arcaded veranda to either side of the front tower. Little is known about the interior of the house, except that it had central heating, gas lights, and running water, all rarities at the time.

After the house was built, Thompson continued to prosper, becoming president of the First National Bank in 1870. An avid sportsman, he

Horace Thompson house, about 1880

had a great adventure in 1876 while hunting in southern Minnesota. He stumbled on three members of the James gang after the Northfield bank robbery and held them at bay with a shotgun until help arrived. Thompson died in 1880 at age fifty-two when he caught pneumonia on a business trip to New York. Like so much else in Lowertown, his house fell to the railroads. The Northern Pacific, which began pushing tracks through the Trout Brook valley in the 1880s, needed still more land by 1900. In 1904 the railroad bought Thompson's house, razed it, then graded the lot. Subsequently large warehouses occupied the site of the house and its surroundings, and entire blocks of Woodward Avenue itself disappeared.

BOHEMIAN FLATS

West bank of Mississippi River beneath Washington Avenue Bridge, Minneapolis. Owner built. 1860s–1963.

The hierarchy of altitude was especially strong in the Twin Cities in the late nineteenth century. While the rich resided in their mansions on Summit Hill in St. Paul and Lowry Hill in Minneapolis, the poorest Twin Citians were tucked away—out of sight and mind—in deep holes like Swede Hollow or on the floodplains below the river bluffs. Isolated from the city by barriers of language, culture, and geography, these enclaves were often identified with a particular ethnic group, although most were actually quite diverse in their makeup.

Bohemian Flats in Minneapolis was perhaps the largest of all the river-flat settlements in the Twin Cities. Occupying two shelves of land at the bottom of a low gorge, the flats were first settled in the 1860s and by 1900 were home to twelve hundred people. What attracted immigrants to this flood-prone place was land so cheap that even the poorest families could build homes of their own. The St. Anthony Water Power Company, which owned the flats, charged an annual rent of only twelve dollars in the 1880s for a house lot, although rates eventually rose as high as twenty-five dollars a year. It is thus no surprise that 95 percent of the flats' residents identified themselves as homeowners in the 1890 census.

The houses—described by one resident as "looking like little cigar boxes on a stage street"—were all small and built of wood on

Bohemian Flats under the Washington Avenue Bridge after a spring flood, about 1900

cramped lots. Board fences surrounded most houses, providing a measure of privacy and also corralling the cows kept by many residents. A few stores and saloons, a brick apartment building, and a tiny church—Holy Emmanuel Slovak Lutheran—provided the rest of the flats' architectural ensemble. Three main streets—Mill, Cooper, and Wood—ran parallel to the river through the center section of the flats north of the Washington Avenue Bridge. Other parts of the settlement had no discernible streets, however, and houses were "dropped about in strange fashion and in irregular lines."

The site of Bohemian Flats was far more picturesque in the nineteenth century than it was in the twentieth, when dams raised the level of the Mississippi River through much of Minneapolis. Before the dams were built, the river poured through a fast, rock-strewn channel below the Falls of St. Anthony. Sawmills upriver sent a tremendous volume of flotsam tumbling over the falls. Residents of the flats built platforms out into the river from which they were able to harvest this treasure, which could then be sold or used for heating or even home construction. "Of this harvest there is, from April to November, an almost uninterrupted stream," a magazine correspondent wrote in 1887. "You can see slabs, shingles, strips, blocks, boards and sometimes entire logs hurrying down the river." Most men in the flats held day labor jobs, so wood gathering was left to the very young, the very old, and women. In a good season, a skillful gatherer could collect three hundred or more cords of wood from the river.

Despite its name, Bohemian Flats had a mixed population that swelled with a surge of immigrants in the 1880s and 1890s. The 1900 census reported 613 Slovaks, 123 Czechs, 41 Irish, and a sprinkling of Norwegians, Germans, Austrians, Danes, and Russians living in the densely settled section of the flats north of the Washington Avenue Bridge. The smaller part of the flats south of

the bridge was actually more "Bohemian" in character, with Czechs forming the largest ethnic group.

The Bohemian Flats, published in 1941 by the Works Progress Administration, painted a rather sunny picture of life on the flats, but it cannot have been all that wonderful. Nils Vaag—the young hero of O. E. Rølvaag's novel, *The Boat of Longing*, set in Minneapolis in about 1912—thought the small houses dotting the flats resembled "black scorch flecks in the bottom of a huge kettle. Nils had often wondered how human beings could endure living down there." But they did endure, despite the lack of sewer and water service, the annual spring floods, and the grinding poverty that sometimes manifested itself in violence and alcoholism.

The flats developed gradually over a period of years and ended that way as well. In 1915 the city, interested in building a municipal barge terminal, began proceedings to condemn parts of the flats. Years of litigation followed with the inevitable result. Most of the flats' residents were finally evicted in 1931 to make way for the terminal. Fourteen homes remained, but they vanished one by one over the next three decades—the last being demolished in 1963.

Bohemian Flats, about 1895

FIRST WASHINGTON SCHOOL

East side of Third Avenue South between Fourth and Fifth streets, Minneapolis. Abraham Radcliffe. 1867–88.

SECOND WASHINGTON SCHOOL

South side of Sixth Street between Park and Chicago avenues south, Minneapolis. Long and Kees. 1888–1971.

These two schools, built just twenty-one years apart, reflect how quickly both education and architecture changed in Minneapolis in the nineteenth century. The first Washington School, which opened in 1867, was a small, plain building that initially served all of the city's public school students. Its design is attributed to Abraham Radcliffe, one of the busiest architects of the period in the Twin Cities. The building was actually the second school on the site. It replaced Union School—the first in Minneapolis—which was built in about 1857 and burned to the ground eight years later in a fire set by a disgruntled student.

The first Washington School was utterly unpretentious. Constructed of Platteville limestone, the school was basically a four-story box fitted out with a few simple French Second Empire adornments. These included window hoods on the third floor, corner quoins, a small balcony over the entrance, a bracketed cornice, and an ill-proportioned mansard roof. The rooms inside were simply finished, with first through eighth graders on the lower floors and high school students above.

Next to the building was a brick and wood bell tower that had survived the Union School fire. With its arched, open belfry and low-pitched roof, this delightful little tower was essentially Italianate in character. Its bell had a four-part mission: to summon the children, to ring out fire alarms (this was before Minneapolis installed a telegraphic fire alarm system in 1872), to celebrate special events (such as Union victories during the Civil War), and to provide a standard by which to set the city's watches and clocks. All of this was clearly in keeping with Minneapolis' small-town character in the 1860s and 1870s. The school and bell tower lasted until 1888 when they were demolished to make way for the Minneapolis City Hall–Hennepin County Courthouse.

By this time Minneapolis had shed its village garb and was a booming city, with eighteen thousand public school students occupying almost forty buildings. In 1887–88 alone, nine schools were built in Minneapolis, among them the new Washington Elementary School on Sixth Street. Although not the largest school of its time in Minneapolis, Washington Elementary was—from a purely design point of view—the most unusual and exciting.

First Washington School with bell tower to the right, about 1875

The school was designed by the prolific firm headed by Franklin Long and Frederick Kees, who must have been in a festive and not altogether rational mood when they drew up plans for the building. Three stories high with walls of light brick, the school consisted of a wide central section flanked by heavy round towers that contained small rooms. Although generally considered a mix of Gothic and Romanesque Revival, the school's elusive style might best be described as Early Space Age due to the numerous rocket-like turrets (or "minarets," as one newspaper called them) that were attached to the outer walls. These turrets gave the building an almost palpable sense of thrust, as though it might at any moment shoot off into the sky, never to be seen again.

The school also featured a phenomenally overwrought profile with a mad profusion of chimneys, turrets, towers, gables, and dormers bursting up and out from its mansard roof. Not much is known about the interior, although the arrangement of windows visible in photographs suggests there were about twelve classrooms on the first two floors.

Alas, this wild and woolly product of the late 1880s did not remain intact for long. About 1916 the school's top floor was lopped off, destroying all the visual fun created by Long and Kees but doubtlessly making roof maintenance a much easier chore. The building also acquired additions in 1925 and 1950 that further altered its original appearance. Presumably there was a good deal of interior updating over the years as well. In 1965, with its enrollment down to fewer than one hundred students, the school was closed for elementary purposes but continued to be used for special education classes. The end came in 1971 when Washington was torn down and replaced by the mammoth Hennepin County Medical Center, a building every bit as ugly as the old school but not nearly as endearing.

Architect's drawing for the second Washington School

ACADEMY OF MUSIC

Southwest corner of Hennepin and Washington avenues, Minneapolis. Robert Alden. 1872–84.

Theaters could be found in the Twin Cities by the early 1850s, but it was not until after the Civil War that large opera houses made their appearance. The Pence Opera House in Minneapolis and the St. Paul Opera House, both built in 1867, were the first of their kind. The largest of these early opera houses, however, was the Academy of Music. It specialized in "high-class" plays and concerts, although by 1878 the Academy also was booking the likes of Professor Bosco, a low-rent magician whose act was so inept that he was driven off stage one night by a volley of vases, pencils, and other potentially lethal missiles.

The audience was mellower at the theater's opening on January 2, 1872. Hailed locally as the finest opera house west of Chicago, the Academy was built at a cost of more than one hundred thousand dollars by Joseph Hodges, an investor from Providence, Rhode Island. The four-story building, like most opera houses of the time, combined rent-producing commercial space with a large upstairs hall. Occupying what was then Minneapolis' "100 per cent" corner, the building appears to have been a financial success for Hodges, who sold it a year later to a local syndicate headed by Thomas Lowry.

The designer, Robert Alden, was a Minneapolis pioneer whose first project had been the Winslow House hotel in St. Anthony. For the Academy of Music, Alden produced a fairly standard design with iron storefronts at street level, brick walls above broken by pilasters and string courses, simple arched windows, and a big mansard roof, signalling the building's membership in the grow-

Academy of Music, about 1874

ing French Second Empire fraternity. The mansard, ornamented with terra-cotta window caps and a galvanized iron cornice, was more than just a pretty hat: it covered huge, curving wooden roof trusses that provided a clear span for the opera hall on the third and fourth floors.

The horseshoe-shaped hall was about eighty feet square with thirteen hundred seats (almost all upholstered) on the main floor and balconies. The interior was gussied up with statuary, a big portrait of Beethoven, and frescoes. Stage equipment included a painted drop curtain and eleven sets of scenery, plus all the usual mechanisms of theatrical deception. Only two staircases (both less than ten feet wide) led up to the gaslit hall, which had all the elements of a spectacular firetrap. There were, in fact, persistent fears about the building's safety. In 1880, for instance, Minneapolis architect Frederick G. Corser worried out loud in a letter to the newspaper that the theater might be too weak structurally to support large crowds expected to gather there for high school graduation ceremonies. However, a committee of architects, engineers, and builders formed to investigate these concerns concluded four days later that the Academy was perfectly safe. Despite such assurances, the public never seems to have had complete confidence in the building.

Over its short life, the Academy attracted violinist Ole Bull, Buffalo Bill, and—perhaps most notably—the Irish poet and dandy Oscar Wilde. "The Apostle of Aestheticism," as one newspaper called Wilde, spoke to a curious crowd of three hundred on March 15, 1882. Wilde, then just twenty-eight and sporting long bushy hair, was jeered on stage, although it is not clear whether the audience was reacting to his ideas or his attire. His outfit was certainly bold: a low-necked shirt, a large white necktie, a black velvet cutaway coat, knee breeches, long black stockings, and white kid gloves. A reviewer found little of merit in Wilde's aesthetic theories, complaining

Academy of Music under construction, showing the arched roof trusses

that the "youthful speaker was imbued with the egotistical idea that the American public know nothing of art." What Wilde thought of Minneapolis is not known.

Wilde turned out to be one of the Academy's last big draws. In 1883 the theater closed, largely because of competition from the city's new Grand Opera House. Lowry and the syndicate owning the Academy then turned the building into an office structure, engineering one of the first big historic reuse projects ever undertaken in the Twin Cities. The renovated building contained five stories, including three stories of offices arranged around a skylit atrium carved out of the old theater. But the new Academy of Music building did not last long. On Christmas Day 1884 it was destroyed by fire, and two years later a new eight-story office building—Temple Court—filled the site, which subsequently became home to a nondescript federal office building.

WILLIAM S. JUDD HOUSE (EVERGREEN)

Block bounded by Fifth and Sixth streets, Fifth Avenue South and Portland Avenue, Minneapolis. Joseph Haley. Ca. 1873–1926.

A. T. Andreas's 1874 *Atlas of Minnesota* depicts this house as one of the great ornaments of Minneapolis. A drawing shows the towered house, known as Evergreen, set well back from the street on a block-square lot ringed by an iron fence. To one side of the dwelling is a delightful carriage house. On the other side, a fountain (probably added by the artist) sends up its spray amid a forest of small evergreens. The entire scene is as romantic as a fairy tale, perfectly exemplifying the domestic ideals expounded by Andrew Jackson Downing and other advocates of the picturesque.

William S. Judd, born in New York in 1823, was an all-purpose capitalist who at various times was a hotelkeeper, grain merchant, lumberman, woolen manufacturer, and part owner of the Cataract and Union flour mills in Minneapolis. By 1875 he was also insolvent, having lost most of his fortune speculating in grain futures. His wife

William Judd house, engraving from the Andreas atlas

Mary, in fact, appears to have possessed most of the family's financial acumen, and it was she who owned the land on which the house was built.

The house, which dates from about 1873 (possibly earlier), was apparently designed by Joseph Haley, a New York native who began his architectural practice in Minneapolis in 1869. Several large houses, including the nearby Alonzo Rand mansion of 1874, are also attributed to Haley, but little of his work survives. Built of cream-colored brick, the building was an Italian Villa-French Second Empire hybrid. The body of the house, three stories high, was textbook Italian Villa,

with double entry doors, an open front porch, tall paired windows, and bracketed eaves below a low-pitched roof. Shooting up from the center of the house was its most fanciful feature, a five-story tower topped by a steep French Second Empire mansard. A variety of projections, bays, and balconies completed the house's willfully picturesque profile.

The interior, loaded with black walnut and mahogany woodwork, included an elegant drawing room that ran the whole length of the house. One of the bathrooms was also said to contain the city's first fully plumbed bathtub. If so, Minneapolis was well behind its municipal rival in the personal hygiene department, since at least one house in St. Paul—the Horace Thompson house—had indoor plumbing as early as 1860.

As late as 1881 the Judd house was described as "the most showy residence in the city." But its proximity to the business district soon made it undesirable as a private home. By 1884 it had become a high-class rooming house, whose residents included the popular interior decorator John Bradstreet. Known as "Judd's Castle," the house was still considered "a prominent landmark" in 1902 when Judd died. The house was razed in 1926 and replaced ten years later by the Minneapolis Armory.

William Judd house, about 1925

MINNEAPOLIS CITY HALL

First and Second streets between Hennepin and Nicollet avenues, Minneapolis. Franklin Long. 1873–1912.

Minneapolis City Hall, about 1880

Minneapolis has seldom paid much heed to proper siting of its public buildings. But this rather ungainly structure was an exception. It occupied a prominent position overlooking Bridge Square, which in the 1870s was the commercial heart of the city. The building's choice location was a matter of economics rather than farsighted civic thinking. Bridge Square was public property, and by putting its new city hall there, Minneapolis saved the cost of acquiring a site elsewhere downtown. The city further improved its economic position by renting much of the building to private tenants.

Before 1873 Minneapolis city government had operated out of rented quarters in the Pence Opera House Block. But this arrangement was so clearly unsatisfactory that Minneapolis' normally parsimonious voters in 1872 approved a fifty thousand dollar bond issue for a new city hall. Franklin Long, by this time the city's best-connected architect, won the commission and produced an oddly imposing little four-story building (with a small fifth floor beneath a central tower). The wedge-shaped building was 160 feet long but only 20 feet wide at its narrow end on First Street. Its walls were built of local limestone with granite window frames and trim. The building's salient feature was its multitowered mansard roof, which from certain vantage points had the look of an oversized tricorn hat. The overall effect was supposed to be French Second Empire. It is doubtful, however, that anyone in Paris would have recognized the building as such.

Detailed descriptions of the interior are hard to come by, but the most impressive space appears to have been a large lobby with entrances off both Hennepin and Nicollet. The building also had a steam-powered passenger elevator, possibly the first in Minnesota. Initially the city leased out all but the basement and one floor of the building. Tenants included the U.S. Post Office (1873–82), the *Minneapolis Tribune*, the Northwestern Telegraph Company, and even

Franklin Long himself. City offices occupied the second floor, where the city council chambers were located. The *Tribune* reported in October 1873 that council members "blushed becomingly when they saw the nice new room into which they were ushered."

It did not take long for the building to prove to be inadequate. Ventilation was so poor that sewage fumes sickened many postal clerks on the first floor. The building was also a firetrap, described by one newspaper in 1882 as being "noto-riously dangerous in its construction." But the basic problem was that by 1890 the building was simply too small to house all of the offices necessary to govern a city of 165,000 people. A new city hall–courthouse was authorized in 1889 and completed in 1906. Once city agencies moved out, the old building was doomed. In 1912, not long after the city had signed a demolition contract for the vacant structure, it was destroyed by fire. Three years later Gateway Park was built on the site.

Minneapolis City Hall, amid the decoration for the first Industrial Exposition, 1886

U.S. CUSTOMS HOUSE

Northwest corner of Fifth and Wabasha streets, St. Paul.
Supervising architect of the U.S. Treasury. 1873–1939.

U.S. Customs House shortly after completion

When this building opened in February 1873, it was hailed by one commentator as "truly an ornament to our city." It is a measure of how quickly St. Paul grew that barely fifteen years later the Customs House was considered entirely inadequate, "worthy of notice only on account . . . of its palpable incongruity with the surroundings." Yet it was an important structure, both historically (it was the first downtown federal building in the Twin Cities) and as a fine example of the Romanesque Revival style.

The Customs House was built to hold the U.S. Post Office, federal courtrooms, and the offices of other federal agencies. Like all federal buildings of its period, it was designed by the office of the Supervising Architect of the U.S. Treasury, which tended to produce standardized designs in the fashion of the moment. Local architects were always called in to supervise the work, collecting a nice fee in the process. Both Edward Bassford and Augustus Knight served in this capacity, but neither was really involved in the design of the Customs House.

The building occupied the site of the old Mansion House hotel, which carried on St. Paul's tradition of combustibility at the inn by burning down in 1867. Excavation for the Customs House began that fall, but work moved at a glacial pace due to the usual political dillydallying, and it was not until February 1873 that the post office finally moved in.

Built of local limestone with trim of St. Cloud granite (possibly the first use in St. Paul of this handsome material), the three-story Customs House was plain and solid, if not especially inspiring. Its symmetrical facades featured rows of round-arched windows to either side of pedimented central pavilions defined by columnlike chimneys. Triple-arched openings marked entrances. Quoins, carved column capitals, and a denticulated cornice provided a modest level of ornamentation.

The post office was on the ground floor with

Interior of U.S. Customs House, about 1895

courtrooms and other offices above. Some rooms had ornate wooden ceilings and most had fireplaces. With its broad hallways (said to take up a third of the interior), the building was inefficient and quickly proved to be too small. The courtrooms also drew complaints, one judge calling them "notoriously bad for their purpose." Horse and cow markets nearby made the building an olfactory nightmare in summer and attracted swarms of insects. This condition led postmaster David Day to remark in 1882 that his offices were at times "worse than Egypt when plagued by flies."

Despite periodic expansion plans, the government's space crunch was not solved until 1898 when the first section of a new federal building (later Landmark Center) opened two blocks away. As for the old Customs House, it survived in an auxiliary role until 1939 when the government tore it down. A two-story commercial building was then constructed on the site.

PLYMOUTH CONGREGATIONAL CHURCH

Southeast corner of Eighth Street South and Nicollet Avenue, Minneapolis. Russell Sturgis. 1875, 1885–ca. 1909

The Plymouth congregation built its first church in 1858 at Fourth and Nicollet. Two years later the church was burned down by an arsonist who resented the pastor's temperance views. A new church went up on the same site in 1863 but was too small. The congregation then bought land at Eighth and Nicollet for a new church, its third in seventeen years.

The designer, Russell Sturgis, was a well-connected New York architect who had studied in Germany and whose staff at various times included George F. Babb and Charles F. McKim. Sturgis began his career in the polychromatic grip of the Ruskinian Gothic style advocated by his early mentor, Leopold Eidlitz. But by the mid-1870s Sturgis had managed to stifle his flamboyant tendencies and was gravitating toward a plainer, more overtly functional brand of architecture.

FAR RIGHT:
Plymouth Congregational Church, 1890

BELOW:
Auditorium of Plymouth Congregational Church, about 1881

This approach suited the Plymouth congregation, which had a limited budget but wanted a large church with a straightforward auditorium. Sturgis met the challenge by providing a sort of decorated Gothic barn, as rugged and homely as its urban surroundings. Built mostly of local limestone, the church enclosed a large amount of space with more attention to efficiency than style. Its gabled front facade, with a pair of wheel windows above triple entry doors, evoked at least a hint of Italian Gothic. But the church's awkwardly mounted octagonal corner tower, surmounted by a wooden spire with louvered panels, was like nothing ever seen in Europe. The side elevations were equally unusual, having unbuttressed clerestories rising above a row of tall arched windows. There was little or no ornament.

Inside, the ninety-foot-square auditorium offered twelve hundred seats on two levels, arranged in a tight horseshoe under a high central roof supported by two huge trusses. The gallery, tucked directly beneath smaller sloping roofs, offered such excellent sight lines that many church members preferred it to the main floor. Simple frescoes, carved oak woodwork, and stained glass provided the only ornamental flourishes. An addition completed in 1885 included Sunday school rooms, prayer rooms, and a kitchen. The church was considered shockingly utilitarian in its day and "was greatly ridiculed," according to one member of the building committee. But another critic, while acknowledging the church's unpopularity, wrote in 1878 that it was "the best designed . . . building in town."

As the Nicollet Avenue shopping district moved south in the 1880s and 1890s, the corner occupied by the church became increasingly valuable. In 1907 the congregation cashed in, selling the property for $234,000 and moving two years later into a new church farther south on Nicollet. The old church was then razed to make way for a department store, which was itself replaced in 1969 by the Midwest Plaza Building.

EASTMAN FLATS

13–59 Eastman Avenue, Nicollet Island, Minneapolis.
Architect unknown. 1877 to 1882–ca. 1959

Franklin Steele laid the first claim to Nicollet Island in 1848 and cut down most of its virgin hardwood forest before losing the property to foreclosure in 1861. Entrepreneurs William W. Eastman and John L. Merriam acquired the island four years later and offered to sell it to the city as a park. City voters, to the regret of future generations, refused to spend the money. Eastman and Merriam then decided to develop the south end of the island for industry, but it was not until 1879 that they managed to obtain a reliable source of power via a rope cable driven by turbines at the Falls of St. Anthony. Meanwhile, the two men worked to turn the northern part of the island (above Hennepin Avenue) into a fashionable residential retreat. Eastman himself had built a mansion on the island in 1868, and a few other businessmen, such as William S. King, followed suit in the 1870s.

But the double row of town houses Eastman built between 1877 and 1882 were far more impressive. The *Minneapolis Tribune* called them the city's "star block of tenement houses," and it would be hard to dispute that judgment. Although row houses had already appeared in the

Eastman Flats in wintertime, about 1930; note the stone and brick facades

96

Eastman Flats, about 1936

Twin Cities by this time, the Eastman Flats set new standards for size and elegance. The project ultimately included fifty houses, thirty in a row on the north side of Eastman Avenue (located one block north of Hennepin) and twenty on the south side. The northerly row extended all the way across the island, forming one of the young city's most extraordinary architectural ensembles.

The first houses were built of stone quarried right on the island, but later units had brick fronts. Four stories high (including tall basements), the houses were treated simply on the exterior with narrow arched windows (topped by the usual heavy hoods), classically inspired detailing, and mansard roofs. The style was French Second Empire. The houses varied in size, but some corner units were as large as twenty-four by forty-five feet and contained fourteen rooms. Interior finishing included oak woodwork, fireplaces, and French plate-glass windows (the best

on the market) in the front parlors. All units had central heating and hot and cold running water.

Initially the houses proved to be highly attractive to the upper-middle class clientele Eastman had in mind, and by July 1878 all but two were rented. This early success convinced Eastman to build more units over the next several years. But Nicollet Island, like the nearby Gateway District, began to slip after 1900. The row houses were then subdivided into apartments (generally one to a floor), and a less well-to-do clientele moved in. It appears that part of Eastman Flats vanished as early as the 1920s when De La Salle High School built an addition on the site. But some of the old row houses survived until 1959, when the school expanded again. By 1991 only the eight-unit Grove Street Flats (a separate development also built by Eastman in 1877) remained as a reminder of the great row house era on Nicollet Island.

CENTRAL HIGH SCHOOL

Eleventh Street and Fourth Avenue South, Minneapolis.
Long and Haglin. 1878, 1888–1936.

CENTRAL HIGH SCHOOL

Northeast corner of Tenth and Minnesota streets, St. Paul.
Gurdon Randall. 1883, 1888–1929.

Minneapolis Central High School, about 1885

The first public high school buildings in St. Paul and Minneapolis were strikingly similar. Both were built about the same time, both were Victorian Gothic in style, both received major additions in 1888, and both were replaced by new buildings in 1912–13.

Minneapolis acquired its first Central High School in 1878. Before then, both elementary and high school students attended the old Washington School. But as the city's population increased dramatically in the decade after the Civil War, there was pressure to build a separate high school. City voters approved bonding for the project in 1875, but construction did not begin until two years later.

Franklin Long and his then-partner, Charles Haglin, were awarded the job following a national design competition. They produced a rock-solid essay in Victorian Gothic that was one of the most impressive buildings of its time in Minneapolis. Four stories high (counting the basement), the building was constructed of rock-faced Platteville limestone with Kasota stone trim. Its dominant feature was a massive corner tower, more than one hundred feet high. Two smaller round towers and a profusion of steep gables added further romance to the proceedings, while a big front porch provided a welcoming domestic gesture. The building was also strongly detailed with trefoil window frames, checkerboard stone work, ornamented column capitals, and a banded roof of red and black slate.

Despite its picturesque outline, the building was all business inside. Carefully planned, the school contained twenty classrooms, a gymnasium, a large auditorium, laboratories, and offices.

Demolition of Minneapolis Central High School

St. Paul Central High School, about 1908; note the observatory at the top of the tower at the right end of the school

Staircases tucked neatly in the round towers provided up-and-down circulation. The educational program included Latin and Greek as well as English, history, and math. In 1880 the school enrolled two hundred students, a number that was to increase fourfold over the next decade.

In the early morning hours of April 28, 1882, the building's environs were the scene of a grisly civics lesson. A man named Frank McManus, accused of raping a four-year-old girl, was pulled from his cell in the Hennepin County jail by a mob of sixty men, dragged to a huge oak tree across from the high school, and summarily hanged. "A Leper Lynched," exulted one newspaper the next day. Later, however, the newspapers—as well as many citizens—began having second thoughts about the wisdom of mob justice, and the lynching apparently was the last in Minneapolis.

As Central's enrollment swelled in the 1880s, the building became overcrowded, and an addition was completed in 1888. The addition was nearly as large as the original building and followed the same style. It contained twenty-three classrooms, shops in the basement, and a third-floor assembly hall. In 1913 the city built a new Central High School in south Minneapolis. The old building stood until 1936, however, when a new vocational school replaced it.

St. Paul built its first high school in 1883. The city had been conducting high school classes since 1870 at Franklin School in Lowertown, but by the late 1870s more room was needed. After rejecting an initial bond proposal in 1879, voters finally approved funding for a new high school two years later. The site chosen was on the block bounded by Tenth, Eleventh, Minnesota, and Robert streets. Adams School—built in 1858 and the second oldest in the city—occupied a part of this site and was torn down in 1882 to make way for the high school.

A competition was held for the project, and the winner was Gurdon P. Randall of Chicago. Randall—a reputable if not especially inspired architect—was best known for designing large public and institutional buildings and a series of thundering limestone churches in Chicago, the most prominent of which was probably his First Congregational Church of 1869. Central High School was to be his only commission in St. Paul, and the record suggests that he may have ended up regretting it.

Randall's design makes for an interesting comparison with Long and Haglin's school completed only five years earlier in Minneapolis. Although both buildings were Gothic in style, Randall chose to build his of red brick, whereas Long and Haglin had relied on the local stone. (Minneapo-

Students assembled in the auditorium of St. Paul Central High School, about 1903; note the hammer beam, bracketed ceiling

lis Central, in fact, was one of the last big buildings in the Twin Cities constructed of Platteville limestone, which lost popularity around 1880 as brick and other types of stone became readily available and as clients' tastes became more sophisticated.)

Three stories high with white stone trim offsetting its brickwork, St. Paul Central was a less powerful design than its Minneapolis counterpart. Randall's building offered a big central tower and plenty of agitation at the roof line, but the design was rather dainty and mannered compared to the rough-hewn solidity of Long and Haglin's work. The design also proved to be extremely costly, much to the displeasure of the St. Paul School Board. Noting that the building had cost more than double its fifty thousand dollar budget, the board president in March 1883 accused Ran-

dall of "perpetrating a fraud on the people and every architect who made a bid on the work."

Cost overruns notwithstanding, the school opened in September 1883 with about 225 students. It was originally known as St. Paul High School, but the name was changed to Central a few years later. Enrollment grew so swiftly that by 1888 a fourteen-room addition was built along the east side of the building toward Robert Street. The addition included a small observatory perched atop a round corner tower. By 1909 the school was bursting at the seams with thirteen hundred students, and St. Paul began laying plans for a new Central High School on Lexington Parkway. This building was completed in 1912. The old high school was then converted to an elementary school before being torn down in 1929 for a new Public Safety Building (extant).

SMALL COMMERCIAL BUILDINGS OF THE 1880S AND 1890S

A LARGE NUMBER of small, often highly ornamented commercial buildings were constructed in downtown St. Paul and Minneapolis during the late nineteenth century. Usually no more than six stories high, these buildings established the basic scale and rhythm of downtown streets for many years. Virtually all are gone.

MINNEAPOLIS

SARNOFF-IRVING HAT
COMPANY BUILDING
328 Nicollet Avenue, ca. 1880–ca. 1958.

GOLD SEAL
BUILDING
308 Hennepin Avenue,
ca. 1882–1963.

WINDOM BLOCK (Loring and Windom Block)
221 Second Avenue South, George M. Goodwin, 1882–ca. 1910.

DOLLY VARDEN BUILDING
219 Nicollet Avenue, 1882–1960.

CITIZENS BANK BUILDING
416 Nicollet Avenue, William H. Dennis,
1884–1941.

MORRISON BLOCK
Southeast corner of Washington Avenue
and Second Avenue South, 1884, 1887
(rebuilt after fire)–ca. 1960.

JOURNAL BUILDING
47–49 Fourth Street South, William H.
Dennis, 1890–1941.

NORTHWESTERN
MILLER BUILDING
118 Sixth Street South, William
Channing Whitney, 1898–1955.

ST. PAUL

GILFILLAN BLOCK
Southeast corner of Fourth and Jackson streets,
Edward P. Bassford, 1882–1920s.

RICE BLOCK
Southwest corner of Fifth and Jackson streets,
Edward P. Bassford, 1884–1955.

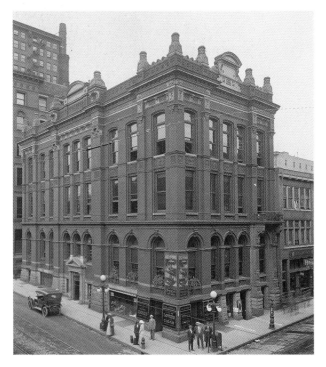

FIRST NATIONAL BANK
Northwest corner of Fourth and Jackson streets,
Denslow W. Millard, 1885–1941.

MANNHEIMER BLOCK
Southeast corner of Third and Minnesota streets,
Abraham Radcliffe, 1882–ca. 1928.

FOREPAUGH BUILDING (Daily News Building)
94 East Fourth Street, Willcox and Johnston, 1888–1970.

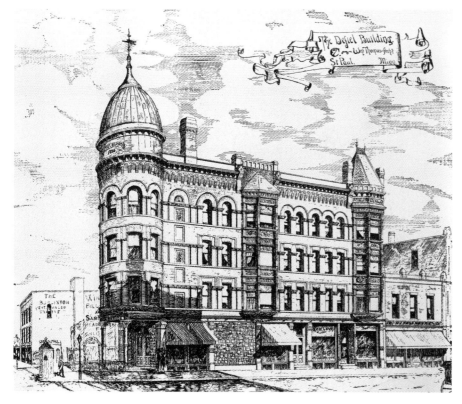

DEFIEL BLOCK
215 West Third Street (at Seven Corners), Hermann Kretz, 1889–1936.

STEES BUILDING (Frost Building)
28–30 East Fourth Street, J. Walter Stevens,
1887–1936.

COMING
OF AGE,
1880-1900

In late May 1882 Mark Twain concluded a sentimental steamboat journey up the Mississippi River with a stop in the Twin Cities. What he found was cause for astonishment. "When I was born [in 1835]," he wrote later in *Life on the Mississippi*, "St. Paul had a population of three persons; Minneapolis had just a third as many. The then population of Minneapolis died two years ago; and when he died he had seen himself undergo an increase, in forty years, of fifty-nine thousand nine hundred and ninety-nine persons. He had a frog's fertility."[1]

Yet even Twain, for all his supreme gifts of exaggeration, might have been amazed by what was about to happen next. Fueled by waves of immigration, a booming economy, and almost limitless optimism, the Twin Cities embarked in the 1880s on a fabulous adventure. Both cities began the decade as gangly urban teenagers, with populations of less than fifty thousand. By the turn of the century, despite the great depression that began in 1893, they were full-fledged adults. St. Paul's population reached 163,000 by 1900, while Minneapolis—displaying its increasing dominance—exploded to 202,000 people. "St. Paul has been developed from the frontier trading-post of the earlier days by an evolution, the successive stages of which have left their several records," Montgomery Schuyler wrote in 1891, "but Minneapolis has risen like an exhalation, or, to adopt even a mustier comparison, has sprung from the heads of its projectors full-panoplied in brick and mortar." Municipal boundaries expanded with the population. By 1887 St. Paul had reached its present size of more than

fifty-five square miles, and Minneapolis was close to its ultimate size of fifty-eight square miles.[2]

The building boom that accompanied this growth in population and territory was unprecedented. The boom began in the early 1880s as the Twin Cities climbed out of the recession that had marked much of the 1870s. By 1883 St. Paul and Minneapolis reported a combined total of $17.8 million in new construction, a figure exceeded only by New York (with $37.2 million) among American cities. This was an incredible statistic, considering that St. Paul, which alone ranked fourth among all American cities with $9.5 million worth of construction, had not even been listed in a similar survey three years earlier. Eastern capital, attracted by rapidly rising land values in the two downtowns, played a prominent role in the boom. "There are very many Eastern capitalists in town, all seeking favorable investments," wrote the St. Paul correspondent for the *Inland Architect and Builder* in 1883. On a recent day, he noted, out-of-town investors had purchased six downtown St. Paul lots worth a total of more than fifty thousand dollars.[3]

So many new buildings were springing up that local newspapers, which never wearied of civic boosterism, had trouble keeping an accurate scorecard. A writer for the *Daily Pioneer Press* noted that "one needs to be pretty constantly on the alert to keep track of the new business-block schemes which are now formulating, and an equally constant goer upon the streets to make note of the new foundations which are going in almost daily." On his visit to the Twin Cities in 1891, Schuyler found an electric atmosphere "where antiquity means the day before yesterday, and posterity the day after to-morrow, the present is the most contemptible of tenses, and men inevitably come to think and live and build in the future-perfect." As it turned out, the future was imperfect, and the boom finally came crashing to a close with the great depression of 1893.[4]

Skyrocketing land prices accompanied the building rush. Property values in parts of downtown St. Paul were said to be increasing at the rate of 100 percent or more a year in the early 1880s. The market was equally spectacular in downtown Minneapolis, where a lot purchased for two hundred dollars a front foot in 1882 was worth five times as much by the end of the decade. With vast amounts of money to be made, real estate speculation was endemic. "Men attended sales of lots, purchased without proving the property, then went home boasting of the fact, only to discover later that their land was a foot underwater or otherwise inaccessible," said one historian. "Money in this way passed from buyer to buyer with such surprising swiftness that Minneapolis was credited with thirty-eight millionaires [by the late 1880s]—a number sadly decreased in the time of trouble that followed."

St. Paul, meanwhile, was said to have forty millionaires by 1889.[5]

In this heady atmosphere, a champagne sensibility prevailed, and all manner of ideas bubbled and frothed to the surface. Minneapolis architect LeRoy Buffington prepared plans in 1887 for a twenty-eight-story skyscraper, which if built would have been the tallest in the world. About the same time, another Minneapolis architectural firm, Long and Kees, unveiled plans for a twelve-story luxury hotel faced entirely in marble that was to be built at Eighth and Hennepin. Proposals for giant opera houses, monumental public buildings, and vast downtown arcades also poured forth from the offices of local architects.[6]

Other dreamers were at work as well. In 1886 the *St. Paul Daily Globe* published its vision of what downtown would look like by 1919. The *Globe* foresaw downtown St. Paul as a kind of gigantic Rube Goldberg contraption, complete with trains running fifteen stories above the street and huge transportation balloons moored to the tops of skyscrapers. Not all dreams were quite so grandiose. In 1888, for example, there was a serious proposal for an elevated train connecting St. Paul and Minneapolis. Two years later a St. Paul entrepreneur tried to win support for building an eight-block-long underground railroad to distribute freight through Lowertown, saying John D. Rockefeller himself had expressed interest in the idea.[7]

Amid these dreams of urban magnificence, reality could be sobering. Despite tremendous development, much of downtown St. Paul and Minneapolis remained raw in the 1880s and 1890s. Municipal services, none too good to begin with, were especially troublesome and seldom kept pace with the burgeoning population. Complaints about foul air, dirty unpaved streets, inefficient garbage collection, overflowing sewers, badly maintained sidewalks, poor streetlighting, overcrowded schools, and inadequate police and fire protection were endemic.[8]

The Globe's *vision of St. Paul, 1886*

SAINT PAUL IN 1919.

Streets were a particular sore point, in part because nobody was sure how best to pave them. Although St. Paul had begun paving in 1873 and Minneapolis in 1882 (installing cedar blocks on part of a mile-long section of Washington Avenue and granite on the remaining part), the debate over paving materials raged for twenty years. Cedar blocks, brick, and various kinds of stone were tried in both cities, but all had significant drawbacks. Cedar block did not wear well, brick was expensive, and stone—usually granite—was extremely noisy and could be treacherous for horses in wet weather. The problem was not ultimately solved until the widespread introduction of asphalt and concrete paving in the twentieth century.[9]

Electric, telephone, and telegraph wires were another urban nuisance. Telephone and telegraph service had arrived in the Twin Cities by the 1870s, but electricity did not appear until 1882 when the Minnesota Brush Electric Company built the nation's first hydro-electric generating plant at the Falls of St. Anthony. There being a fine sense of priorities at the time, saloons were among the first customers for this new power source, as was the Big Boston Clothing store on Washington Avenue. The store advertised in March 1882 that the new lights made it "easier than ever before" to find bargains.[10]

In 1883 Minnesota Brush Electric installed Minneapolis' first electric arc lamps along Washington Avenue and also built a 257-foot-high light mast at Bridge Square. Eight huge arc lights atop the mast were intended to serve as a kind of man-made moon over Minneapolis. The lights cast a shadow a mile away, but otherwise proved to be unsatisfactory, and the mast was taken down in 1892.[11]

St. Paul also moved rapidly to exploit the newly discovered power of electricity, installing its first electric street lamps in Rice Park by late 1883. As demand for electricity grew, overhead power lines sprouted up along downtown streets

Bridge Square, showing light mast and city hall behind the light mast (center) and temporary street arch for a celebration (left center)

and soon proved to be a serious problem. They made fire fighting especially difficult, interfering with efforts to raise ladders. Despite loud objections from the power companies, both St. Paul and Minneapolis by 1890 began requiring that downtown utility wires be put underground.[12]

THE MOST PROFOUND visual change in the 1880s was the arrival of the skyscraper. At the beginning of the decade, no commercial or industrial structure in the Twin Cities rose much above one hundred feet, and church spires dominated the

Lighting structure lowered from top of light mast

skyline, much as they had in medieval Europe. The twin spires of Assumption Church at 208 feet were probably the highest structures in either city before 1880. But as the 1870s drew to a close, it became clear to observers of the local building scene that dramatic changes were in the wind. "The era of large business structures is at hand," wrote a correspondent for the *St. Paul and Minneapolis Pioneer Press* in November 1879. These words proved prophetic because within a few years the Twin Cities embarked on the sky-scraper age.[13]

Although the origin and development of the skyscraper remains a subject fraught with controversy, there is no question that technological advances—including the passenger elevator, the metal structural frame, and improved methods of fireproofing—opened the way for high-rise construction. New York City in the 1870s and Chicago in the 1880s were the centers of skyscraper design, and their influence was quickly felt in the Twin Cities. In some cases, the design of early Twin Cities skyscrapers can be traced to specific buildings in New York or Chicago. For example, the Minnesota Loan and Trust Building (1885, gone) in Minneapolis bore a striking resemblance to the Tribune Building of 1873 in New York City.[14]

It appears that improvements in elevator technology played an especially crucial role in attracting tenants to high-rise office buildings. "The elevator has come to be regarded with favor in this city, and the era of tall buildings seems to have been reached," a Minneapolis newspaper reporter wrote in 1885. He added:

Two years ago, builders very reluctantly put on the fourth story, and tenants hesitated about going into the upper portions of the blocks built. But very recently a number of six, seven and eight-story buildings have been put up, supplied with fast elevators. These structures have been made fire-proof [sadly, not true],

and tenants have been as readily found for the upper stories as for the lower. . . . The new buildings, with elevator accommodations, are rapidly depopulating the buildings without them, and which have heretofore been regarded as eligible office buildings. The occupants of offices were slow to appreciate the elevator, but in not to exceed two years they have found themselves in favor, and taller buildings are the order of the day.[15]

Montgomery Schuyler thought competition also had something to do with the sudden eruption of tall buildings. In St. Paul, he remarked, high-rise buildings were necessary because the city's cramped business quarter "leaves only the vertical dimension available for expansion." But in Minneapolis, he said, "the altitude of the newest and tallest structures . . . could scarcely be explained without reference to the nearness of St. Paul, and the intensity of the local pride born of that nearness."[16]

If a skyscraper can be loosely defined as a commercial building that seeks to express itself vertically, is tall enough to require elevators, and uses some kind of frame construction, then the Minnesota Loan and Trust Building probably qualifies as the Twin Cities' first example of this genre. Located on Nicollet Avenue, the building had only seven floors, the same number as the recently finished Minneapolis Tribune Building and one fewer than the West Hotel, built a year earlier. But Minnesota Loan and Trust sought to rise above its competitors via a slender, purely decorative rooftop tower that reached a height of more than one hundred feet. This may not have made Minnesota Loan and Trust the tallest commercial building of its day in the Twin Cities, but it seems to have been the first consciously to strive for great height.[17]

Other tall office buildings, ranging in height from seven to twelve stories, quickly followed in Minneapolis. These included the Lumber Ex-

1885

change (1886) at Fifth and Hennepin, Temple Court (1886) at Washington and Hennepin, the Bank of Minneapolis (1887) at Third and Nicollet, the Boston Block (1881, rebuilt 1887) at Third and Hennepin, the Oneida Building (1888) at Fourth and Marquette, the Globe Building (1889) on Fourth near Hennepin, the Masonic Temple (1889) at Sixth and Hennepin, the Sykes Block (1889) on Hennepin near Third, the Wright Block (1889) on Hennepin near Fourth, the New York Life Insurance Building (1890) at Fifth Street and Second Avenue South, and, of course, the Northwestern Guaranty Loan (Metropolitan) Building. At twelve stories, the Guaranty Loan was to reign atop the city's skyline for twenty-four years. Of these early Minneapolis skyscrapers, only two—the Lumber Exchange and the Masonic Temple—survived in 1991.

Although the depression of 1893 was the main factor in bringing the tall-building boom in Minneapolis to a halt, city government also played a role. There had been a 125-foot height limit for commercial buildings in Minneapolis as early as 1886, although it is not clear whether the ordinance was faithfully enforced. But in March 1890 the Minneapolis City Council, disturbed by the recent onslaught of skyscrapers, unanimously passed an ordinance reducing the height limit to one hundred feet. The council may have been motivated in part by a tragic fire four months earlier at the Tribune Building. Seven people trapped on upper floors died, some plunging to their deaths as they tried to escape the flames. Fresh memories of this fire may also explain why the *Tribune* strongly supported the ordinance in an editorial the next day:

Excessively high buildings damage all the property in their vicinity. Their shadows keep the sunlight away. Their great mass shuts off the air currents. They obstruct the outlook from other buildings. They dwarf neighboring

Boston Block, 1892

structures and disfigure the streets they occupy. In case of fire their upper stories are beyond the effective reach of the fire department. . . .

In short, these sky-scraping buildings are detrimental to the comfort and interest of so many people, that they may well be forbidden.[18]

No similar bout of acrophobia appears to have struck St. Paul, where tall buildings also flourished in the 1880s. The first commercial structure in St. Paul to advance beyond the old four-to-five-story standard was the seven-story Ryan

RIGHT: *St. Paul Chamber of Commerce building, from Inland Architect (1889)*

BELOW: *In 1896 the Bank of Minnesota became the Scandinavian American Bank (about 1906).*

Hotel, completed in 1885 at Sixth and Robert. A number of six-story buildings—including the Union Block (1885) at Fourth and Cedar, the Chamber of Commerce (1886) at Sixth and Robert, and the Bank of Minnesota (1886–1924) at Sixth and Jackson—were built about the same time. Then, in 1887, came the ten-story Globe Building at Fourth and Cedar, which for a brief period was the tallest commercial building in the Twin Cities. The key year for St. Paul, however, was 1889, which saw the completion of four significant tall office structures: the Germania Bank Building at Fifth and Wabasha, the New York Life Insurance Building at Sixth and Minnesota, the Germania Life Insurance Building at Fourth and Minnesota, and the Pioneer Building at Fourth and Robert. The Pioneer Building, which was thirteen stories counting a penthouse (four more stories were added around 1910), remained the tallest in the city until 1915. It and the Germania Bank (later St. Paul) Building were all that remained of this early skyscraper legacy in 1991.[19]

Although twelve stories turned out to be the maximum height for Twin Cities' skyscrapers in the nineteenth century, much higher buildings were already on the drawing boards of local architects, including Buffington's twenty-eight-story "cloudscraper." As it turned out, however, it took more than forty years before a Minneapolis building—the Foshay Tower of 1929—reached the height envisioned by Buffington.[20]

Besides growing taller during the 1880s, buildings grew much larger. Most public and commercial structures before 1880 were quite small, with widths of twenty-five to forty feet (the typical lot size). Few if any downtown buildings took up as much as a quarter of a square block. By 1881, however, the Twin Cities had their first block-long public building—Market Hall on Seventh between Wabasha and St. Peter streets in St. Paul. A year later the first block-long commercial structure appeared when the Auerbach,

Finch, and Van Slyck Building (also known as the Drake Block) opened in St. Paul on the west side of Sibley between Fourth and Fifth streets. In Minneapolis the year 1883 saw completion of the huge Syndicate Block. With more than five acres of floor space, it was the largest commercial building of its day in the Twin Cities and said to be one of the largest in the country. In 1886 the immense Industrial Exposition Building, more than a square block in size, opened in southeast Minneapolis near the Falls of St. Anthony. All of these early giants are gone, although parts of the Syndicate Block (which later became a J. C. Penney Department Store) survived until 1989.

THESE LARGE PUBLIC and commercial buildings not only changed the architectural scale of St. Paul and Minneapolis but also brought about a fundamental downtown realignment. Before 1880 St. Paul's commercial core centered on Third Street from roughly Wabasha to Wacouta. But by the mid-1880s the city's banking and retail trade, along with much of its hotel and office space, began to migrate north away from the river. The First National Bank relocated in 1885 to a new building at Fourth and Jackson. That same year the National German-American Bank moved to Fourth and Robert, leaving behind a building on Third completed six years earlier. The first large department store to move uptown

Auerbach, Finch, and Van Slyck Building, about 1885

*Schuneman's store,
about 1900*

was Dickinson's store, which relocated at Fourth and St. Peter in 1885. In 1890 Schuneman's, one of the city's biggest retail emporiums, occupied a glassy new structure at Sixth and Wabasha. Another prominent retailer, Mannheimer Brothers, left its ten-year-old building on Third in 1892 to move into a much larger new store at Sixth and Robert. Office development followed a similar trend, concentrating along Fourth, Fifth, and Sixth streets. Construction of the palatial Ryan Hotel at Sixth and Robert also helped to create a new downtown center north of Third.

By 1894 *Northwest Magazine* reported that "Third Street . . . is still a busy thoroughfare but is no longer a shopping street for ladies. Commission houses now occupy many of the stores once tenanted by dry goods firms, jewelers and milliners." The ultimate result of this shift north was that Lowertown evolved into an almost exclusively wholesaling district while the office-bank-

ing-retail core of St. Paul came to occupy the approximate area it did in the 1990s.[21]

Downtown Minneapolis saw a similar shift in its center of gravity as development moved away from the old Bridge Square district and south along Hennepin and Nicollet avenues. Said one newspaper in 1887: "Ten years ago most of the business transacted in Minneapolis was done on Bridge Square and a small section of Washington avenue. . . . Now on Nicollet avenue above [south of] Third street . . . is done more business than on all the rest of the street."[22]

The strongest impetus for the move south, away from the historic riverfront district, came from the Syndicate Block, located on Nicollet between Fifth and Sixth. "An enterprising merchant who had previously started in on the corner above the Syndicate block was regarded as a fit subject for the insane asylum," a writer observed in 1886. But within a few years, the merchant's prescience was rewarded as Nicollet became the city's "great retail street." Donaldson's Glass Block was among the first big retail stores to stake out this new territory, opening at Sixth and Nicollet in 1883. The store proved to be an instant success. In 1884 the opening of the luxurious West Hotel at Fifth and Hennepin gave a boost to that avenue, which gradually developed into an entertainment strip.[23]

In the meantime, bank and office development spread along Nicollet, Marquette, and Second avenues south. By 1890 large office structures, such as the ten-story New York Life Insurance Building at Fifth Street and Second Avenue South, were encroaching on neighborhoods that only a decade earlier had been largely residential. Wholesaling, meanwhile, began to concentrate north of Hennepin. In the 1890s massive brick warehouses began to line First, Second, and Third avenues north, creating what remained a century later one of the city's most impressive architectural ensembles. Land values reflected these changing patterns. The most expensive property in Minneapolis by 1890 was along Nicollet between Third and Seventh streets and on parts of Fourth and Fifth streets.[24]

As the downtown commercial cores expanded, driving up property values, homes and churches were forced out. "Scores of old frame houses will be moved out of the [downtown St. Paul] fire limits this spring, to make room for brick structures," the *St. Paul and Minneapolis Pioneer Press* reported in 1885. "Houses on wheels are seen frequently on the prominent streets." Some businessmen even moved or demolished their own homes to cash in on the real estate bonanza. In 1883 H. G. Sidle moved his substantial brick house from the corner of Fifth and Nicollet, replacing it the next year with a four-story office block. So rapid and extensive was commercial expansion that by 1884 virtually all of the private residences remaining in the center of downtown Minneapolis had become boardinghouses.[25]

THE WEALTHIER CLASSES by this time were already relocating to exclusive new neighborhoods beyond the reach (or so it was thought) of commercial development. In Minneapolis the well-to-do businessman of the 1880s could choose from among several high-class neighborhoods. Just northwest of downtown near Sixth and Lyndale avenues north was Oak Lake, a genteel subdivision platted in 1880. Now vanished as a residential district, Oak Lake offered rolling, heavily wooded terrain, two small ponds, and graceful winding streets. "There is no part of the town in which so many pretty houses are being erected," a newspaper reported in 1882, and for the next twenty years or so, Oak Lake remained a desirable locale. So, too, was the Loring Park-Hawthorne Avenue district where many large houses were constructed in the 1880s, culminating with Samuel Gale's huge stone fortress of 1889 at Sixteenth and Harmon.[26]

But the gold coast in Minneapolis in the 1880s was concentrated on and around Lowry Hill and

south along Park Avenue. William Washburn, a millionaire miller whose first home had been near Seventh Street and Fifth Avenue South, was among those who led the southward parade of wealth. In 1884 Washburn moved into Fairoaks —a palatial estate (gone) on a two-square-block site at Twenty-second Street and Stevens Avenue. This was considered to be a distant location, but Washburn's isolation did not last long. The city's business elite soon began building mansions along nearby Park Avenue, which a newspaper in 1887 proclaimed to be "the finest residence section of Minneapolis." Park Avenue's exalted status was reflected in the quality of its improvements. It was the first Minneapolis street to receive asphalt paving (in 1889), a project financed by its wealthy residents. By the 1990s few private homes remained along the once grand avenue, and many of its most splendid mansions were gone.[27]

In St. Paul the residential shuffle was equally pronounced in the 1880s. The old Lowertown mansion district was hit especially hard, and within thirty years it had all but vanished:

W. L. Hathaway house, on James Avenue in Oak Lake neighborhood, about 1890

Uri Lamprey house on Cedar Street, about 1900, overlooked Central Park near the present State Capitol

Andrew Muir house, 545 Summit Avenue

Interior of Muir house just before demolition

Summit Avenue quickly emerged as St. Paul's most prestigious residential address. In 1881 the *Pioneer Press* reported that "St. Anthony Hill [the area through which lower Summit Avenue runs] is the scene of the greatest activity in house-building operations, and its supremacy as the favorite locality for homes for the better class of citizens appears to be now well assured." Summit's place as St. Paul's showpiece avenue was further secured in 1884 when Norman Kittson completed a vast house on the present site of the St. Paul Cathedral. Over the next five years, forty-six new houses were built on lower Summit, almost half of which remained in 1991.[29]

For the cities' poor, however, finding a decent place to live was almost impossible. Housing of all sorts, but especially low-cost housing, was in chronically short supply. A St. Paul newspaper advised its readers in 1882 that it was "absolutely impossible" to obtain a house for rent in the city. By the end of the decade, the situation was not much better. "The scarcity of small houses has driven a larger element into boarding houses, hotels and flats," the *St. Paul Daily News* reported in March 1889, noting that there was a glut of expensive houses on the market.[30]

Those with the least money usually lived in ghettos of one sort or another. In Minneapolis, for example, there was "Hell's Half Acre," a dense collection of shanties between Eighth and Ninth streets near Second Avenue South. A police historian, who does not appear to have been bashful in the presence of hyperbole, described this small corner of the city as "a place of utter darkness, wailing and woe. Bloody frays were a nightly occurrence. . . . The alleys were strewn with empty beer kegs and whisky bottles, and the latter were often used as weapons of warfare."[31]

Other squatters lived in hidden-away places like Swede Hollow or along the river flats in shacks built from drift lumber. For poor immigrants these makeshift communities offered an inexpensive start on life in a new and alien

By 1880 circumstances had conspired to force a new alignment of residence districts. The lower town region, once so attractive, became too constricted, too central and from the multiplication of railway trains and tracks through the Trout Brook valley, too noisy for comfort, and a rapid hegira for the hills was underway. The movement continued until practically all the former inhabitants of the Grove and Woodward street region had disappeared. Such of their houses as remain are now mostly transformed into hospitals, tenements, etc., while many have been demolished to make space for railroad terminals.[28]

Although Wabasha (Capitol) Hill, Dayton's Bluff, and the Upper West Side all saw significant upper-class home building in the 1880s,

west of Chestnut Street. Located near a huge city garbage heap—described by the reporter as a "stinking, loathsome hole"—the settlement included scores of small shacks, a few stores, and at least one saloon. Its hundred or more occupants supported themselves by fishing, rag picking, and theft, according to the reporter, who viewed this community—particularly its children—as a grave threat to St. Paul: "With stinted intellects, depraved habits, and a lawless disposition, it is easy enough to predict that in the children playing on the sands to-day lie the nucleus of future mobs that will throng the streets of St. Paul." The reporter also saw an ominous cloud of radicalism looming on the horizon, likening the children's "spirit of abandon" to that of "the fully developed Chicago socialist." St. Paul survived (as did Chicago, for that matter), but the Upper Levee flats and communities like it have not.[32]

In addition to individual housing of all kinds, the 1880s produced the first large array of multiple-dwelling units in the Twin Cities. These ranged from lavish row houses to crowded, cheaply built tenements. The Minneapolis version of the *Globe* reported in 1889 that "tenement rows have become a favorite style of residence building," especially "among that class of

ABOVE:
Hell's Half Acre, 1905; the Church of the Redeemer is in the background

BELOW:
Upper Levee flats under the High Bridge, about 1889

world, and many families moved up to better neighborhoods as their fortunes improved. Periodically, newspapers would take a look at how this other half lived, often in sensational stories laced with intolerance and bigotry. In 1886, for example, a *Pioneer Press* reporter toured the "Bohemian" settlement on the Upper Levee flats

tenants who can afford lake residences in the summer and who prefer to be within easy reach of the business center in the winter." In Minneapolis most of the big row houses were around the southern rim of downtown in an area that eventually came to be dominated by apartment buildings. Among the larger row houses were the Warman Block (1882) at Eighth and Portland, Spring Grove Terrace (1885) at Seventeenth and Clinton, Nicollet Terrace (1886) at Nicollet and Oak Grove, La Veta Terrace (1888) at Seventeenth and Nicollet, and Zier Row (1889) at Ninth Street and Fourth Avenue South. All are gone. St. Paul also acquired a number of splendid row houses during this period, including Laurel Terrace (also called Riley Row) at 286–94 Laurel Avenue and Lauer Flats at 226 South Western Avenue. Both stood in 1991.[33]

Most tenements of the period were a far cry from these gracious row houses. Tenements were generally two to four stories, sometimes with stores on the ground floor and apartments above. Bathrooms, if they existed indoors, usually were shared. Unlike the narrow, deep tenement buildings of New York City, those in Minneapolis and St. Paul tended to have long fronts that provided relatively decent amounts of light and air. Probably the largest tenement of the 1880s in the Twin Cities was Beard's Block (gone), built in 1880–81 at Twelfth Avenue and Second Street South in a part of Minneapolis teeming with Scandinavian immigrants. More than a block long and three stories high, it harbored so many families that it became known as "Noah's Ark." In St. Paul one of the biggest tenements was the three-story Portland Block (gone), built in 1885 and located on Broadway between Eighth and Ninth streets.

The modern rental apartment building with several units per floor and individual bathrooms did not really arrive until the end of the decade. Large apartment hotels—such as the Aberdeen and Barteau (at Ninth Street and Smith Avenue), both in St. Paul and both completed in

ABOVE:
Zier Row (detail), about 1890, showing a strong French influence

BELOW:
Hotel Barteau, about 1895

1889—were among the first to provide this kind of living. By the 1890s developers were constructing large numbers of apartment buildings around the fringes of both downtowns.[34]

Some architects thought row houses and apartments would eventually predominate in the Twin Cities. "The time must soon come when a twenty-five-foot lot will be considered ample, and many people will prefer to live in a 'city house'. . . to the pleasure and inconvenience of a little grass plot, a fancied healthy space and a good deal of side-walk to keep clean for eight months of the year," wrote William Channing Whitney in 1887. It was a logical argument, especially in view of the area's extreme climate, which would seem to have favored compact, densely clustered housing.[35]

But multiple dwelling units never proved highly popular with the middle and upper classes in the Twin Cities. Land outside the two downtowns was plentiful and relatively cheap throughout the 1880s and 1890s, and most people with enough money to build a separate house did so. "The Western man loves elbow room and doesn't like to live squeezed up against his neighbors," a magazine writer explained in 1895. "Apartment houses have enjoyed a certain popularity in recent years as abodes of small families and of quiet, elderly people. . . . Nevertheless, with all the recent growth in city ways, more than nine-tenths of the population [of Minneapolis] still live in separate houses, in accordance with the good old New England village system."[36]

INSTITUTIONAL BUILDINGS AND churches also saw a flurry of development in the 1880s. Hospitals, clubs, and private schools, which had often been housed in small residential-scale structures before 1880, all felt the need to expand. New buildings of this type in downtown St. Paul included Turner Hall (1882), an odd "German Renaissance" style wooden building at Sixth and Franklin (Auditorium) streets; St. Joseph's Hospital (ca. 1885) at Ninth and Exchange streets; the delightful Minnesota Club (1886) at Fourth and Cedar streets; Cathedral School (1889), located at Sixth and Main streets and dominated by a massive Romanesque tower; and the domed Visitation Convent and School (1889) at Robert Street and University Avenue. All are gone.

In Minneapolis lost institutional and club buildings of this period include the Minnesota Hospital College (1886) at Sixth Street and Ninth Avenue South; the Union League Clubhouse (1887) on Sixth Street near Hennepin Avenue; Normanna Hall (1889), a gathering place for the city's Norwegian community located at Third Street and Twelfth Avenue South; the Minneapolis YMCA (1892), a large and impressive Romanesque pile at Tenth Street and LaSalle Avenue; and the elegant Renaissance-inspired Minneapolis Club (1892) at Sixth Street and Marquette Avenue.

Soaring population also created a demand for new churches. Congregations that had built small wooden, stone, or brick churches in pioneer days needed more room, touching off a wave of ecclesiastical building. Significant lost churches of this era include Trinity Evangelical Lutheran (1886), Central Park Methodist (1887), and the People's Church (1889) in St. Paul, and Westminster Presbyterian (1883), the Unitarian Church (1887), and Free Will Baptist (1891) in Minneapolis.

NEW ENTERTAINMENT FACILITIES were also much in demand in the 1880s. The first large "downstairs" theater in the Twin Cities was the Grand Opera House (1883), built as part of the Syndicate Block in Minneapolis. St. Paul responded the same year with its own Grand Opera House, which actually was a reconstruction of the old St. Paul Opera House of 1867. Other large theaters followed in both cities. In Minneapolis these included the Hennepin Avenue Theater (1887), the Bijou Opera House (1887, rebuilt

LEFT:
Minneapolis YMCA, about 1900

BELOW:
Entryway to Minneapolis YMCA

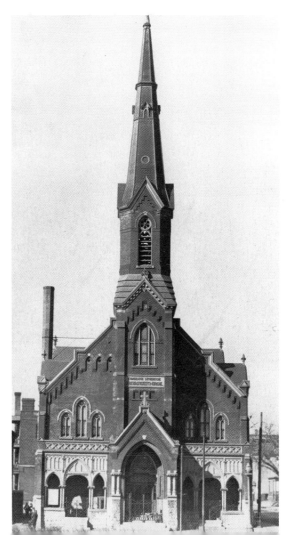

Trinity Evangelical Lutheran Church, 1930

121

*Minneapolis Metropolitan
Opera House, 1904*

1890), and the Metropolitan Opera House (1894). Among the major additions to St. Paul's theatrical scene were the Olympic Theater (1884) and the Metropolitan Opera House and Litt's Grand Opera (both opened in 1890 after the old Grand Opera House burned down). None of these theaters survives, and some had very brief lives. The Minneapolis Grand Opera House, for example, stood for only fourteen years.

Besides live theater, the Twin Cities of the 1880s and 1890s offered numerous other forms of entertainment. Some were old-fashioned, such as drinking, gambling, and visiting "sporting houses." Others were decidedly novel. Roller skating was a huge fad in the 1880s. A newspaper writer complained during the height of the craze that "there are more people in the rinks then than attend church on Sundays." By 1885 Minneapolis had eleven rinks, including the large Washington Avenue Rink (1883) at Tenth and Washington avenues north and the Crocker Rink (1884) at Sixth and Marquette. Roller mania was less pro-

*Litt's Grand Opera
House, 1905*

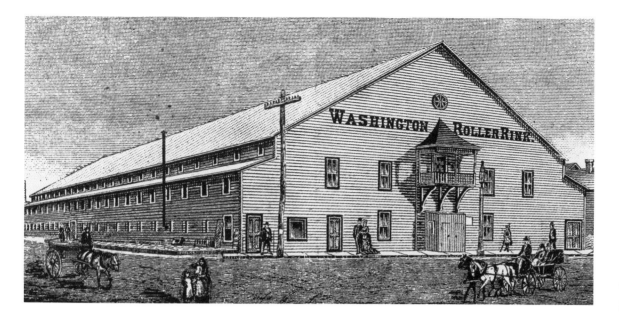

Washington Avenue Rink, 1895

nounced in St. Paul, which made do with four rinks, the largest being the Exposition Rink (1884) on Fourth near Wabasha.[37]

For cheap thrills, a good bet was one of the dime museums, which offered a variety of oddities, curios, and freak shows and were especially popular with youngsters. These establishments—the first opened in Minneapolis in 1883—offered something for everyone: displays of curiosities such as a piece of George Washington's coffin, vaudeville shows, shooting exhibitions by Annie Oakley and Calamity Jane, plus "innumerable . . . specimens of Nature's detours," including Jo-Jo the Dog-faced Boy, the Crawling Fat Woman, and the ever popular and amazing Joltum, whose specialty was catching cannonballs and living to tell about it. An 1887 editorial in the *Saturday Evening Spectator* complained that dime museums promoted "unhealthy excitement" as well as "vulgarity and immorality," which, of course, is precisely what attracted young people. Dime museums remained popular until the arrival of motion pictures after the turn of the century.[38]

For those with a taste for subterranean amusement, there was the Felsenkeller ("cellar in the

rocks"), an underground saloon and bowling alley that opened on St. Paul's West Side in the 1880s. A man named Fandel spent seven years carving the place out of a sandstone cliff below Prospect Terrace near Winslow Avenue. Perhaps the most astonishing feature of this peculiar establishment—only two drawings of which are known to

Felsenkeller, 1886

exist—was a winding underground staircase, hewn from solid rock, that led all the way up to the top of the cliff. Much later, in the 1930s, St. Paul would acquire an even more popular underground establishment just a few blocks away—the Castle Royal Night Club.[39]

Minneapolis had no true cave saloons, but it offered several underground "blind pigs" (illegal bars) in the Gateway District. In 1886 a *Minneapolis Journal* reporter entered one of these "subterranean dives" beneath Washington Avenue. He found it to be "a dark little room under the sidewalk" where drinks were served by an eager bartender in a white apron. Most "blind pigs" appear to have been spectacularly vile, offering rotgut liquor, gambling, and other vices in an environment of filth and stench.[40]

Minneapolitans in search of more edifying entertainment could take in the "Battle of Atlanta," a gigantic panorama that went on display in June 1886 in a specially constructed building at Fifth and Marquette. Not to be outdone, St. Paul countered in 1887 with the Capital City Panorama at Fifth and St. Peter. This offered a vast painting of another Civil War battle—Gettysburg. Both panorama buildings were short-

lived, with the Capital City Panorama surviving only two years.

Organized baseball, which had been played in the Twin Cities since the late 1860s, was another form of entertainment available in downtown Minneapolis. Athletic Park, at Sixth Street and First Avenue North, opened in 1889 as the new home of the Minneapolis Millers, formed five years earlier. By the end of the decade, however, the Millers had moved to Nicollet Park in south Minneapolis, and warehouses replaced Athletic Park.[41]

FESTIVAL ARCHITECTURE—in the form of temporary street arches, ceremonial columns, and the like—was an especially wonderful part of life in the Twin Cities in the 1880s and 1890s. The granddaddy of such festivals was a celebration in September 1883 to mark the completion of the Northern Pacific's rail line from the Twin Cities to the West Coast. In St. Paul more than one hundred thousand people—or so it was claimed —thronged the streets for a grand procession led by the Northern Pacific's president, Henry Villard, and a host of dignitaries, including President Chester A. Arthur and Ulysses S. Grant. The parade passed beneath six ceremonial arches, some seventy feet high. At one point, a group of young women tossed rose petals on the startled Villard, who might have benefited more from an outpouring of cash, given the shaky finances that characterized his railroad career. As the parade wound through downtown, it passed numerous buildings lavishly decorated for the occasion. "St. Paul put on such gala garb as she has never even aspired to before, and will not wear again for years," rhapsodized one newspaper in describing this orgy of pomp and circumstance. Minneapolis also feted Villard with a parade along Washington Avenue.[42]

Three years later St. Paul demonstrated that its taste for spectacle was still strong, staging its first Winter Carnival. The carnival was inaugu-

One of the arches built for the Northern Pacific celebration

rated to prove to a skeptical world that Minnesota in general and St. Paul in particular were not the American version of Siberia but were in fact a great winter pleasure ground where happy citizens cavorted in frosty frolics. To support this dubious proposition, the first carnival included a torchlight parade in which five thousand uniformed members from a variety of clubs marched down Third Street in fourteen-degree-below-zero weather, past buildings decorated with so many glittering candles that one awestruck reporter likened the scene to a vision of "celestial glory." For the 1888 winter carnival St. Paul put on perhaps the biggest parade in its history—a seven-mile-long extravaganza that took three hours to pass a given point.[43]

As part of the 1886 carnival St. Paul built its first large ice palace, the only building type for which the city was to become famous. The palaces of 1886, 1887, and 1888 were among the most dazzling works of architecture in the history of the Twin Cities and among the largest structures of their kind ever built anywhere. Besides ice palaces St. Paul built many other temporary structures for early winter carnivals. The 1886 carnival featured four toboggan slides (including

ABOVE:
Ice palace in 1888

LEFT:
Toboggan slide on Ramsey Hill like the one for the 1886 carnival; this one was built in 1917

125

what must have been a terrifically fast half-mile-long run down the precipitous Ramsey Street Hill), an array of ice sculptures, and a one-hundred-foot-high illuminated ice tower atop Dayton's Bluff.[44]

Warm weather and grumbling from the business community eventually put a damper on the city's enthusiasm for winter carnivals. Joseph Bookwalter, a St. Paul railroad executive whose nose seems to have been pressed firmly to the grindstone, complained in 1890 that "for widespread and lasting ruin the ice palace and winter carnival surpasses the combined influence of all other evils." Instead of wasting time in frozen frivolity, he argued, the citizens of St. Paul should "devote their energy and money to judicious investment in manufacturing enterprises." But it was unusually mild winter weather, which put a stop to ice palace building in 1889 and 1890, that seems to have melted St. Paul's chilly devotion to January frolics. A scaled-down winter carnival was held in 1896, but after that the institution went dormant for twenty years.[45]

Minneapolis never built ice palaces of any note, preferring to celebrate its municipal might with permanent structures such as the Industrial Exposition Building at Main Street and Central Avenue. This mammoth building was constructed for the Minneapolis Industrial Exposition, a great indoor fair of commerce and art modeled on similar annual events in other cities. Opening day on August 23, 1886, drew fifty thousand people, and much of downtown assumed a gala appearance for the event. Nicollet Avenue merchants staged the most elaborate spectacle of all, decorating the street with gaslit arches that at night formed "a blaze of glory and a monument of enterprise," according to one newspaper.[46]

Perhaps the largest nineteenth-century celebration in Minneapolis was the Harvest Festival of 1891. Put together in only two weeks, this festival by one (undoubtedly inflated) estimate drew three hundred thousand people for a gigantic parade on September 23, 1891. The festival was a vast sigh of relief after several hard years for the Upper Midwest's farmers, who by the late 1880s were experiencing the beginnings of the depression that was soon to strike the entire American economy. But 1891 bought temporary respite in the form of a bumper harvest, and Minneapolis decided to throw a party. The Harvest Festival's seven-mile-long parade offered all manner of startling sights—five hundred butchers on horseback, giant vegetables, plumbers demonstrating their craft, a mobile prison cell (courtesy of the Hennepin County sheriff), and even a burglar-proof safe, mounted on a float and attended by mock "cracksmen" trying to open it. The parade route, over ten miles long, was lined with hastily constructed grandstands and numerous decorations, including precisely arranged flour barrels that in places formed pyramids twenty-seven feet high. Viewing the procession as it made its way down jam-packed Nicollet Avenue beneath an array of ceremonial arches, a reporter wrote that "no one could gaze unmoved upon such an inspiring scene. Streamers were flying, festoons swaying, banners were fluttering in the playful breeze." He summed up by saying, "The Harvest Festival of 1891 will be remembered as long as those who beheld it and participated in it—and all who saw participated—shall live."[47]

ALONG WITH PUBLIC celebration, public architecture took on a new scale in the 1880s and 1890s. The government buildings, markets, and schools built in the pioneer period proved to be inadequate as the population mushroomed, and many of these structures—including the first St. Paul City Hall, the first Ramsey County Courthouse, and the Minneapolis Market House—were replaced before the turn of the century. In addition to Market Hall, the second State Capitol, and Central High School, large public buildings of the period in St. Paul included the U.S. Quartermaster's Department Building (1884) at Second and Robert and the St. Paul City Hall–Ramsey County Courthouse (1889) at Fourth and Wabasha. All are gone.

St. Paul also undertook a number of huge engineering projects, most notably the so-called Seventh Street fill, which at a cost of $1 million in 1883 significantly reduced the grade along Seventh between downtown and Dayton's Bluff. In addition the city built two new bridges over the Mississippi—the first Robert Street Bridge (1886) and the first High Bridge (1889). Several new downtown parks also made their debuts, including Central Park (1883), just south of the present State Capitol and site of the 1886–88 ice palaces; Summit Park (1883), a grassy triangle at Summit and Third Street; Lafayette Square

Robert Street Bridge; note flooding of the West Side

High Bridge, about 1891; the West Seventh Street district is in the foreground

Lafayette Square, about 1888

electric-powered streetcars. Electrification was virtually complete by 1893.[49]

Among the significant public and institutional buildings of this time in Minneapolis were the Industrial Exposition Building, the public library at Tenth and Hennepin, Washington School, and the U.S. Post Office (1889–1960) at Third and Marquette. Despite having a 152-foot-high central tower with a clock whose four faces were lighted by gas jets, the white Ohio sandstone post office was quickly overshadowed by its awesome next-door neighbor, the Northwestern Guaranty Loan Building. Still standing is the Minneapolis City Hall–Hennepin County Courthouse, designed in 1888 but not completed until 1906. The Minneapolis park system also began to take shape in the 1880s, but aside from Loring Park (1883), most of this development was outside the downtown area.[50]

(1884–86) in Lowertown; and Park Place (about 1880), near Tenth and St. Peter and occupying the site of the old Park Place Hotel, which—in standard St. Paul fashion—had burned to the ground in 1878. With the exception of the Seventh Street fill, now pierced by freeways, all of these architectural and engineering works are gone, as are the parks.

Another major public improvement in St. Paul was the first Union Depot, opened in August 1881 at the foot of Sibley Street. With seven railroads already operating in the city, the depot quickly proved to be too small and was rebuilt in 1884 after a fire. By 1889, when St. Paul was the third busiest rail hub in America, the depot was said to be handling up to 268 trains a day and more than eight million passengers a year.[48]

Public transportation in St. Paul also took a quantum leap forward during this period. Until the late 1880s, horsecars—operating along nine lines—remained the only form of mass transportation. In 1888 a steam-powered cable-car system began operating between downtown and Summit Hill. Two years later, cable cars also began lurching up the long hill on East Seventh Street. The cable system, however, was a technological dinosaur, and in 1890 St. Paul began the switch to

U.S. Post Office in Minneapolis, about 1890; the Metropolitan Building is in the background

With fairly level terrain, Minneapolis did not require the kind of massive street-grading projects undertaken in St. Paul. As its population and industry grew, however, the city needed more bridges across the Mississippi, and several were built in the 1880s. By far the noblest of these—and the greatest work of nineteenth-century engineering in Minnesota—was the Stone Arch Bridge (1883) built by the Great Northern Railway across the Falls of St. Anthony. It remained one of the most impressive structures of any kind in Minneapolis in 1991. Other bridges constructed in the 1880s have not survived. These included the Plymouth Avenue Bridge (1882), the Washington Avenue Bridge (1886), and the Northern Pacific Bridge (1886), all iron-truss structures that were later replaced by modern spans. Another important engineering project, completed in 1885, was the widening and deepening of the canal that powered the west side milling district.

Minneapolis was never quite so large a railroad center as St. Paul was, and the city's first Union Depot was not built until 1885. It was at the foot of Hennepin Avenue, opposite the site of the later Great Northern Station. Two other sizable depots—the Great Western (1886) and the Chicago, Milwaukee, St. Paul and Pacific (1898), both on Washington Avenue South—were also built before the turn of the century. The Milwaukee Depot, no longer used by trains, was the only one that remained standing in 1991.

Like St. Paul, Minneapolis relied largely on horsecars for mass transportation through much of the 1880s. This system was extensive, with sixty-six miles of track, 218 cars, and more than a thousand horses in use by 1890. There was also a "steam motor"—essentially a small railroad—that began operating in 1879 between downtown and Lake Calhoun. The smoke, soot, and noise from these trains provoked bitter protests, especially from William Washburn, near whose estate the line ran. Complaining that the passing trains frightened his horses, Washburn called the line "a curse to the street it is on and to the city" and expressed outrage at the "idea of a full-fledged steam train running down what you might call the finest avenue in the city! It will not be tolerated. It's absolutely a ruin to property on First avenue, which might as well be confiscated." After failing to obtain satisfaction from the Minneapolis City Council, Washburn made his horses happy in 1886 by foreclosing on the motor line (he was its major bondholder) and threatening to shut it down.[51]

Three years later, technology came to the rescue when the first electric streetcar made a trial run along Fourth Avenue South. The run was highly successful, and Minneapolis quickly electrified its entire mass transit system. In both Minneapolis and St. Paul these improvements in mass transit played a vital role in opening up new neighborhoods once considered too distant from downtown to attract residents.[52]

First Minneapolis Union Depot, 1891, showing the train shed at the left

THE STREETCARS BROUGHT thousands of people daily into the two downtowns, and what these riders saw by the end of the century was an environment of extremes. With zoning still years away, splendor and squalor cohabited on downtown streets in a landscape of startling juxtapositions. Skyscrapers rose next to shanties, elegant retail emporiums overlooked rotting wooden sidewalks and streets choked with mud and manure, backyard privies stood in the shadow of grand hotels. Although both downtowns by 1890 were densely built up along most streets, blocks tended to remain open in the middle, where a disorderly collection of sheds, shacks, and other outbuildings formed a now-vanished back-alley world that might be called the interstitial city.

Created almost overnight as though exploded out of a cannon, downtown St. Paul and Minneapolis were also paradigms of a society addicted to change. In this helter-skelter urban world, the shock of the new was so pervasive that no one could escape its electrifying touch. Everything seemed to be moving and changing all at once: great office towers rising out of mud holes, houses wheeling through the streets on their way to new destinations, old monuments falling to the relentless roar of progress.

Here was the incomparably energetic bourgeois world Karl Marx, in faraway Europe, had visualized years before, a world of "everlasting uncertainty and agitation" where "all that is solid melts into air." It is hard, now, to fathom the effect this unprecedented rate of change had on human beings, but Twin Cities newspapers of the day suggested that all was not well. For the common worker in an unregulated, profit-hungry world of fast-moving machinery, life seems to have been extremely dangerous. Gruesome industrial accidents—decapitations, crushed skulls, scaldings, severed limbs—were astonishingly common in the 1880s and 1890s, if the newspapers are to be believed. Railroad mishaps were also an almost daily occurrence in both cities, where most trains ran at grade and where crossing gates and other safety measures were as yet unheard of. Another startling feature of life in the Twin Cities at this time was the prevalence of suicide, which was often accomplished publicly, much to the delight of the local press. Newspapers reported an "epidemic of self-destruction"

St. Paul, about 1886, looking north from the corner of Fourth and Robert; Ryan Hotel, second State Capitol, and Assumption Church appear on the horizon; livery stable in the foreground

while running advertisements for various tonics guaranteed to keep people from doing away with themselves.[53]

Yet for those able to function in a world that seemed to rearrange itself by the minute, the Twin Cities of the 1880s and 1890s offered many wonders and curiosities. David and Goliath confrontations were especially common. When the ten-story New York Life Insurance Building was completed in St. Paul in 1889, it stood beside one small wooden house and directly across the street from another. The new skyscraper's elegance was also diminished by the fact that it overlooked dirt streets, since paving had not yet reached that part of downtown St. Paul. Similar incongruities could be found throughout downtown Minneapolis. The *Minneapolis Tribune* was so upset by this visual chaos that it editorialized in favor of European-style design controls to "prevent the sense of glaring discord that now offends the eye."[54]

Where development was especially intense, such as along parts of Jackson and Fourth streets in St. Paul or Nicollet Avenue in Minneapolis, the cities managed by the early 1890s to attain a kind of rambunctious grandeur. There was an almost solid wall of buildings in these places, and the result was urban congestion at its best. The 1880s marked the beginning of the Twin Cities' great downtown age, which was to last until the end of World War II. In a sense that is difficult to imagine today, the downtowns were the absolute centers of community life, places where everyone came to work, shop, eat, and drink, be entertained, or simply watch the passing procession. In fact loafing seems to have been a prime pastime, so much so that there were numerous complaints in the newspapers about gangs of "rowdies" who idled about downtown streets and amused themselves by subjecting passing females to "impudent" stares.[55]

An amazing amount of visual clutter characterized both downtowns at this time. Sidewalks were carnivals of boisterous capitalism, a chaotic medley of sights, sounds, and smells. They were crowded not only with people but also with a wide assortment of freestanding and overhanging signs, numerous clocks (almost every jeweler had one in front of his shop), rows of huge multi-masted utility poles, plus a generally mismatched array of lamps, benches, water fountains, and trash bins. Zoning laws, along with standardization brought about by the automobile, gradually cleaned up this endearing mess, and downtown streets today seem as antiseptic (and about as interesting) as hospital corridors.

THE ARCHITECTURAL LOOK of this new urban world was strongly eclectic. In part this reflected the availability of a wide range of new building materials. In the 1860s and 1870s, Twin Cities' architects and builders had relied on a limited assortment of materials, mostly of local origin. But the situation quickly changed after 1880 in response to improved railroad transportation, rapid advances in technology, and the demands of an increasingly wealthy class of clients. Platteville limestone, for example, fell out of favor as new regional building stones were introduced. These included the soft reddish-brown sandstone (often called Lake Superior brownstone) quarried in Wisconsin and Michigan; beige-colored Hinckley sandstone from east-central Minnesota; and so-called Jasper stone, an extremely hard reddish-pink quartzite from southwestern Minnesota. Architects could also choose from a huge variety of other stones—white Ohio sandstone, buff-colored Indiana limestone, Tennessee and Georgia marbles, and various granites. More exotic materials, such as Mexican onyx and tropical woods, were also readily available.[56]

Brick, however, remained the Twin Cities' principal building material in the 1880s, especially for commercial architecture. There was almost no limit to the variety of local and imported brick available. Deep red brick was a favorite, particularly in the warehouse districts. Terra cotta—a form of molded, fired clay ideal for cornices, architectural ornament, and fireproofing—also came into wide use. In addition, a variety of newly invented building materials appeared on the scene, although few proved to be successful. The St. Paul Roofing and Cornice Works, for example, promoted an elaborate facade system using sheets of copper made to resemble stone blocks. An old building on Third Street in St. Paul was given the copper treatment in about 1890 as a demonstration, but the idea never caught on.[57]

Although it is widely assumed that buildings are no longer constructed as well as they used to be, the truth is that shoddy work was extremely common in the great boom of the 1880s. Building collapses, usually during construction, were a fairly regular occurrence. In May 1886, one wall of a five-story building under construction in downtown Minneapolis collapsed, killing five men. A coroner's jury later cited "gross neglect" as the cause of the accident. That same year a five-story tenement building erected—unwisely—atop the treacherous ground of the Seventh Street fill in St. Paul came loose from its foundations, tumbled with a great crash into Swede Hollow, and burst into flames, only moments after all of its undoubtedly surprised residents had scrambled to safety.[58]

Fire safety provisions were also terribly inadequate. In the Tribune Building fire, occupants of the upper floors were trapped because the only staircase—made of wood—wrapped around an open elevator shaft that acted as a great flue for spreading the flames. Corner-cutting by busy contractors also appears to have been common. In 1948 St. Paul building inspectors ordered sixteen families to vacate an 1880s-vintage apartment house that had buckled badly in one section. Demolition crews later discovered that two-by-fours had been used for some of the building's floor joists, rather than the much larger members required for safe construction.[59]

Poor construction was so pervasive in the 1880s that both cities were forced to approve long-overdue building ordinances. "The almost unparalleled rapidity with which our business and residence streets are being covered with buildings, and the slipshod and hasty manner in which some of these buildings are constructed, demand the passage of such an ordinance," stated a newspaper article in 1883. The law enacted that year by St. Paul established a permit system and minimum safety requirements. Minneapolis followed suit with a similar ordinance in 1884.[60]

AS THE TWIN CITIES came of age, so too did the local architectural profession. The demand for architects and draftsmen, especially in the early 1880s, was tremendous. "There is a great scarcity here of good architectural draughtsmen," St. Paul architect George Wirth wrote to the editors of American Architect and Building News in 1883. "A dozen good draughtsmen could find plenty of employment here and in Minneapolis." Wirth need not have worried, because architects from around the nation and across the seas had already begun to arrive. These newcomers formed the first generation of academically trained architects in St. Paul and Minneapolis. While older architects from the master builder tradition—such as Bassford and Radcliffe—continued to flourish, the new arrivals quickly made their mark. Their skill and sophistication as designers endowed the architecture of this period with a richness and quality that remains unsurpassed in the history of the Twin Cities.[61]

Little is known about the lives of most of these architects. They appear in passing newspaper references, in an occasional magazine article, in city directories, or on the lists of architectural societies. A few left correspondence or drawings behind, and occasionally an obituary will shed some light on a life and career. But none (not even Gilbert) has been the subject of a biography, and most remain virtually unknown outside a small circle of architectural aficionados.

There were at least four newcomers in the 1880s who were to have a great effect on St. Paul. The first was J. Walter Stevens, who followed his father to St. Paul and opened an office of his own in 1879 or 1880. Details of Stevens's life are sketchy, but it is known that he was born in Massachusetts, that his father was also an architect-builder, and that he was young—perhaps twenty-two or twenty-three—when he arrived in St. Paul. Although not a gifted designer, Stevens appears to have been an adept organizer and a shrewd judge of talent. By the mid-1880s his office was one of the busiest in St. Paul, employing several outstanding draftsmen, including the legendary Harvey Ellis. Much of Stevens's work was in Lowertown, where a half dozen of his buildings survived in 1991.[62]

In 1882 the man who was to become one of

Charles Zimmerman house, about 1890

Minnesota's most prolific architects—Clarence H. Johnston—established his first independent practice in the city. Born in nearby Waseca, Johnston worked as a draftsman in St. Paul in the 1870s, then left in 1880 for a year of study at the Massachusetts Institute of Technology. Upon his return, he designed a number of Summit Avenue houses before forming a partnership in 1886 with William Willcox, who had arrived from Chicago three years earlier. This partnership lasted until 1890 and produced two lost buildings of particular significance—the Bank of Minnesota (1886) at Sixth and Jackson and the Amherst Wilder house (1887) on Summit.[63]

One of Johnston's classmates at MIT was Cass Gilbert, the only Twin Cities architect of the nineteenth century who was to achieve national renown. Born in Ohio but raised in St. Paul, Gilbert began his career as a draftsman for Radcliffe in 1876. He went to MIT for more schooling in 1878, then worked for the celebrated New York firm of McKim, Mead and White before returning to St. Paul in late 1882. In 1884 he formed a partnership with St. Paul native James Knox Taylor that lasted for eight years. The partners designed numerous houses, churches, and office buildings in St. Paul (and elsewhere) in the 1880s and early 1890s. Gilbert shot into national prominence in 1895 with his winning design for the new Minnesota State Capitol. He later moved to New York City and designed such familiar monuments as the Woolworth Building and the U.S. Supreme Court Building.[64]

Another outstanding designer who moved to St. Paul in the 1880s was Allen H. Stem. In partnership with Edgar Hodgson, Jr., from 1886 to 1890, he designed several distinctive houses, including a delightful small town house in 1887 for photographer Charles A. Zimmerman. This delicate, almost toylike house, which is long gone, was an example of the Moorish Revival style that enjoyed a brief period of popularity in the Twin Cities in the 1880s. Stem also designed one of

Clarence Johnston

Cass Gilbert

the city's most urbane small apartment buildings, the now vanished Capitol (also known as the Costanza), completed in 1889 on St. Peter near Fourth. Later Stem teamed up with engineer Charles Reed to design the first St. Paul Auditorium and the Saint Paul Hotel. Reed and Stem were subsequently consulting architects for Grand Central Station in New York City.[65]

St. Paul experienced an influx of European-born and educated architects in the 1880s, with Germans predominating. Among them were Emil Ulrici, who designed several fine residences, including the wonderfully romantic George Benz house (1888) that once stood near the present State Capitol; Albert Zschocke, perhaps best known for his splendid Hotel Barteau (1889); and Hermann Kretz, whose firm specialized in commercial buildings and apartment houses. From England came Walter Ife, an apparently quite proper gentleman whose most renowned commission turned out to be a house in 1887 for the notorious madam, Nina Clifford. Another English immigrant, Louis Lockwood, also arrived in the late 1880s and designed what was perhaps St. Paul's first bungalow in 1899. In addition St. Paul attracted a talented Scandinavian-born designer, Didrik Omeyer, who later teamed with master builder Martin Thori to produce some wild and woolly Queen Anne-style houses and at least one startling church.[66]

Other architects who set up shop in St. Paul in the 1880s included Charles E. Joy, a New Hampshire native who designed the second and third St. Paul ice palaces and later specialized in Shingle Style houses; William H. Castner, another practitioner of the Shingle Style who in 1886 designed one of St. Paul's most charming buildings, the Minnesota Club (gone) at Fourth and Cedar; John H. Coxhead, who moved to St. Paul from Illinois in 1887 and designed several highly unusual houses over the next several years; and Charles T. Mould and Robert McNicol, best known for the John Merriam house (1887, gone), the design of which is often attributed to the firm's draftsman at the time, Harvey Ellis.

Ellis cut an alcoholic swath across the Twin Cities between 1886 and 1889, going from one architectural firm to another as the spirits moved him. So many legends swirl about him that separating fact from fiction can be difficult. It is known that he was with Mould and McNicol in early 1886, moved over to Stevens's office later that year, and then went to work for LeRoy Buffington in Minneapolis in 1887. He also worked briefly for another Minneapolis architectural firm, Orff and Orff. By 1889 he had left the Twin Cities for good.[67]

He was welcome in all of these offices because of his phenomenal ability as a renderer, abetted by an intensely romantic imagination. A number of significant Twin Cities buildings are attributed to Ellis, including the Germania Bank in St. Paul, the Samuel Gale house (1889, gone) in Minneapolis, and Pillsbury Hall (1889, extant) on the

George Benz house, about 1915, showing Merriam's Overlook in the foreground

main campus of the University of Minnesota. But it is not clear to what extent Ellis was involved in the design of these and other buildings, and he may have functioned primarily as a renderer who skillfully presented the work of others. What is certain is that his pen-and-ink drawings, especially those for unbuilt projects, remain stunning works.

In Minneapolis some of the largest and most successful architectural firms of the period were headed by men such as Buffington, Dennis, Whitney, and Long who had arrived in the 1870s. But several important new faces appeared in the 1880s. Among them was Maryland-born Frederick Kees, who settled in Minneapolis about 1880 after working as a draftsman for architects in Baltimore and Chicago. He was in Buffington's office briefly, then went into partnership with Burnham W. Fisk in 1882. Kees's most important design with Fisk was the Syndicate Block-Grand Opera House complex, completed in 1883. In 1885 Kees formed a new partnership with Franklin Long. The firm of Long and Kees, which survived until 1897, was among the most prolific and influential in Minneapolis, designing public and office buildings, schools, churches, and houses. Long and Kees's Minneapolis City Hall–Hennepin County Courthouse remains one of the city's most powerful works of architecture. But much of the firm's legacy has vanished, including the Corn Exchange (1885), the Oneida Building (1888), Donaldson's Glass Block (1888), the Minneapolis Public Library, Washington School, and the splendid Free Will Baptist Church. Kees went into partnership with Serenus Colburn in 1897 and remained in practice until 1921.[68]

In 1882 the building boom attracted Isaac Hodgson from Indianapolis. Hodgson and his eldest son soon built a flourishing practice in

The National Bank of Commerce featured attractive tall arched entrances, each surmounted by a triangular panel of richly carved stonework (1903).

Minneapolis, designing such Victorian extravaganzas as the Chamber of Commerce Building (1884) and the Minnesota Loan and Trust Building. Hodgson and Son quickly proved themselves to be adaptable to new ideas, however, and in 1887 produced the strikingly modern Bank of Minneapolis. Hodgson also served for a time as local supervising architect for the U.S. Post Office in Minneapolis, an overwrought pile of stone that seems to have been widely reviled from the day it was built.

Perhaps the most talented designer to arrive in Minneapolis in the 1880s was Harry Wild Jones. Born in Michigan, Jones attended school in Providence, Rhode Island, where he graduated from Brown University in 1882. He then went on to MIT and worked briefly for H. H. Richardson in Boston. Jones settled in Minneapolis in 1884 and soon established his own office. A tremendously eclectic designer with a knack for the unexpected, Jones left major monuments in virtually every building type and style. His outstanding nineteenth-century works in Minneapolis include the National Bank of Commerce (1889–

Frederick Kees

Harry Wild Jones

Temple Court, 1895

Building. Mix was based in Milwaukee for most of his career and designed scores of buildings there before moving to Minneapolis in about 1886. He had actually begun expanding into the Twin Cities market as early as 1882, when he competed for the Syndicate Block commission. A year later he was chosen to design Fairoaks, William Washburn's mansion. But it was large commercial buildings for which Mix became best known. In addition to the Metropolitan Building, he designed Temple Court (1886), an eight-story office building in Minneapolis, and the Field, Mahler, and Company Department Store (1890) in St. Paul. He also designed two office buildings for the *Globe* newspaper, one in St. Paul in 1887 and another in Minneapolis in 1889. All of these were among the most significant buildings of their time in the Twin Cities, and all are gone.[70]

Other prominent figures in the Minneapolis design community included Carl F. Struck, a native of Norway who designed schools, churches, fraternal buildings, and commercial blocks, among them Harmonia Hall (1884, gone), a striking Gothic structure that once held down the northeast corner of Third Street and Second Avenue South; Warren B. Dunnell, a talented designer with a statewide practice who made a specialty of institutional buildings; E. E. Joralemon, a peripatetic draftsman in the Ellis mold, noted for his romantic and well-detailed residential designs; Charles S. Sedgwick, whose wild Queen Anne-style work included the amazing John E. Bell house (1885–1961) on Park Avenue at Twenty-fourth Street; Alexander Murrie, a Scottish immigrant who designed the improbable Spectator Terrace (1889, gone) on Fourth near Hennepin; Warren H. Hayes, a prolific church architect who found commissions in both Minneapolis and St. Paul; the brothers George W. and Fremont D. Orff, who in combination with various designers produced a large number of commercial and industrial buildings, including the giant Mutual Block (1888, gone); George

1939) at Fourth Street and Marquette Avenue, a handsome Richardsonian Romanesque essay with a tinge of Gothic; the delightfully picturesque Bethesda Church (1889) at Eighth Street and Twelfth Avenue South; and numerous residences, among them the elegant Shingle Style W. C. Tiffany house (1889) on Lowry Hill. All three of the works from 1889 are gone. Jones's career continued well into the twentieth century.[69]

Another important figure in the 1880s was E. Townsend Mix, best known as the designer of the Northwestern Guaranty Loan (Metropolitan)

Bertrand, who designed Queen Anne houses before linking up with Arthur B. Chamberlin in
1897 to form a firm that became noted for its
skillful, stripped-down classicism; and John S.
Bradstreet, a popular artist and interior decorator
who was one of the city's taste makers throughout
the 1880s and 1890s.[71]

ONLY A FEW out-of-town architects, generally
from New York or Chicago, managed to secure
commissions in the Twin Cities at this time. But
when they did so, it was often a plum. In 1883,
for example, New York architect Bradford L.
Gilbert (no relation to Cass) designed one of
St. Paul's largest office buildings of the early
1880s—the Northern Pacific Railroad headquarters (1883, gone). The chief New York contribu-
tion, however, came from the firm of Babb,
Cook, and Willard, which designed the New

York Life Insurance Company buildings (1889, 1890) in St. Paul and Minneapolis.[72]

But the influence of Chicago and its distinctive brand of commercial architecture proved to be far more significant in the Twin Cities. Chicago architects, led by William Boyington, seem to have been especially attracted to St. Paul, whose railroad and warehousing titans often had strong links to the Windy City. Besides Boyington, Chicago architects who designed major buildings in St. Paul in the 1880s and 1890s included Gurdon P. Randall, architect of Central High School; James J. Egan, who was responsible for St. Paul's dominant work of nineteenth-century commercial architecture, the Ryan Hotel (1885); and Solon S. Beman, whose Pioneer Press (later Pioneer) Building (1889), remained the city's finest surviving nineteenth-century skyscraper in 1991. In downtown Minneapolis there were no really prominent buildings by Chicago architects until around the turn of the century.

The so-called Chicago Commercial style, which emerged from that city's rebuilding after the fire of 1871, left a strong mark on Minneapolis as well as on St. Paul. The style—used principally for tall office buildings—emphasized blocky forms, gridlike facades with large plate-glass windows, flat roofs, and modest use of ornament. Generally seen as a forerunner of architectural modernism, the style reached its summit in the work of such giants as John Root and Louis Sullivan, although the Chicago firm of Holabird and Roche was perhaps its most dedicated and consistent practitioner. The proximity of Chicago, the influence of such Chicago-based publications as the *Inland Architect and Builder*, and the style's inherent simplicity and directness all contributed to its popularity in the Twin Cities.[73]

Probably the first full-blown, Chicago-style building in the Twin Cities was Hodgson and Son's remarkable Bank of Minneapolis. Other Chicago-style buildings of varying degrees of purity cropped up in the Twin Cities over the next few decades, although never in sufficient numbers to create a distinctive look.

FOR THE MOST part, St. Paul and Minneapolis stayed well within the eclectic mainstream of American architecture in the late nineteenth century. Although both cities had designers of real talent (Gilbert and Jones come immediately to mind), neither could boast of a form-giver capable of creating a unique and widely influential body of architecture. Schuyler, writing in 1891, found the Twin Cities architectural scene to be a decidedly mixed bag, contrasting its "western" exuberance with the more refined work of the East. Yet he found cause for optimism, detecting the "hopeful beginnings of a national architecture" in several of the buildings he saw. As it turned out, however, the Twin Cities was not to play a major role in shaping the future of American architecture. Without the presence of a dominating figure such as Richardson, Root, or Sullivan, the architectural mishmash of the 1880s and 1890s in the Twin Cities never effervesced into the pure juice of style. Even so, many delightful, odd, daring, and beautiful buildings emerged during this period, which was the closest the Twin Cities ever came to a Golden Age of architecture.[74]

The early 1880s were characterized, above all else, by tremendous eclecticism in design. With a wealth of materials available to them and with popular taste running toward the picturesque, Twin Cities architects strove for color, variety, and surface elaboration. They also took a wonderfully carefree approach toward historical styles, mixing up great architectural salads with a pinch of Gothic and a dash of Romanesque, and then throwing in something a little more exotic—how about a nice Moorish arch?—simply for the fun of it.

This restless eclecticism began showing up on commercial buildings in the 1870s and reached full flower by the early 1880s, as one local newspaper reported:

A few years ago architects adhered quite closely to certain styles, but of late there has been a tendency to break away from traditions and work upon an entirely different plane. Whatever produces the best effect is what the architect of today makes an effort to attain, and the result is there is a combination of most of the old styles into something that is newer, and consequently, more attractive. The tastes of the people are constantly changing, and modern architects simply strive to meet the demand for something that is fresh and original. . . . You will find in most of the business blocks lately erected in St. Paul that certain one-idea styles have been followed in but few instances. As a rule, there is a mixture, and sometimes you will see the plain Gothic, the arch French, the Romanesque and the Queen Anne all combined to produce a unique and striking effect.[75]

Although no single style dominated in the Twin Cities at this time, Victorian Gothic seems to have been as popular for commercial and public buildings as anything else. The Ryan Hotel in St. Paul was the ultimate statement of this style, while the Minnesota Loan and Trust Building in Minneapolis was an equally definitive demonstration of its excesses.

As used in the Twin Cities, this style was not the elaborately detailed and patterned Gothic Revival specified by John Ruskin, but a more casual and less pure American version. Features of the style included tall narrow windows, pointed Gothic arches (although these were sometimes left out), towers with high saddle roofs, and deeply incised floral ornament. Marked color contrast, often accomplished by threading horizontal bands of white stone through walls of deep red brick, was also common.

Although St. Paul newspapers first noted the popularity of these "red and white buildings" in 1882, Gothic Revival public and commercial structures began appearing in the Twin Cities by the late 1870s. An early example in Minneapolis, designed by Buffington, was the Farmers and Mechanics Bank Building (1878) at Nicollet and Washington. Kees and Fisk's Syndicate Block, also on Nicollet, was probably Minneapolis' largest Gothic-influenced commercial building. Jefferson (1877) and Central High schools in Minneapolis were among the first public buildings to offer the Gothic look. St. Paul's Central High School followed suit, as did many others. But aside from the Ryan Hotel, none of the Gothic-inspired commercial or public buildings in the Twin Cities was a nationally significant example of the style.[76]

A variety of other styles also appeared on the architectural smorgasbord. Minneapolis architect

Farmers and Mechanics Bank, about 1878

Jefferson School, about 1880

William H. Dennis specialized in French Renaissance Revival confections, culminating in 1885 with the richly decorated Vendome Hotel (also known as Stillman's Block). Located on Fourth near Nicollet, the Vendome offered, among other wonders, a replica of the Statue of Liberty's head. Dennis designed two other buildings on the same block, creating a sort of mini-French Quarter that survived until the 1960s.

The highly varied and badly named Queen Anne style also had a short commercial heyday, thanks largely to LeRoy Buffington. His West Hotel (1884) and Tribune Building (1885) defy stylistic pigeonholing, but both seem as close to Queen Anne as any other style. First popularized by English architects for half-timbered houses based on Elizabethan models, Queen Anne was primarily a residential style. H. H. Richardson is generally credited with introducing the style to this country in his Watts Sherman house (1876)

in Newport, Rhode Island. In American hands the style gradually lost much of its medievalism and took on a Colonial overlay, with classic columns, Palladian windows, and similar features providing a quiet counterpoint to busy spindle-work, incised ornament, and richly patterned wall surfaces. The style began appearing in the Twin Cities around 1880 and received one of its most memorable early expressions in the Shipman-Greve house (1884, extant), designed by Buffington and located on Summit Avenue in St. Paul. This house was built just a few blocks from St. Paul's last great French Second Empire gasp, the Kittson mansion.[77]

By about 1885 the relentless quest for architectural novelty had begun to wane. "The rage for the Queen Anne style is fast abating," a newspaper reporter wrote in late 1884. However, this did not signify a sudden return to chaste classicism, since the reporter went on to note that "strong colors are still in vogue. . . . [and] at least four colors should be used in painting a house to give it the proper appearance." Meanwhile architects themselves began calling for a little restraint. In December 1884 Minneapolis architect James K. Wilson complained in a speech that too many new buildings were being "bedecked and bedizened with every manner of projections and gee-gaws, any kind of trash, so that it be a 'new style,'—God save us!"[78]

As it turned out, God did not intervene, but a figure of almost equal weight and authority—H. H. Richardson—did. Although Richardson died in 1886, his giant shadow cast a measure of order upon the Twin Cities architectural scene that was to last well into the 1890s. With his design for Boston's Trinity Church, completed in 1877, Richardson had developed a massive masonry style that was to sweep the country. Usually known as Richardsonian Romanesque, the style emphasized heavy walls of stone or brick, round-arched window openings, and rich ornament based on Romanesque and Byzantine models.

But what really set Richardson apart from his contemporaries was his command of powerful, straightforward forms. Richardson rediscovered simplicity, as architects seem to do at least once every century, and his ability to break free from the busy excesses of Victorian design soon made him the most imitated architect in America.[79]

For Twin Cities architects, superb examples of Richardson's work could be found a few hours away by train in Chicago. Richardson's Chicago buildings included the Marshall Field Wholesale Store (1885–87, gone), which was to be the model for a generation of Twin Cities warehouses, and the tautly composed J. J. Glessner house (1885–87, extant), a fortress-style residence. More influential than Richardson himself, at least in the Twin Cities, was the Chicago architect John Root. In a number of Chicago office buildings, most notably the Rookery (1885–88, extant), Root brilliantly reworked the Richardsonian aesthetic and quickly won many imitators.[80]

Franklin Long's Kasota Block (1884, gone) on Hennepin Avenue in Minneapolis appears to have been the first Richardsonian commercial building in the state. One of the first Twin Cities residences with a strong Richardsonian flavor was the William W. McNair house (1884–86, gone) at 1301 Linden Avenue in Minneapolis, designed by E. E. Joralemon for Long's firm. Scores of other works in the master's manner soon followed, and competitions for such important buildings as the Minneapolis City Hall–Hennepin County Courthouse even specified a Richardsonian design.[81]

Pure examples of the style were rare: the city hall and courthouse, modeled on Richardson's Allegheny County Courthouse in Pittsburgh, was perhaps the best. In other cases architects simply added a few round arches to the usual Victorian miscellany and labeled the result Richardsonian. Bassford's ineptly designed St. Paul City Hall–Ramsey County Courthouse fell into this catego-

Vendome Hotel, about 1948

ry. In rare instances Twin Cities architects were able to assimilate lessons from Richardson and produce distinctive variations on his work. The Samuel Gale house (1889), attributed to Harvey Ellis during his employment in Buffington's office, is an example. In its final stages, Richardsonian Romanesque was sometimes mixed with

W. W. McNair house, about 1890

elements of the so-called Chateauesque style, derived from sixteenth-century French models. Perhaps the best example of this mixed style is the old Federal Courts Building (1898, 1902), renamed Landmark Center, in St. Paul.

The Richardsonian style, or something aspiring to it, was used for everything from public and commercial buildings to churches to apartments and homes. The year 1889 seems to have been the peak of the Richardsonian era in the Twin Cities, especially in Minneapolis, which saw the completion of such splendid specimens as the

National Bank of Commerce, the Globe Building, the public library, and the Gale mansion. Richardsonian-Chateauesque houses, such as William Donaldson's house on Groveland Avenue in Minneapolis, were still being built as late as 1893, but by this time various classically inspired styles had already moved to the forefront of public taste. In fact the crusade for a new national style in the 1880s ended not in the promised land of a uniquely American architecture but at the ancient walls of classicism.

The Chicago World's Fair of 1893, with its famous White City, is sometimes depicted as the dawning of a new classical age in American architecture. This was not really the case, however. Well before the fair, classicism in one form or another was gaining ground in the Twin Cities and elsewhere as a reaction against the overindulgence of Victorian design. In 1887 Minneapolis architect William Channing Whitney wrote that there is "no better way of attaining good principles of design than by studying classic forms, going back to the work that was the foundation of all the styles that have since arisen." Classicism is the one guest that never leaves the American architectural party, always standing ready to take the floor if the conversation lags. Even in the wildest period of the early 1880s, a few local architects—Dennis, most notably— were working in an essentially classical idiom. But it was not until the late 1880s that classicism began to become a strong and consistent force in the Twin Cities.[82]

Residential design showed the way. Queen Anne and the related Stick Style had been all the rage in the early 1880s, but their popularity waned quite rapidly. Leading Twin Cities architects then began to embrace new East Coast styles that were moving toward the simplified, classically inspired forms of American Colonial architecture. The New York firm of McKim, Mead, and White was the pacesetter in this regard. In 1883 the firm produced one of the first houses in the so-called Shingle Style in Newport, Rhode Island. This style put Queen Anne on a Colonial diet, resulting in houses that retained a picturesque profile but shed much of their Victorian fat in favor of plain walls and modest ornament. Often mounted on high stone bases, these houses usually featured a continuous shingle surface covering the walls and roof.[83]

The Shingle Style—confined to houses and a few small churches—was never especially popular in the Twin Cities, although some excellent examples were built. The style, or at least some-

thing approaching it, seems to have made its first appearance in Minneapolis about 1884 in the George Campbell house (gone), designed by Harry Jones. Later Jones designed two splendid examples of the style—the W. C. Tiffany house (1889) on Lowry Hill and Bethesda Church (1889) at Eighth Street and Twelfth Avenue South. Both are gone, as is a Shingle Style beauty from Buffington's office—the Francis E. Little house (1888), which was located at 1414 Harmon Place. In St. Paul the Daniel Noyes house (1884), located on Summit Avenue and designed by Chicago architect H. R. Marshall, was an early if not entirely pure example of the style. Although several St. Paul architects worked in the style, four in particular—Allen H. Stem, William Castner, Charles Joy, and John Coxhead—were among its most skillful practitioners. Their Shingle Style houses, a few of which remain, were all

Francis Little house, about 1890

Bethesda Church (African-American), 1902

built before 1890, which seems to have been about the end of the Shingle era in the Twin Cities.[84]

By this time, the more familiar Colonial Revival style was beginning to gain popularity. Also pioneered by McKim, Mead, and White in New York, the Colonial Revival was another effort to bring the Victorian architectural free-for-all under control. With its compact and simple volumes, modest classical detail, and dignified formality, the Colonial Revival house—in a hundred different guises—has proved to be a favorite for more than a century. William Channing Whitney appears to have introduced this style to the Twin Cities in 1886–87 with his William H. Hinkle house (extant) in Minneapolis. Cass Gilbert was also among the first local masters of the Colonial Revival. In such designs as the A. P. Warren house (1889, gone) in St. Paul, Gilbert was able to breathe new life into an old model. Allen Stem in St. Paul and Jones in Minneapolis also designed in this style with considerable flair. But much Colonial Revival architecture in the Twin Cities was predictable and derivative, and in its watered-down form it became the style of choice for innumerable four-square tract houses built between 1890 and 1910.[85]

A different form of classicism—based generally on northern Italian Renaissance models—gradually came to dominate commercial and public architecture in the Twin Cities in the 1890s. Here again, the work of McKim, Mead, and White proved extremely influential. Their two houses for Henry G. Villard (both 1886) in Manhattan set the standard, offering a vision of Renaissance elegance, restraint, and solidity that proved irresistible to architects in the Twin Cities and elsewhere. Equally important was the firm's Boston Public Library (1887–95), the great early showpiece of an era that is sometimes called the American Renaissance.[86]

In St. Paul, Bassford introduced Renaissance elements on the lower floors of his Germania Life Insurance Building in 1889. Classicism with an odd Flemish flavor turned up that same year on the New York Life Building. Cass Gilbert was among the first St. Paul architects to exploit the classical revival. He turned out a full-bodied Italian palace facade for his Endicott on Fourth Building (extant), completed in 1890. Five years later Gilbert designed the Bowlby Building, also known as the Boston Clothing Store (gone), at Sixth and Robert Streets in the approved neo-

144

A. P. Warren house, about 1889

Bowlby Building, 1915

Detail of cornice and upper floor of Bowlby Building

classical manner. In that same year he also won a competition for the city's ultimate Renaissance-inspired architectural spectacle—the State Capitol.[87]

In Minneapolis, William H. Dennis continued to churn out work in the classical mode, including the Minneapolis Journal Building (1890), the delightful little Nicollet National Bank (1893), and the S. E. Olson Department Store (1893). The first big office building in Minneapolis to adopt a Renaissance look was the New York Life Insurance Building of 1890 by Babb, Cook, and Willard of New York. The Minneapolis firm of Bertram and Keith contributed the urbane eight-story Dayton (later known as the Besse) Building, completed in 1895 at Sixth and Nicollet. Harry Jones, adept at any style, chipped in with a number of elegant, classically inspired apartment houses, such as the Lombardy (ca. 1895). The U.S. Post Office in Minneapolis, designed by

Minneapolis Club, about 1900

George Partridge house, about 1904

committee, took a running leap at classicism but never quite got there. It was left to William Channing Whitney, that apostle of good taste, to design the city's most faithful Renaissance revival exercise of the nineteenth century—the Minneapolis Club (1892–ca. 1925) at Sixth and Marquette. All of these buildings are gone.

Classicism in its many guises was also popular for residences, perhaps because the style was associated with great wealth and good taste, two attributes that do not always coincide. Among the grandest Beaux-Arts mansions of the 1890s was the George H. Partridge house (1897, gone) at 1 Groveland Terrace in Minneapolis. This estate, designed by Long and Kees and expanded by Kees and Colburn in 1904, included a circular

garage in which vehicles were parked with the aid of a turntable.[88]

The theme of classicism is continuity. The classically styled buildings that rose in the two downtowns at the turn of the century were intended to suggest a visible link to an older order of things. But the link to the past has always been weak in American cities, where every day is the day of the dollar and commerce prefers the future tense. The new century, despite its classical beginnings, was to prove to be not much different from the old—change, not continuity, was its hallmark. As it progressed the monuments of the past were swept away one by one, until downtown St. Paul and Minneapolis had once again made themselves into new urban worlds.

BUILDING PROFILES

ST. PAUL CITY RAILWAY COMPANY-DICKINSON'S DEPARTMENT STORE

East side of St. Peter Street between Fourth and Fifth streets, St. Paul. George Wirth, LeRoy Buffington. Ca. 1878, 1880, 1885–93.

The idea of converting an industrial building into a trendy shopping spot is far from new, as the history of this horsecar-barn-turned-department-store demonstrates. The building had its beginnings in the late 1870s when the St. Paul City Railway Company built a two-story brick barn for its horses and equipment at Fourth and St. Peter streets. In 1880 the company, which by then had 160 horses, added a third floor (for storing grain and hay) to the original barn and also built a new structure directly to the north along St. Peter. The new building, three stories high, housed the company's thirty-six horsecars, a turntable, repair shops, offices, and a dormitory for drivers and conductors. In the narrow space between the two buildings was a steam-operated elevator that lifted cars to the second floor.

As designed by George Wirth, both brick buildings were quite straightforward, with simply arranged windows and a minimum of ornament. The top floors offered one nice touch in the form of horseshoe-shaped windows that provided an amusing visual comment on the building's function while also anticipating the Moorish fad of the 1880s.

The streetcar company did not stay long in its buildings. In 1884 a group of investors led by Thomas Lowry bought the company and moved the stock and offices elsewhere. This created an opportunity for Samuel G. Dickinson, a successful retailer who owned a large dry goods store on Third Street. Dickinson wanted to move into better quarters up town, and in 1884 he struck a deal to lease the streetcar buildings for ten years for use as a department store.

Architect LeRoy Buffington was then called in, and by May 1885 he had worked an astonishing transformation. Buffington installed plate-glass windows on the ground floor, redid the interiors, and connected the two buildings with a new pavilion, which had a spectacular Moorish arch in the shape of—what else—a horseshoe. Buffington may also have been asked at one point to add another floor—drawings, in fact, show the store with four stories—but written accounts indicate this was never done. Even so, the changes wrought in the building seemed magical to a *Pioneer Press* reporter who wrote: "This abode of mules and horses has, as if the lamp of Aladdin had been utilized, been changed into the most elaborate guildhall in the Northwest."

The new store's forty-five thousand square feet of space included a two-story rotunda, forty departments spread over three floors, and a small café. Dickinson advertised his establishment—perhaps with more enthusiasm than accuracy—as the "largest department store in the country." But the store encountered financial troubles in the grim days of the early 1890s, and in 1893 Dickinson surrendered his lease and closed the business for good. The building was then razed to make way for a three-story arcade and office structure financed by William Davidson. The Lowry Medical Arts Building, constructed in about 1910, subsequently occupied the site.

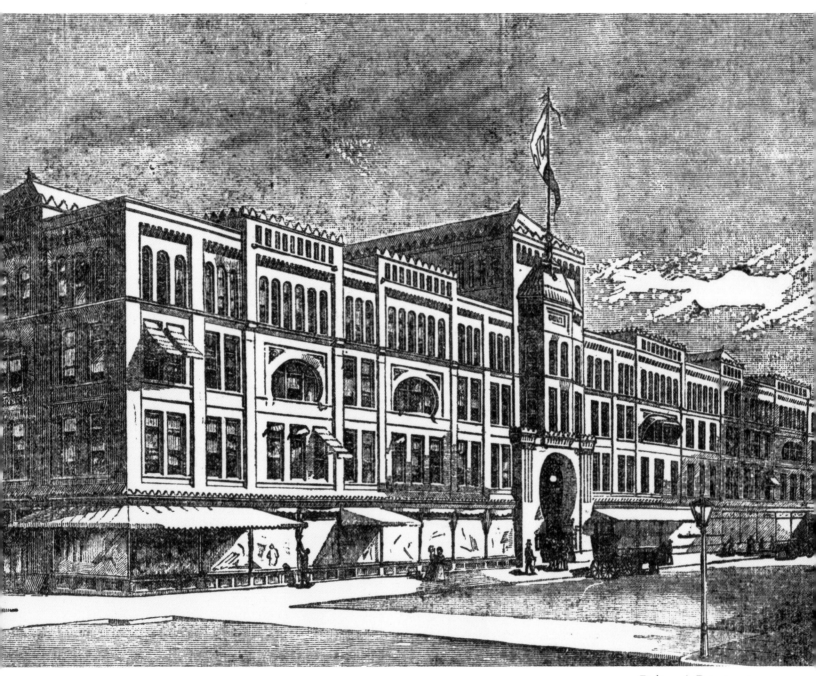

Dickinson's Department Store as it appeared after Buffington redesigned it in 1885

MARKET HALL

North side of Seventh Street between Wabasha and
St. Peter streets, St. Paul. Abraham Radcliffe. 1881–1915.

The second Market Hall, about 1890

This was the first major public building of the 1880s in St. Paul. Intended as a kind of civic center, the building turned out to be a "burden on the city treasury," as one newspaper put it, and served its original purpose for less than twenty years. The building occupied the site of the city's first public market, which was erected in 1853 but had become far too small by the 1870s, when planning began for a replacement.

Abraham Radcliffe won the commission after a contest with at least one other prominent local architect, Edward Bassford. The early 1880s was a time of dizzying diversity in architectural styles, and Radcliffe's design for Market Hall—which mixed Victorian Gothic, Romanesque Revival, and classical elements with considerable gusto—was no exception. Built of yellow brick with stone trim, the two-story structure extended an entire block along Seventh. Rows of big arched windows, pilasters, pedimented pavilions, and a tightly bracketed cornice gave the composition a classical feel. But the building's off-center, 115-foot-high tower (which later had to be reinforced to accept a three-ton bell) added a Gothic Revival touch to the proceedings, as did richly patterned brickwork above some of the windows.

The interior was simply organized. The ground floor was basically open space for market stalls, while the upper floor included a large hall, a dining room, and a municipal courtroom. The building, however, never quite worked the way it was supposed to. Only a week after Market Hall opened, the State Capitol burned down, and for the next two years state government took over much of the building. When the politicians cleared out in 1883, the ground floor was finally opened up entirely for market use, with thirty-two stalls, some beneath a sidewalk canopy. There was also an open air hay market to the rear.

During the late 1880s when Seventh and Wabasha was the city's busiest intersection, Market Hall was at the center of St. Paul life. On Saturday morning—market day—thousands of people swarmed around the building, buying and selling food in a scene that one newspaper described as "bewildering to one not accustomed to it."

Market Hall quickly proved to be too small, and by 1890 supplementary markets had already sprung up elsewhere downtown. The upstairs hall—never a financial success for the city—housed a theater company for awhile, but otherwise remained largely vacant. In 1899 the city transferred ownership of the building to the St. Paul Public Library, which spent ninety-eight thousand dollars on remodeling and then moved into the upper floor. The ground floor was leased for commercial use. Meanwhile the city built a new public market at Tenth and Jackson streets. Market Hall—renamed the Library Building—survived until April 26, 1915, when it burned down, taking more than a hundred thousand books with it. The St. Francis Hotel-Palace (later Orpheum) Theater occupied the site after 1916.

Market Hall after the 1915 fire

UNION DEPOT

Foot of Sibley Street, St. Paul. LeRoy Buffington.
1881, 1884–1913.

The first railroad depots in St. Paul were small, crude affairs built to serve only one or two lines. By the late 1870s when St. Paul had eight railroads, there were still at least three separate depots clustered along the downtown riverfront. The inconvenience of this arrangement was apparent, and in March 1879 the railroads, after much legal maneuvering, formed a company to build and operate a new Union Depot.

The depot's site, on the east side of Sibley Street at the Mississippi River, offered ready access to existing tracks along the riverfront and in the Trout Brook-Phalen Creek valley to the east. But the site was also flood prone and had terrible soil conditions. Much of it had once been swampy bottomland, a "literal 'slough of despond,'" according to one historian. As a result it took a year to prepare the site, mainly by adding fill and raising track levels to stay clear of high water.

LeRoy Buffington was selected as the depot's architect—possibly after a limited competition—

in April 1880. The depot company's directors were, as one writer put it, "actuated by economical motives," and rejected anything elaborate in favor of a rather bare-bones building, which opened in August 1881. Built of red brick with white sandstone trim, the two-story depot presented an unassuming front facade with a central pavilion flanked by lower pavilions to either side. One newspaper described the design as "Italian," but in fact it was an elusive jumble of classical, Romanesque, and Gothic Revival elements.

The interior was straightforward. A skylit central hall, forty feet high, formed the spine of the building, with rooms arranged to either side. On the first floor were waiting rooms (one for each sex), a ticket office, a large dining room, and, to the rear, baggage rooms. Upstairs were offices and crew rooms, a mail room, and a waiting room for emigrants. Virtually every room had a fireplace, although the building was heated by steam and had incandescent lighting. Nine tracks separated by platforms were at the rear of the depot. There was also a platform on the south side serving the Chicago, Milwaukee and St. Paul Railroad. The depot was set well back from Sibley, creating a staging area for the "fiery, untamed hackmen" who whisked passengers to and from their hotels.

The depot did not lead a charmed life. Huge cracks developed as it settled into the boggy soil, and for a time there was talk of abandoning the structure and building a new depot elsewhere. Then, on June 11, 1884, a fire raced through the building, leaving the interior in ruins. A new depot on a new site was now given serious consideration, but the idea presented too many complications, so the old depot was simply rebuilt from the inside out. As a result of this rebuilding, the depot acquired a new profile, including a saddle-roofed central tower much higher and more ornate than the old one. A new baggage room was also added to the rear of the building. The rebuilt interior followed the general arrangement of the original but appears to have been a bit more lav-

Union Depot as it appeared upon completion in 1881

Union Depot after the reconstruction following the fire

ish. All told, the rebuilding cost $150,000, about $25,000 more than the original depot had.

Five years later the depot acquired its most extraordinary feature—a 710-foot-long, 170-foot-wide iron and glass train shed that may have been one of the longest ever built in America. It replaced platform canopies that had provided limited protection from the elements for passengers as they went to and from trains.

By 1887 the depot was said to serve eight million passengers a year with up to 280 trains—most of them locals—arriving and departing daily. Many famous travelers passed though the depot, among them Chief Joseph of the Nez Perce, who was photographed in 1904 on his way to the World's Fair in St. Louis. The depot's heavy use proved to be its downfall. Despite several later additions, the depot was never large enough to handle all the traffic. As a result there were frequent calls in the newspapers and elsewhere to build a replacement. By 1910 one newspaper reported that final plans for a new and much larger train station would be approved

shortly. But nothing happened until fire, once again, forced action. On October 3–4, 1913, a spectacular blaze that lit up the night sky over Lowertown destroyed the depot. Work began four years later on a new Union Depot, which was completed in 1923, just as the great age of the passenger train was about to end. This depot's concourse and part of an elevated train platform leading to it occupied the site of the old depot.

The iron and glass train shed behind the depot, about 1890

153

BEARD'S BLOCK

East side of Twelfth Avenue South between Washington Avenue and Second Street South, Minneapolis. Architect unknown. 1881–ca. 1931.

This huge tenement, often referred to as "Noah's Ark" because it housed immigrant families of all nationalities, was probably the largest of its kind ever built in the Twin Cities. It was financed by Henry B. Beard, a Connecticut-born and Yale-educated businessman who combined a knack for real estate speculation with a strong social conscience. Beard began his career in Minneapolis in 1869 as an insurance agent, quit ten years later to pursue his dream of becoming a minister, then returned to a successful career in real estate. During the 1880s Beard developed property in northeast Minneapolis, on Lowry Hill, and in the lake district. Known for his public-mindedness, he donated much of the land around Lake Harriet for use as a park.

Beard's Block under construction

Beard's tenement was one of his most ambitious projects. Completed in 1881 (and enlarged about 1890), the three-story building was intended to provide something rare in Minneapolis then and now—decent low-cost housing for poor working families. In its original form, the U-shaped building extended for a full block along Twelfth and about half a block on Washington and Second. This gave it a total street front of nearly eight hundred feet, probably more than any other building of the time in Minneapolis. Constructed of brick, the building was simply detailed with repetitive three-window bays, segmental arched windows and doors, and a standard corbelled cornice topped by large roof ornaments along Washington. The entire building, except for seven storefronts facing Washington, was de-

ied from thirteen dollars a month for a four-room apartment on the ground floor to eight dollars a month for a third-floor unit. Hansen said the building had no indoor plumbing and instead provided separate privies (and separate wood-sheds as well) for each apartment, all located in a courtyard reached through an arched passageway off Twelfth Street. Other sources, however, stated that the building had its own private sewer, which was tunneled through twelve hundred feet of sandstone to the Mississippi River. Gas and running water, uncommon amenities for low-cost housing in the 1880s, were also provided.

Beard's Block apparently was torn down about 1931 when it was last listed in city directories. A modern office structure later occupied the site.

CENTER:
The Washington Avenue facade of Beard's Block, about 1912

BELOW:
A 1912 insurance map shows the extent of Beard's Block

voted to apartments—more than eighty in all—which were "immediately taken and duly appreciated by a good class of workmen," according to one newspaper. Little is known about the overall layout of the building, although it appears that apartments on the top floor could only be reached by back steps with entry through the kitchen.

Among the early residents of Beard's Block was Carl Hansen, who left a brief account of the building in his memoir, *My Minneapolis*. "It is doubtful," Hansen wrote, "if anywhere in America so many Norwegian families have lived under one roof." Other nationalities—including Swedes and Irish—were also well represented, producing an ethnic stew that must have rivaled the tenements of New York's Lower East Side. Rents var-

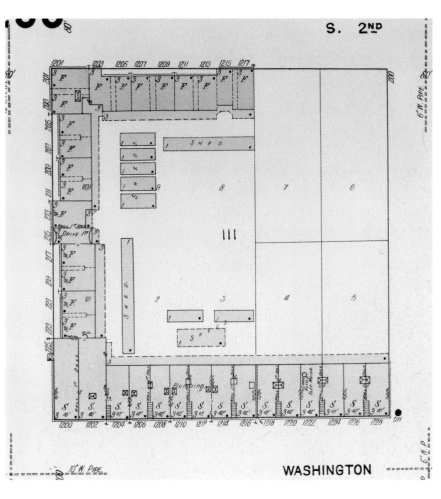

SYNDICATE BLOCK AND GRAND OPERA HOUSE

East side of Nicollet Avenue between Fifth and Sixth
streets, Minneapolis. Kees and Fisk, Oscar Cobb.
1883–97, 1989.

In 1881 a dozen Minneapolis businessmen
formed a syndicate, bought a choice lot on Nicollet Avenue for $77,500, and laid plans for a huge
office and retail building. The syndicate invited
several leading architects—including William
Dennis, E. Townsend Mix, and Frederick Kees—
to submit plans. Kees, then in partnership with
Burnham W. Fisk, won the competition, and
work on the project began in 1882.

Syndicate Block, about 1905

The original design called for a four-story structure, but the owners—apparently at the architects' urging—decided in 1882 to add a floor to improve the building's proportions. Despite a fire that set back the pace of construction, the building was completed in 1883. Extending three hundred feet along Nicollet, with 250,000 square feet of space, the building was the city's first block-long commercial structure and far larger than anything seen before in Minneapolis. Civic boosters, who trod fearlessly in the realm of hyperbole, even went so far as to describe the structure as "the largest business block under one roof in America."

Such inflated claims aside, the Syndicate Block was a powerful piece of Victorian street architecture, its facades of light Ohio sandstone bristling with knobby columns, fluted pilasters, and heavily hooded windows, all set off by crisply incised floral ornament. Much of this ornament had a strong Gothic flavor, although the building's symmetrical massing and light color evoked Renaissance classicism. The deeply indented, richly layered windows were especially impressive and must have provided a wonderful field for the play of light and shadow.

Inside, the Syndicate Block was mostly loft space that could be adapted to a variety of uses. The biggest tenant initially was the furniture and decorating firm of Phelps and Bradstreet, which occupied all six floors in the center of the building. Shops and offices, some located off a small arcade, filled in the remaining space.

The Syndicate Block was to enjoy an excep-

157

Grand Opera House, 1883

tionally long life despite several damaging fires. The original exterior, however, expired long before the building. After a fire in 1911, the south half of the building received a new brick and terra-cotta facade along with a classical cornice. This schizophrenic arrangement lasted until the 1950s when the J. C. Penney Company leased the entire building and encased everything in metal panels. After Penney's moved out in the 1980s, the building stood vacant for several years until it was finally demolished in 1989 to make way for a new shopping mall and skyscraper, which also occupied the site of the old Grand Opera House.

As originally planned, the Syndicate Block was to consist solely of office and retail space. But by 1882 there was intense agitation in Minneapolis for a new opera house that would supersede the Pence and Academy of Music, both of which were viewed as being antiquated "upstairs" halls. Various proposals floated around until the money men behind the Syndicate Block decided in April 1882 to include an opera house in their project. Oscar Cobb, who had grown up in St. Anthony before embarking on an architectural career in Chicago, was called on to plan the interior of the opera house, while Kees and Fisk designed the facade. Cobb was a prolific theater architect who claimed to have designed opera houses in every state, although he mostly worked in the Midwest.

The new Grand Opera House, which opened on April 2, 1883, was located next door to the Syndicate Block on Sixth Street. It was the Twin Cities' first big "downstairs" theater, having a main floor at ground level and seating for fourteen hundred. Although the Grand's facade followed the general lines of the Syndicate Block, the theater, which had a large balcony and arch above the main entrance and an ornate parapet, presented a more festive appearance than its mammoth neighbor.

The auditorium itself was of the triple-tiered horseshoe variety and was so compactly arranged that even patrons in the most remote reaches of the gallery were no more than fifty feet from the stage. At least one critic claimed before the theater opened that it was badly built and lacked sufficient exits in case of fire. This allegation prompted a lengthy reply from Kees, who called the theater's fire-safety precautions "second to none in the country." In truth most opera houses of the period were flimsily constructed—with lots of glitter and little architectural substance—but the Grand does not appear to have deserved any particular opprobrium in this regard. Moreover theatrical managers in New York were said to be fond of the Grand, referring to it as "the ideal playhouse" because of its good sight lines and intimate seating.

The interior decoration by C. N. Atwood of Boston was done in an olive, crimson, and green color scheme that must have satisfied even the heartiest Victorian appetite for decorative overkill. "The whole effect," wrote one admiring if not very prescient critic, "will for a long time provide a feast for the eye and quiet comfort and contentment to the patrons." In fact the decorative scheme survived only four years before John Bradstreet was called it to redo everything with a new Moorish look.

Opening night, according to one newspaper, attracted "a brilliant audience" that heard "an exceptionally brilliant concert." After the recitation of a sappy ode entitled "A Hymn to Art" and a brief speech by Cobb, the program went ahead with the performance of orchestral and vocal pieces from well-known operas.

Considered the city's "first-class" theater, the Grand presented everything from Shakespearean tragedies to Italian grand opera to a one-time viewing of a six-thousand-foot-long panorama of Yellowstone Park. But it was never a financial success. The Grand closed in 1895, a year after the opening of the Metropolitan Opera House three blocks away on Marquette, and was torn down in 1897.

Interior of the opera house showing Bradstreet's Moorish decor

CENTRAL PARK

Block bounded by Summit Avenue (later Columbus Avenue), Central Avenue (later Constitution Avenue), and Central Park Places East and West (both gone), St. Paul. 1883–ca. 1960.

CENTRAL PARK METHODIST EPISCOPAL CHURCH

Southwest corner of Twelfth and Minnesota streets, St. Paul. George Wirth. 1887–1961.

This park and church were once part of an exceptionally urbane residential neighborhood on the northern fringes of downtown St. Paul. Located a block south of the park, the church featured one of the city's most conspicuous steeples, 165 feet high and with unusually graceful proportions. Meanwhile the park provided an elegant oasis of greenery in the heart of a densely populated apartment house district and was also the site of the first three Winter Carnival ice palaces.

The church was actually the third built by the city's oldest Methodist congregation, formed in 1848 by a group of eight faithful that included a former slave named James Thompson. The con-

Central Park, looking northwest; the Uri Lamprey house is far right and Trinity Lutheran Church is far left, about 1900

gregation erected its first church (also the first Protestant church in Minnesota) in 1849 on Market Street overlooking Rice Park. A schism soon developed in the congregation, however, and some members left to form the Jackson Street Methodist Church. A small brick church built in 1856 at Ninth and Jackson streets served this congregation until the mid-1880s when the need for a larger church became evident. In 1886 the congregation bought land at Twelfth and Minnesota streets for a new church, which took its name from its location.

Central Park was just being developed at this time, much of the site having been donated to the city in 1883. The park was quite small—less than two and a half acres—but at its prime in the 1880s and 1890s it was a delightful spot with a large central fountain and an impressive array of buildings around its edges. These included several mansions, most notably the Blood-Hardenbergh house (1889, gone), along with such elegant apartment buildings as the Elsinore and the Virginia (both 1893, gone). But it was the church, designed by George Wirth, that dominated the park environs until the completion of Cass Gilbert's State Capitol in 1904.

Wirth reportedly went to Chicago to study churches there before designing Central Park Methodist, and he must have learned something of value because the building he produced upon his return to St. Paul was an impressive, cheerfully eclectic performance. With its playful silhouette, pale walls of Dresbach limestone, and bulging corner turrets garnished with a jolly assortment of

Central Park, looking toward downtown; the dome of the State Capitol is far right, about 1898

Central Park Methodist Episcopal Church, about 1925

conical roofs, Central Park Methodist seemed almost to be a "light" version of the normally dark and heavy Richardsonian Romanesque. The placement of the corner tower and some of its detailing, however, suggest that Wirth had not entirely shed the English Gothic model so prevalent for Protestant churches.

As befitting a Methodist church, the interior, which underwent at least one major remodeling (1916), was plain. The main floor offered six hundred seats built on a sloped floor and arranged in a semicircle around the pulpit and choir. A gallery above provided an additional three hundred seats. Illumination came from a pair of large wheel windows in the two main gables and a central skylight. The auditorium was finished in oak, pine, and cherry, all treated simply. There was also "a cosy [sic] fireplace," which was said to give "added cheerfulness to the scene." A two-story annex to the rear of the auditorium contained a pastor's study, lecture rooms, a kitchen, two dining rooms, and a pair of parlors for "young men" and "young ladies."

The neighborhood began to lose its residential character around the turn of the century as the new Capitol brought an ever-expanding governmental presence. Encroachment also came in the form of a baseball park erected diagonally across the street from the church in 1903. Sunday baseball became a heated issue with the congregation, which did not favor such an irreligious Sabbath pastime, and the dispute was not resolved until the Saints baseball team moved to Lexington Park in 1910.

While the church could survive baseball, it was no match for Interstate 94, which came barreling through the Capitol area in the 1960s. The church was demolished to make way for the freeway in 1961, two years after the congregation had moved to a new church a few blocks away on Jackson Street. Central Park vanished at about the same time when it was converted into a parking lot for the state's new Centennial Office Building, completed in 1958. Some years later, a ramp was built on the site, wiping out all traces of the historic park. Because the land was covenanted and had to be used for park purposes, the state added a rooftop park to the ramp.

Demolition of the church, October 20, 1961

163

NORMAN W. KITTSON HOUSE

201 Summit Avenue, St. Paul. Abraham Radcliffe.
1884–1905.

This gigantic house—on the site where the St. Paul Cathedral was later built—was one of the last great gasps of the French Second Empire style in the Twin Cities. Costing an estimated $175,000, it was also the most expensive and visually prominent house of its day in St. Paul, if not necessarily the most beautiful. One local critic, in fact, described the house's details as "horrible" while admitting that its overall effect was "quite imposing."

The Canadian-born Kittson arrived at his mansion on the hill after a long and colorful career that began in 1830 in the fur trade in Michigan. By the 1840s Kittson was established in Pembina on the Red River of the North where he helped to develop the famous ox cart trade that brought furs to Mendota and St. Paul. He also operated a steamboat line on the river and thereafter was always known as "Commodore." Later he formed the Red River Transportation

The front hallway and stairs of the Kittson house, about 1888

Company with James J. Hill and became involved in railroading. Like many of his contemporaries, he made the bulk of his fortune from real estate speculation in St. Paul. His personal life seems to have been as colorful as his business career, since he fathered twenty-six children by at least four wives.

Kittson's first residence in St. Paul was a modest house on Jackson Street. But in 1881 he hired Abraham Radcliffe to design something more overwhelming on Summit Avenue. Radcliffe responded with a vast, rambling house—built largely of Kasota stone—that embraced all the excesses of the already passé French Second Empire style. There was a distinctly parvenu quality to the mansion, which strove for grandeur at all

A cable car rolled along Selby Avenue past the Kittson house about 1889.

costs. Radcliffe tacked on everything he could think of: porches, bays, big hooded windows, and the inevitable mansard roof bursting at the seams with dormers, chimneys, and other decorative extrusions. Rising above all this clutter was a truly impressive lookout tower—one of the most massive ever built for a house in the Twin Cities.

The interior was a sort of miniature deforestation project, with more than twenty rooms sporting hundreds of linear feet of oak, mahogany, sycamore, and cherry woodwork. Decorators from Chicago turned these rooms into a Cook's Tour of architectural history, finishing them in period styles that ranged from Louis XIV to French and German Renaissance. Many rooms came with stained-glass windows (those in Kittson's library featured portraits of famous authors), ceilings hand painted in oil, frescoed walls, and heavy draperies in such popular colors as "chocolate brown" and "electric blue."

Legend has it that Kittson never locked the doors of his mansion and that nearby residents routinely used its main hall as a shortcut on their way to and from downtown. Perhaps because of all this pedestrian traffic, Kittson reportedly spent little time in the house before his death in 1888. Kittson's family (after a long squabble over the estate) moved out in 1895, and by 1898 the mansion had become a boardinghouse. The Archdiocese of St. Paul bought the property for $52,500 in 1904 and razed the house a year later to make way for the Cathedral.

WEST HOTEL

Southwest corner of Fifth Street and Hennepin Avenue, Minneapolis. LeRoy Buffington. 1884–1940.

The West Hotel, about 1905; the Cream of Wheat Building is down the street to the right

"In the . . . development of the West," Montgomery Schuyler wrote, "it is not surprising that the chief object of local pride should not be the local church, but the local hotel." The sort of lavish hotels Schuyler had in mind first appeared in the United States around 1809 when the two-hundred-room Exchange Coffee House opened in Boston. Although the Twin Cities had notable hotels before the West, such venerable establishments as the Nicollet House in Minneapolis and the Merchants Hotel in St. Paul were basically oversized inns with only limited pretensions to grandeur. The West, on the other hand, aspired to be, and was, the Twin Cities' first truly grand hotel.

The hotel was named after Charles W. West,

a Cincinnati millionaire, and his nephew John West, who settled in Minneapolis in 1875 and later managed the Nicollet House. Charles West was a frequent visitor to Minneapolis, and in 1881 he agreed to invest some of his millions in a new hotel to be operated by his nephew. Streetcar magnate Thomas Lowry headed a group of businessmen who helped to secure a site at Fifth and Hennepin on property once owned by the city's first resident, John Stevens.

This group of investors selected LeRoy Buffington, then a rising star on the Twin Cities architectural scene, to design the hotel. Construction began in 1882, just as the Queen Anne craze hit the Twin Cities. Buffington had recently designed a fine Queen Anne-style residence, the Shipman-Greve house (1884, extant) on Summit Avenue in St. Paul. He continued in this vein with the hotel, which was basically a Queen Anne house inflated to gigantic scale. The design's extreme eclecticism held limited appeal for Schuyler, but a promotional pamphlet described the hotel "as one of the most striking architectural studies to be found anywhere."

The building's base was white Joliet marble with alternating courses of marble and red brick on the second story. Everything above was brick and terra cotta. A profusion of oriels, chimney-like columns, arched recesses, and irregular balconies rambled across the upper facades, while gables and dormers erupted at the roof line. The original design also called for an open, domed tower, but it was never built. The hotel's main entrance was on Hennepin. A handsome porte cochere on Fifth served patrons arriving by carriage.

Dominating the interior was a seventy-by-ninety-foot lobby with a skylit roof supported by massive iron girders. It was advertised as the nation's largest hotel lobby. Located at the base of an inner light court, this great room was finished in marble, onyx, and mahogany. A second-floor corridor, reached by a grand staircase, wrapped around the lobby and led to several ornate public rooms, which one critic scorned for their "crude and inharmonious decorations." The Moorish-style dining room, done by Herter and Company of New York, fared better with the critics. John Bradstreet also decorated several rooms in what Schuyler described as a "rich and quiet" fashion. Male guests, however, may have preferred the barroom, which offered a stained-glass representation of "Bacchus and the Drinking Tribe." The hotel had 407 sleeping rooms and 140 baths, all luxuriously furnished.

The hotel opened in time to host a Grand Army of the Republic convention in July 1884, but the formal dedication did not take place until November 19. This "triumphant event," as the *Minneapolis Tribune* called it, featured a seven-course banquet of stupefying length (five hours) topped off by a rich dessert of self-congratulatory speeches.

The West remained Minneapolis' grand hotel for twenty years. As such, it attracted numerous celebrities, among them Mark Twain. It housed delegates to the 1892 Republican National Convention and was also the scene of glittering social events. But the depression of 1893 hit the hotel hard, and after John West's death in 1899 a new owner took over. A year later the hotel made more news when a man named Lannie Day was mysteriously stabbed to death in the billiard room. A far greater tragedy occurred in 1906 when eleven people, including two who jumped to their deaths, perished in a fire on the seventh floor. The West never quite recovered from this disaster, nor was it able to meet the competition of new hotels such as the Radisson, which opened in 1909. The hotel slipped into bankruptcy in 1928, although it managed to stay open. As the losses continued to mount over the next decade, the owners finally threw in the towel. After an auction of its contents, the West was torn down in March 1940. The site remained a parking lot in 1991.

The dining room, showing its Moorish decoration, about 1914

The lobby and grand staircase, 1887

WILLIAM D. WASHBURN HOUSE (FAIROAKS)

Block bounded by Stevens Avenue, Third Avenue South, and Twenty-Second and Twenty-Fourth streets, Minneapolis. E. Townsend Mix. 1884–1924.

Every midwestern city had its great showpiece mansion in the 1880s. Norman Kittson's Summit Hill extravaganza was, for a time at least, the house to see in St. Paul. In Minneapolis the mansion that stood out above all others belonged to William Drew Washburn. Situated on a ten-acre estate at what was then the south edge of Minneapolis, the house was known to thousands, in part because the Washburns threw the place open once a year for a public tour, with proceeds from the one dollar admission charge going to charity. "The Washburn residence . . . is an object of personal pride to every individual citizen of Minneapolis," proclaimed the *Northwest Magazine* in 1885. "To hear it spoken of one would think it were as much a piece of public property as Central [Loring] Park or Nicollet Avenue."

The man who built this tourist attraction hailed from a remarkable family. Born in Maine in 1831, William was one of eleven children, several of whom went on to fame and fortune. One brother, Israel, was governor of Maine. Another, Cadwallader, was a pioneer Minneapolis miller and later governor of Wisconsin. Yet another, Elihu, served as minister to France under President Ulysses S. Grant. William Washburn continued in the family political tradition, serving in the U.S. House of Representatives and later as a U.S. Senator.

A lawyer by training, Washburn arrived in Minneapolis in 1857, practiced law briefly, and then became secretary and later an owner of the Minneapolis Mill Company, which controlled waterpower on the west side of the Falls of St. Anthony. Although known to be "dogmatic

and even arrogant," his intelligence, good looks, and oratorical skills brought him success. Over the years, Washburn branched out from milling into lumbering and railroading and was one of the richest and most powerful men in Minnesota when he moved into his mansion in 1884.

Washburn's house—which probably cost well over one hundred thousand dollars—was the first commission in Minnesota for E. Townsend Mix, who had spent much of his career in Milwaukee where he was a favorite of the local Yankee families. When the Milwaukee market dried up around 1880, Mix began competing for jobs in the Twin Cities. His name first appeared in the local press in 1881 when he was listed as one of several candidates for the design of the Syndicate Block.

Mix was an adept designer who worked in many styles, and for Washburn he turned out a Tudor-heavy Queen Anne house with hints of Romanesque Revival. Nearly one hundred feet square and sixty feet high, the house strove for a romantic profile, using dormers, bays, and other projections to mask its basically foursquare form. Other elements included an off-center tower,

Library at Fairoaks, about 1893

The Washburn house, 1886

steep gables, chimneys with a decided Tudor twist, and even a wooden side porch right from the Queen Anne pattern books. Yet for all its pursuit of the picturesque, the house—built of Kasota stone—lacked panache. In fact the entire design seemed slightly out of step with itself, as though Mix did not quite know how to play really wild Queen Anne jazz.

The interior was decorated under the direction of Washburn's wife, Lizzie, a famous hostess whose parties attracted such luminaries as former President Grant and General William T. Sherman. A New York firm, with help from local decorating guru John Bradstreet, executed much of the interior design and did not err on the side of restraint. Solid doors of Spanish mahogany, a marble floor with Washburn's monogram, frescoed walls and ceilings, onyx fireplaces, stained glass, Circassian walnut paneling, luxurious tapestries, and oriental cushions arranged "for smoky reveries" were but a few of the wonders to be found within, according to the *St. Paul Daily Globe*, which concluded in an 1889 article that "there is a strong suggestion of royalty here."

The grounds, attributed to Frederick Law Olmsted (designer of Central Park in New York), may have been even more spectacular than the house. The estate, beautifully manicured by a team of gardeners, included a pond, a stream crossed by a rustic footbridge, and a large greenhouse, as well as the usual carriage house.

As was so often the case with the great mansions of the 1880s, the house more or less died with its original occupants. After Washburn's death in 1912, the house was donated to the Minneapolis Park Board. But it survived for only twelve years as a youth recreation center before it was razed to make more room for what became Washburn–Fair Oaks Park.

The rustic bridge, stream, and pond of the Washburn estate

RYAN HOTEL

Northeast corner of Sixth and Robert streets, St. Paul.
James J. Egan. 1885–1962.

Ryan Hotel, about 1900

When news of the proposed West Hotel surfaced in 1882, reaction in St. Paul was swift. The West, according to the *Pioneer Press*, "threatened the supremacy of St. Paul as a hotel center," making it "necessary for St. Paul to build a big hotel in the latest palatial style." A businessmen's committee went to work on the problem but made little progress. Then someone had the bright idea of calling on Dennis Ryan for help. Ryan, a newcomer to St. Paul, had made a fortune mining gold and silver in Utah and seemed ready to spend some of his millions. He soon agreed to finance a hotel, provided leading businessmen would commit two hundred thousand dollars to the project. Within months, the money had been raised—James J. Hill alone chipped in twenty-five thousand dollars—and work began on the $1 million hotel project.

The hotel's designer was James J. Egan, a prolific Chicago architect whose oeuvre included many large churches and the Cook County Courthouse (1882–85, gone). He also designed the Hotel St. Benedict Flats (1883) on Chicago's North Side. The Ryan was to be Egan's only commission in St. Paul, and he made the most of it, creating a seven-story Victorian Gothic extravaganza that extended nearly a block along Sixth Street. The models for the Ryan were the Midland (St. Pancras) Hotel of 1871 in London and Egan's own hotel in Chicago.

Victorian Gothic was an additive style, and Egan made sure not to leave anything out for the Ryan, producing a great architectural stew chock full of piquant ingredients. To provide vivid color contrast—a Victorian Gothic hallmark—Egan sheathed the Ryan's facades in red brick threaded with undulating bands of white Ohio sandstone. He then stirred in a potpourri of polished granite columns, rich terra-cotta ornament, windows with trefoil arches, stained-glass transoms, and no fewer than twenty-two bracketed balconies.

The roof line was even spicier. This was the Ryan's glory, an Old World profusion of dormers, pinnacles, spires, and towers. Schuyler, who could be a sourpuss at times, dismissed the whole design as "a multiplicity of features . . . confused by a random introduction of color." A local newspaper writer was kinder, saying the Ryan "presents a massive appearance of solidity and strength."

Gothic touches continued in the hotel's magnificent lobby, which occupied the bottom of a huge open light court at the center of the hotel. The two-story-high lobby was one of the great rooms in St. Paul's history, a spectacular space rimmed by an arcaded balcony and lit by stained-glass clerestory windows to either side of a vaulted ceiling. Ornate marble columns held everything up, while lavish frescoes, dark oak woodwork, and colorful stenciling augmented the decorative splendor.

The hotel's other public spaces included a barroom (where John L. Sullivan, legend has it, once cracked the solid mahogany bar with an angry smash of his fist), various parlors and ladies' rooms, a billiard hall, and a truly spectacular grand dining room. The upper six floors contained 335 sleeping apartments (ranging in size from one to six rooms), three hundred of which had at least one fireplace. Fully one hundred of these rooms also came with private baths.

The hotel's grand opening on July 2, 1885, was one of those marathons of oration and gluttony so beloved by Victorians. The banquet began with a ten-course meal (the menu included soft shell crabs, spring lamb, and larded green peas), followed by an interminable round of toasts, after which a battery of speakers droned on into the night. The event concluded with St. Paul Mayor Edmund Rice leading three cheers for Dennis Ryan.

During its long life, the hotel hosted its share of celebrities, among them President Grover Cleveland. But after the Saint Paul Hotel opened in 1910, the Ryan declined in status, and in 1923 there was even a plan to tear it down. Fortunately the plan fell through and the Ryan endured.

Over the next thirty years, the hotel suffered various financial crises while undergoing a series of remodelings. Yet the old place never lost its charm. As late as 1961 it was still "a pleasant, comfortable hotel, with three restaurants and good food." By this time, however, the Ryan was losing money, and its owners finally decided to demolish it. The wrecking crews went to work in 1962. Within weeks, the "magnificent pile," as one newspaper had called it, was gone, replaced by the inevitable parking lot. The loss of this wonderful building was a great and lasting blow to the city. A twenty-story office tower built in 1981 for the Minnesota Mutual Insurance Company later occupied the site.

The hotel lobby, about 1890

MINNESOTA LOAN AND TRUST BUILDING

311–15 Nicollet Avenue, Minneapolis. Hodgson and Son.
1885–ca. 1920

The Minnesota Loan and Trust Company, organized in 1883, was one of many financial institutions that sprouted during the great boom of the
1880s. The company set out at once to build a
home for itself, and the result was this peculiar
structure—arguably the Twin Cities' first skyscraper and certainly the most bizarre. One later
critic dismissed the building as "an enormously

RIGHT: *Minnesota Loan and Trust, about 1890*

BELOW: *Construction of the Minnesota Loan and Trust*

large but ill-adjusted and unstable toy," and even contemporaries struggled to describe its style, calling it everything from "English-Venetian Gothic" to "English street style."

Wedged into a forty-nine-foot-wide midblock site, the building resembled a bad piece of Victorian furniture exploded to gigantic scale. Its designer, Isaac Hodgson, had begun his career in Indianapolis, where he became best known for monumental French Second Empire style courthouses. After moving to Minneapolis in 1882, he quickly established himself as the local master of mad-dog eclecticism with his Chamber of Commerce Building (1884, gone). For Minnesota Loan and Trust, Hodgson took an even longer walk on the wild side, creating a facade of white Ohio sandstone that compressed all the excesses of high Victorian design into one delightfully insane package. Treating each story as an independent entity, Hodgson threw in a profusion of Gothic arches, columns, bays, balconies, and other maladjusted elements, then topped the whole concoction with a gawky tower.

In New York in 1873 Richard Morris Hunt had decked out his Tribune Building with a strikingly similar tower, which critics dubbed a "brick and mortar giraffe." Hodgson's equally long-necked tower housed a large clock that instantly became a Nicollet Avenue landmark. But the 150-foot tower's underlying purpose was to give Minnesota Loan and Trust identity on the skyline by making its building the tallest in Minneapolis. It held this title for less than a year, however, being eclipsed in 1886 by the ten-story Lumber Exchange Building.

Structurally the building was quite sophisticated, with an interior iron frame clad in terra cotta. This construction prompted Minnesota Loan and Trust to claim (dubiously) that its new skyscraper was "The Model Fire Proof Building." No interior photographs of the building are known to exist, but descriptions suggest that it was finished luxuriously. Minnesota Loan and

Trust's first-floor offices included bronze and brass grillwork, carved mahogany trim, marble staircases, and counters of Mexican onyx. The building had two elevators, which apparently were set in a small central light shaft.

In 1909 Minnesota Loan and Trust merged with Northwestern National Bank, leaving Hodgson's great curiosity piece without its major tenant. Although records indicate that the city issued a demolition permit for the building as early as 1911, photographs reveal that Hodgson's goofy creation stood until about 1920, when a new F. W. Woolworth store went up on the site. Later the Sheraton-Ritz Hotel (1963–1990) occupied the entire block, which by 1991 had become a parking lot.

Chamber of Commerce, Minneapolis, about 1895

NATIONAL GERMAN-AMERICAN BANK

Northwest corner of Fourth and Robert streets, St. Paul.
George Wirth. 1885–1913.

National German-American Bank, about 1901

In 1856 two German immigrants—Ferdinand Willius and Henry Meyer—opened a banking firm in St. Paul. Their firm weathered the financial panic of 1857 (although Meyer died that year) and by 1873 had evolved into the German-American Bank of St. Paul. As its name suggests, the bank drew most of its customers from the city's large German population. In 1879 the bank moved into a new building on East Third Street. Four years later the bank obtained a national charter and then enriched itself by pooling funds with backers of a proposed new bank. Soon thereafter, bank officers made plans to construct this building, one of the largest and most ornate office structures of its day in St. Paul.

Not surprisingly the bankers called on a German-born architect, George Wirth, to undertake the design. After emigrating to America in 1869 at age eighteen, Wirth studied architecture at Cornell University, made a grand tour of Europe, and arrived in St. Paul in 1879. With a formal background few local architects could match, Wirth quickly built a career designing office buildings, houses, and churches. The National German-American Bank was the biggest of all his projects in St. Paul—and also one of the best.

Rising from a high base of red sandstone, the five-story brick building demonstrated Wirth's considerable skills as a designer. The building—as close to Renaissance Revival in style as anything else, although one newspaper called it "Norman"—offered richly composed facades with groups of arched and flat-headed windows set off by pilasters, terra-cotta cartouches, and bands of vigorous geometric ornament. There was also a spectacular arched entrance on Robert framed by columns of red jasper and black porphyry. Carved around this portal were allegorical medallions representing thrift, industry, and other virtues beloved by the banking profession.

The main banking hall inside appears to have been the largest in St. Paul, measuring 102 by 42 feet. It had paneled walls, tile floors, wood-beamed ceilings, and a long tellers' counter made of cherry and carved with no fewer than twenty-seven ornamental patterns. Above the banking hall, from the second through fifth floors, were one hundred offices arranged around what may have been the first big atrium in a Twin Cities office building. Drawings of this skylit space, which measured twenty-eight by eighty-five feet, suggest it was elegant and airy. Wirth also took great care with such practical matters as plumbing and heating, grouping all utilities in a central vertical core.

Unfortunately this handsome and well-detailed building did not have a long life. The bank began experiencing financial reverses in the depression of the 1890s (it closed briefly in 1893) and finally merged with the Merchants Bank in 1912. A year later, Wirth's bank was demolished and replaced by a sixteen-story building. The Merchants Bank Building, completed in 1915 and later part of the First Bank Saint Paul, remained on the site in 1991.

The main hall and light court on the second floor, 1885

TRIBUNE BUILDING

Northwest corner of Fourth Street and Marquette Avenue, Minneapolis. LeRoy Buffington. 1885–89.

As newspaper competition intensified in the Twin Cities in the 1880s, the big dailies turned to architecture as a marketing tool, constructing what a century later would come to be called "signature buildings." The *Minneapolis Tribune*, founded in 1867, was the first to adopt this strategy. Ironically, by the time the *St. Paul Daily Globe* and *St. Paul and Minneapolis Pioneer Press* followed suit a few years later, the Tribune Building was already on the verge of destruction.

When the Tribune Building was under construction, the local press said two things about it that were false. The first was that it would be "very different from anything Buffington has yet designed." In fact the building was strikingly similar to a project that preceded it on Buffington's drawing boards—the West Hotel. Like the West the seven-story Tribune Building was a Queen Anne-Renaissance Revival hybrid, its most notable feature being a ground-floor arcade of Joliet marble (a stone also used on the hotel). Above the arcade was a busy red brick facade sporting bays, patches of terra-cotta ornament, and other familiar items from Buffington's bag of tricks. A gaggle of gables and a tower were shown on drawings, but much of the ornament was simplified during construction.

Tribune Building, 1886

176

The *Tribune*, its large job printing operation, and space leased to other newspapers—including the *Pioneer Press*—occupied the four upper floors of the building, with rental offices below. The newspaper's main presses were in the basement. Smaller presses—probably for job printing—were on the upper floors. When operating, these presses apparently caused the floors to shake so much that at least one tenant feared a collapse.

The second untruth about the building was that it would be "fire-proof throughout." Although the building had masonry walls and fire-resistant iron framing, its interior was full of wood, paper, cloth, and other combustibles. Moreover its design was manifestly unsafe. There was only one staircase, made of wood. Even worse, it wrapped around the building's only elevator shaft, which in the event of fire would act like a great chimney, drawing smoke and flames upward. Later a newspaper that had once praised the building for being fireproof described it "as the most complete firetrap in the city." The city's Trades and Labor Assembly, many of whose members worked as printers and compositors on the building's upper floors, called attention to the fire danger in 1886 and asked for changes to be made. Nothing was done.

The price for this negligence was paid three years later, on November 30, 1889. A fire—probably ignited by careless smoking—began on the third floor about ten o'clock at night and eventually worked its way up the staircase and elevator shaft, trapping scores of people on the upper floors. As firemen arrived (including some who came from St. Paul by train), they found themselves largely helpless. A network of utility lines around the building made it difficult to raise ladders, which were not tall enough to reach the two upper floors in any event.

A huge crowd gathered as the fire raged, and what followed was one of those spectacles of death and salvation that remain lodged in the memory over a lifetime. A few of the building's

Ruins of the building after the fire

occupants saved themselves by acts of desperate courage. One was Billy Lown, a compositor, who became stranded on a top-floor ledge. With the flames coming at him, he somehow managed to jump one story down to a lower ledge. Another compositor followed him, also landing safely, and the two men were later rescued by ladder as the crowd below cheered.

Others were not so fortunate. One man attempted to crawl across a wire to safety and fell six stories to his death. Another man, or so newspaper accounts claimed, shot himself rather than face the flames. Milton Pickett, an editor for the Minneapolis bureau of the *Pioneer Press*, plunged to his death from a red-hot fire escape. By the time it was all over, seven men were dead and thirty others injured. There were recriminations and an investigation following the fire—the first ever in a high-rise office building in Minneapolis—but it would be years before fire codes improved safety in tall buildings.

What remained of the building's walls was torn down after the fire, although the foundations apparently were left in place and used for a new office building—called, appropriately, the Phoenix—completed in 1893. The Phoenix Building was torn down in 1961 and replaced by a parking ramp for the Sheraton-Ritz Hotel. The ramp, like the hotel, vanished in 1990.

INDUSTRIAL EXPOSITION BUILDING

Main Street and Central Avenue, Minneapolis.
Hodgson and Son. 1886–1940, 1946.

Industrial fairs were extremely popular in the nineteenth century, and several cities—including Cincinnati and Chicago—staged annual expositions. In 1885 the idea caught on in Minneapolis, which was smarting because the State Fair had moved to St. Paul. Spurred by an editorial in the *Minneapolis Tribune*, a committee of businessmen pledged one hundred thousand dollars for an exposition and set about selling public stock. By year's end, nearly twenty-four hundred stockholders, "from all classes and conditions," had paid a total of $250,000 and elected a board of directors (led by William Washburn) to oversee construction of a suitable building for the event.

The directors initially sought a downtown site, but property was too expensive. Other interests then agreed to donate the site of the old Winslow House near the Falls of St. Anthony, and their offer was quickly accepted. In January 1886 the directors asked six local architects to submit plans for a building. Even though a multidomed iron and glass structure proposed by LeRoy Buffington made "the most showy and unique appearance," the directors chose a design from Isaac Hodgson and Son. The cornerstone was laid on May 29, and the huge edifice—the largest public building of the nineteenth century in the Twin Cities—was completed less than three months later.

The building was 356 feet long, 336 feet wide, and 80 feet high. Rising from one corner was a 260-foot tower, the tallest structure of its day in the city, with an open-air lookout (reached by elevator) that could accommodate four hundred people. A pedimented entry pavilion broke up the roof line, as did several smaller towers. De-

Industrial Exposition Building, about 1888

scribed as "modified Renaissance" in style, the building was actually quite eclectic, mixing vaguely Gothic elements (such as the tower) with other details (such as banded entry columns) cribbed from French classicism. The outer walls of cream-colored Mankato stone and brick were treated plainly except for a few bursts of terra-cotta ornament. Large windows pierced the exterior walls at every floor. The vast, open interior—framed mostly in timber—offered eight acres of floor space organized around a central light well, at the bottom of which was an oval-shaped pond complete with fountain.

The exposition itself opened on August 23, 1886, amid much pageantry. A procession left the West Hotel at two in the afternoon, moved down Nicollet Avenue (splendidly lighted and decorated), and then crossed the river to the new building, whereupon oratory broke out. This lasted until four o'clock, when the wife of President Grover Cleveland (who had been invited to attend but who went fishing instead) touched a telegraph key in New York and set the exposition's machinery in motion. The exhibits included everything from candy making to the manufacture of barbed wire to (naturally) flour milling. There were also restaurants, sales booths, a Mexican cavalry band, an art gallery (highlighted by Albert Bierstadt's epic paintings of the West), and a sculpture hall filled with fig-leafed nudes. The exposition ran for six weeks, drew 338,000 people, and made a profit of fifty-six thousand dollars.

Annual expositions were held through 1890, when the event attracted Johann Strauss and his orchestra from Vienna. But by 1891 the exposition had played its last waltz, a victim of declining attendance and a sour economy. In June 1892 the building had its final moment of glory, becoming the scene of the Republican party's national convention. The building was altered for this event, with the light court turned into a twelve-thousand-seat auditorium. Mrs. Cleveland

may have been tempted to touch that telegraph key again and turn off the power because the convention renominated her husband's old nemesis, Benjamin Harrison, for a second term as president. But this time, Harrison lost the election.

As for the exposition, it finally went bankrupt in 1895. Stuck with a huge white elephant, the directors tried to pawn it off on the state for use as a capitol, but that idea went nowhere. Then, in 1903, Marion Savage (best known as the owner of the great pacer, Dan Patch) bought the building for his stock-food company. Savage turned the place into a mail-order warehouse, manned by young clerks on roller skates. In 1935 Savage's company vacated the building, which was torn down five years later to make way for a Coca-Cola bottling plant (since demolished and replaced by a parking lot). The tower, however, stood until 1946, functioning in its last years as a signboard for Coca-Cola. Although the Exposition Building is gone, stone salvaged from the structure can still be seen in several public works projects from the 1940s, including the Harriet Island pavilion (1942, extant) in St. Paul.

The tower following demolition of the rest of the building, about 1940

Delegates and guests filled the hall during the Republican National Convention, June 11, 1892.

MINNESOTA CLUB

Southeast corner of Fourth and Cedar streets, St. Paul.
William Castner (Charles Mould?).
1886, ca. 1890–ca. 1928.

Minnesota Club, about 1913

Members of St. Paul's business and social elite, among them Henry Sibley and Norman Kittson, founded the Minnesota Club in 1869. Intended for "gentlemen" (women were not admitted as full-time members until the 1970s), the club in its original form survived only six years before succumbing to the financial depression brought on by the Panic of 1873. In 1883, however, with the economy much improved, St. Paul business leaders reorganized the club and began planning a new clubhouse, which opened in 1886.

There is some question about who designed the clubhouse. The *St. Paul Pioneer Press*, in an article published in August 1884, attributed it to Charles Mould. But six months later *Inland Architect and Builder* identified William Castner, another St. Paul architect, as the designer. While one of the publications may simply have made a mistake, it is also possible that Mould was initially hired for the project and then replaced by Castner.

Regardless of who may have had a hand in the design, the clubhouse—domestic in scale, yet possessed of a dignified formality suitable to its purpose—was one of downtown St. Paul's architectural delights. Built of red brick over a brownstone base, the three-story structure was in no readily identifiable style, although it was probably as close to Queen Anne as anything. Its most notable feature was a round corner bay capped by a small, steep dome. Sporting a pair of eyelike circular windows, this peculiar dome resembled nothing so much as the head of a giant insect that had somehow attached itself to the building. More pleasing was the building's graceful double staircase, which led up to the main entrance on Cedar Street.

The club's membership in the 1880s included only one architect, Cass Gilbert, who found that hobnobbing with the city's social and financial elite could be quite good for business. Gilbert also took charge of furnishing the club, which consisted of several dining rooms, a large main floor

lounge, a billiard room, a card room, a library, and guest and servants' rooms on the top floor. The furnishings—heavy leather chairs, solid oak tables, rich oriental carpets—were not only in keeping with Gilbert's tastes but also provided a suitable aura of masculine gentility.

The one thing the clubhouse lacked was sufficient room. Around 1890 the club built a large addition to the south on Cedar. This new wing was adjacent to a rooming house where Nina Clifford—the celebrated madam whose loyal clientele included many club members—had first set up shop in St. Paul. Clifford moved to a new, more luxurious brothel on Washington Street a few years later. The club, pressed for space, built a new home (extant) on the same street in 1915. The old clubhouse was used for several years by the Women's City Club before being torn down and replaced in 1929 by the Minnesota Building (extant).

Interior of a club room, 1888

PANORAMA BUILDING

Southwest corner of Fifth Street and Marquette Avenue, Minneapolis. Long and Kees. 1886–1921.

CAPITAL CITY PANORAMA

Southeast corner of Sixth and St. Peter streets, St. Paul. Denslow Millard. 1887–89.

Panoramas—huge paintings of landscapes or historic events—were to the nineteenth century what wide-screen movies became to the twentieth. First painted in Europe after the Napoleonic Wars, panoramas (also known as cycloramas) appeared in the Twin Cities as early as the 1850s and were a common form of touring entertainment by the 1870s. Some of these panoramas, usually displayed by being rolled through a frame, were up to one thousand feet long and twelve feet high. Panoramas so large that they needed a building of their own did not arrive until the 1880s when a businessman named William Wehner swang into action.

Wehner decided in about 1884 to undertake the production of panoramas that would equal those of Europe. Establishing his headquarters in Milwaukee, Wehner built a large circular studio (complete with a movable painting platform mounted on rails), gathered a team of fifteen European artists (led by F. H. Heine), and set about

Panorama Building, Minneapolis, about 1886

producing—on something like an assembly-line basis—gigantic Civil War panoramas. The first work out of his studio depicted the famous Union charge at Missionary Ridge near Lookout Mountain, Tennessee, in 1863. Wehner's next and most famous panorama, shown first in a building constructed especially for it in Minneapolis, was "The Battle of Atlanta."

The building required to house Wehner's monstrous panorama—it was 368 feet long by 50 feet high—was completed in 1886. Attributed to the partnership of Franklin Long and Frederick Kees (although there is some uncertainty on this point), the building was essentially a big, twelve-sided brick drum, with the only windows appearing at the very top and in the roof. A small pavilion, sporting a tower and battlements, provided entrance to the structure. Inside, visitors walked to a central platform to view the panorama, which was mounted all the way around the walls.

The "Battle of Atlanta" opened on June 28, 1886, and drew its largest crowds—up to twelve thousand a week—during the Minneapolis Industrial Exposition that September. "Here old soldiers love to linger," wrote one magazine, "and here the younger generation come to see how battles were fought and won in the great War of the Rebellion." The panorama building was open from eight in the morning to ten at night daily and cost fifty cents for adults and twenty-five cents for children—a fairly steep price in those days. The admission price included a lecture explaining the panorama.

Meanwhile St. Paul had also caught panorama fever. Henry Castle, a prominent St. Paul newspaperman who later wrote an indispensable history of the city, opened the Capital City Panorama in 1887 with the "Battle of Gettysburg." The building, which appears to have been similar to the one in Minneapolis, was designed by St. Paul architect Denslow Millard. More than one hundred thousand people supposedly took in the panorama during its first year in St. Paul.

Twice that many viewers were said to have seen the "Battle of Atlanta" in Minneapolis before it moved on to its next venue in March 1888. A month later, a new panorama—"Jerusalem on the Day of the Crucifixion"—opened in Minneapolis. The next year, "Gettysburg" left St. Paul and was replaced by the "Merrimac and Monitor."

By this time, however, panorama glut seems to have set in. There was also the problem that the huge paintings did not tend to inspire repeat visits. Moreover the panorama buildings were huge heat hogs in winter, making it difficult for the operators to turn a profit. As a result, both panoramas were closed for good by the end of 1889. The St. Paul building was replaced the next year by Jacob Litt's Grand Opera House. The Minneapolis building stood vacant until it was remodeled in about 1893 by the New England Furniture Company, which remained on the site until 1921 when a new Federal Reserve Bank (extant, designed by Cass Gilbert, later altered) wiped out the last traces of the Twin Cities' brief love affair with panoramas. At least one of the panoramas— "The Battle of Atlanta"—survived and was later restored for display at Grant Park in Atlanta.

The Capital City Panorama is the circular building shown in this 1888 panorama map.

FIRST UNITARIAN CHURCH

Southeast corner of Eighth Street and La Salle Avenue, Minneapolis. LeRoy Buffington. 1887–1927.

Ecclesiastical architecture in the Twin Cities tended to be numbingly predictable in the 1880s, with a few exceptions. This handsome little structure was one of them. It was built for the First Unitarian Society of Minneapolis, which had been organized in 1881 by some of the city's leading citizens. The society met in rented quarters for several years before commissioning a building of its own in 1885. What the society sought was a structure that, as one newspaper put it, "would be taken for a club room . . . rather than a church." As designed by LeRoy Buffington, the church indeed resembled an urban clubhouse. "The architect has had in view, in the designing of all parts, the domestic character desired by the society," wrote the *Saturday Evening Spectator* in 1887, "and nothing was spared to make the building as home-like as possible."

Like J. Walter Stevens's People's Church of 1889 in St. Paul, First Unitarian used architecture as a means of expressing disdain for orthodoxy. Built with solid walls of red Sioux quartzite from southwestern Minnesota, the building in its basic form was a rather conventional essay in the Richardsonian Romanesque style. But it flaunted its individuality by means of peculiar detailing. Instead of the usual cut stone moldings, for example, Buffington used rough-faced stone for everything from window sills to the dwarf columns around the double-arched entry on Eighth Street. Schuyler thought such tricks were "a caprice that seems . . . to proceed from the pursuit of novelty and that gains nothing in vigor for what it loses in refinement." The building's rough detailing, however, may actually have been a matter of necessity, since Sioux quartzite is so hard that it is difficult and costly to finish in any detail.

As part of his design, Buffington also took great pains to make the building's exterior reflect interior function. This effort was most evident along the La Salle Avenue side, where Buffington used projecting stones to echo the lines of interior staircases. Inside, the church featured a sixty-five-by-forty-seven-foot auditorium with seating arranged in amphitheater fashion. There were two small galleries above the main floor, and the total seating capacity was about six hundred people. The auditorium was finished quite simply in cherry and mahogany woodwork and apparently had brick walls. The main floor also included two comfortably furnished parlors and a pastor's study. Clubrooms, a music hall, a kitchen, and other facilities were located in the basement.

Unfortunately this urbane little building did not have a particularly long life. The society moved elsewhere in 1927, and its old clubhouse-cum-church was torn down to make way for an office building. A parking ramp later occupied the site.

First Unitarian Church, about 1900

185

BANK OF MINNEAPOLIS

Southwest corner of Nicollet Avenue and Third Street,
Minneapolis. Hodgson and Son. 1887–1958.

*Bank of Minneapolis,
about 1890*

Detail of the bank building showing the second-floor windows tilted open from the top

This early skyscraper was remarkable in several respects. With its glassy, cellular facades, it was perhaps the first building locally to exploit the aesthetic possibilities of metal framing. It may also have been one of the first tall office buildings anywhere in the United States to rely entirely on a metal-frame structure. Equally remarkable is that it came from Hodgson's office, which only a year or so earlier had produced, almost directly across Nicollet, that great piece of Victorian clutter, the Minnesota Loan and Trust Building. In fact the amazing difference between this building and earlier works by Hodgson and Son suggests that an outside hand—perhaps an itinerant draftsman—may have been involved in the design.

The Bank of Minneapolis, established in 1867, had occupied various rental quarters before commissioning its new building in 1885. In April of that year, the *Real Estate Review* of Minneapolis reported that architect William Dennis would

design the bank's building. But somewhere along the line Hodgson's firm won the commission and produced a building so distinctive that the local press had trouble describing it. Said one newspaper: "The form and features of the walls are not in any of the so-called 'styles,' but may be termed a structure of 'Modern American' model."

The seven-story building was indeed strikingly "modern," with a blunt squared-off shape, repetitive facades, and large expanses of glass. The windows on the second floor, where the bank maintained its offices, were ten-by-fourteen-foot panes of plate glass that must have been the largest of their day in Minneapolis. (Surprisingly these huge windows could be tilted open to provide ventilation in warm weather.) Paired double-hung windows, also extremely large, filled in the five stories above. The building's rounded piers of white Ohio sandstone were quite thin and served visually as little more than window frames.

The building's straightforward appearance was a logical expression of its structural skeleton, which consisted of steel beams and girders supported by cast-iron columns. A newspaper in 1887 described this structural system as "a complete iron and steel cage . . . from top to bottom." The building may have relied to some extent on masonry piers, however. Even so, the Bank of Minneapolis appears to have been as technologically advanced as anything of its time in Chicago, including William Le Baron Jenney's famed Home Insurance Building of 1885. This building, long gone, is often credited (wrongly, it now seems) as being the world's first all-metal-frame office structure.

Like so many other historic buildings in the Gateway District, the Bank of Minneapolis endured years of indifferent treatment but could not survive the ravages of urban renewal. It and several other fine old nineteenth-century business blocks came down in 1958 to make way for the new Minneapolis Public Library.

GLOBE BUILDING

Southwest corner of Fourth and Cedar streets, St. Paul.
E. Townsend Mix. 1887–1959.

The *St. Paul Globe*, founded in 1878, had become one of the most successful daily newspapers in the Northwest by the mid-1880s. A staunch supporter of the Democratic party, the *Globe* promoted itself as the "people's newspaper" and published editions in both St. Paul and Minneapolis. In 1887 the newspaper proclaimed its power and influence by erecting the tallest office building to date in St. Paul.

E. Townsend Mix, one of the Twin Cities' busiest commercial architects in the mid-1880s, designed the ten-story building. The Globe was Mix's first big commission in St. Paul, and he responded with an eclectic design executed in red brick, sandstone, and terra cotta. The general style was Romanesque, although Mix added a few classical touches, such as a split pediment (which held a three-foot-diameter globe) over the main entrance. At a time when most skyscrapers were still struggling to escape the wedding-cake look, Mix managed to endow the Globe Building with a good deal of vertical thrust by recessing spandrels beneath some windows and grouping others into six-story-high oriels. He kept this skyward momentum going right up past the roof by attaching a pair of turrets, four big chimneys, and a forty-foot-high lookout tower to a castlelike parapet. The tower's base formed an open-air arcade for viewing the city. Adventurous visitors could go even higher in the tower, climbing a spiral staircase to a crow's-nest lookout more than 150 feet above Fourth Street.

Inside, the Globe Building was most notable for its central light court, or atrium, a standard feature in Mix-designed office buildings. In the 1980s atriums were constructed largely as a matter of show, but in the 1880s, before electric lighting had been perfected, they were essential for bringing daylight into tall office buildings. The light court that cut through the Globe Building was quite small—about twenty feet square—and not nearly as elaborate as the famous atrium Mix designed three years later for the Northwestern Guaranty Loan Building in Minneapolis. Arranged around the Globe's central light court were the usual array of small offices. The newspaper itself occupied only the first, ninth, and tenth floors of the building.

The Globe Building's reign atop St. Paul's skyline lasted only until 1889 when the *St. Paul Pioneer Press* completed a thirteen-story skyscraper two blocks away on Fourth Street. The *Globe* itself soon encountered financial troubles and was purchased in 1896 by James J. Hill. He kept the newspaper going until 1905 when it folded for good. The *Globe's* building enjoyed a longer life. Despite several extensive remodelings (the first in 1932) and the loss of its tower (in 1950, after wind damage), the building remained for many years a powerful presence in downtown St. Paul. But old age, and an era that worshiped the new, finally caught up with the Globe in 1959 when it was razed to make way for a modern office tower.

RIGHT: *The light court viewed from one of the top floors, about 1959*

LEFT:
Drawing of the Globe Building in St. Paul, 1887

BELOW:
Tower of the Globe shortly before it was demolished

JOHN L. MERRIAM HOUSE

Northwest corner of University Avenue and Cedar Street, St. Paul. Mould and McNicol (possibly with Harvey Ellis). 1887–1964.

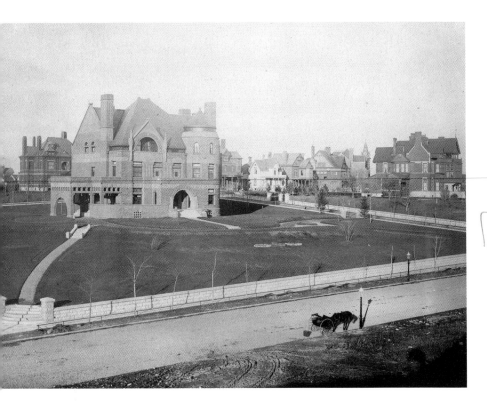

The Merriam house in its setting on Capitol Hill, about 1890; the William Merriam house is far right

Set on a high hill, this house was once part of a great row of mansions that extended along University and Sherburne avenues overlooking downtown St. Paul. William Merriam (son of John and governor of Minnesota from 1889 to 1893) was the first member of the family to build in the area, constructing a large house on University Avenue east of Cedar Street in 1882. But it was John L. Merriam's glorious Richardsonian Romanesque mansion that dominated the neighborhood until it fell under the shadow of Cass Gilbert's State Capitol at the turn of the century.

The son of a New York iron manufacturer, John L. Merriam arrived in St. Paul in 1860 and quickly made his mark in the world of business. He was greatly assisted in this regard by certain family connections, since in 1858 he had married Helen M. Wilder, the only sister of Amherst Wilder, who eventually became one of St. Paul's wealthiest men. Merriam's initial venture was a partnership with Wilder and James Burbank in a stagecoach line. Later he became involved in a foundry business, railroading, construction, and real estate. He also organized the Merchants Bank of St. Paul and was its president for many years.

Like many of the city's elite, Merriam built his first house in Lowertown, not far from that of his brother-in-law. As railroads began to consume great chunks of Lowertown, Merriam and Wilder headed for the hills. Wilder went to Summit Avenue while Merriam, following his son's lead, decided to build north of downtown.

The designers Merriam chose, Charles Mould and Robert McNicol, were partners in a small St. Paul firm patronized by many well-to-do clients in the 1880s. In 1886 they attracted Harvey Ellis as a draftsman, and he is generally credited with playing a major role in the design of the Merriam mansion. The house's romanticism and certain aspects of its detailing do indeed suggest that Ellis had a hand in the design. Charles Mould, however, was a talented designer in his own right, and the extent of Ellis's involvement in the project remains conjectural.

What is clear is that the house was one of the great works of nineteenth-century architecture in the Twin Cities. Built of reddish brown and pink sandstone, the mansion was an exercise in controlled romanticism, its picturesque tendencies held in check by the discipline of geometry. The house's most powerful feature was a huge entry arch that cut into a low covered porch like the mouth of a cave. This porch, which seemed to grow out of a big corner tower on one side of the house, led on its other side to an elegant terrace. Above, the house rose to a steep front gable punctured by yet another gaping arch. Profuse

190

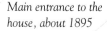

The winged dog is perched on the right front corner of the roof, about 1915

detailing in the form of clustered columns, bold diamond and checkerboard patterns, clumps of carved foliage, and even a grotesque winged dog (who crouched atop one corner of the house) combined to animate what easily could have been a gloomy, static design.

The interior was equally magnificent. "The house is a palace," wrote one newspaper in 1887. "Every room is finished in a different wood, richly carved from special designs." The most memorable space was a two-story-high entry hall finished in dark oak, much of it exquisitely carved. Here, too, was the grand staircase, which led past a landing lit by stained-glass windows to an open gallery above. A library (done in baywood) and a dining room (mahogany) opened off the hall, as did a large drawing room. The second floor contained bedrooms, while a spacious billiard room and servants' quarters filled the third floor.

Merriam enjoyed his house for only eight years. After his death in 1895, his widow remained in the house. Around 1905 she offered it for use as a governor's mansion, but the state, regrettably, rejected the proposal. Mrs. Merriam apparently continued to live there until her death in 1915. In 1927 the St. Paul Institute bought the house and turned it into a museum. The institute, later renamed the St. Paul Science Museum, gradually became cramped for space and in 1939 built a large, and not very handsome, addition at the rear of the house. The state, eager to expand in the Capitol area, became the house's final owner in 1959. When the Science Museum moved into a new building downtown in 1964, the state immediately demolished the mansion. There were a few unhappy murmurs from architecture lovers, but otherwise the destruction of this splendid and irreplaceable house seems to have occasioned little public protest. The state then built the bland Administration Building on the site.

Main entrance to the house, about 1895

AMHERST H. WILDER HOUSE

226 Summit Avenue, St. Paul. Willcox and Johnston.
1887–1959.

This "baronial castle," as one newspaper called it, occupied perhaps the most beautiful vantage point in St. Paul at the crest of what later became known as Cathedral Hill. Located just two doors down from the James J. Hill house, the Wilder mansion—with its distinctive conical-roofed tower and adjacent chimney—was long a familiar silhouette on the St. Paul skyline. The house's destruction in 1959, well documented in newspaper photographs, was especially unfortunate because its builder, Amherst H. Wilder, was one of St. Paul's most influential citizens, establishing a charitable trust that remains a vital force in the life of the city.

Wilder was born in the mountainous Adirondack region of New York State. After finishing school there, he went to work in his father's small iron manufacturing and merchandising business. In 1859, at the relatively advanced age of thirty-one, Wilder came west to St. Paul, where he was marked for success both by virtue of his business acumen and his family connections. His cousin, John C. Burbank, was already operating a flourishing stagecoach and express business in St. Paul and immediately admitted Wilder as a partner in the firm. Wilder also benefited from his sister Helen's marriage to John Merriam. From his beginnings in the express business, Wilder gradually branched out into other enterprises—provisioning, railroading, and lumbering among them—and by the 1880s had amassed one of the largest fortunes in the Northwest.

Wilder's first home in St. Paul was a large but by no means spectacular dwelling on Woodward Avenue in Lowertown. As this once-exclusive residential district began to succumb to railroad incursions, Wilder decided to make the move up to Summit Avenue. In late 1885 he bought a house and three-acre lot for fifty-two thousand dollars on the bluff side of Summit, had the 1860s-vintage dwelling demolished, and then hired the fashionable firm of William Willcox and Clarence Johnston. The result was not an especially notable design, but the mansion's size (it had more than twenty-five rooms), location, and rich finish made it one of St. Paul's great houses. Constructed of red brick and Lake Superior sandstone, the house was generally Tudor Revival (or as one newspaper called it, "English domestic") in character. There were also strong Richardsonian Romanesque elements, especially evident in column capitals and other detailing.

The house's Summit Avenue front presented a broken arrangement of oriels, bays, and gables behind a Gothic-arched porte cochere. Unlike many houses on the avenue, the Wilder mansion was carefully oriented to exploit views from the bluff, with an open porch at the rear wrapped around a three-story circular tower. A screened

Wilder house viewed from Summit Avenue, about 1908

wooden porch (possibly added later) was located above the open porch. Not everyone liked this arrangement, and one family friend later described the mansion as a "turreted house of red brick and ugly porches."

A two-story hall, complete with a huge "English fireplace," dominated the interior. As was the custom in an age of conspicuous lumber consumption, main-floor rooms were finished in a variety of woods—oak for the hall, bird's eye maple for the main parlor, and cherry for the dining room and the library, which was located in the base of the tower and may have been the home's most memorable space. Marble fireplaces, elaborately carved woodwork, beveled-glass mirrors, and ornate plaster ceilings added to the house's aura of sumptuous overkill. The second floor, reached via a grand staircase offering splen-

did views down Summit, contained several large bedroom suites. Servants' quarters and a ballroom occupied the third floor.

Amherst Wilder spent just seven years in his house, dying of Bright's disease in November 1894. Both Wilder's widow, Fanny, and the couple's only child, Cornelia Day, died in 1903, and much of the family fortune went to establish the charity administered by the Wilder Foundation. The mansion was acquired by the St. Paul Archdiocese for use as the archbishop's residence in 1918. In 1959 the archdiocese decided to replace the house with a new chancery building. Abandoned and left to vandals, the house was finally town down late that year, depriving future generations of any chance to see what one historian called "the grandest mansion of all the sixty-two [on Summit Avenue] that have been destroyed."

ABOVE LEFT:
The drawing room, about 1890

ABOVE RIGHT:
The house in the last stages of demolition with only the tower left standing

LA VETA TERRACE

Southeast corner of Seventeenth Street and Nicollet
Avenue, Minneapolis. William A. Hunt. 1887–1932.

*La Veta Terrace as it
appeared in an 1888 drawing*

In the 1880s, just before the electric streetcar
began opening up large new areas of the Twin
Cities for residential settlement, row houses enjoyed a brief period of popularity. The *Minneapolis Tribune*, for example, noted in May 1884 that
"an unusually large number of tenement rows"
were being erected in the city. Because they required less land than detached dwellings did, row
houses proved to be especially attractive to developers in Minneapolis, where there was intense
demand for good housing close to downtown.
The most fashionable row houses—often called
"terraces" to give them an aura of English respectability—were built on downtown's southern
fringes. Some of them were enormous. Spring
Grove Terrace, completed in 1885 at Seventeenth Street and Clinton Avenue, had twenty-
four units and a total street frontage of nearly six
hundred feet. La Veta Terrace—a few blocks west
along Seventeenth—was not as large, but it may
well have been the most lavish row house of the
1880s in Minneapolis.

La Veta Terrace's architect, William A. Hunt,
practiced in Minneapolis only briefly (between
about 1885 and 1888) before moving to Duluth.
There he designed many houses as well as such
important public buildings as the Duluth Normal

School (1898). La Veta Terrace appears to have been Hunt's largest commission in Minneapolis, and it is evidence of his considerable skills as a designer that he obtained the job after winning a competition.

Built of pink quartzite, red pressed brick, brownstone, and terra cotta, La Veta Terrace put on Richardsonian Romanesque airs but could not quite escape its Victorian Gothic heritage. The building was intensely pictorial, its Romanesque features (such as large entry arches) functioning more as scenes in a great street show than as essential elements of the design. Like so many Victorian buildings, La Veta Terrace went wild at the roof line, where the Nicollet facade alone offered ten gabled dormers (in four sizes and shapes), three towers (the largest, on the corner, sporting

La Veta Terrace shortly before its 1932 demolition

a Gothic-style spire), and five chimneys, all jutting out from a steep mansard roof.

Inside were eleven three-story rental units, each with anywhere from ten to thirteen rooms. All first and second floor rooms contained fireplaces and were finished in oak, birch, and magnolia. Standard amenities included electric bells, hot and cold running water, and gas, but there was only one bathroom per unit (on the second floor). Rental rates are unknown, but the units were definitely intended for an upper-middle-class clientele.

As with most Twin Cities row houses, La Veta Terrace did not remain fashionable for very long. Shortly after the turn of the century, the building was subdivided into thirty-two units. A man named John H. Musgrave later purchased the building, which was thereafter known as Musgrave Flats. The elaborate facades were still largely intact when the old row house fell to the wrecker in 1932.

THEODORE HAMM BREW HOUSE AND MANSION

Swede Hollow near Minnehaha Avenue, St. Paul.
August Maritzen (brew house), Augustus Gauger
(mansion). 1887, 1894–1940s, 1954.

Brew house and mansion viewed from Swede Hollow, about 1900

Breweries were once among the largest and most picturesque buildings in the Twin Cities. Because of the vertical nature of the brewing process, breweries tended to be quite tall, and they were almost always located in gorges or other romantic locales that offered a reliable supply of water and easy access to sandstone storage caves. St. Paul—with its large German population, numerous streams and springs, and deep sandstone hollows—was a brewer's dream. By 1887, with twelve breweries, it was the beer capital of Minnesota.

Theodore Hamm was already a successful brewer at this time, even though he had fallen into the business by accident. Born in Herbolzheim, Baden (Germany), in 1825, he emigrated to Chicago in 1854 and arrived in St. Paul two years later. His first venture was a boardinghouse and saloon in Lowertown that he operated with his wife, Louise. Later he ran another saloon. In 1864 Hamm foreclosed on a mortgage he held on a small brewery located near the upper end of Swede Hollow. Although not a brewer himself, Hamm had a knack for business and by 1882 had turned his establishment—originally known as the Excelsior Brewery—into St. Paul's largest, with an annual production of thirty thousand barrels.

In 1894 the brewery took a quantum leap forward with the completion of a new main brew house that was to be a St. Paul landmark for half a century. This huge project—under the direction of Theodore's son, William, who by 1890 ran the business on a daily basis—doubled the brewery's capacity and pushed it far ahead of its local competitors. The Hamms called in one of the nation's leading brewery architects, August Maritzen of Chicago, to design their new brew house, and he produced an impressive specimen of industrial architecture. Built of red brick and stone, the brew house was five stories high and had long rows of arched windows, ornate North Germanic-inspired gables, and a splendid baroque dome surmounted by a cupola. Spread around this building over an area of two square blocks were other parts of the brewery complex, including an office building, paint and wagon shops, a blacksmith shop, and a stable for sixty draft horses that hauled beer wagons.

The opening of the expanded brewery on September 27, 1894, drew a crowd estimated at ten thousand people, most of whom appear to have been more interested in consuming the plant's product than in contemplating its architecture. All of the brewery's buildings, "elaborately decorated" with American and German flags, were open for tours. One stop was at the employees' refreshment room, where—claimed one newspaper—some workers fortified themselves with "forty or fifty glasses [of beer] a day," although the average employee was said to find "twenty to thirty sufficient."

A 1900 advertisement featured the brewery.

Like other brewing dynasties of their time, the Hamm family resided within eyesight of their business, in an enclave of houses overlooking Swede Hollow. Theodore originally lived in a modest house but in 1887 moved into a new mansion perched on the crest of the bluff. The house was built by William while Theodore was traveling in Germany and presented to him as a present on his return. Designed by St. Paul architect Augustus Gauger, the house was a Queen Anne confection with a round corner tower, a profusion of gables, and large arched windows on the second floor that echoed those of the brewery down the hill. A side porch overlooked the ravine near a staircase that angled down to the brewery. Inside, the house offered twenty rooms, eight fireplaces, and all the other accoutrements of the good life in the 1880s.

Theodore Hamm lived in the house until his death in 1903, after which William moved in. William, who took his exercise in moderation, walked down the steps to work every morning but had his chauffeur drive him back up the hill in the evening. He died of a heart attack in 1931, his widow two years later, and the house went into decline. It was later converted into a nursing home but was vacant when a fourteen-year-old arsonist torched it in April 1954.

By this time, much of Maritzen's brew house, including the dome, had disappeared beneath a series of remodelings and expansions, although some original walls and windows remained visible. These expansion projects, begun in 1946, made the brewery the fifth largest in America by 1954. The company's efforts to make its beer a national brand ultimately failed, and in 1965 the Hamm family sold out to Heublein, Inc., of Connecticut. There have been three other owners of the building since then, the latest being the Stroh Brewery Company of Detroit.

Hamm mansion, about 1900

DONALDSON'S GLASS BLOCK

Southeast corner of Sixth Street and Nicollet Avenue, Minneapolis. Long and Kees, Kees and Colburn. 1888, 1903, ca. 1910, 1924, 1949–82.

The department store was invented in Paris, where free-trade policies spawned by the French Revolution opened the way for large shops selling a variety of goods. It was not until the 1860s, however, that advances in iron framing made possible great, glassy stores such as the Bon Marché (1869–79), a Parisian institution that became a worldwide model for aspiring retailers.

The first modern department store in Minneapolis was built by two Scottish immigrant brothers, Lawrence S. and William Donaldson, who began their careers in 1882 in a one-story building at Sixth and Nicollet. This modest structure, originally known as "Colton's Glass Block," proved to be inadequate, and in 1888 the Donaldsons replaced it with a five-story store built of iron and glass. Designed by Franklin Long and Frederick Kees, Donaldson's Glass Block changed forever the experience of shopping in Minneapolis. At a time when most dry goods stores were housed in narrow buildings with cramped aisles and dim lighting, the Glass Block offered bright, spacious interiors, an elegantly furnished "waiting room" for those who presum-

Donaldson's Glass Block, about 1925

The Donaldsons' first store at Sixth and Nicollet, 1883

ably had shopped until they dropped, a restaurant, the latest "cable cash delivery system" (the cash register had not yet arrived), and an unparalleled array of merchandise. Following the French model, the store had a central light well, which not only provided illumination but also helped shoppers to orient themselves.

The gleaming white exterior, illuminated after dark by thousands of lights, offered a dramatic main entrance through a forty-foot-high archway on Nicollet. Stylistically the building was notable for its straightforward expression of structure in the manner of the best Chicago buildings of the period. But there was also one decidedly Parisian touch—a lighted, sixty-foot-high corner dome capped by a small lookout tower.

Over the next thirty years, the store continued to grow until it eventually stretched a full block along Nicollet between Sixth and Seventh. The first major addition, designed by the firm of Kees and Colburn, was completed in 1903. Other large additions were built around 1910 and in 1924. In the 1940s there were two notable exterior changes. The first came in 1942 when the big corner dome was dismantled, its metal frame used as scrap for the war effort. Seven years later the entire store was sheathed in a sleek Moderne

style stone facade, obscuring all traces of its original design.

Donaldson's remained on the site until 1982 when the store moved across Nicollet to new, smaller quarters. Workers then began to demolish the old store, but fire finished the job on Thanksgiving Day in 1982. This fire, one of the largest in Minneapolis history, also destroyed the Northwestern Bank. Subsequently Gaviidae Common, a shopping mall, occupied the site of Donaldson's old store. The Donaldson's name also vanished from the Twin Cities retail scene a few years later when Carson Pirie Scott of Chicago acquired the company's stores in 1987.

The Sixth Street entrance to Donaldson's, 1900

199

GLOBE BUILDING

20 Fourth Street South (between Hennepin and Nicollet avenues), Minneapolis. E. Townsend Mix. 1889–1958.

Globe Building, about 1895

With its playful gables and witch's-hat tower, this building was the great romantic among early Twin Cities skyscrapers. It may also have been Mix's finest essay in the Richardsonian Romanesque, rock solid yet not the least bit ponderous. The building's magnificent angle tower was its dominant feature. Like a model seen slightly in profile, the tower struck a distinctive diagonal pose that added enormously to the building's presence, which otherwise might have suffered due to a cramped midblock site. The tower, which Schuyler admired, was an arresting design in its own right, its heavily rusticated walls encaged in a framework of smooth stone piers that anticipated the cellular look of skyscrapers to come.

The building was also quite colorful. Its narrow facade on Fourth Street was clad almost entirely in red Minnesota granite and reddish-brown Lake Superior sandstone. The long and highly visible side walls, however, had to settle for common brick. As originally designed, the building was even more picturesque than it turned out to be. A drawing in the *Globe* to celebrate the opening of the building showed four side gables, two front balconies, and oriel windows on the ground floor. The four gables were indeed built, but the other features were not.

Inside, the building was arranged much like the newspaper's earlier one in St. Paul and had a small light court containing two elevators. Unfortunately no photographs, drawings, or detailed descriptions of this space have been found. Newspaper offices occupied most of the first floor and all of the eighth, with renters in between. Among them were many prominent lawyers and a young man named Richard Sears, who went on to considerable success in the mail-order business.

The Globe was also associated with a legendary figure known as Sid the Ratman. His real name was Tom H. Goodale, and he was a contractor for the building. One day Goodale's son, who worked with him, died in a fall from the roof. This accident, it was said, unhinged Good-

ale, who later took to haunting downtown streets where he would buttonhole passersby with strange stories about rodents and other unpleasant creatures. Goodale usually concluded these bizarre narratives by telling his audience: "I believe the Globe Building is better than the Guaranty Loan, the Guaranty Loan." This coda become so familiar that listeners would chant it in unison, like the refrain to a popular song.

The building came to an equally unhappy end. A writer had predicted in 1889 that "fifty years from now . . . the Globe Building will still be an ornament." By 1939, however, the Globe was an empty hulk, its last twenty-eight tenants having vacated six years earlier. Hennepin County took title to the building in 1942 and sold it for sixteen thousand dollars in back taxes. Its new owners turned the building into a parking garage, and it served in that capacity until 1958 when it was demolished to make way for the new Minneapolis Public Library (extant).

Architect's drawing for the Globe Building, showing slightly different detailing

SAMUEL C. GALE HOUSE

1600 Harmon Place (at Maple Street), Minneapolis.
LeRoy Buffington (Harvey Ellis). 1889–1933.

Among the great nineteenth-century mansions of Minneapolis, few could match this one for sheer masonry muscle. Built of pinkish-red Sioux quartzite, the hardest stone quarried in America, the house seems to have been designed with defense in mind, as though Gale feared that proletarian armies might one day appear at his doorstep. Yet despite its overwhelming solidity—a newspaper said the house was "put up to stand for ages"—its life as an occupied dwelling was brief.

Gale house, about 1900

Samuel C. Gale, a Harvard-trained lawyer, was one of many transplanted Yankees who formed the social and financial elite of Minneapolis. He arrived in 1857 at age thirty and three years later opened a real estate-insurance office with his brother, Harlow. Together, the Gales bought and platted large tracts of land. By 1864—when he built his first house at Fourth and Marquette— Samuel Gale was already a rich man. He became even richer as land prices skyrocketed in the early 1880s. In 1887 Gale took advantage of these prices and sold his property on Marquette to the National Bank of Commerce. He then built this house on a fine corner lot overlooking Central (later Loring) Park.

The architect Gale chose was LeRoy Buffington, who at that time employed Harvey Ellis as a

The front hallway and main staircase, about 1893

draftsman. Ellis's inimitable hand is evident in the design of the mansion, which emerged as a sort of Richardsonian Romanesque fairy tale. The exterior, said to possess "castle like grandeur," included a fragmented entry arch, a swooping front gable rising from an open porch, and an incredible round tower topped by a cone of stone. The most faithfully Richardsonian aspect of the composition was the adjoining carriage house, which offered rock-ribbed simplicity.

Within, no expense was spared, especially in the house's thirty-by-forty-five-foot entry hall. This relentlessly substantial space featured oak paneling, beamed ceilings, stencil- and mosaic-work, an alabaster fireplace, and a truly grand staircase. Also on the first floor were a reception room, drawing room, library, morning room, dining room, and a conservatory complete with a central fountain. The predominant style of these rooms was French Renaissance, a marked con-

trast to the exterior. Upstairs were all sorts of marble-heavy bathrooms and six bedroom suites, many with views of the park. In his own bedroom Gale allowed himself a sentimental touch—the apple wood came from the orchard of his boyhood farm in Massachusetts. Servants' quarters were tucked away on the third floor, as was a gymnasium.

Gale spent one hundred thousand dollars on his mansion and claimed that it was "built to last 100 years." But for unknown reasons, he moved out only six years after the house was built. In 1897 Judge Martin B. Koon bought the house, but he, too, moved away as commercial and institutional development encroached on the neighborhood. Later the house was converted into a nursing home, acquiring an unsympathetic addition in the process. The building was finally torn down in 1933, outliving Gale by only seventeen years.

MINNEAPOLIS PUBLIC LIBRARY

Southeast corner of Hennepin Avenue and Tenth Street, Minneapolis. Long and Kees. 1889–1961.

Minneapolis Public Library, about 1890

The Minneapolis Public Library grew out of an earlier institution—the Minneapolis Athenaeum. Founded in 1860 the Athenaeum was a private circulating library whose shareholders—mostly from the upper classes—paid an annual fee. Agitation for a free public library soon developed.

Leading the campaign was Thomas B. Walker, a millionaire lumberman and art collector who believed public libraries could help educate the masses, thereby elevating the moral tone of society. Under Walker's insistent prodding, a public library free to all replaced the Athenaeum in 1885.

The newly appointed library board's first step was to find a building site. After much discussion, the board chose a location on the southern edge of downtown near what was then an elegant residential district. The next step was to select an architect, which the board did by means of a

The main stairwell, about 1895

competition in 1886. Nine firms (all but one of them local) submitted designs in the dominant style of the day—Richardsonian Romanesque. The winners were Franklin Long and Frederick Kees, who later went on to design a much larger Richardsonian monument—the Minneapolis City Hall and Hennepin County Courthouse.

For the library, which opened in December 1889, the architects designed a sort of Richardsonian clubhouse in Lake Superior sandstone. With its arcaded windows, corner towers, and heavy-set massing, the library resembled a compact version of Long and Kees's great city hall–courthouse to come. The library, L-shaped in plan, fronted on Hennepin. Squat granite pillars framed a magnificent split entrance, surmounted by a large curved bay with four windows and a central niche sheltering a statue of Minerva, goddess of wisdom.

The interior was organized around a skylit foyer finished in red brick and featuring exquisite iron stair railings made by the celebrated Chicago firm of Winslow Brothers. On the first floor was the main reading room, which offered eighteen-foot ceilings, mahogany wainscoting, and a fireplace. Because there were no open shelves, books had to be requested from an adjoining delivery room. The upper floors contained offices, a natural history room, and an art museum.

The building generally won praise for its design. Schuyler found it "distinctly successful," while a local newspaper called it "by far the most beautiful building in the city." One grumpy critic for the *Building Budget*, however, complained that the designer had failed to "hold himself down." Within a few years, the library became part of a superb urban trio along Tenth that also included First Baptist Church (1888, by Long and Kees, extant) and Charles Sedgwick's YMCA Building (1892, gone). Like other public buildings of its era, the library ultimately proved to be too small. Additions in 1905 and 1925 completed the square started by Long and Kees, but there was no room for expansion after that. The building was torn down in 1961 and replaced by a new, blandly utilitarian library six blocks away on Hennepin. The site of the old library became a parking lot.

The main reading room and circulation desk, about 1890

ST. PAUL CITY HALL AND RAMSEY COUNTY COURTHOUSE

Block bounded by Fourth, Fifth, Wabasha, and Cedar streets, St. Paul. Edward Bassford. 1889–1933.

The St. Paul City Hall–Ramsey County Courthouse in the last stages of construction; the windows had not yet been installed

This ungainly hulk of a building never won many popularity contests. Schuyler called it "unfortunate in design . . . a congeries of unrelated and unadjusted parts," while a *Harper's Weekly* correspondent thought it "a sad failure." A county grand jury went even further, describing the structure in 1925 as "antiquated, inconvenient and an architectural mistake." Yet for all its deficiencies, this big stone pile was an imposing presence

along Fourth Street for almost half a century, its two-hundred-foot tower a highly visible symbol of local government.

Prior to completion of this structure, city and county government in St. Paul occupied separate buildings, both dating from the 1850s. County government was especially cramped in a small courthouse at Fifth and Wabasha that one newspaper described as "a great eyesore." As St. Paul's population began to explode in the 1870s, agitation developed for a new city hall–courthouse. Civic pride was at stake, a newspaper noted, because "all through the state cities and towns were surpassing St. Paul in the character of their public buildings." In the early 1870s the state legislature authorized three hundred thousand dollars in bonding for the project, and a design was prepared by the firm of Radcliffe and Buffington. But a depression had begun in 1873, and it took eight years before St. Paul voters finally approved the bonding. Because of rising costs, the original three-hundred-thousand-dollar amount had to be doubled before work finally started on the building's foundation in 1884.

By this time, there were already fears that the building would prove to be too small, and some local businessmen advocated incorporating rental office space into the structure as a cushion for future expansion. Most people, however, wanted a traditional public building, and that is exactly what Bassford designed. When the cornerstone was laid on October 13, 1885, a long line of speakers—not all of them riveting—predicted the building would be one of the wonders of the ages. Similar sentiments were voiced at the building's dedication four years later when a newspaper writer said that the structure was "capable of standing for centuries." This forecast did not turn out to be the case, in part because the building was so poorly designed.

Bassford had won the commission—one of the plum jobs of the decade—not because of his great skills as a designer but because of excellent politi-

The city council chambers, about 1900

cal connections. The building he produced was a muddled attempt at Richardsonian Romanesque, with none of the power or grace of the real thing. Early drawings show that Bassford initially had something more or less Victorian Gothic in mind, but he performed last-minute cosmetic surgery in an effort to achieve a more up-to-date Romanesque look.

The block chosen for the building was a public square, empty except for the old courthouse and the county jail along Fifth. The historic courthouse was razed in 1884, but the jail remained until the county built a new one a block away in 1903. With most of the block to work with, Bassford put the new building's main entrance and tower along Fourth, creating side entries on Wabasha and Cedar. The building's massive walls were of rock-faced Kasota stone, which held its pinkish color for only a few years before being turned a dirty brown by the coal smoke in the city's polluted air. Fifty gargoyles stared down from these darkened, quite powerful walls. Nevertheless the overall composition, especially Bassford's off-handed placement of the tower, left much to be desired.

Inside, 150 rooms were organized around wide central corridors. The finish was generally plain, although Mexican onyx and Tennessee marble, used for wainscoting, added a touch of elegance. In addition to the usual government offices, the building included six courtrooms and a large city council chamber. Fifty feet square with a forty-foot-high coved ceiling, this chamber was quite ornate, with plenty of plaster- and stencilwork and wildly overwrought chandeliers. Unfortunately the chamber had wretched acoustics, as the council discovered all too soon.

The building, in fact, turned out to be a municipal lemon—too small, inefficiently laid out, and costly to heat. By the 1920s the structure had become so overcrowded and dilapidated that a grand jury condemned it as unsafe. Three years later voters approved $4 million in bonding for a new city hall–courthouse (extant), which was completed in 1932. No one was interested in saving the old building, and it was demolished in 1933. Much of the stone was salvaged, however, and went into at least one church in West St. Paul, several park buildings, and Acacia Park Cemetery in Mendota Heights. The site was occupied by the St. Paul Pioneer Press building and a parking ramp in 1991.

The clock tower, about 1923

PEOPLE'S CHURCH

Northwest corner of Pleasant Avenue and Chestnut
Street, St. Paul. J. Walter Stevens. 1889–1940.

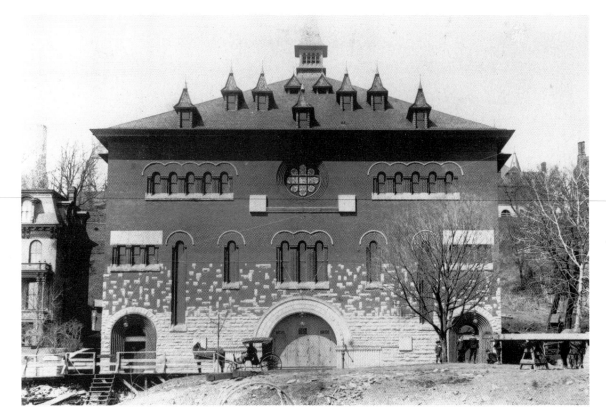

The People's Church,
about 1900

Among the most dynamic religious leaders of
his day in St. Paul was the Reverend Samuel G.
Smith. A man of "vigorous and progressive
views," Smith began his career in the Methodist
Episcopal church, where he developed a large
following, and then struck off on his own in 1887
to form the People's Church. Organized on the
Congregational model, the church drew from
"the best of all forms of worship," according to
Smith, and soon proved to be highly successful.
Services initially were held at St. Paul's Grand
Opera House. In 1889, however, the congrega-
tion moved into a new building—said to be
America's largest Protestant church—located on

Pleasant Avenue almost directly below the site of
James J. Hill's Summit Avenue mansion.

As designed by J. Walter Stevens's office, the
church building deliberately avoided the usual
trappings of religious architecture, resembling a
large clubhouse more than a place of worship.
This aspect did not go unnoticed. "The building
suggests no current form of ecclesiasticism," the
Pioneer Press observed when the church opened
on April 14, 1889. Schuyler, however, thought
the church exhibited the "wild, free theology of
the West." This free-spirited quality was especially evident on the building's lower facades where
chunks of stone randomly erupted from brick

The church auditorium, about 1939

walls, creating what one newspaper called "an original and peculiar appearance." Three great arched entrances punctured the building's stone base along Pleasant. A variety of windows, including two extremely tall lancets, were arranged in the brick above. These lancets, and a wheel window below the eaves, were about all that hinted at the building's religious purpose. A colony of dormers roosting on a steeply pitched roof culminated Stevens's rather bizarre composition.

The first floor of the building contained as-

The church in 1915 as its was rebuilt after the fire

sembly and lecture rooms, classrooms, a ladies' parlor, and a kitchen. One floor above was the main auditorium, which seated twenty-five hundred people (thirty-five hundred with extra chairs brought in), and was the largest first-class meeting hall of its time in St. Paul. The auditorium, including the large balcony, was finished rather simply in keeping with the Reverend Mr. Smith's desire to avoid ostentation.

A 1901 fire destroyed the roof and interior of the church. The building survived but with a less picturesque roof line and a new arts-and-crafts style sanctuary. Because of its size and fine acoustics, the church auditorium attracted many notable lecturers and musicians on national tours. Mark Twain spoke there in 1895, twenty-six-year-old Winston Churchill in 1901, and Teddy Roosevelt a few years later. Among the musicians who played at the church (in 1925) was Serge Rachmaninoff.

In the 1930s the church began to lose both its members and its endowment fund, and the decline proved to be irreversible. The congregation voted in 1939 to disband and merge with the Highland Park Community Church. A year later fire destroyed the old building on Pleasant. The church site is gone as well, vanished beneath Interstate 35E.

ABERDEEN HOTEL

Southwest corner of Virginia Street and Dayton Avenue,
St. Paul. Willcox and Johnston. 1889–1944.

Aberdeen Hotel, about 1900

The late 1880s introduced a new building type to the Twin Cities—the luxury apartment hotel. Among the grandest of these was the Aberdeen, located three blocks from Summit Avenue, St. Paul's most exclusive residential precinct. Built by entrepreneur J. J. Watson, the eight-story hotel offered only a few rooms for transients and advertised itself as a place "for those seeking the comforts of home without the annoyance and routine of keeping house."

The Aberdeen's architects, William Willcox and Clarence Johnston, produced a crisp, clean design inspired by Renaissance classicism. The two-story base of rusticated Ohio sandstone had large arched windows and a triple-arched entrance beneath a small loggia. The six stories above were faced in light brick with the top floor—set off by a string course—receiving a slightly darker treatment. A smartly executed cornice completed the composition in appropriately classical fashion. Octagonal corner turrets, their flat tops supporting corner lookouts, provided the only touch of Victorian quaintness to an otherwise sober design.

Initially all but fourteen of the hotel's seventy-eight units were arranged as two- to eight-room suites. Large suites included a reception room, kitchen, pantry, dining room, library, private bath, and "every convenience for comfortable family living." Most single rooms also had baths (not a universal hotel amenity at the time) but were expensive at five dollars a night (three dollars was then the going rate in St. Paul). On the main floor, the hotel offered a café and a ballroom, which one magazine described as "a novel and excellent feature that will be popular with the society of 'The Hill.'" The city's elite gathered in the ballroom on June 9, 1893, to celebrate completion of the Great Northern Railway's transcontinental route to Seattle. Naturally James J. Hill was the guest of honor. Chicago luminaries such as George Pullman and Marshall Field were also on hand for the banquet, which was said to be one of the most costly ever staged in St. Paul.

As befitting a hotel that catered to a well-to-do clientele, the Aberdeen attracted some notable tenants in its early years, including Minnesota Governor John A. Johnson, who from 1904 to 1910 occupied a sixth-floor suite with a view of the State Capitol. Emmanuel Masqueray, architect of the nearby St. Paul Cathedral, was also a resident. Like other hotels of its period, the Aberdeen began to slip as it grew older. In 1920 the federal government bought the hotel and operated it as a veteran's hospital for the next seven years. The building, which had cost $250,000 to construct, was later sold at auction for $750, but no use could be found for it during the depths of the depression. In 1937 the vacant building came into the spotlight when the burned, mutilated body of Ruth Manson, a waitress, was found inside. Her murder was never solved, but the incident stimulated community efforts to have the old hotel condemned. In 1944 the Aberdeen finally succumbed to the wrecking ball. Its structural frame yielded five hundred tons of scrap iron for the war effort. A parking lot and a YWCA building occupied the site in 1991.

Dayton Avenue entrance to the hotel, about 1937

NEW YORK LIFE INSURANCE BUILDING

Southwest corner of Sixth and Minnesota streets, St. Paul. Babb, Cook, and Willard. 1889–1967.

NEW YORK LIFE INSURANCE BUILDING

Southwest corner of Fifth Street and Second Avenue South, Minneapolis. Babb, Cook, and Willard. 1890–1958.

In the late 1880s the rapidly expanding New York Life Insurance Company built skyscrapers in five midwestern cities, including St. Paul and Minneapolis. (The other three were in Chicago, Kansas City, and Omaha. The Omaha building was the only survivor in 1991.) The company decided to build in the provinces both as a way of investing spare capital and increasing its sales. In Minneapolis, for example, New York Life agreed to put up a new building only after extracting a promise from local business leaders to help the company sell $4 million worth of insurance. A design competition for these two New York Life buildings attracted such prominent Twin Cities architects as Allen Stem, Cass Gilbert, and LeRoy Buffington, but the commission for both structures ultimately went to Babb, Cook, and Willard of New York.

For St. Paul the firm produced a highly quaint design, which Montgomery Schuyler described as "a still small voice of scholarly protest on the part of an 'Eastern' architect against a 'boisterous and rough-hewn' Westernness." The building's asymmetric wings (one was twice as wide as the other), daintily scaled ornament, and picturesque gables were indeed unusual features in St. Paul and gave the structure a fairy-tale air.

The ten-story building, however, was not as irrational as it looked. Its oddly asymmetric massing was in fact a logical response to the fact that the building abutted property on Minnesota Street not owned by New York Life. Anticipating that an adjoining structure might one day block out light and air, the company made the south wing of its new building very narrow so that all offices would face north toward an open light court. (This precaution, as it turned out, was unnecessary because no tall building was ever constructed next door.)

New York Life Insurance Company Building, St. Paul, shortly after completion; note the neighboring small frame structures

More or less Flemish Renaissance in style, the New York Life Building presented an extremely romantic profile with a steeply pitched roof and the only stepped gables ever seen on a Twin Cities skyscraper. The gables were not part of Babb, Cook, and Willard's original design, which showed a more Germanic treatment of the upper floors. In September 1888, however, a St. Paul newspaper reported that "the original designs for the upper stories have been greatly modified and elaborated upon. Their style has been completely changed, and will be something on the Flemish order." Beneath these peculiar gables were three ornate round windows that added yet another distinctive touch to the building. "The treatment of the upper stories," boasted a company publication with some justice, "is perhaps the most novel and original of any to be found in the country."

The building's colorful facades were composed of red St. Cloud granite (basement), reddish-brown Lake Superior sandstone (first two floors), and cherry-red pressed brick (upper floors), all embellished with terra-cotta and cast-iron ornament. Structurally the building was fairly standard, with load-bearing exterior walls supporting an interior metal frame. The main entry on Minnesota Street was spectacular—a two-story-high archway framed by ornamental panels and crowned by a great bronze eagle, the company's symbol, sculpted by Augustus St. Gaudens.

Inside, the building's most notable feature was a barrel-vaulted, skylit entrance corridor wedged between the office wings. This space was purely ceremonial, designed to impress visitors with the power, majesty, and financial strength of the New York Life Insurance Company. Walls and columns of Italian, French, and Tennessee marble enforced an aura of sumptuousness, as did a stained-glass skylight and fine mosaic floors. Ascending a series of steps, the visitor then reached a cross corridor connecting to another entrance on Sixth. Here, providing access to the building's four hydraulic elevators, was a more intimate

LEFT:
The main entrance to the St. Paul building before installation of the eagle

BELOW:
The entrance corridor of the St. Paul building, about 1890

The New York Life Insurance Company Building, Minneapolis, 1890

space ornamented with elaborate wrought- and cast-iron grillwork. Gilded plaster, cherry doors and trim, marble wainscoting, and frescoed ceilings completed the decorative ensemble. The offices above all had doors with sidelights, washstands, ten-foot or higher ceilings, marble window sills, and hookups for gas and electricity. Most of the building's early tenants were lawyers, attracted by a free law library on the third floor. The lower floors contained retail space, including a large banking hall.

Over the years, the building settled slightly (a common problem in downtown St. Paul's treacherous soil) but otherwise appears to have weathered the ravages of time quite nicely. In 1931 the building received its first significant alterations, which included a full-height addition to the

south and reconstructed windows on the lower floors. The owners also performed an art-deco facelift on the lobby, destroying virtually all of its original features. By the mid-1960s, the building remained in sound condition, but it had the misfortune of being located in the heart of the Capitol Centre renewal district where nothing old was allowed to stand. There was hardly a whisper of opposition when the building was torn down in 1967 and replaced by a parking ramp conspicuous only for its ugliness.

A year after completing its St. Paul building, New York Life opened a larger and even more splendid structure in Minneapolis. For this project Babb, Cook, and Willard forsook the picturesque Flemish touches used in St. Paul, choosing instead a more recognizable form of Renaissance Revival with Romanesque overtones. Ten stories high and organized around a rear light court invisible from the street, this building was among the first tall office structures in the Twin Cities to embrace the neoclassical revival begun in New York by McKim, Mead, and White. It was far from a chaste embrace, however, and the building's massive facades fairly hummed with old-time Victorian diversity, presenting an abundance of layers, windows in all sizes and shapes (including several of the bull's-eye variety), and an extensive ornamental program executed in sandstone, granite, and two shades of red terra cotta.

The building rose from a high base of rusticated granite, through middle stories of pressed red brick, and culminated with a colossal terracotta cornice. This extravagant projection inaugurated a great era of cornice envy in the Twin Cities as tall buildings vied with one another to display ever more outrageous overhangs. But one feature of the New York Life Building was never duplicated—the four five-thousand-pound honeysuckle anthemions that sprouted like big plants from the roof. The main entrance on Fifth Street featured four banded granite columns beautifully carved in St. Cloud. These distinctive neo-Grec columns framed three pairs of oak entry doors. Like the building as a whole, the grand entrance was designed to display "the solidity and dignity . . . [of] the great corporation which erected it."

Within, more splendors awaited. The main entrance led directly to an elevator lobby fitted out with all the marble, tile, ornamental iron, and decorative plaster the architects could muster. The building's pièce de résistance lay just beyond in the form of a space called the Inner Court. Forty-five feet long with a flight of marble stairs cascading through its center, this elegant skylit space seems to have been intended more than anything else to instill a feeling of secular awe. Marbles from around the world, rich mosaics, and fine wrought ironwork filled the Inner Court. The court also featured a huge electric clock and a magnificent double spiral staircase. The ornate clock, set high in the court's rear wall, became an instant tourist attraction, which "on every holiday the country people around Minneapolis come to see in shoals." The sinuous double staircase, built of iron with marble treads, was at the opposite end of the court toward the main entrance. It led to a small balcony and from there to the second-floor elevator lobby.

Two side passages opened out from the court,

one leading to a subsidiary entrance on Second Avenue South and the other to a narrow one-story arcade attached to the west side of the building. The arcade, which had room for only small shops, was a sort of architectural insurance policy, since its real purpose was to create a shaft of open space, thereby assuring light and air to the office windows above even if another tall building were constructed next door.

Like its counterpart in St. Paul, this building contained first-floor banking halls, elegantly finished offices, and a free law library. The eight-thousand-volume library, plus a location close to the courthouse, quickly turned the structure into a "legal hive where the lawyers make honey, at least for themselves," according to one contemporaneous account.

Despite this early skyscraper's size and magnificence—only the Guaranty Loan (Metropolitan) was its equal in Minneapolis at the time—little of its history has been documented. It appears, however, that the building remained in good condition through the mid-1950s. Even so, the end came in 1958 when the building was razed to make way for the twenty-eight-story First National Bank, the first of the post-World War II skyscrapers that soon dominated the Minneapolis skyline.

The inner court, showing the winding double staircase, 1890

GERMANIA LIFE INSURANCE (GUARDIAN) BUILDING

Southeast corner of Fourth and Minnesota streets,
St. Paul. Edward Bassford. 1889, 1902–70.

This big hunk of granite and sandstone was the first building constructed in the Midwest by the Germania Life Insurance Company, a multinational firm based in New York. Like its great contemporaries—the New York Life Insurance buildings of 1889 and 1890—the Germania Life was an exercise in image enhancement, the marble-saturated sumptuousness of its lobby intended to impress customers with the company's financial might.

The building also showed that Edward Bassford could still compete with the aggressive young architects who had invaded St. Paul in the 1880s. Bassford's design was an interesting mix of classical and Richardsonian Romanesque elements. He treated the building's base quite classically with rusticated walls of red granite framing tall arched windows in the fashion of the Renaissance Revival. The main entrance on Minnesota was more Romanesque in character, however, with a band of intertwining floral ornament surrounding a tall arch. Above, the eight-story building was divided into two wings separated by a deep court facing Minnesota. A short colonnade bridging the wings provided a platform for a huge bronze statue of Germania, who was later to prove to be unpopular. The upper stories were faced in rugged Lake Superior sandstone laid in at least two different patterns. Here, Bassford followed a standard Richardsonian model with midfloor windows grouped into a broad arcade.

Inside, a grand staircase ascended through a skylit corridor to a second-floor elevator lobby. The staircase and much of the lobby were executed in creamy Italian marble, while railings, light fixtures, and elevator grilles were made of brass. "The building may be described as palatial without the least exaggeration," reported the *Northwest Builder* in 1890. "In fact there are few royal palaces in Europe that could be compared

Germania Life Insurance Building, about 1890

with it." This, of course, was a notable piece of hyperbole, but the building certainly was among the most lavish of its day in the Twin Cities.

The first major change to the structure came in 1902 when two stories were added. Extra stories had been contemplated as early as 1888, and the new floors did not significantly compromise the building's appearance. The next major surgery on the building was of an entirely different character, however. As anti-German frenzy mounted during World War I, local patriots agitated for the removal of the statue of Germania,

and the big bronze lady came down on March 3, 1918. "The loyal Americans of St. Paul feel that Germania fails in representing the Americanism of the city," said one newspaper in endorsing this ugly act of vandalism. That same year, Germania Life Insurance Company became Guardian Insurance.

The building itself survived until 1970 when it was demolished for the Kellogg Square apartment complex. Ten carved heads mounted along the Fourth Street side of Kellogg Square are all that remain of the Germania Life Building.

ABOVE LEFT:
The main staircase and skylit lobby, 1890

ABOVE RIGHT:
The statue of Germania being removed from the building in March 1918

ATHLETIC PARK

Block bounded by Fifth and Sixth streets and First and Second avenues north, Minneapolis. Orff Brothers. 1889–96.

DOWNTOWN BASEBALL PARK

Block bounded by Summit Avenue (later Columbus Avenue) and Twelfth, Minnesota, and Robert streets, St. Paul. 1903–08.

Organized baseball began in the Twin Cities as early as 1858 when a team called the Olympics was formed in St. Paul, but professional baseball did not arrive until 1884. In that year the Minneapolis Millers and their arch rivals, the St. Paul Saints, became charter members of the Northwestern League, which later evolved into the Western Association. The Millers, however, failed to draw sizable crowds until 1889 when they posted a winning record and, equally important, moved into a new downtown ball park. Known as Athletic Park, this small stadium was also used for University of Minnesota football games and thus qualifies as an early, undomed example of a multiuse sports facility.

Athletic Park, Minneapolis, about 1890

Athletic Park, Minneapolis, with the West Hotel looming in the background, about 1892

Plans for Athletic Park caused quite a political ruckus when presented to the city council. The issue was Sunday baseball, which certain Presbyterian ministers objected to on moral grounds. The *Daily Globe* labeled these opponents "cranks" and assured its readers that baseball would be played decorously in the new ball park. The Millers' manager, a character by the name of Morton, even allowed as how there would be "no loud or boisterous noise of any kind at any time" during games. He also promised a ban on liquor, noting that "no baseball player can drink and play good ball," a proposition not entirely supported by the historical record. Despite opposition from religious leaders, the park finally managed to open in May 1889.

As designed by the prolific team of brothers George and Fremont Orff, the park was a simple affair built entirely of wood. It seated about eighteen hundred people in a covered grandstand and another sixteen hundred or so in bleachers down the first and third base lines. Home plate was located near First Avenue North and Sixth Street, as were the park's two entrances. The block occupied by the park was about 330 feet square, which made for a field with cozy dimensions. In fact it appears that both the left and right field foul poles were only about two hundred feet from home plate. Right field was so short that some fly balls hit over the fence were ground-rule doubles. A white line painted on a wire screen above the right field fence was the deciding factor. A ball hit to the right of this line (but to the left of the foul pole) was a double. A ball clearing the fence to the left of this line, in the deeper portions of the park, was a home run. The left field fence also had its eccentricities. In a game against Kansas City, Miller outfielder Elmer Foster clambered up a plank bracing the fence and caught a ball headed out of the park. This spectacular catch precipitated a mighty rhubarb and later become a celebrated episode in Miller lore.

Foster and the other boys of the brief midwestern summers enjoyed only five seasons in Athletic Park, which was torn down in 1896 after the land on which it stood was sold. The Millers then moved to Nicollet Park in south Minneapolis where they were to remain for more than sixty years. The site of Athletic Park was eventually filled with large warehouses, among them Butler Square.

At the time of Athletic Park's demise, the St. Paul Saints were still trying to move downtown. In the 1890s the team played at several sites, including Lexington Park in the Midway area, but none was satisfactory. The team also had various owners, including Charles A. Comiskey. In December 1902 the team's owner, George Lennon, made what was to become a familiar threat to later generations of baseball fans. Lennon announced he would move the team, which by then had become a member of the fabled American Association, unless the city allowed him to build a new stadium downtown. He eventually found a site just south of Central

Park, but there was stiff opposition from occupants of nearby mansions and from Central Park Methodist Episcopal Church. The city council, however, could not resist the urge to play ball, and in 1903 Lennon received approval for his stadium.

Like its vanished Minneapolis counterpart, the St. Paul park was cheaply built of wood and offered minimal amenities. A crude grandstand with room for 1,760 people provided about half the seating, with everyone else consigned to the bleachers. The grandstand and home plate were located near Twelfth and Robert streets at the southeast corner of a typically small downtown St. Paul block.

St. Paul baseball fans were eager to have the park, and a cartoon in the *Pioneer Press* on July 13, 1903—a week before the stadium opened— showed people rushing from their jobs downtown to attend an afternoon game. About four thousand people did indeed flock to the park for its grand opening on Monday, July 20, 1903, when the Saints took on the hated Millers. Longtime

Downtown St. Paul baseball park, 1903

St. Paul Mayor Robert Smith threw out the first pitch, and the Saints went on to reward their faithful by trouncing the Millers eleven to three.

The park does not appear to have had any particular name, but it soon become known to fans as "the pillbox" because of its exceptionally modest dimensions. The stands were only ten to twenty feet from the playing field, which gave fans a wonderful view of the game but left little room for catching pop-ups in foul territory. The outfield fences were even shorter than those at Athletic Park, with the right field foul pole probably no more than 175 feet from home plate. Right fielders, it is said, routinely played with their backs to the fence, and slow runners were sometimes thrown out at first on one-hop line drives to right. Balls hit over the fence down either the left or right field lines were ground-rule doubles, and the rarest achievement of all in this intimate little ball park was a triple.

St. Paul's downtown park, like its predecessor across the river, was short-lived. It appears that the Saints played their last season in the park in 1908, since in October of that year a fire destroyed the grandstand. By 1910 the Saints were back at a refurbished Lexington Park, and downtown baseball in St. Paul was gone forever. A large bakery was later built on the site of the old ball park. This bakery closed in 1991 and may eventually be razed to make way for another state office building.

Fans sitting in the bleachers could see the spire of Central Park Methodist Episcopal Church and the tower of the second State Capitol.

NORTHWESTERN GUARANTY LOAN
(METROPOLITAN) BUILDING

Southwest corner of Third Street and Second Avenue
South, Minneapolis. E. Townsend Mix. 1890–1961.

*Northwestern Guaranty
Loan Building, about 1900*

The Northwestern Guaranty Loan Company was founded by Louis F. Menage, one of the most successful and flamboyant of the real estate speculators who made fortunes in Minneapolis in the 1880s. In 1888, with his young company prospering, Menage laid plans to erect what would be the city's largest and tallest office structure. Menage spared no expense on the project, pouring well over $1 million into the building that, as one newspaper later said, was intended to be "in every way a world beater." And in many respects, it was, even if not all critics of the time agreed. Schuyler, for instance, thought the building lacked "refinement" while Cass Gilbert found it "stupid and in bad taste." Later critics have come to see the building as a remarkable essay in solid and void and Mix's ultimate achievement as an architect (in more ways than one, since he died of tuberculosis only four months after its completion).

The building's colorful—if not especially remarkable—exterior featured walls of red Lake Superior sandstone set above a three-story base of green New Hampshire granite. It was a measure of the Guaranty Loan's cost and splendor that all four sides were faced in stone, whereas the usual practice was to use less expensive brick on any facades not overlooking the street. Because its outer walls were all of rock-faced stone and featured large protruding bays, the Guaranty Loan had an extremely rugged, almost crude appearance. Above these walls a forty-foot-high corner lookout tower, along with several smaller companion pieces, dominated the roof line. The overall style, evident in the building's arcaded base and elaborate arched entries, was Richardsonian Romanesque.

If the building's outside was an essay in the sober gravity of stone, the inside was a fantasy of light and space, a delicate act of dematerialization in which the experience of architecture was reduced to wavering lines of iron and great expanses of glass. The heart of this "wondrous

Main entrance to the building, about 1900

place," as the *Minneapolis Journal* called it, was the building's light court, which extended from the second floor to the roof. Notable for the quality of its detailing and its breathtaking expanse (about fifty by eighty feet), the glass and iron atrium was one of the supreme spaces of its kind in the history of American architecture. The four hundred offices around the court were reached by

ABOVE LEFT:
The light court, looking toward the main entrance and the elevator shaft

ABOVE RIGHT:
The light court viewed from the second floor upward toward the skylight

cantilevered balconies featuring one-inch-thick glass floors—helpful in distributing light—and magnificent ornamental railings made by Crown Iron Works of Minneapolis. Six open-cage elevators and a marble staircase moved people from floor to floor.

Although most of the building was devoted to offices, there was a popular twelfth-floor restaurant, which also served a roof garden above. On warm summer nights when an orchestra played, the garden was a favorite haunt for lovers, who found the view (and presumably the darkness) conducive to romance and who often carved their names on the soft sandstone parapets. The lookout tower, for years the highest vantage point in Minneapolis, also attracted crowds, who paid twenty-five cents for the view. Unfortunately at least one young woman used the tower as a jumping platform, and it apparently was closed after this suicide.

The building's lavishly orchestrated grand opening (see Introduction) represented the high-water mark of the great flood of money, ambition, and energy that transformed the Twin Cities in the 1880s. When depression hit in 1893, however, Menage and his company were found, like so many others of their time, to have been floating on a sea of questionable financial dealings. Within months, Northwestern Guaranty Loan went under, and Menage, wanted by the law, went south. Detectives followed his trail to Guatemala and South America but never were able to nab the slippery financier in his tropical refuge. (Menage later returned to the United States.) Thomas Lowry bought the building after Menage's hasty exit and then sold it in 1905 to the Metropolitan Life Insurance Company. Although there were several subsequent owners, the building was known thereafter as the Metropolitan.

The razing of this building in 1961–62 during the height of urban renewal fever was perhaps the most inexcusable act of civic vandalism in the history of Minneapolis. The building was in good condition and almost fully occupied at the time the city condemned it, and it is hard to find anything in the historical record to justify its wanton destruction. Little remains of the building except its ironwork, much of which has been reduced to the status of incongruous yard art, decorating patios, walls, and even motel balconies in the Twin Cities area.

Last stages of demolition of the Metropolitan Building

METROPOLITAN OPERA HOUSE

100 East Sixth Street (south side between Robert and Minnesota), St. Paul. Charles A. Reed, McElfatrick and Sons. 1890–1936.

Metropolitan Opera House, 1903

When St. Paul's Grand Opera House, which had been rebuilt in the early 1880s, burned down on January 21, 1889, the city found itself in desperate need of a place of amusement. Various schemes were immediately trotted out in the lo-

cal press, and within months work began on what would have been a spectacular replacement—an open-air arcade and adjoining opera house on Fourth Street near Wabasha. Funding for this ambitious project, designed by LeRoy Buffington, ran out after the foundation had been built. A syndicate led by retailing tycoon Robert Mannheimer then came to the rescue, raising five hundred thousand dollars for a new opera house, to be called the Metropolitan, on Sixth Street.

Some confusion exists as to who actually designed the opera house. McElfatrick and Sons, a New York firm specializing in theaters, was initially retained for the job in November 1889, but descriptions of the completed structure identify Charles A. Reed as the architect. The New York–born Reed, who came to St. Paul in the 1880s, was an engineer by training and is best known as the longtime partner of Allen H. Stem. This connection has led some sources to attribute the opera house to the firm of Reed and Stem. Their partnership, however, was not formed until 1891, a year after the opera house opened. The most likely scenario is that Reed acted as engineer and construction supervisor for the project, while McElfatrick and Sons handled the design work.

From the outside the Metropolitan was hardly theatrical, presenting an almost grim appearance. The structure was, in fact, a combination office building and theater—a common arrangement at the time, since large opera houses were too costly to build as separate entities. The Metropolitan's eight-story front—featuring brick walls and simple squared-off windows above a high base of rusticated granite—was as plain and direct as could be, with barely a hint of ornament. Only an arched glass and iron canopy over the main entrance and the opera house's name inscribed in heavy blocks revealed what lay within.

Judging from contemporary descriptions, the opera house itself was a real beauty. Its only superior, claimed one local newspaper, was Chicago's great Auditorium Theater, completed a year ear-

Main entrance to the opera house, 1916

lier. Reached via a corridor through the office building, the Metropolitan offered an elegant foyer that overlooked the auditorium through plate-glass windows. The interior also contained art-glass windows designed by Louis Millet, a Chicago artist best known for his work with Louis Sullivan. The auditorium itself was nearly square, allowing its eighteen hundred seats to be arranged in a wide horseshoe (with two balconies) that put almost everyone close to the stage.

The decor appears to have been reasonably subdued, with ivory, gold, and brown tones predominating and with decorative plasterwork providing most of the ornamental pizzazz. The stage and its equipment were top of the line, as were the creature comforts, which included unusually wide seats and a primitive air-conditioning system that operated by circulating water over blocks of ice. Because of its size and amenities, the Metropolitan from the outset enjoyed a reputation as St. Paul's classiest theater.

Opening night on December 29, 1890, attracted a capacity crowd, which was subjected to the usual oratorical punishment before seeing the light opera *Robin Hood*. One newspaper noted that the "beautiful women for whom St. Paul is justly celebrated were to be seen at their best and fairest." No mention was made of any handsome men. Governor William Merriam was the chief notable on hand, and the guest list formed a roster of Summit Avenue blue bloods of the sort F. Scott Fitzgerald (not yet born) would immortalize in *The Great Gatsby*.

For the next thirty years the Metropolitan was to be St. Paul's premier opera house, featuring Shakespearean dramas and other high-class entertainment. Occasionally there were less exalted forms of amusement, such as pictures of the Jeffries-Sharkey heavyweight fight shown in 1900. By the 1920s the Metropolitan's days as an opera house were largely over, and it became a movie theater. Competition from such new downtown movie houses as the Capitol, along with the devastating impact of the depression, eventually caught up with the old opera house, and in 1936 the Metropolitan was demolished. The American National Bank Building later took up the entire block where the opera house had stood.

Seating arrangement of the opera house, 1890

FIRST FREE (FREE WILL) BAPTIST CHURCH

Northwest corner of Fifteenth Street and Nicollet Avenue,
Minneapolis. Long and Kees. 1891–ca. 1930.

Free Will Baptist Church, about 1904

During their long partnership, Franklin Long and Frederick Kees produced a number of powerful buildings inspired by the work of H. H. Richardson, including the Minneapolis municipal building and Long's own house (1894, extant) near Lowry Hill. But few if any of the firm's Richardsonian buildings were better than this compact, tautly composed church, which achieved a clarity of form and a command of detail worthy of the master himself.

The First Free Baptist Church was founded, with six members, in 1851. The congregation built a church on Washington Avenue in 1855 and then moved in 1873 to a much larger Gothic-style building at Marquette Avenue and Seventh Street. Like other downtown congregations, the Free Baptists soon saw their church hemmed in by commercial development, and in 1890 they decided to sell out and move south. The two hundred members of the congregation began worshiping in their new church in early 1891, although it was not formally dedicated until June 28 of that year.

Built largely of Lake Superior brownstone, the church proper was square in plan with gables to either side of a corner tower. This tower, which was decisively incorporated into the main mass of the church and ended in an open belfry, gained a strong sense of vertical thrust from rounded stone piers attached to its sides. Richardson had designed a very similar tower for the city hall in Albany, New York, in 1882. Beneath the church's gables were large flat-bottomed wheel windows defined by bold arches of smooth stone. The main entrance, off to one side of the tower, was reached through a triple arcade sheltering an inset porch with exquisite iron gates and railings. Seamlessly integrated into the overall design of the church was a two-story wing.

The Akron-plan interior offered about one thousand seats on the main floor, gallery, and in an adjoining conference room that could be thrown open during services. Stained-glass windows and geometric stencilwork on the walls provided most of the decoration. There was also a large organ directly behind the pulpit. The wing off the auditorium included a dining room and kitchen, Sunday school rooms, and a pastor's study. A pamphlet marking the congregation's fiftieth anniversary in 1901 noted that "this edifice,—artistic, convenient and commodious, may well be the permanent home of our people in Minneapolis." It was, but not for long. Around 1914 the congregation appears to have disbanded, since the church ceased to appear in city directories after that date. Although the church building was scheduled for demolition, it remained standing until at least 1922 when it was occupied by something called the Unity Society of Applied Christianity. It is not clear exactly when the church came down, but atlases show it was gone by about 1930.

Entrance to the church, about 1891

TEMPLES AND PALACES

DURING THE CITY BEAUTIFUL era, templelike buildings inspired by Greek, Roman, and Renaissance architecture were a common sight in downtown St. Paul and Minneapolis. Banks especially favored this classical pose, although other kinds of buildings—from homes and churches to hospitals—also adopted the temple format. These buildings generally were quite small and provided a nice counterpoint to the dark, wildly decorated structures of the 1880s. Virtually all of these turn-of-the-century temples and palaces have vanished.

MINNEAPOLIS

GUARANTY SAVINGS AND LOAN
ASSOCIATION BUILDING
517 Marquette Avenue, ca. 1895–ca. 1925 (new facade).

FRIENDS' MEETING HOUSE
Southeast corner of First
Avenue South and Fourteenth
Street, ca. 1895–1988.

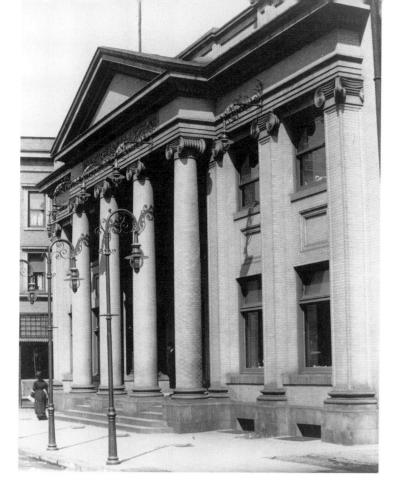

MINNEAPOLIS GAS AND LIGHT
COMPANY BUILDING
16–20 Seventh Street South, Long and Long, 1903–ca. 30.

MIKRO KODESH SYNAGOGUE
720 Oak Park Avenue, ca. 1905–34.

ST. PAUL

STATE SAVINGS BANK
93 East Fourth Street, Reed and
Stem, 1907–29.

FIRST NATIONAL BANK
331 Minnesota Street, Louis Lockwood,
1908–67.

EMPRESS (LYCEUM) THEATER
479 Wabasha Street, Buechner and Orth,
1911–78.

ST. PAUL FIRE AND MARINE
INSURANCE COMPANY BUILDING
111 West Fifth Street, Louis Lockwood,
1909–ca. 59.

VISIONS OF CHANGE: THE TWENTIETH CENTURY

TRAFFIC CHANGE

ooking back on the previous century, the *Minneapolis Journal* in May 1904 found a less than impressive architectural environment:

> There was a day in Minneapolis when a store was anything which would protect a stock of goods from the weather and a dwelling house was a collection of lumber, plaster, paint and hardware combined after the individual ideas of the carpenter or owner. A few good buildings were put up in the early days; but in the excusable haste to house a population which was growing most extraordinarily and to care for the commercial needs of both city and country, architectural principles were very commonly forgotten or thrust aside.

> Later this condition was aggravated by the operations of speculators who built solely for profit and without any notion of present honor or of permanently benefitting the community. To them Minneapolis is indebted for sundry rows of tawdry tenements and a few shaky business structures which still dot the city.[1]

But a new vision was now at work in Minneapolis; the *Journal* proclaimed:

> With the accumulation of wealth and the general diffusion of culture and the broadening of ideas there has been a steady growth of attention to architecture; a development which has now reached such a stage that there is a strong public sentiment in favor of good building, whether it be in the public edifices, commercial structures or in the home. . . .

> Minneapolis stands now for good, substantial, architecturally correct buildings, and the present state of mind of the city is such that it is safe to predict that the next ten years will see a wonderful change in the general aspect of the place.

The *Journal's* expectation of architectural change was borne out in the decades that followed, but not always with "wonderful" results. Created out of a wilderness in the nineteenth century, downtown St. Paul and Minneapolis almost completely remade themselves in the twentieth. Inevitably this change came at the expense of historic buildings. Before 1900 downtown development had occurred mainly on undeveloped

Seventh Street South, Minneapolis, looking toward Hennepin, about 1915

sites or on sites containing only crude structures. But by the turn of the century both downtowns were densely built up, and to construct a new building on a prime site usually required tearing down something old.

The *Journal*, reflecting the certainty and optimism of the City Beautiful era, welcomed such destruction as a sure sign of progress. The dignity, order, and permanence of a classically inspired architecture, the newspaper believed, would displace the chaotic sprawl inherited from the nineteenth century. As an exemplar of this new architectural order, the *Journal* cited Harry Jones's elegant Cream of Wheat Building, completed in 1904 at First Avenue North and Fifth Street. The Cream of Wheat Building, the newspaper predicted, "will set a style which it will be diffi-

cult for future builders to depart from." There was similar thinking in St. Paul where Mayor Andrew R. Kiefer predicted, apparently with a straight face, that his city would one day become "an American Dresden."[2]

The fluid realities of American urbanism, however, contradicted this dream of a timeless architecture. In the nineteenth century, St. Paul and Minneapolis had been shaped by the demands of a growth-oriented market economy and the ceaseless pressure of real estate speculation. Similar forces continued at work in the twentieth century, abetted by new agents of change, most notably the automobile. These forces were far more potent than the *Journal* imagined, and there was a profound irony in the newspaper's belief that Minneapolis could achieve a sense of beauty

Seven Corners in St. Paul, showing midday traffic congestion, about 1935

and permanence in its architecture only by wiping away all traces of the past. Unfortunately this attitude, in one form or another, came to dominate American city planning for much of the twentieth century. The dream cities that emerged from such thinking varied with the taste of the times, so that the *Journal's* vision of a City Beautiful eventually gave way to more modern fantasies of isolated towers, immense green spaces, and endless freeways. The bottom line, however, was always the same: creating this new world would require vast acts of urban destruction.

With nothing to protect them, old buildings in most American cities stood little chance of surviving once market forces began to act on

Traffic signal installed in downtown St. Paul, about 1923

them. This was to be true until the passage in 1976 of federal tax incentives for renovating historic buildings. In many instances, however, the incentives came too late. The Cream of Wheat Building is a case in point. Its elegant classicism proved as ephemeral as everything else in downtown Minneapolis, and in 1939 the building— once described by the *Journal* as "a thing of beauty, attractive, harmonious and fitting"—was torn down. It had stood for only thirty-five years.[3]

THE FIRST THREE decades of the twentieth century were a period of growth and consolidation in both downtowns, which remained the undisputed hubs of their communities. Street-level density reached its ultimate level during these years, with buildings crowded tightly together on almost every downtown block. Yet while there was plenty of construction and demolition, change tended to occur incrementally rather than in great destructive bouts of urban renewal.[4]

The rate of population growth remained impressive, particularly in Minneapolis, which established once and for all its position as the dominant twin. Between 1900 and 1920 the city's population nearly doubled, from 203,000 to 381,000. By 1930 Minneapolis had 464,000 people, close to its ultimate size of 522,000 recorded twenty years later.[5]

St. Paul's population, meanwhile, grew more slowly during those thirty years. A local newspaper had contended just before the turn of the century that St. Paul was destined to become the "chief metropolis of an empire" while Chicago and other lesser places in the Midwest would "sink back into their oozy malodorous slime." But instead of overtaking Chicago, or even Minneapolis, St. Paul's population showed more modest growth between 1900 and 1930, rising from 163,000 to 272,000. St. Paul did not reach its peak population of 313,000 until 1960.[6]

Population growth expanded the boundaries of both downtowns, although their central business

*East Seventh Street,
St. Paul, looking east from
Wabasha, about 1914*

districts did not move much. In Minneapolis, Nicollet Avenue between about Fourth and Tenth streets continued to be the heart of the city, paralleled by a growing entertainment district along Hennepin and a banking-financial district on Marquette. St. Paul never organized itself quite so neatly, but the area bounded roughly by Fourth, Seventh, St. Peter, and Robert streets gradually solidified as the city's main business district.[7]

Other parts of the downtowns, however, began to take on new characters. In Minneapolis commerce and manufacturing spread west toward Loring Park and south along the area from about Portland to Tenth avenues, displacing many old houses. Meanwhile, the warehouse district continued to grow north of Hennepin. The first two decades of the century saw construction of numerous warehouses in this area, including the

magnificent Butler Brothers Warehouse (later Butler Square) at Sixth Street and First Avenue North, designed by Harry Jones and completed in 1908. Further commercial expansion occurred on the downtown's western fringe, along such streets as Harmon Place, where the city's first automobile dealers located as early as 1907. Left stagnating behind was the old Gateway District where new construction virtually stopped. By 1930 the Gateway was firmly established as "hobohemia."[8]

St. Paul's compact downtown had less room for growth during these thirty years. Even so auto dealers and other smaller businesses gradually pushed into an area west of Rice Park that had once been largely residential. To the east, in Lowertown, a flurry of warehouse construction replaced buildings dating from the 1870s and 1880s. Meanwhile St. Paul's version of the Gateway—the old Third Street commercial district—

continued to deteriorate, leaving it ripe for clearance. This process began in 1928 with the construction of Kellogg Boulevard.

As commercial development spread past its old boundaries, housing units were either displaced or became less desirable. By 1930 only the Lowry Hill area of Minneapolis and the Summit Hill section of St. Paul continued to offer upper-class living close to downtown. The decline of some residential neighborhoods came with astonishing speed. The Oak Lake neighborhood in Minneapolis began to lose its cachet as early as 1900, largely as a result of nearby industrial development but also because of an influx of Jewish families. Ten years later blacks started to locate nearby, and white flight began in earnest. By 1927 the well-to-do had departed en masse, and the neighborhood was considered a slum. Similar trends became evident in St. Paul. By 1920 the metamorphosis of the eastern part of Lowertown from a high-class residential neighborhood into an industrial-railroad district was complete. Meanwhile the old mansions along College Avenue and north of the new State Capitol evolved into rooming houses as their owners moved to better parts of town.[9]

THE CITY BEAUTIFUL remained a tantalizing ideal in St. Paul and Minneapolis during these years, but reality had a nasty way of contravening visions of urban grandeur. Besides coping with the inevitable budget squeeze brought on by the demands of a swelling population, Minneapolis had to face the problem of municipal corruption. Scandal erupted during the notorious administration of Mayor Albert Alonzo ("Doc") Ames, whose conduct attracted the attention of muckraker Lincoln Steffens. In a 1903 article for *McClure's Magazine*, Steffens described the "Shame of Minneapolis," unveiling such curiosities as the "Big Mitt Ledger," used for recording a variety of payoffs and kickbacks to dishonest city officials. Claiming that the city's elite was too preoccupied

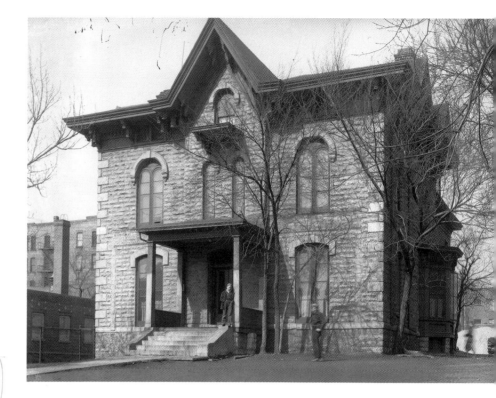

with making money to worry about "public business," Steffens found Minneapolis to be governed by "loafers, saloon keepers, gamblers, criminals, and the thriftless poor of all nationalities."[10]

In St. Paul, where really spectacular municipal misdoing did not surface until the gangster era of the 1930s, the problem was not so much corruption as it was the age-old desire to keep taxes low. Government displayed an immense capacity for indifference; the city and county spent so little for so many years that basic civic responsibilities—such as maintaining public buildings—sometimes were ignored. In early 1900, for instance, the city's building inspector was forced to condemn the forty-three-year-old Ramsey County jail after discovering that its bulging stone walls were being held together by eighteen "hog chains" and little else. Low levels of public spending characterized St. Paul government for much of the twentieth century, and this parsimony frustrated the high ideals advanced by advocates of the City Beautiful.[11]

Morris Lamprey house, 137 West College Avenue, St. Paul, 1937

Despite such problems, the period from 1900 to 1930 saw the construction of important civic buildings in both downtowns. In St. Paul these included a new Ramsey County jail (1903) at Fourth and St. Peter streets; the second St. Paul Armory (1904), a grim stone fortress at Sixth and Exchange streets; and the St. Paul Auditorium (1906), designed by Allen H. Stem and notable for its interior stencilwork and flexible floor plan. All three buildings, which replaced earlier structures, are gone. The Minnesota Historical Society building (1917), designed by Clarence Johnston, has survived, although it began a new life in 1992 as home to the state's judiciary. Still standing as well is the St. Paul Public Library and Hill Reference Library (1917), one of the finest public buildings of any era in St. Paul. A popular downtown recreational facility, the Harriet Island baths on the Mississippi River, also opened in

ABOVE:
St. Paul Armory,
about 1905

RIGHT:
Harriet Island baths (left)
and pavilion (right),
about 1905

St. Paul at the turn of the century. The baths attracted more than two hundred thousand people a year until about 1920, when pollution forced everyone out of the water.

Meanwhile, in 1906, Minneapolis finally saw completion of its mammoth City Hall–Hennepin County Courthouse after nineteen years of planning and construction. Like most other public buildings in Minneapolis, the city hall–courthouse was built on a site that allowed no room for a mall, plaza, or other ceremonial space. The architects initially had hoped to create a large open space along Fourth Street in front of the building, but nothing ever came of their plans or various subsequent schemes. Over the years the city hall–courthouse also suffered from indifferent treatment, and some of its most memorably overwrought spaces, including the city council chambers and main courtroom, were

destroyed by remodeling. The completion of this building left little need for either the old Hennepin County Courthouse (1857) or the old Minneapolis City Hall (1873) at Bridge Square, and both had disappeared by 1914.[12]

Other important public buildings completed during this time included the first Minneapolis Auditorium (1905–73), built as part of the Northwestern National Life Insurance Company's new headquarters at Eleventh Street and Nicollet Avenue; the Minneapolis Armory (1907) at Lyndale Avenue and Kenwood Parkway; the U.S. Post Office (1915) on Washington Avenue South; Gateway Park and Pavilion (1915); the Minneapolis Institute of Arts (1915), which was the only Twin Cities building designed by McKim, Mead, and White; and Cass Gilbert's Federal Reserve Bank (1921) at Fifth and Marquette. Of all these buildings and places, only the post office, later used as a federal office building, and the Institute of Arts remained in anything like their original form in 1991.[13]

First Minneapolis Auditorium, about 1905

TALL OFFICE BUILDINGS, spacious banking halls, and large department stores dominated commercial architecture of this era. In Minneapolis the drive to build higher was frustrated for many years by the one-hundred-foot height limit imposed in 1890. Later raised to 125 feet, or about twelve stories, this cap remained in effect until 1909 when the Radisson Hotel managed to reach fourteen stories. Five years later came the nineteen-story, 252-foot-high First National-Soo Line Building (extant) at Fifth and Marquette. Its lofty appearance apparently caused fear and trembling in local real estate circles, and a twelve-story limit was quickly reimposed in late 1914 at the request of the Minneapolis Civic and Commerce Association.[14]

The Soo Line Building reigned over the city's skyline until 1929 when it was eclipsed first by the twenty-seven-story Rand (later Dain) Tower (extant) and then by that fabulous skyscraper-cum-obelisk, the Foshay Tower (extant), which at thirty-two stories remained the city's tallest building for almost half a century. The last big skyscraper to appear in Minneapolis before the Great Depression was the twenty-six-story Bell Telephone Building (extant), completed in 1931. Evidence of Minneapolis' experiment in downtown height control was long visible on Second Avenue South, which featured an array of twelve-story buildings dating from the early twentieth century.

St. Paul, growing much more slowly than Minneapolis, saw fewer additions to its skyline in the early years of the century. The thirteen-story Pioneer Building of 1889 was finally outdone in 1915 when the Merchants Bank Building (extant) went up across Robert Street. This sixteen-story building, cleaned in 1989 to reveal its sparkling facade of glazed white brick, contained a magnificent neoclassic banking hall, long since remodeled out of existence. The First National Bank of St. Paul eventually absorbed the Mer-

The Soo Line Building (center) dominates the horizon, about 1924. The Gateway Pavilion is across the street from the Pick-Nicollet Hotel, which replaced the Nicollet House.

Lobby of the Merchants Bank, about 1915

chants Bank and completed a thirty-two-story skyscraper next door in 1930–31. Surmounted by a huge lighted sign that animated the night sky, the First National Bank kept its place as St. Paul's tallest building for more than fifty years.

Numerous less lofty office buildings appeared during the first three decades of the century, and a surprisingly large number are gone. St. Paul has lost the eight-story Manhattan Building (1911) on Fifth between Robert and Jackson; the seven-story Northwestern Telephone Exchange Building (1912, 1917) at Fifth and Cedar; and the twelve-story Builders Exchange (1924) at Sixth and Jackson. The ranks of the vanished in Minneapolis included the eight-story Studebaker Building (ca. 1910) at Sixth Street and Second Avenue South; the twelve-story Builders Exchange (1918) at 609 Second Avenue South; and the fourteen-story Northwestern National Bank Building (1929) at Sixth and Marquette.[15]

Although banks as early as the 1880s had incorporated their banking halls into office buildings and did so again after 1910, there was a period in between when they took a different approach. During this short-lived era, from about 1895 to 1910, financial institutions favored the bank-in-a-temple, constructing relatively small, free-standing banking halls modeled on the classic architecture of Greece, Rome, and the Renaissance. The Farmers and Mechanics Bank (1893, enlarged 1908) at 111 Fourth Street South in Minneapolis appears to have been the first such temple of finance in the Twin Cities. A variant—the bank as miniature Renaissance palazzo—also appeared in 1893 when the Nicollet National Bank opened its doors a block away on Fourth Street.[16]

Outstanding examples of temple or palazzo banks in Minneapolis included the Northwestern National Bank (1904) near Fourth and Marquette and the First National Bank (1906) at Fifth and Marquette. The Northwestern offered an Ionic portico but only a modest degree of classical ornament. The First National was larger and showier, bypassing the Ionic in favor of the more elaborate Corinthian order. St. Paul, always a bit less flamboyant in its commercial architecture than Minneapolis, completed its first temple bank in 1907—the First National Bank at Fourth and Minnesota. The State Savings Bank, half a block away on Fourth, also appeared in full Ionic regalia in 1907. Only one of these temple banks—the Farmers and Mechanics—still stood in 1991. After serving for years as the home of Schiek's Restaurant, the building in 1988 became a nightclub featuring topless dancing and pay-as-you-go mud wrestling, presumably done in a restrained classical manner.

The period from 1900 to 1920 developed into a great era for department stores. In Minneapolis, George Dayton in 1901 opened a store at Seventh and Nicollet that eventually became the city's largest. E. E. Atkinson's new store, across Nicollet from Dayton's, opened two years later in an elegant four-story building. Meanwhile, older stores, such as Donaldson's Glass Block and S. E. Olson's (later Powers), built large additions. Donaldson's began to expand and remodel in 1903, and by 1910 the store had acquired 350,000 square feet of floor space spread over half a block. Powers rebuilt its store on Nicollet in 1905–06. Of these stores, only Dayton's remains in its original building (designed by Charles Sedgwick in 1901–02 and restored to something like its original exterior appearance in 1990). In St. Paul the two largest department stores constructed in this era, the Emporium (1911, 1915) and the Golden Rule (1915), faced each other across Seventh Street at Robert. Both buildings remained in 1991, but the original classical facade of the Emporium (later the Metro Square Building) disappeared beneath a modern glass sheathing.[17]

At least two fine examples of a relatively new building type—the multistory shopping arcade—appeared at this time. Small arcades, generally of only one story, had been built in the Twin Cities beginning in the 1880s as part of larger retail or office buildings, but it was not until after the turn of the century that large, self-contained arcade buildings became fashionable. In St. Paul the best known was the Bremer (or St. Paul) Arcade at Seventh and Robert, completed in 1916. At that time a three-story, skylit section was added to an existing (ca. 1885) building. Later the Bremer was completely altered inside and out. The Twin Cities' finest arcade, the Loeb (1914, gone) at Fifth and Hennepin in Minneapolis, had an unusual L-shaped plan and contained four (later five) levels of shops.[18]

THE EARLY YEARS of the century also saw an important structural innovation—the concrete frame—that proved to be especially suitable for warehouses. Before about 1910 most Twin Cities warehouses were constructed around a frame of massive timbers that would be slow to burn in the event of fire. Iron or steel columns were sometimes used with timber beams in a system known as "mill construction." Late in the nineteenth century, however, architects and engineers in the United States and abroad began experimenting with a new kind of construction using a frame of concrete reinforced with steel bars. Concrete framing had many advantages: it was stronger than mill construction, it allowed for extremely large windows so that interiors could be made brighter, and it was fireproof.[19]

New York engineer Ernest Ransome patented one of the first concrete-frame structural systems in the United States in 1903. Later refinements in technology permitted a flat slab of concrete to be substituted for beams and girders. A Minneapolis engineer, Claude A. P. Turner, patented a highly efficient column-and-slab structural system for concrete in 1908.[20]

Perhaps because of this local connection, builders used concrete framing extensively in the Twin Cities during the first two decades of the century. In fact it appears that by 1915 the Twin Cities had the nation's greatest concentration of tall concrete-frame buildings. Concrete framing was even more popular for warehouses, the first example appearing in the Twin Cities around 1905. Grain elevators and other industrial structures, many of which survived into the 1990s, also employed this type of construction.[21]

A number of important concrete-frame industrial buildings are gone, most notably the huge Janney, Semple, Hill and Company Warehouse (ca. 1916). The firm of Kees and Colburn designed this block-long, six-story-high warehouse located at First Street and Second Avenue South in Minneapolis. Despite the creation of historic districts that gave some protection to old ware-houses in both cities, a few were lost every decade. In 1989, for instance, the Nicols, Dean and Gregg building (1906)—an early and especially handsome concrete-frame warehouse at 205 East Eighth Street in St. Paul—was razed by the owner at the very moment that preservationists were working to nominate it for the National Register of Historic Places.[22]

FOR THE TRAVELER the early 1900s offered new railroad stations, showrooms and garages for the increasingly popular automobile, and an array of just-opened hotels in both cities. Many bridges also appeared, including one of national significance completed in 1909. This rather unprepossessing structure, which carried Lafayette Street across the Soo Line tracks in St. Paul, was one of the first bridges anywhere to use Turner's flat-slab concrete structural system. It has vanished, but

Janney, Semple, Hill Warehouse, about 1916

other elegant concrete bridges of this period—such as the Third Avenue (1916) in Minneapolis and the Robert Street (1926) in St. Paul—remain as impressive as ever.[23]

Unfortunately the new railroad depots, both designed by Chicago architect Charles Frost, lacked a similar degree of elegance. For the Great Northern Station (1914) in Minneapolis, Frost produced a standard Beaux-Arts pile, ponderous but nonetheless impressive. He located it directly across Hennepin Avenue from the city's old Union Depot, which was torn down soon thereafter. Although not a lively design, the Great Northern Station succeeded as a City Beautiful object, nicely terminating the view north on Nicollet Avenue. The depot was razed in 1978. Frost's new Union Depot (1923, extant) in St. Paul was larger than its Minneapolis counterpart and also more somber, with nary a hint of ornament or color to ease the severity of its overweening Doric colonnade.

In 1907 another transportation monument—the Selby Avenue streetcar tunnel in St. Paul—was completed. The tunnel solved an old problem, allowing streetcars to ascend the steep Summit Hill without having to resort to cables or counterweights. The tunnel closed in 1958 when the last streetcars ran.

Automobile garages and showrooms began to appear around 1900, and many were elegantly appointed in keeping with the look of the times. The Pence Auto Company garage (1909, extant but remodeled) at Eighth and Hennepin in Minneapolis, probably the first big garage in either downtown, was said to be one of the largest in the country. Auto dealers soon began to cluster around the downtown fringes in new two- or three-story buildings. The Frederick Murphy and Company showroom (1913) at Thirteenth Street and Hennepin Avenue in Minneapolis was especially urbane, displaying three floors of vehicles behind huge plate-glass windows. The automobile's popularity brought about an abrupt drop in the number of livery and boarding stables. As late as 1905, there were still seventy stables in Minneapolis and forty in St. Paul. By 1930 only three remained in each city.[24]

An unprecedented wave of hotel construction took place during the first two decades of the century, particularly in Minneapolis. Although none of these establishments compared in size or splendor to the grand hotels of New York and Chicago, such hotels as the Radisson and the Saint Paul offered superb accommodations. New hotels appeared largely as a response to changing client demands. The great downtown hotels of the 1880s—such as the West and Ryan—had been built at a time when a bath with each room was considered a luxury. By 1900, however, this was regarded as a standard amenity, and a new generation of hotels began to provide it. Hotel construction also followed trends in downtown development, especially in Minneapolis where most of the major hotels built after 1900 were south of Sixth Street.

Among the numerous Minneapolis hotels of this period, some catering primarily to long-term residents and others designed for the transient trade, were the Plaza (1906) at Hennepin and Kenwood Parkway; the Radisson (1909) on Seventh Street between Nicollet and Hennepin; the Dyckman (1909) on Sixth between Nicollet and Hennepin; the Andrews (1911) at Fourth and Hennepin; the Curtis (1905, 1911) at Tenth Street and Third Avenue South; the Leamington (1912), across Third from the Curtis; the Hastings (1912) at Twelfth and Hawthorne; the Sheridan (ca. 1920) at Eleventh and Marquette; the Pick-Nicollet (1924), replacing the historic Nicollet House at Hennepin and Washington; and the Ritz (1924) at Washington and Second Avenue South. The Nicollet, the last survivor among this group of hotels, fell to the wrecker in 1991.

St. Paul's one and only top-of-the-line hotel from this period was the Saint Paul, which in

1910 replaced the old Windsor Hotel at the corner of Fifth and St. Peter. Most of the other new St. Paul hotels seemed quite plain, including the Boardman (1902) at Ninth and Wabasha, the Frederic (1903) at Fifth and Cedar, the Wolf (1916) at St. Peter and Exchange, and the Lowry (ca. 1920) at Fourth and Wabasha. The Saint Paul, elegantly restored in 1979, remains in use as a hotel, and the Lowry became an apartment building. The others are gone.

AN ABUNDANCE OF theaters also sprang up to serve the growing population. St. Paul's entertainment district concentrated along Wabasha and Seventh streets, while in Minneapolis Hennepin Avenue (and a short section of Seventh Street nearby) emerged as the Upper Midwest's version of Broadway. By 1916, according to one count, at least twenty-five theaters were operat-

ing in downtown Minneapolis and seventeen in downtown St. Paul. Many had been built or significantly remodeled since the turn of the century. They ranged from legitimate playhouses to gaudy vaudeville palaces to crude nickelodeons for motion pictures. The 1920s produced another surge of new theaters, including two magnificent movie palaces—the Capitol (later Paramount) on Seventh Street between St. Peter and Wabasha in St. Paul and the incomparable Minnesota (later Radio City) at Ninth and LaSalle in Minneapolis. Both have vanished.[25]

Minneapolis theaters included the first Orpheum (1904), 25 Seventh Street South, an eighteen-hundred-seat vaudeville house; the New Garrick (1907), 40 Seventh Street South, another vaudeville house; the Gayety (1909), 101 Washington Avenue North, offering burlesque; the Crystal, 305 Hennepin, said to have the largest movie screen in the Twin Cities when it opened in 1909; the Shubert (1910), 20 Seventh Street North, which started as a playhouse and later evolved into a movie theater under various names; the New Palace (1914), 414 Hennepin, the city's largest vaudeville house with two thousand seats; and the Strand (1915), 36 Seventh Street South, transformed in 1930 into one of the city's great art-deco monuments, the Forum Cafeteria. All except the Shubert, vacant and marooned on an otherwise empty block, are gone.

New St. Paul theaters included the Star (1901), on Seventh near Jackson, for many years the city's most celebrated burlesque house; the first Orpheum (1906), at Fifth and St. Peter, a large and elegant vaudeville house; the Princess (1910), 21 East Seventh Street, another vaudeville house; the Shubert (1910), on Exchange near Wabasha, later known as the World and as

ABOVE LEFT: *New Palace Theatre, 1929*

BOTTOM LEFT: *New Palace Theatre interior*

Orpheum Theater, St. Paul, about 1910

the home of Garrison Keillor's "Prairie Home Companion" radio show; the Alhambra (1911), 16 East Seventh Street, which appears to have been an early movie theater; the Empress (1911), 479 Wabasha, a vaudeville house that ended its days as a porno theater; and the New Palace (later Orpheum), completed in 1917. The World, beautifully renovated in 1986, and the vacant Orpheum were the only survivors in 1991.

By the 1920s, as motion pictures grew in popularity, lavish new theaters specifically designed for movies began to appear. The largest of these movie palaces, such as the Capitol and the Minnesota, also came equipped with full stages, orchestra pits, and other traditional features, because live entertainment was usually offered along with the movie. The second Orpheum (1921) and the State (1922), both in Minneapolis, were the only surviving 1920s-vintage downtown theaters in 1991. The State, however, was beautifully restored and renovated in 1991, bringing at

least a little old-time glitter back to Hennepin Avenue.[26]

As commercial development drove up land prices, churches began moving out of both downtowns. Many of the cities' older congregations—such as Westminster Presbyterian, Hennepin Avenue United Methodist, and Plymouth Congregational in Minneapolis and House of Hope Presbyterian and the Cathedral in St. Paul—had built large churches in the nineteenth century on prime downtown sites. By 1900, or even earlier in some cases, these churches had become too small, while the land they occupied was so valuable that their congregations could not resist selling out and using the profits to build larger churches elsewhere.

The great migration began as early as 1895 when Westminster Presbyterian sold its twelve-year-old church at Seventh and Nicollet to George Dayton and built a much larger church

Swedish Tabernacle, 1934

standing in 1991. But there have been at least two notable losses—First Covenant Church (the Swedish Tabernacle) of 1904 in St. Paul and the Wesley Temple Building of 1928 in Minneapolis. The Swedish Tabernacle was at Edgerton Street and Minnehaha Avenue on St. Paul's East Side. Double towered, with a rounded central gable and vaguely baroque detailing, the tabernacle was a true curiosity, unlike any other church in the Twin Cities. It was designed by Didrik Omeyer and Martin Thori, whose inspiration for this peculiar building is unknown. The church, said to have excellent acoustics, was razed in 1963.[28]

The twelve-story Wesley Temple Building, at 123 East Grant Street, was also a curiosity—the Twin Cities' only attempt at a "sky church." Skyscraper churches enjoyed a brief vogue in the 1920s and were based on the idea that one could serve God and Mammon in the same building. The Chicago Temple (1924) emerged as the prototype for this sort of office building-church. The original grandiose design of the Wesley Temple Building called for something along similar lines, with office wings flanking a central church tower

(1899, extant) at Twelfth and Nicollet. Plymouth Congregational moved from the central part of downtown in 1907, Hennepin Avenue United Methodist in about 1910. The same trend was evident in St. Paul, although some of the city's biggest churches made their moves only after 1910. House of Hope Presbyterian Church moved to Summit Avenue in 1914, leaving its old church (gone) at Fifth and Exchange streets. The huge new St. Paul Cathedral—the largest church structure in the Twin Cities and one of the largest in America—opened in 1915, a year after the old Cathedral Church at Sixth and St. Peter had been razed. A number of other downtown congregations did not relocate in new churches until the 1920s.[27]

Most of the big churches constructed in the Twin Cities between 1900 and 1930 remained

RIGHT: *Wesley Temple Building, 1929*

nearly thirty stories high. But this audacious plan had to be scaled back, and only a twelve-story office building, used in part for church administrative purposes, was built before the Great Depression set in. This handsome building, which featured some exceptionally fine terra cotta, was demolished in 1986 to make way for the new Minneapolis Convention Center.[29]

Churches were not the only institutions that built at this time. Fraternal and social organizations such as the Masons, Elks, YMCA, and YWCA also felt the need for new, larger quarters. While a few of these buildings—such as the Minnesota Club (1915) in St. Paul and the Minneapolis Club (1908)—were still used for their original purpose decades later, many other institutional buildings disappeared. St. Paul, for example, lost the old YMCA (1907) at Ninth and Cedar, the Elks Hall (1908, rebuilt ca. 1912) on Washington Street overlooking Rice Park, the Masonic Temple (1910) at Sixth Street and Smith Avenue, and the old YWCA (1912) on West Fifth Street. In Minneapolis the Elks Hall (1913) at Seventh Street and Second Avenue

ABOVE:
YWCA, Minneapolis, 1929

LEFT:
Masonic Temple, St. Paul, about 1928

South and the YMCA (1919) at Ninth and LaSalle were still standing in 1991, but both buildings had been significantly remodeled for other uses. Minneapolis, however, lost one of its finest institutional buildings of this period—the beautifully designed YWCA (1929) at 1130 Nicollet Avenue.

MUCH OF THE new housing built in and around the two downtowns after 1900 took the form of apartments. "The tendency of the age in building is toward concentration," a St. Paul newspaper noted in 1907, "and the popularity of the flat [apartment] building seems to increase rather than diminish." Apartments also became popular downtown as improved public transportation opened up more distant areas for single-family housing. In Minneapolis the growing apartment house district south of Grant Street filled with three-story walk-up buildings. Most were straightforward affairs with some sort of ornamental front and walls of common brick to the sides and rear. A few were more elaborate, such as Harry Jones's wonderfully sophisticated Imperial Apart-

ments (ca. 1900) at Grant and LaSalle. The Imperial is gone, but many other apartment buildings of its era remain, often as condominiums.[30]

High-rise apartment buildings, which had made their first appearance in the Twin Cities about 1890, became increasingly popular after the turn of the century. Some assumed the form of elegant apartment hotels, such as the six-story Groveland (1927, extant) in Minneapolis. Others, like the ten-story St. Michael Apartments (1916, gone) at 512 St. Peter in St. Paul, seem to have been built for a less wealthy clientele.

A few new single-family houses appeared in such exclusive near-downtown neighborhoods as Lowry Hill in Minneapolis and lower Summit Avenue in St. Paul. One of the most splendid of these was the Frederic W. Clifford house (1905) at 325 Clifton Avenue in Minneapolis, designed by Harry Jones. The Clifford house is gone, as are at least two other large Tudor-style houses that once stood nearby—the William H. Dunwoody house (1905) at 104 Groveland Terrace and the C. D. Velie house (1906) at 225 Clifton. In St. Paul only about a dozen single-family houses,

Imperial Apartments, 1894

Velie house, about 1910

all of which survive in one form or another, were built along lower Summit Avenue between 1900 and 1930. But many expensive new houses appeared in nearby neighborhoods such as Crocus Hill where land was more readily available than on Summit. Meanwhile the middle class spread out along the streetcar lines as new residential tracts opened.[31]

For the poor, little changed. They continued to live in squalid conditions in ramshackle old buildings around the downtown fringes or in isolated pockets of poverty such as Swede Hollow and Bohemian Flats. The situation appears to have been especially desperate in St. Paul where a notoriously inattentive city government had let the city's housing stock deteriorate for years. This predicament came to light in a devastating report

issued in 1917 by the Amherst H. Wilder Charity and its impassioned new director of social services, Carol Aronovici. The report included photographs of children sitting in garbage-strewn yards or playing by crude outhouses that lined Phalen Creek. The city passed a long-overdue housing ordinance in response to Aronovici's report, but almost twenty years later, in 1936, *Fortune* magazine still called St. Paul's slums "among the worst in the land."[32]

DRAMATIC CHANGES OCCURRED in the Twin Cities architectural community after the turn of the century. The day of the master builder, at least for important commissions, had passed, and formally trained architects, capable of working skillfully with classical forms, rose to dominance.

At the same time, some leading designers, especially in St. Paul, left for opportunities elsewhere. Cass Gilbert's departure for the East Coast reflected his growing national reputation, but other important St. Paul figures from the 1880s—such as William Willcox, William Castner, Charles Joy, and George Wirth—moved away primarily for economic reasons as work became scarce following the depression of 1893. Several notable Minneapolis architects, including William H. Dennis, also left by 1900. Meanwhile death claimed many members of the older generation of master builders. Isaac Hodgson, Jr., died in 1909, Edward P. Bassford and Franklin B. Long in 1912, and Charles Haglin in 1921.[33]

Still, many familiar names continued to appear well into the new century. In Minneapolis, LeRoy Buffington remained on the scene until his death in 1931, although his practice declined sharply after 1900. Frederick Kees, in partnership with Serenus Colburn after 1900, continued in practice until 1921. This firm, one of the city's most versatile, designed everything from theaters to office buildings to houses. Harry Jones also remained active but after 1908 devoted himself almost exclusively to designing churches, which usually lacked the panache of his earlier work. The most successful commercial firm in Minneapolis was the one formed by Franklin Long and his son Louis in about 1900. In 1909, Lowell Lamoreaux, who had been the firm's chief designer for several years, became a third partner. Long, Lamoreaux, and Long designed hotels (including the Radisson), office buildings in both St. Paul and Minneapolis, auto showrooms, warehouses, and a variety of other buildings, although business seems to have fallen off after Franklin Long's death. For residential architecture, especially of the costly variety, William Channing Whitney became Minneapolis' designer of choice. His tasteful, restrained houses and small club buildings, while not particularly imaginative, were models of good civic deportment that

perfectly expressed the ideals of the City Beautiful.

In St. Paul, J. Walter Stevens's office continued to pour out warehouses in Lowertown, but the quality of design declined after 1900. The romance and energy also seems to have gone out of Allen Stem's work after 1900, although he continued to win important commissions for railroad stations and large commercial buildings such as the Saint Paul Hotel and the St. Paul Athletic Club (1918, extant). The establishment architect of this era in St. Paul was Clarence Johnston, whose office churned out an abundance of houses, office buildings, department stores, and institutional structures until Johnston's death in 1936. Most of Johnston's well-to-do clients seem to have liked their architecture as bland as possible, and he generally obliged them.

Meanwhile a few new architects appeared, including several who left lasting marks. Edward H. Hewitt—a Red Wing, Minnesota, native who became a star pupil at the École des Beaux-Arts in Paris—opened a Minneapolis office in 1904 and teamed with Edwin H. Brown seven years later to form a successful partnership that lasted until 1930. Hewitt's own office (ca. 1907) at 716 Fourth Avenue South was one of the finest small buildings of its period in Minneapolis, mixing classicism with the sleek lines of Frank Lloyd Wright's emerging Prairie Style. The firm's largest commission was the Bell Telephone Building (1931, extant) in Minneapolis.

A French-trained (and born) architect destined to have an even greater impact on the Twin Cities' skyline arrived in St. Paul in 1905. Emmanuel L. Masqueray, steeped in the École des Beaux-Arts tradition of classical grandeur, was invited to St. Paul by Archbishop John Ireland to design the new Cathedral. He also won the commission for the Basilica of St. Mary in Minneapolis, which opened in 1913, two years before the Cathedral. These two vast churches—done in a rather coarse but overwhelming neobaroque

Emmanuel L. Masqueray

masqueray

style—remain awesome presences, splendidly oblivious to anything as insignificant as the passage of time. Masqueray, who died in 1917, also designed several smaller churches, including the delightful St. Louis Catholic Church (1910, extant) in downtown St. Paul.[34]

The other prominent newcomer was William Gray Purcell, who more than anyone else brought modern architecture to the Twin Cities. Purcell arrived in Minneapolis in 1907 and set up a small office with engineer George Feick. Born in the Chicago area and trained at Cornell University, Purcell was a dreamer who took his inspiration from the leading progressive architects of the day, Louis Sullivan and Frank Lloyd Wright. Earlier

Purcell had met George Elmslie, Sullivan's longtime chief draftsman, and the two became close friends. In 1910 the Scottish-born Elmslie, a brilliant designer and draftsman, agreed to go into partnership with Purcell. Over the next decade, the firm of Purcell and Elmslie (Feick was a minor player and left in 1913) designed a series of magnificent Prairie Style banks and houses that remain among the finest of their kind in America. Many of these houses are in the lake district of south Minneapolis. The firm completed only a few small projects in downtown Minneapolis, including two automobile garages and an elegant shop (1914, gone) for the Minnesota Phonograph Company offices at 612 Nicollet.[35]

William Gray Purcell

Minnesota Phonograph Company office

All of these architects faced increasingly stiff competition from out of state. New York or, more commonly, Chicago architects secured a number of important commissions in the Twin Cities. Robert W. Gibson of New York became one of the first outsiders to win a major commission in Minneapolis after the turn of the century. He began by designing the First National Bank in 1906 and then was awarded the commission for its much larger replacement—the First National-Soo Line Building. Another New Yorker, Electus Litchfield, produced the St. Paul Public Library and Hill Reference Library. Architectural contributors from Chicago included the firm of Ottenheimer, Stern, and Reichert, who were architects of the Loeb Arcade. Chicagoan Charles Frost was also active in the Twin Cities where he designed three railroad depots and the large downtown St. Paul office building later known as First Trust Center (1914). Many theaters built in both cities at this time were also the work of Chicago architects, as were several of the skyscrapers that sprouted in the late 1920s and early 1930s.[36]

Still most downtown buildings continued to be designed by local architects, and the old truism remained in effect: St. Paul architects seldom worked in Minneapolis, and vice versa, although at least one Minneapolis firm—Kees and Colburn—enjoyed some success in St. Paul.[37]

THE WORK OF these thirty years, whether by local or outside architects, often attained the highest quality. Unlike most eras, this was one in which the largest buildings tended to be the best. Such monumental works as Gilbert's State Capitol, Masqueray's two great churches, Jones's imposing Butler Brothers Warehouse, and Litchfield's superb library remain architectural touchstones in the Twin Cities, buildings that define their places with an authority not equalled before or since. With the exception of Jones's stern, Gothic-tinged warehouse, all of these monuments also serve as examples of the dominant architectural style of the time—Beaux-Arts classicism. Taking its name from the era's premier school of architecture, the École des Beaux-Arts in Paris, this style emphasized grandeur, lavish decorative detailing, and the use of classical forms derived primarily from Rome and the Renaissance. Best when teetering at the brink of excess, Beaux-Arts classicism appeared largely as an institutional style, if for no other reason than that few individuals could afford it.

The emphasis on classically inspired design during these years brought a certain stateliness to both downtowns, which for the first time began to acquire those qualities of finish and urbanity that Montgomery Schuyler had found so conspicuously lacking in 1890. Yet this restrained and dignified brand of architecture was not entirely a blessing. For one thing, most of it did not meet the high standards set by Gilbert, Masqueray, and Litchfield. When an architectural style is used for almost everything—as classicism was in the Twin Cities between 1900 and 1920—it invariably becomes watered down. This phenomenon showed up especially in commercial and apartment buildings of the period. Although almost all were draped in some sort of classicism, the gown often was either quite coarse or so thin that the bones beneath poked through.

There was also a stultifying sameness to many of these buildings, which tended to be as proper, solid, and restrained as a Victorian gentleman and, quite often, just as stuffy. In an interview with the *Minneapolis Journal* in 1902, Harry Jones, who by this time had acquired the classical religion, remarked that "the business center of Minneapolis is being very much improved in appearance . . . by the prevalent architectural style of classic and renaissance forms which present more elements of simplicity than those styles which predominated a decade or more ago. . . . The uselessness of parapets, towers and gables has become as apparent as their unsuitability is obvious." Jones neglected to mention that other, equally "useless" architectural devices—such as gigantically overscaled cornices—were very much in style at the moment. He concluded the interview by noting that "cities can only be really beautiful when they have attained some uniformity in the height of buildings."[38]

Jones's comments suggest that, whatever else it may have been, the City Beautiful was no place for nonconformists. The idealists of the Progressive Era sought to make life better and safer for people by filing away the raw edges of unbridled capitalism. Smoothing out the skyline appears to have been part of the same process. Yet there was still enough wild stuff from the 1880s left in St. Paul and Minneapolis to provide a sort of architectural counterweight to Beaux-Arts sobriety. In fact the mix of old and new in the two downtowns was probably never better than it was between about 1910 and 1920.

Not everything built during these years came swathed in heavy classical drapery. The warehouse architecture of the period, often magnificently plain, emphasized structure over style. The Minneapolis firm of Bertrand and Chamberlin, in such buildings as the Leslie Paper Company warehouse (1904, gone) at 305 Fifth Street South, showed particular skill in this regard. In other cases local architects looked to Chicago and Louis Sullivan for inspiration. Kees and Colburn at the opening of the century turned out three distinctively Sullivanesque buildings—the Minneapolis Grain Exchange (1900–02, extant) at Fourth Street and Fourth Avenue South and the adjoining Advance Thresher Company (1900, extant) and the Emerson-Newton Plow Company (1904, extant) buildings at 700–08 Third Street South.

Much greater variety appeared in domestic design, where the compact, efficient, and informal bungalow-style house became extremely popular with the middle class after 1900. The only detached houses being built near either downtown at this time were mansions, and these tended to look to the past rather than the future, with Colonial or Tudor Revival the preferred styles.[39]

The Progressive Era effectively ended with World War I, as did the Beaux-Arts age in America. By the 1920s it was back to business as usual in the Twin Cities, and architecture went through another strongly eclectic period. Toward the end of the decade art deco made its appearance in the Twin Cities. With its sleek lines, jazzy ornament, and lush palette of materials, art deco (also known as Zigzag Moderne) was unabashedly theatrical, a style for strutting in public. Not surprisingly, such indecorous architectural behavior was frowned upon in Minnesota, and art deco in the Twin Cities tended to be much less flamboyant than it was in, for instance, New York or Los Angeles.

In the 1930s art deco evolved into a second—and much more restrained—phase that is often called Streamline Moderne. Characterized by rounded corners and windows, smooth surfaces, and extensive use of metal and glass, the streamline phase of art deco was quite popular in the Twin Cities, especially for new facades on old commercial buildings. One of the purest expressions of the style locally was the Minneapolis Greyhound Bus Terminal (1936, extant but barely recognizable after being remodeled into a nightclub). When used for large public buildings, the Moderne style was often mixed with classical elements, as in the U.S. Post Office in Minneapolis (1933, extant) and the Minneapolis Armory (1936, extant).

Only one Twin Cities architectural firm, Liebenberg and Kaplan of Minneapolis, made a real specialty out of art deco, mostly of the later Moderne variety. Jack Liebenberg, the firm's designer, produced a delightful series of small movie theaters (some new, others remodeled) in the 1920s and 1930s, but almost all were in outlying neighborhoods rather than downtown.[40] A few other local architects, such as Magnus Jemne of

St. Paul, who designed the Women's City Club (later the Minnesota Museum of Art) at 305 St. Peter in 1931, also proved adept at art deco. The two finest art deco buildings in either downtown—the St. Paul City Hall–Ramsey County Courthouse (1932) in St. Paul and the Rand (later Dain) Tower in Minneapolis—were the work of the Chicago firm of Holabird and Root, although the St. Paul firm of Ellerbe Associates played a major role in the city hall–courthouse project.

Most of the major art deco monuments in the two downtowns remained in 1991, but there have been some notable losses. The Woolworth store (1937), a handsome Moderne structure at Seventh and Nicollet designed by the Minneapolis

firm of Larson and McLaren, has vanished. Also gone (in spirit and to a lesser extent in form after being dismantled and then partly reassembled) is the marvelous Forum Cafeteria (1930) at 36 Seventh Street South in Minneapolis. Designed by architect George B. Franklin of Kansas City, the Forum was actually carved out of the old Strand Theater. The Forum was in many respects the Twin Cities' most delightful art deco fantasy, one still remembered fondly by those who had the good fortune—especially as children—to experience its sleek, silvery splendor.[41]

IN 1936 *FORTUNE* MAGAZINE produced a lengthy profile of the Twin Cities. It was not favorable. Minneapolis received a few grudging compli-

F. W. Woolworth Company store, about 1938

ments—"its streets are broad, clean, and crowded, its stores well filled"—but for the most part, *Fortune* depicted Minneapolis as a city on the decline, its social fabric riven by labor unrest (such as the violent teamsters strike of 1934) and its industrial might fading in the face of stiff competition from elsewhere. St. Paul fared even worse. It was portrayed as a decaying, crime-infested city that had lost all economic vitality. "St. Paul is cramped, hilly, stagnant," the story said. "Its streets are narrow and its buildings small. . . . Its slums are among the worst in the land." Although much of the unsigned article was little more than a long East Coast sneer, it hit at some uncomfortable truths, because by the mid-1930s both downtown St. Paul and Minneapolis were in serious trouble.[42]

Much of the trouble stemmed from the Great Depression, which was as hard on buildings as on people. The war that followed further depressed the downtown building market. With the exception of large public projects, such as new post offices, little construction took place in either

downtown between 1930 and 1950. The 1940s, however, produced at least one skyline icon, the Northwestern National Bank weather ball in Minneapolis. This seventy-eight-ton illuminated globe atop the sixteen-story bank building first began beaming its weather message—white: cold in sight; red: warmer weather ahead; green: no change foreseen; blinking light by night or day: precipitation on the way—in 1949. It remained in operation until fire destroyed the bank on Thanksgiving Day in 1982.

But the era from 1930 to 1950 was more notable for acts of destruction in the two downtowns than for any new works of architecture. Many buildings that fell to the wrecker were not immediately replaced, leaving open wounds in the downtown fabric that took years to heal. After St. Paul tore down its old city hall and courthouse in 1933, the block bounded by Wabasha, Cedar, Fourth, and Fifth streets stood largely vacant for the next twenty years. It was turned into a makeshift park called Victory Square, a name that must have rung hollow in a city whose

Depression

259

Pawnbroker district along East Seventh Street in St. Paul in 1936

downtown had grown old and tired for lack of new blood.

Aging, inefficient buildings were especially vulnerable during the depression years when money for maintenance or repair was hard to come by. This applied to both publicly and privately owned buildings. In St. Paul the 1930s saw the destruction of the second State Capitol and the old Customs House on Wabasha in addition to the old city hall and courthouse. All were worthy of preservation, but there was simply no money for such luxuries. Meanwhile private building owners struggled to pay property taxes, and many ended up forfeiting their property, which the city then sold or razed.

The depression and its aftermath hit old office buildings, theaters, and houses especially hard. Between 1930 and 1945, Minneapolis lost such important monuments as the West Hotel, the Samuel Gale house, the Francis Little house, the Metropolitan Opera House, the first Orpheum Theater, the Boston Block, the National Bank of Commerce, the Citizens Bank, the Northwestern National Bank (1904), the Oneida Building, and the Nicollet National Bank. St. Paul lost the Aberdeen Hotel, the old Chamber of Commerce Building, the first Orpheum Theater, and the Metropolitan Opera House, among others.

By the time of World War II both downtowns

were showing their age. Returning to Minneapolis in 1942 after a long absence, Sinclair Lewis found a grim scene. "Minneapolis is so ugly. Parking lots like scars. Most buildings are narrow, drab, dirty, flimsy, irregular in relationship to one another—a set of bad teeth." But this situation was soon to change so drastically that if Lewis had come back just twenty-five years later he might not have recognized the old downtown he once detested.[43]

THE ERA FROM 1945 to 1970 was, in many respects, the most destructive in the history of the Twin Cities. To be sure, the destruction of historic buildings was not a strictly modern phenomenon. The fate of the log Chapel of St. Paul built in 1841 by Father Lucien Galtier offers a case in point. In 1856 the tiny building—by then no longer in use—was dismantled. All the pieces were marked and numbered, with the idea that the structure would someday be rebuilt elsewhere. No one, however, conveyed this message to certain workmen, who mistook the logs for common firewood and burned them all. By the 1880s local newspapers frequently published reminiscences of life in the "early days," with sketches of vanished buildings. Even so, buildings in the nineteenth century—especially houses—were often moved rather than demolished, and large-scale urban destruction in the Twin Cities did not really begin in earnest until the twentieth century.[44]

Until the 1950s the power of the marketplace—more than anything else—determined the fate of downtown buildings. Fine old buildings that occupied prime sites were ruthlessly eliminated when money could be made by doing so. In other cases historic buildings survived (although sometimes with massive amounts of cosmetic surgery) because they still turned a dollar or were not located on especially desirable blocks. Change thus tended to occur in increments on relatively small sites, and there was at least some sense of urban continuity, with the

Abandoned house at 449 Iglehart Avenue, St. Paul, 1969

typical block holding a mixture of both new and old buildings. Beginning in the 1950s, however, as both downtowns battled for survival, a new way of doing things—federally financed urban renewal—wrought unprecedented changes.

URBAN RENEWAL AS it was practiced in most American cities in the 1950s and 1960s has acquired an unsavory reputation. The process did, in fact, go terribly wrong, as Jane Jacobs demonstrated as early as 1961 in her angry book, *The Death and Life of Great American Cities*. Yet urban renewal was welcomed in many cases by people who saw it as a surefire way to revitalize decaying neighborhoods. In the Selby-Dale area of St. Paul, for example, a neighborhood group in 1969 placed signs on dilapidated old houses that asked, "Why Can't the Wreckers Take This One?" Nor did urban renewal invariably dictate the destruction of old buildings, although that is generally what happened in the Twin Cities. In parts of Philadelphia, by contrast, urban renewal funds were actually used in the 1950s to rebuild historic neighborhoods. It is also important to remember that urban renewal represented a response to very real problems.[45]

Those problems, in the Twin Cities and elsewhere, have been well documented. As America moved to the suburbs after World War II, money, jobs, and industry were sucked out of the old downtowns. With their customer base rapidly eroding, downtown stores and shops soon began to close or follow the migration out of the city. The depression and war years had also left most downtowns with an aging stock of buildings that were hard pressed to compete with gleaming new shopping malls and office complexes in suburbia. In St. Paul downtown retail sales declined by $15 million between 1948 and 1954. Property values, meanwhile, were in the midst of a startling drop. Between 1930 and 1956 the total assessed value of property in downtown St. Paul plummeted by more than 50 percent. The picture was nearly as bleak in Minneapolis.[46]

In short, plenty of evidence existed in the 1950s to suggest that downtown America was dying. At the same time theories spawned by pioneers of architectural modernism, such as the French architect Le Corbusier, had gained wide currency in American urban planning circles. These theories emphasized complete rebuilding—urban towers set amid open green spaces, separation where possible of vehicular and pedes-

Loewy's vision of the Kellogg Boulevard area

trian traffic, and careful zoning intended to force out traditional downtown activities such as manufacturing and warehousing. St. Paul received a taste of what was to come as early as 1945 when Raymond Loewy—a celebrated industrial designer and urban planner—proposed modernizing downtown by stripping away historic facades, constructing large parking garages, and demolishing old buildings on Kellogg Boulevard to make way for a new apartment complex.[47]

A strong social vision underlay these modernist design theories. Arthur Nichols, a landscape architect who helped to design the Capitol Mall in St. Paul in the 1940s, once told an interviewer: "Lack of space is at the root of much of our social ills. . . . When you pack buildings together, you cramp people. . . . you create tensions and

slums and ghettoes. People need space. It means freedom and beauty." The new downtown, leading urban thinkers said at a conference in 1957, would have "a great deal of grass and flowers; there would be birds and fountains and fine buildings generously spaced." Frank Lloyd Wright, on one of his periodic nose-tweaking visits to the Twin Cities in 1956, went even further, arguing that "centralization of cities is just plain murder." A few mile-high buildings surrounded by vast parks would solve the problem, he said.[48]

Other architects sounded less extreme, but their message was similar: downtown America needed to be sanitized, reorganized, and modernized in order to compete with the suburbs. And because the patient was so sick, the surgery would have to be extensive and radical. Most American cities—including St. Paul and Minneapolis—ultimately went under the knife of urban renewal, and while it may have saved them, it also changed them forever.

Two primary instruments were used for the operation. One was the Federal Housing Act of 1949, which provided funds for clearing slums or other "blighted" areas. "Blight" became the operative word, and in time it served as a kind of all-purpose justification for egregiously destructive acts. City officials quickly discovered that "blight was in the eye of the beholder" and used housing act funds for all sorts of clearance projects that generally eliminated more housing than they replaced. The other key urban renewal instrument was the federal highway aid program. For essentially political reasons, planners significantly expanded the interstate highway program beyond its original format to include new inner-city routes. The Federal Highway Act of 1956 provided for more than sixty-one hundred miles of in-city highways, a figure later increased to eighty-six hundred miles. The impact of these huge multilane highways on both downtown St. Paul and Minneapolis proved to be enormous.[49]

URBAN RENEWAL DURING this era was especially destructive because it was so extensive and so complete. Like the great northern pineries at the turn of the century, the old sections of downtown St. Paul and Minneapolis were subjected to clear cutting. And once the boundaries of devastation had been established, nothing was allowed to stand.

In St. Paul the first great assault came in the State Capitol area. This decayed landscape of old rooming houses, churches, apartments, and small commercial buildings undoubtedly needed renewal. *Fortune* magazine in its 1936 article had used a painting of the area to illustrate its thesis that St. Paul's slums were among the nation's worst. The neighborhood—which gradually became pockmarked with parking lots—had not improved by the early 1950s when redevelopment began in earnest. Yet for all of its blight, the area had many buildings of real quality and a nice residential scale. Selectively rehabilitated, it could have formed a beautiful transition zone between the downtown commercial core and the State Capitol area. But with a new interstate highway coming through and with the state intent on creating a new State Capitol approach, the old neighborhood did not stand a chance.[50]

The state had approved plans for the Capitol Mall in 1945 that called for acquiring and clearing 103 acres. Relocation problems caused by the postwar housing shortage delayed the project, and it was not until 1950 that clearance began. In the meantime the St. Paul Housing and Redevelopment Authority worked on its own plan for the Capitol area, which was approved in 1952. All told, the city and state eventually targeted seventy-one acres for renewal. By the time Interstate 94 opened in 1967, virtually every historic building in the renewal area (except those in the Capitol complex itself) had been demolished and the historic street pattern destroyed. The casualty list included one of the state's most important Richardsonian Romanesque mansions, the John

Route of Interstate 94
through downtown St. Paul
as envisioned in 1946

PROPOSED
St. Paul
CROSS-TOWN EXPRESSWAY
AND TRAFFIC DISTRIBUTORS
TO THE ADJACENT CENTRAL BUSINESS DISTRICT

Construction of Interstate
94 in the mid-1960s

*Row house at 117-125 Iglehart Avenue
torn down for Capitol Mall area*

Elsinore Apartments, 50-60 Summit Avenue, about 1960

Merriam house (razed 1964); at least a dozen apartment buildings and row houses, among them the Newport (razed 1952), the Virginia (razed ca. 1956), and the Elsinore (razed ca. 1960); churches such as Trinity Lutheran (razed 1952) and the splendid Central Park Methodist (razed ca. 1960); and such irreplaceable public spaces as Central Park and Park Place.

St. Paul also began taking steps in the 1950s to clear out areas of substandard housing, such as Swede Hollow, the Upper Levee, and the West Side flats. The flats, subject to frequent flooding and home to some of the city's most impoverished residents, had been considered a slum for more than a hundred years. It was also a close-knit community, one that had attracted waves of immigrants, including Polish and Russian Jews and, later, Mexican Americans. Buildings here—such as the Agudas Achim Synagogue (razed ca. 1963) or the exotically decorated Paul Ferodowill

Ferodowill house,
216 West Indiana, 1956

house (razed 1966)—tended to be modest but contained as rich a store of memories as did far grander structures in other parts of the city. Clearance to make way for the Riverview Industrial Park began in earnest in the 1960s. Soon nothing remained of the old world of the flats.[51]

Minneapolis' first foray into large-scale urban renewal at this time was actually a continuation of a slum-clearance program begun in the 1930s. This scheme involved the sprawling Glenwood neighborhood on the downtown's northwestern fringe. In the early 1930s the city had cleared out the Oak Lake section of Glenwood, relocating the municipal market there. Then, in 1938, the city undertook the ambitious Sumner Field project in which thirty acres of dilapidated housing

near Bryant Avenue North and Olson Memorial Highway were bulldozed and replaced by six hundred housing units in two-story brick buildings. The rest of the neighborhood, however, continued to decay and by the early 1950s was widely regarded as the city's worst slum. Once largely Jewish, the neighborhood had become almost 50 percent black by 1950 when the city decided on the harsh medicine of clearance.[52]

The federal government approved the project in 1954, and eventually the city demolished more than 660 structures in a 180-acre area between Glenwood Avenue and Olson Highway. Beginning in the 1960s the Grant neighborhood to the north received a heavy dose of the same medicine. Light industry and public housing, including high-rise apartment buildings of the kind that were to prove a social and architectural disaster, rose from the ruins. Some of these high-rises—hailed in their day as great improvements—have already been demolished. Meanwhile the people who supposedly were to benefit from this massive slum clearance project left in droves. Of the thousand families displaced by urban renewal in Glenwood in the 1950s, only eighteen had returned by 1962, perhaps because there was nothing left worth returning to.

The other great Minneapolis urban renewal project of this era centered on the historic Gateway District. Consisting almost entirely of buildings constructed before 1900, the Gateway had become both a civic embarrassment and a unique urban resource. Despite its architectural and historical significance, the district was little more than an ugly, decayed skid row in the eyes of many Minneapolitans. Much truth lay in this perception. The district's three thousand or so residents, almost all of whom were male, included a goodly share of drifters and dehorns. These unfortunates provided the human cargo for seventy cheap hotels and flophouses, some of which packed 150 men to a floor in five-by-seven-foot cribs, while requiring everyone to use a single bathroom. The Gateway's fifteen square blocks also offered more than sixty taverns, twenty-four pawnshops, and ten hamburger joints. Many of these businesses occupied buildings that could justifiably be described as run-down, rat-infested firetraps.[53]

Yet the Gateway was also a lively place with a quality generally lacking in Minneapolis—urban soul. Not all of its drinking establishments were rotgut dives, and some—such as the Persian Palms nightclub—attracted a middle-class clientele searching, often with considerable success, for a taste of sin. The area also featured bars that catered to blacks, gays, and others not welcome in mainstream Minneapolis. Nor was everyone who lived in the Gateway a derelict, as much of

*Persian Palms,
111 Washington Avenue
South, 1959*

the public assumed. The district's profusion of cheap hotels and rooming houses attracted a sizable population of retirees who simply could not afford lodging elsewhere. And even though many of the district's buildings appeared to be in extremely poor condition, others—such as the elegant old Minnesotan Hotel or the Janney, Semple, Hill warehouse or the Metropolitan Building—were by no means ready for the scrap heap.

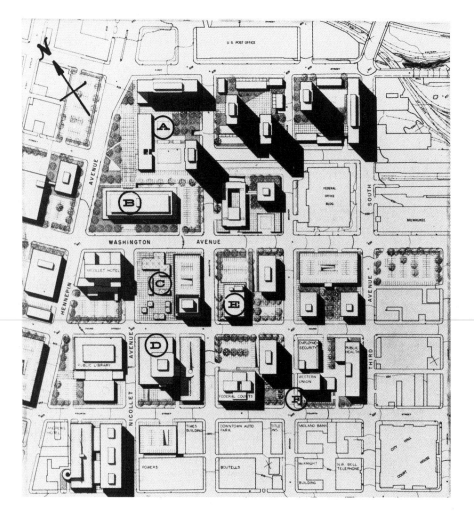

Cerny plan: A. River
Towers Apartments,
B. Northwestern National
Life Insurance Company,
C. Gateway Plaza,
D. Sheraton Hotel,
E. IBM Corporation,
F. Midbank Realty
Company

Schemes for clearing out all or part of the Gateway had been proposed as early as 1906. The first big clearance effort came with the creation of Gateway Park in 1915. Seventeen years later the city demolished an entire block's worth of old buildings to make way for Pioneer Square (gone) in front of the new post office on First Street. But it was not until after World War II that the impetus for really massive renewal began to pick up steam. Minneapolis architect Robert Cerny was a catalyst in this regard. In the late 1940s and early 1950s he prepared plans for a row of civic buildings along Fourth Street, envisioning these structures as great Corbusian slabs of concrete. At first little came of this idea, but after General Mills, Inc., announced in 1955 that

it would move its corporate headquarters to suburban Golden Valley, Cerny's dream of wholesale clearance in the Gateway District won powerful new proponents.[54]

By 1957 the city's government and business leaders had developed a full-fledged Gateway plan, which included private as well as public redevelopment. Federal funds were approved that year, and the wrecking crews soon went to work. Over the next several years the city razed 180 buildings and relocated 2,500 residents, while nearly 450 businesses closed or moved. By the time it all ended in 1965, one-third of downtown Minneapolis had been leveled, as though struck by a precision bombing run, and the historic Gateway was gone forever.[55]

The demolition took a heavy toll on Minneapolis' architectural heritage. Besides the Metropolitan Building, the Gateway project claimed such monuments as the old Federal Courthouse, the Globe Building, the Kasota Block, and the Vendome Hotel, plus scores of lesser known structures. Gateway Park was also destroyed. New apartment and office buildings, most of them devoid of architectural interest, gradually filled in the holes. Some parcels, or even entire blocks, served as parking lots for years, and 40 percent of the Gateway project had not been developed as late as 1971. The site of the Metropolitan Building remained vacant until 1980 when a drab seven-story office structure replaced Mix's masterpiece.[56]

Not everything that happened in downtown Minneapolis in the 1960s was bad. The Nicollet Mall, opened in 1968, gave a much-needed shot in the arm to the city's declining retail trade, while providing a kind of linear park in the center of downtown. Unfortunately the mall lost much of its loopy charm in a 1990–91 rebuilding.

A similar mall might have benefited downtown St. Paul, which found itself locked in an uncomfortable state of inertia during the 1950s and early 1960s. This was not entirely bad. Be-

cause so few new buildings were being constructed, the city's historic commercial core remained more or less intact. Although downtown St. Paul looked old and tired, it enjoyed a kind of amiable frumpiness that gave the city a quality quite distinct from its ambitious neighbor. To be sure, there were significant losses during this period, none more heartbreaking than the demolition of the great Ryan Hotel in 1962. Yet as late as 1967 the central part of downtown still retained such treasures as the New York Life and Guardian buildings, as well as dozens of other nineteenth-century structures.

The beginnings of a great change were already visible by 1960. In that year Dayton's completed its new downtown department store on the block bounded by Sixth, Seventh, Wabasha, and Cedar streets. The Dayton's store, designed by the same architects who had created the trend-setting Southdale shopping mall a few years earlier in suburban Minneapolis, dramatically demonstrated the shape of things to come. A virtually windowless brick box with a parking ramp wrapped around four floors of retailing, the store seemed far more amenable to automobiles than to pedestrians. In its imagery and organization, it

Gateway demolition

The area of downtown
St. Paul cleared for
construction of the new
Dayton's store

was essentially suburban, an antisocial cube that shut itself off from the traditional life of the city. Yet it also represented a vision of the future that proved to be irresistible to St. Paul's leaders.[57]

Those leaders had seen downtown's long decline, as well as the abundant evidence of "progress" in Minneapolis, and felt compelled to act. "People were hungry for new space," one downtown business leader recalled. "St. Paul was in an absolute flat period, and everybody wanted to see new buildings." There is no question that downtown St. Paul desperately needed redevelopment of its old and increasingly dilapidated building stock. A 1958 city study found two-thirds of downtown building facades to be in "poor" or "very poor" condition. Moreover many buildings were considered too small to meet contemporary needs. But instead of clearing out the worst of its buildings and trying to save the best, St. Paul resorted to the same sort of block-busting that

Minneapolis had employed so ruthlessly in the Gateway.[58]

The impetus for change in St. Paul came from the private sector. Spurred by events across the river, St. Paul's business leaders in 1961 formed an improvement committee and hired architects to prepare a new downtown plan. This plan, known as Capital Centre, became the centerpiece of downtown renewal. It was unusual in that it contemplated rebuilding the core of downtown, rather than the fringes, as had been the case with the Gateway project. Developers promoted the plan in a handsomely printed, spiral-bound booklet that was in many respects a classic of its period. Filled with airy neo-Corbusian drawings depicting a bright, clean world of plazas and office towers, Capital Centre offered a tantalizing vision of a "modern and exciting" downtown. The essence of this vision appeared in an aerial photograph that showed look-alike

Capital Centre vision
of St. Paul downtown
shopping area

modern office buildings (painted in) rising like a mirage along Fifth and Sixth streets. It took about twenty years to make the mirage real.[59]

Capital Centre quickly became the basis for an ambitious renewal plan adopted by the St. Paul Housing and Redevelopment Authority. The plan focused on twelve square blocks in the heart of downtown. Although a few old structures, such as the Pioneer and Endicott buildings, were spared, almost everything else within the borders of Capital Centre was demolished between 1965 and 1970. Photographers for the *St. Paul Dispatch* and *St. Paul Pioneer Press* caught it all—one historic building after another disappearing into rubble—but this stream of melancholy images failed to inspire any strong public sentiment for preservation.

Here and there, a sop was tossed to history. When the New York Life Building came down in 1967, the great bronze eagle over its entrance was salvaged and then mounted, incongruously, on a nearby parking ramp. Preservationists also managed to save ten sandstone heads from the facade of the Guardian Building when it was razed in 1970.[60]

The effect of Capital Centre was profound—and not entirely beneficial. The project shattered the city's retail trade, forcing more than two hundred stores out of downtown between 1963 and 1975. Many left for good, and not until the 1980s did St. Paul—with developments such as Town Square and Town Court—manage to rebuild its retail base.[61]

From a purely architectural standpoint, Capital Centre was less than memorable. The new office towers, parking ramps, apartments, and commercial buildings that rose along Fourth, Fifth, and Sixth streets were generally works of the dullest sort, although here and there a few buildings of real quality—such as the Osborn

The New York Life eagle, trussed and ready for its removal to a parking ramp

pedestrians using second-story arcades and crossing traffic-choked streets on open bridges. In the Twin Cities architect William Purcell was among the first to propose skyways—or "highwalks" as he called them—in 1954. Curiously the Twin Cities' severe climate seems not to have been the main factor in creating skyways. Instead the selling points were safety, modernity, and convenience.[62]

Minneapolis acquired its first skyways in 1962 as part of the new Norstar Center at Seventh and Marquette. These and subsequent skyways in Minneapolis (thirty-seven by 1990) were privately financed and followed no common design. St. Paul's skyway system began in 1967 with a bridge linking the Pioneer and Endicott buildings to the new U.S. Courthouse across Fourth Street. "The sidewalk at the street level will become almost secondary," a St. Paul planner said in 1966. His words proved prophetic. By 1990 the city's skyway system had been extended to thirty-one blocks. The St. Paul system was publicly financed, and virtually all the bridges looked alike.[63]

The skyway systems provided welcome comfort and convenience, especially in winter, but were not an unmitigated blessing. They pulled life up and away the street, damaged historic facades (such as that of the St. Paul City Hall–Ramsey County Courthouse), obscured important vistas (again, a particular problem in St. Paul), and encouraged new building designs that were bleak and uninviting at street level. In 1988 that peerless student of cities, William H. Whyte, dubbed St. Paul the "blank-wall capital of the United States" after touring its skyway system.[64]

THE SWEEPING URBAN renewal projects of the 1950s and 1960s were not repeated in the decades that followed, in part because both cities concentrated on filling downtown blocks left vacant by earlier clearance efforts. Equally important, the federal well began to run dry in 1972

Building (later Ecolab Center)—rose from the ruins. Windswept plazas added to Capital Centre's woes, pulling many of its buildings away from a strong relationship with the street. Yet if this huge development left much to be desired architecturally, it gave momentum to what became a dominant force in reshaping the look of downtown St. Paul and Minneapolis—the skyway.

Skyways were not a new idea when they first appeared in the Twin Cities in the 1960s. In fact schemes for separating vehicular and pedestrian traffic had been around for many years. In his 1929 book, *The Metropolis of Tomorrow*, the celebrated New York delineator Hugh Ferriss proposed something similar to skyways as a cure for urban congestion. "In the minds of many experts," he wrote, "the only adequate solution lies in the realm of the third dimension—for instance, placing all pedestrians on a separate plane above that of the wheel traffic." Ferriss illustrated the idea with a charcoal drawing that showed when President Richard Nixon cut off further funding for large-scale urban renewal projects. The government's new approach in the 1970s offered limited funding for urban redevelopment through a series of grant programs. The net effect was a reduction in federal dollars. As a result, St. Paul, Minneapolis, and other cities turned to new tools—such as revenue bonds and tax increment financing—to stimulate downtown development on a site-by-site basis.[65]

The most visible symbol of development in the 1970s was Philip Johnson's IDS Tower (1973), which not only brought the Minneapolis skyline up to fifty-seven stories, but also gave the city a world-class skyscraper. One of the largest projects in downtown Minneapolis was the Loring Greenway east of Loring Park. This undertaking produced generally uninspired new buildings while obliterating such important works as Harry Jones's Imperial Apartments on Grant Street. St. Paul, meanwhile, enjoyed a sort of miniboom

at the end of the decade, culminating with the opening of the Town Square shopping and office complex in 1980.[66]

Perhaps the biggest boom of all came in Minneapolis in the 1980s. This decade saw an unprecedented series of new skyscrapers in Minneapolis, including Norwest Center (1988), architect Cesar Pelli's elegant paean to art deco New York. Pelli was one of many out-of-town "starchitects" who found work in Minneapolis in the 1980s, as the city—which liked to call itself the "Minneapple"—strove to present a sophisticated face to the world. The 1980s were far less dynamic in downtown St. Paul, which managed to acquire one new building of note—the Ordway Music Theatre (1984)—and several undistinguished skyscrapers, the World Trade Center (1987) among them.

Meanwhile historic preservation, spurred by federal tax incentives, had become a real force in the Twin Cities by the mid-1970s. The move-

Demolition of the Curtis Hotel by explosives, June 1984

ment's signal triumph in St. Paul was the preservation and restoration of the old Federal Courts Building, which reopened in 1979 as Landmark Center. The city—responding to grass-roots pressure—also established historic districts in the Summit Avenue-Ramsey Hill area, Irvine Park, and Lowertown, thereby helping to preserve many buildings of great architectural and historic significance. Nothing quite as spectacular happened in Minneapolis, but many old downtown buildings—such as the Butler Brothers Warehouse, the Lumber Exchange, and the Masonic Temple—were restored, as were important structures in the St. Anthony Falls Historic District. Minneapolis also established a historic warehouse district and several historic residential districts.[67]

Yet even as worthwhile buildings were being saved, others were being lost to development or fire, particularly in Minneapolis. Prominent casu-

alties in the 1970s and 1980s included the first and second Minneapolis auditoriums; the Great Northern Station; the old YWCA; the Hennepin Avenue steel-arch bridge; many large commercial structures, including the Builders Exchange, Northwestern National Bank, Studebaker Building, Syndicate Block, Wesley Temple Building, and Woolworth's Building; the Andrews, Anthony (originally Holmes), Curtis, Dyckman, Leamington, Nicollet, and Radisson hotels; St. Joseph's Catholic Church; familiar entertainment and dining spots, including the Forum Cafeteria, Charlie's Cafe Exceptionale, and the Gopher Theater; and a number of apartments, row houses, and mansions.

St. Paul also lost much during these twenty years, including the original section of the St. Paul Auditorium; the old YMCA; the first High Bridge; the Northwest Airways hangar and terminal at Holman Field (later St. Paul Downtown Airport); several late nineteenth-century commercial structures, such as Lyon's Block, the Moore Building, and the Nicols, Dean and Gregg Warehouse; the historic Yeorg's Brewery complex on the West Side; the New Astor (Riviera), Empress, and Strand theaters; the old Jackson Street Methodist Church; and a scattering of old houses and apartment buildings, among them the Capitol (later Karl) Hotel and the Marlborough.

In some cases the gain clearly outweighed the loss. Construction of the Ordway Music Theatre, for example, required demolition of three early twentieth-century buildings of considerable quality—the first St. Paul Auditorium, the old Elks Hall, and the Wilder Charities Building. Yet the Ordway was a strong addition to the city, both as an institution and as a work of architecture, and it has enhanced the appearance of Rice Park. In other cases, however, decent old buildings were demolished to make way for projects—City Center in Minneapolis comes to mind—that added little except bulk to the skyline.

THE ASTONISHING RECONSTRUCTION of much of downtown St. Paul and Minneapolis between 1960 and 1990 has left a mixed legacy. Much of it is undeniably positive. Physically both downtowns may be in the best shape of their lives. New, well-maintained buildings are everywhere, especially in Minneapolis. The infrastructure—roads, bridges, streetlights, and sewers—is in far better condition than in many American cities. The worst slums are gone, and much new housing has been built. The skyway systems make movement throughout both downtowns easy, safe, and comfortable. Downtown retailing, which seemed on the verge of collapse in the 1950s, has made a comeback. Professional baseball and basketball have also returned to downtown Minneapolis after being absent for years.

Equally important, architectural quality has improved markedly since the dog days of the 1960s. In Minneapolis such works as the IDS Tower and Norwest Center seem sure to become historic landmarks in the twenty-first century. St. Paul also acquired its share of fine buildings,

The Nicols, Dean and Gregg Warehouse shortly before its demolition in 1989

most notably the Minnesota Judicial Building (1990), The St. Paul Companies' headquarters addition (1991), and the Minnesota History Center (1992). Meanwhile attention to good urban design has become more apparent. St. Paul, after some design disasters in the 1960s and 1970s, took dramatic steps in the 1980s to improve its public realm with the rebuilding of Kellogg Mall and improvements to freeway bridges in the State Capitol area. For its part, Minneapolis has completed a new riverfront parkway and plans other improvements in the St. Anthony Falls district.[68]

Yet if both downtowns are cleaner, newer looking, and more rationally organized than ever before, they have also lost a great deal along the road to progress. For one thing, their range has narrowed. The downtowns once expressed and reflected all of life in St. Paul and Minneapolis. In this sense they were complete places. That is no longer true. In the 1980s "exclusive" became a favored word in the lexicon of development, used to describe everything from shopping malls to office buildings. The word seems appropriate. Although bag ladies, winos, and the homeless still haunt downtown streets, they seem—perhaps more than ever before—out of place, trespassers in an environment devoted increasingly to "upscale" imagery. This trend has become especially noticeable in Minneapolis.

Spontaneity is also a missing commodity in an era of mega-developments and obsessive planning. For most of their history, the downtowns more or less made themselves in a carnival of capitalism, and if this free-for-all often produced ugliness and inequality, there was a certain rude vitality to the process. In the 1980s both downtowns began to lose the last of their rough edges—the demolition of "Block E" on

Storefronts of "Block E," looking north on Hennepin from Seventh Street

Hennepin Avenue in Minneapolis being a classic example. The old Minneapolis warehouse district north of Hennepin—occupied by a lively mix of artists, antique dealers, and restaurateurs—is the closest thing left to a spontaneously created urban environment in either downtown. But as developers move in and rents move up, the warehouse district threatens to ossify into one of those packaged "old towns" that are so often a substitute for the real thing in American cities. The travails of St. Paul's Lowertown—beautifully preserved, meticulously planned, yet curiously inert for many years—are instructive in this regard.[69]

Architecturally the same exclusivist tendencies have been at work. Small, humble buildings have all but disappeared, replaced by ever larger and showier structures, usually featuring glitzy lobbies that teem with mirrors, plants, and security guards. So large have these buildings become that one or two to a block is now the rule in the newer sections of both downtowns. Meanwhile the urban street wall has become lost in space, replaced by plazas that separate buildings from the sidewalk and from one another, leaving skyways their only act of connection. This phenomenon is particularly evident in parts of downtown Minneapolis, where new skyscrapers seem to jostle, sometimes rudely, for attention. In this landscape of air-cooled, sun-shielded behemoths, the old fabric of the city, woven out of an intimate tangle of buildings, has disappeared forever.[70]

Developers fueled by fat subsidies and dreams of grandeur stand ready to up the ante. Eighty-story skyscrapers and enclosed multiblock shopping malls still loom on the horizon in downtown Minneapolis, although the real estate bust that began in the late 1980s may defer such dreams for awhile. It is impossible to predict when and where new buildings will appear or how new patterns of growth will shape downtown development in the twenty-first century. Only one thing is certain: Lost Twin Cities will grow.

CREAM OF WHEAT BUILDING

Southeast corner of Fifth Street and First Avenue North, Minneapolis. Harry Wild Jones. 1904–39.

Perhaps more than any other building in the Twin Cities, this handsome factory and office structure expressed the high ideals of the City Beautiful movement. Located on the same block as the West Hotel, the building was one of only a few large factories built downtown after 1900, and its presence was obviously intended as a powerful statement about the need for classical beauty in the modern city.

It appears that the driving force behind this unusual industrial building was Frederic W. Clifford, who had helped to found the Cream of Wheat Company in North Dakota in 1895. Two years later Clifford moved with the company to Minneapolis where he became active in urban beautification projects and served on the city's first planning commission. He was also chairman of the commission that hired Cass Gilbert to prepare a master plan for the University of Minnesota's main campus.

The Cream of Wheat Company itself was an almost magical success story. Its only product was a hot breakfast cereal made from middlings, the first part of the wheat kernel broken down during the milling process. Once scorned by millers,

Cream of Wheat Building, about 1906

middlings became pure gold for Cream of Wheat, and the company grew so rapidly after moving to Minneapolis that within six years it was ready to erect a large building of its own. Instead of simply hiring an architect, however, the company—with Clifford no doubt leading the way—decided to stage a design competition with awards totaling twelve hundred dollars. Ten leading Minneapolis architects submitted entries. All the designs were classically inspired, none more so than Harry Jones's winning scheme, which clearly expressed the company's dedication to beauty and civic harmony. This led the *Minneapolis Journal* to cite the building as strong evidence that "purely utilitarian architecture . . . is gradually passing in Minneapolis."

Six stories high and loaded with classical detailing, the building's walls were of light-colored brick with stone and terra-cotta trim. Stained-glass windows flanked the main entry on Fifth Street, while overhead a pair of ferocious-looking griffins (who presumably liked their cereal hot) perched on a massive balcony. The building's middle stories were organized by means of a giant order of engaged Corinthian columns. Arcaded sixth-floor windows and a massive cornice—along with festoons, swags, cartouches, and other pieces of classical paraphernalia—completed the show.

The result was a piece of industrial architecture in evening dress, unwilling to wear its work clothes in public. "The new building resembles a concert hall or conservatory more than it does a factory," noted a correspondent for the *Engineering Record* of New York. A writer for the *Journal* made a similar observation: "To a certain extent the character of the business carried on inside will be an enigma to the passer-by who is accustomed to link the word factory in his mind's eye with a plain angular building of red brick."

The building's devotion to beauty was such that it included a large side garden for the use of employees. Set off from the street by a superb

iron gate and a row of freestanding Ionic columns, the garden was intended to form an uplifting environment for the company's laborers, although no photographs show it in actual use. Inside, the building hewed to its mission of decency and liberality by offering employees—most of whom were women—such amenities as a café and a rest room complete with wicker rocking chairs. The company's officers also had handsome quarters on the first floor that came complete with mahogany paneling and gigantic fireplaces. Manufacturing took place on the third floor, while other floors were used for storage and offices. The entire building (except for the exterior masonry walls) was framed in iron and steel with floors designed to withstand more than three hundred pounds of weight per square foot.

Despite its devotion to the timeless language of classicism, the building had a short life. Cream of Wheat rapidly outgrew the building and in 1927 moved to a much larger factory in northeast Minneapolis. The old building remained vacant for several years and then suffered the indignity of being turned into a municipal parking garage in 1931. Eight years later it was demolished. The site became a parking lot.

Main facade of the building, showing the garden space at the left, about 1910

JOHN S. BRADSTREET AND COMPANY SHOP AND CRAFTHOUSE

Southwest corner of Seventh Street and Fourth Avenue South. John Bradstreet, William Channing Whitney. 1904–19.

The Bradstreet crafthouse, about 1918

John S. Bradstreet set standards of taste for the monied class in Minneapolis for almost half a century. Born in Massachusetts in 1845, Bradstreet moved to Minneapolis in 1873 and five years later established a furniture business in partnership with Edmund Phelps. By 1883 the firm was so large that it occupied six floors of the new Syndicate Block on Nicollet Avenue. Meanwhile Bradstreet built a reputation as the city's leading interior decorator, furniture designer, and "evangelist of good taste," as Montgomery Schuyler described him.

During the 1880s Bradstreet popularized the Moorish style in Minneapolis. His own apartment was a model in this regard, offering a *mihrab* (arched alcove), a frieze with texts from the Koran, and other bits of exotica. He also designed a lavish "oriental" interior for Phelps's house on Park Avenue, helped to decorate the West Hotel, and redid the interior of the Grand Opera House in 1887. A true dandy who favored impeccably tailored suits and jade cuff links to

complement his striking auburn hair, Bradstreet was also a connoisseur of Japanese art. He traveled to Japan every other year, returning with what he called "plunder" in the form of elegant artifacts.

After moving several times (fire forced him out of the Syndicate Block in 1893), Bradstreet finally designed a place of his own, which opened in January 1904. It consisted of an old Italianate-style house, which was completely remodeled, plus a large addition containing galleries, shops, and even several kilns. Although William Channing Whitney was the architect of record, the design was pure Bradstreet, mixing Japanese, Indian, Moorish, arts and crafts, and art nouveau elements. The building's odd windows and "artistic disregard for the conventional," as one newspaper put it, made the place an immediate sensation.

Set back from the street behind a splendid Japanese garden, the crafthouse was reached by passing beneath an archway (called a *torii*) and then along a curving walk to the front entrance. Inside, the visitor found an entry hall paneled in *jin-di-sugi* (carved Japanese cypress wood) and filled with fine furnishings. The hall led to a showroom and then into a fifty-six-foot-long main gallery, which featured a hammer-beam ceiling, skylights, and cloth-covered walls. Here was displayed work from Bradstreet's own shop, which employed up to eighty craftsmen, including several from Japan.

In a 1905 pamphlet, Bradstreet and Company offered the crafthouse as proof that "Minneapolis has gone beyond the pioneer period and is now a city of culture." But Bradstreet's brand of "culture" survived only briefly after his death (from injuries in an auto accident) in 1914. Although Bradstreet and Company stayed in business until the 1920s, the crafthouse closed in 1919. Parts of it fell to the wrecker immediately, but some of the old shop structures apparently survived for another twenty years. Lincoln Centre, a thirty-one-story office tower, later occupied the site.

Entry gate, about 1918

The Japanese garden, about 1918

FREDERIC W. CLIFFORD HOUSE

325 Clifton Avenue, Minneapolis. Harry Wild Jones.
1905–68.

The period from about 1900 to 1915, before the automobile changed everything, was the last great age of mansion building near the downtown cores of Minneapolis and St. Paul. Many of these big houses—mostly located on lower Summit Avenue in St. Paul and on Lowry Hill and along Park, Groveland, and Clifton avenues in Minneapolis—still stood in 1991. But a sizable number are gone, including this fine Tudor Revival house, built for the man who made a fortune from Cream of Wheat.

It is no surprise that Clifford called on Harry Wild Jones to design his house. Jones, of course, had done the Cream of Wheat Building for Clifford only a year before and was later to design houses for several other company officials. What is a bit surprising is that Clifford, who advocated the rigorous classicism of the City Beautiful, chose not to live in a Renaissance-flavored villa, as did many of the millionaires of the time, but instead opted for an informal and quite consciously romantic house.

Above all else, the Clifford house superbly exploited its site. Jones let the house snuggle up against Clifton Avenue, thereby leaving room for a huge rear lawn that stretched a full block south to Groveland Avenue. A magnificent series of walls—some of brick, some balustraded, others of

The Groveland Avenue facade of the Clifford house, about 1910

The front hallway, about 1910

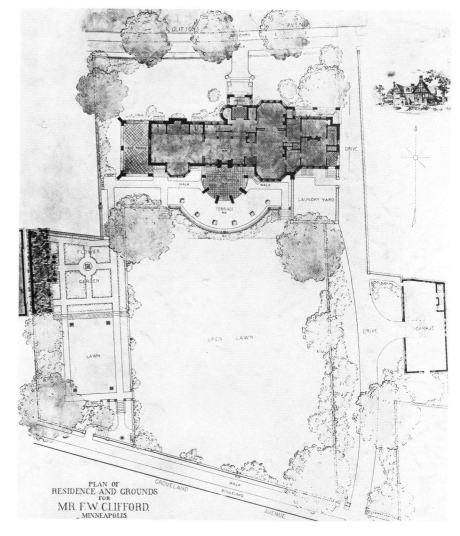

First-floor plan and map of grounds

richly patterned cast concrete—surrounded the property, creating a true urban estate.

The house itself, long and narrow and rising to three stories beneath steep gables, was not as exciting as some of Jones's earlier work, nor was it especially large for its time. But it was exceptional for the quality and consistency of its detailing. Like many so-called Tudor Revival houses, its inspiration actually came from the later Elizabethan and Jacobean eras. Besides its numerous gables (some sporting splendid bargeboards), the house offered such common Tudor Revival features as half-timbering, ornate twisted chimneys, large bay windows, and a split pediment over the main entrance.

Jones, however, almost always managed to incorporate at least one unexpected touch in his best residential designs. Here, it was a rounded, castlelike projection that erupted from the rear of the house between two gables and was cut away at the base to reveal a screened porch. A broad, curving terrace extended out past the porch, connecting the house to the yard and gardens beyond. Inside, the house was all of a piece. The major main-floor rooms, which were arranged to either side of a large entry hall, had a uniformly Tudor-Elizabethan look with dark paneling, elaborate fireplaces, strapwork ceilings, and wide, flattened archways.

Clifford lived in this attractive house until his death in 1947 at the age of seventy-nine. The Osborne McMillan Elevator Company then took over the house for use as its corporate headquarters. In March 1968 the company decided to move elsewhere and sold the house to a real estate developer, who promptly tore it down and built a modern apartment tower in its place.

ST. PAUL AUDITORIUM

Between Fourth and Fifth streets near Franklin (later Auditorium) Street, St. Paul. Reed and Stem. 1907–82.

Entrance to the St. Paul Auditorium, about 1908

St. Paul lacked a large public meeting and exposition hall at the turn of the century. The city had built a primitive auditorium on Eighth Street in 1893 for a huge celebration marking completion of the Great Northern Railway's transcontinental line. This all-wood structure, erected in just one month and never painted, was little more than an oversized shed (not to mention a spectacular firetrap), and it was torn down in 1903.

The modern auditorium that St. Paul opened in 1907 was a far different affair. Built for $460,000, about half of which came from a public subscription campaign, it was one of the most sophisticated multipurpose auditoriums of its day in America. It was also a strong expression of community pride at a time when St. Paul clearly was falling behind in its battle for supremacy with Minneapolis. A writer for the *Pioneer Press*, becoming a trifle carried away in the magic of the moment, said the people of St. Paul "look upon their Auditorium much with the same feeling that Mohammedans regard Mecca. In it are centered their faith and hope for the future, and it rises up like the city of the Moslems as a monument to civic spirit."

The auditorium's architects, Charles Reed and Allen Stem, were especially skilled in planning large spaces and would later serve as associate architects for Grand Central Station in New York City. Stem, who handled the design work while Reed concentrated on engineering, managed to endow the auditorium with real urbanity, a quality seldom found in modern arenas. The main facades, on Fourth and Fifth streets, were Renaissance Revival in style and featured brown brick with terra-cotta trim. On the Fourth Street side, the building presented three floors of rather sober windows above a long entry arcade decorated with simple medallions and plaques. The Fifth Street facade offered a similar arcade but had only one floor of windows above, all of which were strongly pedimented in the classical manner.

Inside, the auditorium was truly ingenious. Instead of relying on simple partitions, it featured an intricate arrangement of movable seats, walls, and floors designed to create three distinct spaces. The heart of the facility was a 125-by-200-foot arena surrounded by six thousand seats. In this form, the auditorium could be used for sporting events, circuses, and similar attractions. For conventions or other events requiring more seating, the arena floor could be removed, creating space for an additional three thousand to four thousand seats and raising the total capacity to ten thousand. There was also a third option, in which some of the floor seating could be pivoted around to form a fan-shaped theater facing a portable proscenium stage. Total seating in this configuration was about thirty-two hundred. So beautifully designed was the whole system that the transformation from theater to arena and vice versa took only about fifteen minutes.

As a sort of bonus this superbly planned interior offered handsome Renaissance-flavored stencilwork, done in carefully coordinated green and red tones. In addition the ornamental program included a series of large panels displaying the names of great composers. The main foyer off the Fifth Street entrance was also quite appealing, with plaster groin vaults rising above large arched windows.

The formal opening of the auditorium on April 2, 1907, was described rather immodestly by the *Pioneer Press* as "an event without a parallel in the West." In truth another event that day—James J. Hill's retirement as president of the Great Northern Railway—may have had a greater impact on St. Paul's future. Nonetheless the auditorium's dedication was indeed an impressive occasion with a symphonic concert, lots of speech making, and a grand ball. "The entire building was aglow with gaiety, beauty and life," reported the *Pioneer Press*, which devoted three pages to coverage of the event.

The auditorium served St. Paul well for many years, hosting everything from auto shows to opera performances to a huge banquet for Secretary of War (and later to be President) William Howard Taft in 1907. In 1932 a new and larger arena was added to the western side of the building. A sixteen-thousand-seat Civic Center arena further enlarged the complex in the 1970s. Mean-

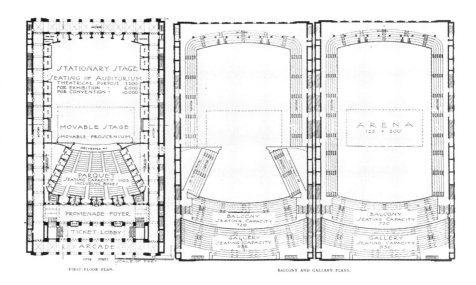

while the old auditorium began to suffer increasingly from the infirmities of age (including a leaky roof), and the city showed no inclination to repair or restore it. The end came in 1982 when the building (by then known as Stem Hall) was torn down to make room for the new Ordway Music Theatre.

ABOVE: *Floor plans*

BELOW: *Auditorium interior*

STREETCAR TUNNEL

Selby Avenue beneath Summit Avenue, St. Paul.
Charles Shepley. 1907–58.

The lower end of the Selby Tunnel, about 1908

St. Anthony (Cathedral) Hill on the western edge of downtown St. Paul was a nightmare for early transit engineers. Selby Avenue was the most direct route up the hill, but its 16 percent grade—nearly as steep as those in San Francisco—presented a daunting challenge. It was not until this 1,472-foot-long tunnel opened that electric streetcars could easily negotiate the hill. The tunnel, which cut the grade to 7 percent, was also a significant engineering work because it was among the first in America built of reinforced concrete.

City planners in the early 1880s had considered an incline railway for the Selby Avenue grade, but as it turned out, cable cars were the first motorized vehicles to conquer the hill. Pioneered in 1873 in San Francisco, cable cars eventually operated in twenty-seven American cities, with Chicago having the largest system of all by the mid-1880s. (By the 1990s, however, only San Francisco still had cable cars.) The cars worked by gripping a constantly moving cable located in a slot beneath the street. Steam engines at either end of the line powered the cable.

In St. Paul cable-car service down Fourth

A streetcar descends into the tunnel in 1951; the Wilder house appears above the streetcar, and the Cathedral is barely visible to the left.

Street, over to Third, and then up Selby began in January 1888. A second cable line commenced running along East Seventh Street a year later. The cable-car system was costly, slow (top speed was about ten miles an hour), and hard to maintain in winter when snow and ice clogged the slots. Accidents were frequent. The most spectacular one occurred on January 27, 1888, a few days after the Selby line had opened, when a two-car train lost its grip and careened down the hill. A car overturned at the bottom, killing one rider and injuring twenty-seven others. The accident was blamed on an inexperienced driver, although cold weather and its effect on largely untested equipment may have been the real culprit.

A much more efficient vehicle—the electric streetcar—eclipsed cable cars in 1890. But streetcars lacked the power to make the climb up Selby Avenue. The solution was a counterweight system, which used the weight of a descending car

to help pull another up the hill. This system remained in effect until the tunnel, envisioned as early as 1887, opened in 1907.

The double-track tunnel, designed and built for the Twin City Rapid Transit Company by Charles Shepley, was a beautiful piece of engineering. It began near Selby Avenue and Third Street and emerged at the top of the hill beside the St. Paul Cathedral (then under construction). Both the tunnel's walls and arched roof were of reinforced concrete. A curve at the lower end of the tunnel was engineered so carefully that a runaway car could hit speeds of sixty miles an hour and still not fly off the tracks.

For half a century, the tunnel was a familiar part of life in St. Paul. When the bus era began in the 1950s, however, the tunnel was doomed. The last streetcar went through the tunnel in 1958. Most of the tunnel was then filled in, although its lower portal remained visible just downhill from the Cathedral.

RADISSON HOTEL

41–43 Seventh Street South (between Nicollet and
Hennepin), Minneapolis. Long, Lamoreaux, and Long.
1909–82.

In December 1909 the *Minneapolis Journal* observed that "no single achievement in the marvelous growth of Minneapolis has so conspicuously marked its approach to metropolitan proportions as the . . . opening for business of the Hotel Radisson." Similar paeans had greeted the West Hotel twenty-five years earlier. By 1909 the West had become passé, and the 350-room Radisson was destined to replace it as Minneapolis' premier downtown hotel. Built at a cost of $1.5 million, the Radisson's central location, high level of service, and modern amenities made it the hotel of choice for well-to-do travelers. It was also, briefly, the city's tallest occupied structure (a rear section rose to fourteen stories) and was advertised (falsely) as the highest concrete-frame building in the world.

One of the city's most prolific turn-of-the-century architectural firms—Long, Lamoreaux, and Long—designed the hotel. The firm's partners were Franklin Long, who had been practicing in Minneapolis since 1868; Louis Long, his son; and Lowell Lamoreaux, who had been a draftsman with the firm for many years before achieving full partnership in 1909. The partners designed scores of commercial buildings in Minneapolis, including the nearby Dyckman Hotel, which also opened in 1909. Generally adhering to the popular styles of the day, the firm's work tended to be competent if not inspiring.

This observation was certainly true of the Radisson. Loosely based on French Renaissance designs, the hotel was best at street level. Here, two-story marble columns formed an elegant framework for the main entrance, which was sheltered by a canopy and had an electric-powered revolving door (controlled by an attendant) said to be the first of its kind in the city. Above its two-story base of rusticated terra cotta, the hotel had plain walls of cream-colored brick

Radisson Hotel, about 1920

punctured by simple double-hung windows. On the top three floors ornament again erupted in the form of thick consoled balconies, fat festoons, and an outrageously plump cornice. These projecting pieces of terra cotta were wildly overscaled, hanging from the upper walls of the building like big, ugly knickknacks.

Inside, however, the hotel conveyed an appropriately Edwardian aura of dense, weighty elegance. The two-story-high lobby, lit by a glass dome, was chock full of marble paneling and leather chairs and also offered eight murals depicting the adventures of the hotel's eponym, Pierre Radisson, who may have been the first white man to visit what later became Minnesota. The hotel's lower floors contained parlors, ballrooms, and several "theme" restaurants. Eateries included the Chateau Restaurant (done in the François Premier style), the Viking Cafe (in which could be found, hanging from the rafters, a miniature Viking ship crafted of silver), and, after 1912, the Teco Inn, whose walls and floors were finished entirely with colorful tiles and landscape panels made by the American Terra Cotta and Ceramic Company of Chicago. There was also a rooftop restaurant.

The most lavish accommodations were a pair of "state suites" on the second floor. Each offered a parlor, a dining room, three bedrooms, and, of course, separate rooms for the maid and valet. Regular accommodations were less posh but still first class for their time. Fully 90 percent of the rooms came with a private bath. The Radisson also had fifty rooms in the rear for its female employees. Perhaps fearing after-hours hanky-panky, the hotel made no such provision for male workers.

The Radisson's numerous amenities included an electric vacuuming system, touted as a great advance. The hotel was also the first building to tap into the Hinckley aquifer that lay beneath downtown Minneapolis, thereby providing guests with a constant source of cool, pure drinking water. In addition the hotel proclaimed itself to be "absolutely fire proof, noise proof, dust proof, [and] vermin proof," none of which, of course, was true.

When the Radisson opened, a newspaper writer predicted that "half a century or more may pass before it will be considered 'old-fashioned' or out of style." This prophecy proved to be accurate. The Radisson (at least on the outside) did indeed remain virtually unchanged for fifty years. In about 1960, however, the original exterior on Seventh Street was buried beneath a garish modern facade of pink and white brick. This updating only postponed the inevitable demise of the grand old hotel, which was demolished by explosives in 1982 and replaced by a new hotel-office building of indifferent design.

The Chateau Room

LOEB ARCADE

Southeast corner of Fifth Street and Hennepin Avenue, Minneapolis. Ottenheimer, Stern, and Reichert. 1914–67.

Hennepin Avenue facade of the Loeb Arcade, 1914

The enclosed urban arcade, which first appeared in Paris in the 1780s, was a popular building type in the nineteenth and early twentieth centuries and continues to flourish in the form of the shopping mall. The vast Galleria Vittorio Emmanuele II (1865–67) in Milan remains the greatest of all arcades, but some splendid specimens also survive in the United States, including the Providence Arcade (1827–29) and the Cleveland Arcade (1888–90). Nothing so grand was ever built in the Twin Cities where the first sizable arcade appears to have been in the Syndicate Block (1883) in Minneapolis. St. Paul also had a number of shopping arcades, including the Grand, Bremer, and Endicott (the latter two of which still stood in 1991, although much altered).

The four-story arcade completed in 1914 by the Loeb Company was in many respects the most intriguing of the lot. The intrigue begins with its principal architect, Henry A. Ottenheimer of Chicago. Largely forgotten, Ottenheimer has one small claim to fame—he once stabbed Frank Lloyd Wright in the neck during a drafting-room dispute. Both men were working for Adler and Sullivan in Chicago at the time, and Ottenheimer took a knife to Wright after being punched in the nose by the great architect-to-be. Neither was seriously injured, but Wright—who never forgot an affront—took revenge in his autobiography, describing Ottenheimer as "insolent," "heavy-bodied, short-legged," and generally lacking in virtue.

Along with bad drafting-room deportment, Ottenheimer had limited talent as a designer. His firm was heavily influenced by turn-of-the-century Viennese architecture but never achieved anything like its crisp elegance. The Loeb, in fact, was a rather clumsy design, its classically inspired facades of creamy terra cotta topped by visually unconvincing pediments. The arcade was noteworthy, however, for its distinctive L shape, formed as it wrapped around a three-story building on the corner.

Inside, the main gallery—finished largely in terra cotta—resembled a boomerang in plan as it curved to follow the shape of the building. Overlooking this skylit gallery were four floors of shops, with those on the upper levels reached via open balconies. The gallery's great height and unusual curving plan made it a memorable space, different from any other arcade ever built in the Twin Cities.

It appears the Loeb was successful in its early years, since a fifth floor, in brick, was added around 1920. In its original form, the arcade had room for nearly ninety shops. Discount clothing stores, jewelers, tobacconists, and small service-oriented shops made up the bulk of the tenants. The arcade was still flourishing in the 1950s but then began to decline rapidly. In the mid-1960s, the Loeb was remodeled and cut down to two stories, but this drastic action failed to revive its fortunes, and in 1966–67 it was demolished and replaced by a parking lot.

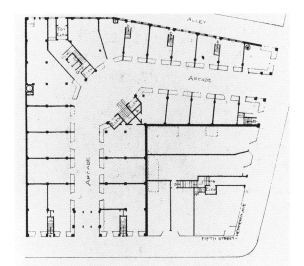

FIRST FLOOR PLAN

First-floor plan of the arcade; the Fifth Street entrance is bottom left and Hennepin is top right

Arcade interior, 1952

GREAT NORTHERN STATION

Hennepin Avenue at Mississippi River, Minneapolis.
Charles Frost. 1914–78.

Great Northern Station, 1914

By the turn of the century, the railroading public considered both union depots in the Twin Cities to be inadequate. In St. Paul the complexities of building a new depot were so enormous that the task was not completed until the early 1920s. Things, as usual, moved a bit more quickly across the river. The City Beautiful movement was especially strong in Minneapolis where a new depot was viewed as vital to plans for rebuilding the decayed Bridge Square area. Among the various schemes advanced for Bridge Square, the most mind-boggling came from LeRoy Buffington, who envisioned a new union depot at the base of two huge towers straddling Hennepin Avenue. While the planners planned and the architects dreamed, James J. Hill took charge of the situation and built a station for his Great Northern Railway. It was located directly across Hennepin from the city's old Union Depot, which was then torn down. Hill's station served a total of five railroads and in effect became Minneapolis' union depot for the next sixty years.

The station was designed by Charles Frost, a respected Chicago architect who had designed Minneapolis' other major railroad depot—the Milwaukee Road station, completed in 1898. Frost's later commissions included St. Paul's new Union Depot and Hill's huge downtown St. Paul office building. A capable if not exactly scintillating designer, Frost relied on familiar Beaux-Arts imagery for the Great Northern Station. Constructed of steel and brick with a facing of light-colored Kettle River sandstone, the station pre-

sented a monumental appearance on Hennepin in the form of arched entry pavilions to either side of a gigantic Doric colonnade. A third-floor attic capped off the exterior, which struck an impressive pose at the northern termination of Nicollet Avenue.

Great Northern employees, who knew a thing or two about how a depot should work, apparently planned the no-nonsense interior. The layout was simple and practical. A large waiting room, 150 feet by 62 feet, was placed between a pair of wide vestibules that led directly from outside to the train concourse. This arrangement allowed the waiting room to function as just that and not as a thoroughfare for everyone boarding or leaving trains. Archways connected the waiting room to men's and women's lounges, the two side vestibules, and the concourse. The trains themselves ran under the depot. Six elevators and a like number of staircases brought travelers down from the concourse to platforms serving the station's twelve tracks. In its peak years, the station handled about 125 trains a day.

If the depot's interior was functional, it was also rather somber, with that heavy institutional feel common to many public buildings of the period. Although the two-story-high waiting room was well illuminated by skylights and clerestory windows, it does not appear to have been an especially inviting space. Large murals later helped to enliven this room, but it grew ever dingier with age. It also suffered from some tacky remodeling that included the installation of a false ceiling about 1960.

The station's location near the heart of Minneapolis' skid row made it a favorite hangout for drifters and bums. One celebrated vagrant—name unknown—would sometimes station himself in the concourse, take a deep breath, and then begin shouting out train departures with great gusto. Unfortunately his command of geography was not precise, and he would sometimes announce the Seattle-bound Empire Builder as

Main waiting room, 1952

heading for "Miles City, Memphis, Winnipeg, Oshkosh, Denver, Atlanta, International Falls and points west." Normally this routine got him tossed out of the station, although it must have been wonderfully entertaining to have such a creative fellow around.

Like other big train depots, the Great Northern—once the pride of Minneapolis—gradually turned into an urban dinosaur, made extinct by the airplane and automobile. After Amtrak took over what was left of railroad passenger service in the 1970s, it built smaller depots in several cities. In the Twin Cities, passenger service was consolidated into a new, utterly unromantic depot in the Midway District of St. Paul. When this facility opened, the Great Northern Station lost its reason for being. While St. Paul managed to turn its old depot into a restaurant-office complex (with mixed results), no one could be found who was willing to take a similar gamble with the Great Northern Station, and it came down in 1978. As of 1991 the site remained vacant, awaiting new development, possibly as a park.

GATEWAY PARK AND PAVILION

Two blocks bounded by First Street and Washington, Nicollet, and Hennepin avenues, Minneapolis. Hewitt and Brown. 1915–53 (pavilion), ca. 1960 (park).

This elegant little park was the most visible product of the City Beautiful era in Minneapolis. It was also an early example of urban renewal, its creation requiring the demolition of more than a dozen historic buildings. Momentum for the project began to build around 1905 when Minneapolis vacated its old city hall building on part of the site. In 1908 the Minneapolis Park Board, after a running battle with nearby property owners, finally voted to acquire two blocks for the park at a cost of $635,000. Work on the park and pavilion did not begin until 1914, however.

A number of Minneapolis architects submitted plans for the project. After consulting with Edward Bennett (then preparing his plan for Minneapolis), the park board awarded the commission to Hewitt and Brown. Edwin Hewitt, the firm's designer, was a Red Wing native whose impeccable credentials included an apprenticeship with Cass Gilbert and a diploma from the celebrated École des Beaux-Arts in Paris. Returning to Minnesota in 1904, Hewitt set up his own office and atelier and quickly acquired an influential clientele. In 1911 he went into partnership with Edwin Brown, who handled the engineering side of the business.

For the Gateway Park pavilion, Hewitt produced a stately, restrained exercise in Beaux-Arts

Gateway Park, before 1924

*Gateway Park, about 1950;
behind the pavilion is the
Pick-Nicollet Hotel*

classicism. The pavilion, faced in smooth stone, consisted of a one-and-a-half-story central section flanked by low, curving colonnades that extended outward in a welcoming gesture. The central part of the pavilion was quite ornate, with large Palladian windows and entry arches, carved panels, and a balustrade around a low domed roof. The colonnades to either side were treated more simply, employing the modest Tuscan order and a minimum of decoration.

Located at the Washington Avenue end of the park, the pavilion contained rest rooms and a public space that was used for many years by the Minneapolis Tourist Bureau. The park itself was basically open green space, sporting potted palms in summer and a municipal Christmas tree in winter. There was also a fountain directly in front of the pavilion and a flagpole said to be the city's tallest.

An inscription carved on the front of the pavilion read: "The Gateway: More than her gates the city opens her heart to you." As time went on, it was mostly the area's huge population of transients who got the message, attracted by the pavilion's free shelter and its public rest rooms. By the early 1950s the pavilion had become a dank, smelly place littered with whiskey bottles and known to its habitués as "the pisshouse." Seeing no hope of improvement, the park board in 1953 demolished the pavilion and put a four-foot-high iron fence around the rest of the park as a deterrent to loafing.

Although the park would have formed an excellent centerpiece for redevelopment, it was bulldozed along with everything else as part of the Gateway Urban Renewal Project in the 1960s. High-rise apartment buildings and office towers subsequently occupied the site.

CAPITOL (PARAMOUNT) THEATRE

22 West Seventh Street (south side between Wabasha and St. Peter), St. Paul. Rapp and Rapp. 1920–65.

Capitol Theatre, 1923

When this sumptuous movie palace opened on September 8, 1920, it was billed, with perhaps some hyperbole, as the "finest and largest west of New York." What is certain is that the twenty-five-hundred-seat Capitol was the first true movie palace in the Twin Cities and the largest ever built in St. Paul. Movie palaces—lavish theaters devoted primarily to showing motion pictures—were a new building type. The first full-blown example had appeared in New York City in 1913, but the golden age of the movie palace did not really begin until the early 1920s.

Before the 1920s most movies were shown either in small, crudely decorated theaters that developed out of the early nickelodeons or in vaudeville houses. In the Twin Cities one of the first sizable theaters devoted solely to movies appears to have been the five-hundred-seat Crystal (1909) on Hennepin Avenue in Minneapolis.

The Capitol brought a new level of sophistication—and a new scale—to the movie-going experience in the Twin Cities. Its owners, the Finkelstein and Ruben circuit, claimed to have spent $1.5 million on the theater, which was incorporated into the new Hamm Building (1920, extant). The Capitol's designers, the brothers George W. and Cornelius W. Rapp of Chicago, were among the nation's premier theater architects, known for their heavy-duty re-creations of French Renaissance splendor. But the Capitol found the brothers in a rare Spanish mood, and for the theater's facade on Seventh Street they produced a terra-cotta extravaganza unlike anything seen before or since in St. Paul. Dominating the Rapps' composition was a trio of tall arched windows complete with outlandishly overwrought moldings and Spanish grillwork. It was not great architecture, but it was great theater, designed to entertain the eye while suggesting a fantasy world within.

In this regard, Rapp and Rapp did not disappoint. The Capitol's two-story-high lobby was a flamboyant Spanish dance executed in Italian travertine marble, polychromed plaster, and wrought iron. The lobby's vaulted ceiling was particularly spectacular with intense hues of gold, red, and blue illuminated by concealed lights. Marble staircases led to a balcony (called the upper lobby), featuring spiral columns, velvet drapery, and other emblems of pomp. It was a show, of course, an architecture of stolen ideas and shameless surfaces, but one newspaper writer was so smitten by it all that he compared the new theater to "the palaces of Sevilla."

The Rapps' Spanish frenzy did not carry over

Lobby of the theater, 1965

ing night's show included singers, an organ recital, symphonic music from the theater's thirty-member orchestra, and a world premiere movie—*The Branded Woman* starring Norma Talmadge—all for just fifty cents.

The Capitol, which became the Paramount under new ownership in 1929, entered a decline in the 1950s as its audience moved to the suburbs and turned to television for entertainment. The theater's size and high operating costs made it especially vulnerable. On June 16, 1965, the theater showed its last movie—suitably enough, it was entitled *Mirage*—and closed for good. A few months later wrecking crews tore out the old theater's splendid interior to make way for a much smaller, modern-style movie house called the Norstar (later converted into an even smaller playhouse). The Capitol's incomparable terra-cotta facade was also destroyed in 1965 and replaced by plain stone panels.

Theater auditorium, 1923

entirely into the auditorium, which was more French in character and relied heavily on ornamental plasterwork for its effects. Domed ceilings under a huge balcony and over the main floor gave the auditorium an extra sense of spaciousness. The proscenium stage, eighty-eight feet wide and thirty-three feet deep, came with all the latest equipment and a large orchestra pit. Of course, no movie palace was complete without a pipe organ, and the Capitol could boast of a ninety-stop monster known for its "thunder drums and the celestial harp effect."

The Capitol's opening attracted a few minor screen moguls, the cream of St. Paul society, and thousands of ordinary people. Attending to the throng were sixteen female ushers attired in "black plush tams set at a rakish angle, black satin blouses, hip length, gathered with a snowy sash, and white satin pegged pantalettes." They also carried swagger sticks, perhaps to keep the male members of the audience in line. The open-

MINNESOTA (RADIO CITY) THEATER

Northeast corner of Ninth Street and La Salle Avenue, Minneapolis. Graven and Mayger. 1928–59.

In 1926 when there seemed to be no limit to the American dream, a group of Minneapolis businessmen led by Sumner T. McKnight laid plans to build the greatest theater ever seen in the Twin Cities. The group formed a corporation, sold bonds, and in 1928 saw their dream come true with the opening of the "show place of the Northwest." Built on a Brobdingnagian scale with a vast lobby and a four-thousand-seat auditorium, the Minnesota was a great monument to optimism and excess, Versailles in a brick box. In the end its size proved to be its undoing because there never were, and never would be, enough people in Minneapolis to fill the place on a regular basis.

Minnesota Theater, about 1929

Theater lobby, 1928

Its designers, A. S. Graven and Arthur C. Mayger of Chicago, were experienced theater architects who by 1928 had completed several movie palaces. For the Minnesota they selected their usual Italian-French Renaissance mix. The exterior, executed in patterned brickwork with terra-cotta trim, was quite plain. A domed corner tower rising from an elaborate marquee was the most distinctive feature. Separated from the tower by a giant arched window was another prominent vertical element—a seventy-five-foot-high sign said to contain (along with the marquee) ten thousand lights. The Minnesota also had a row of small shops fronting the mass of the main auditorium on Ninth.

The real visual fireworks were inside. The lobby was a Grand Central-sized space, 150 feet long, forty-five feet wide, and four stories high. These dimensions made the lobby alone larger than many downtown Minneapolis theaters, as advertisements for the Minnesota frequently pointed out. Colossal marble columns, three monstrous chandeliers of Czechoslovakian crystal, and a vaulted ceiling decorated with blue, rose, and gold coffered panels provided the lobby with a properly sumptuous air, as did a grand marble staircase known as the "stairway to happiness." Opening off the lobby were lavish lounges decked out with statuary, urns, and oil paintings.

The auditorium itself was, as one awed critic reported, a place of "magnificent distances." Seating 4,056 people on three levels, it was advertised as the fifth largest theater in the United States, surpassed only by the Roxy and Paramount theaters in New York, the Uptown in Chicago, and the Michigan in Detroit. Decorated in tan and gold with Renaissance-inspired ornamental motifs, the Minnesota's auditorium was dominated by a spectacular ceiling dome that took on various colors with the aid of hidden lights. The stage, more than sixty feet wide, included a hydraulic orchestra lift as well as a four-manual Wurlitzer organ played for many years by Eddie Dunstedter.

The theater opened amid much fanfare on March 23, 1928, with a special show for various dignitaries (Charles Lindbergh sent his regrets) and invited guests. Serving the crowd were fifty-five ushers, all "Army trained College boys" and all attired in maroon and gold uniforms. The hoi polloi got its first look the next day, and there were long lines for a program that included orchestra and organ concerts, a stage spectacle called "Treasure Ships," a newsreel, a cartoon, and, finally, Minnesota-born Richard Dix starring in the featured film, *Sporting Goods*. The cost was fifty cents for matinees, sixty-five cents evenings.

Operated by the Finkelstein and Ruben circuit with Paramount Publix, the theater attracted such top performers as Burns and Allen, Amos and Andy, Will Rogers, and Duke Ellington. But it was doomed from the start by its size and overhead (it required up to three hundred people to run the place, one of whom did nothing but change light bulbs). The theater shut down for a week in 1931, then went dark for much of 1932 through 1935. It closed down again in 1938, this time for six years. In 1944 new owners bought the theater and changed its name to the Radio City. After the war the theater enjoyed its most successful period as returning soldiers and their families flocked downtown. By the mid-1950s, however, the theater was back to its old money-losing ways. In 1958 WCCO Television bought the theater building and decided to tear it down. The Radio City's last night was October 14, 1958. The movie was *Damn Yankees*, and the organist's final song was "Yours Is My Heart Alone." There was much sentimental writing in the newspapers about the theater but no real effort to save it, and in February 1959 the wrecking crews went to work. A parking ramp replaced the theater.

Auditorium of the theater, 1928

UNBUILT TWIN CITIES

THE BOLDEST AND most imaginative architecture is often the kind that never leaves the drafting board. Since the 1880s, architects have created many incredible works of paper architecture in the Twin Cities. The fact that these works were never built is in many cases cause for regret, although in a few instances it seems just as well that the world was spared their presence. Good, bad, or indifferent, these paper creations offer a window into the architectural thinking of their times, and as such they occupy an important place in the landscape of Lost Twin Cities.

MINNEAPOLIS

SKYSCRAPER
Proposed location unknown, LeRoy Buffington, 1888. Illustrated in *Inland Architect*, July 1888.

APARTMENT BUILDING
Proposed location unknown, LeRoy Buffington (drawn by Harvey Ellis), 1888. Illustrated in *Western Architect*, June 1912.

NORWEST CENTER
Marquette Avenue between Sixth and Seventh streets, Cesar Pelli and Associates, 1984. This is a design for a nine-hundred-foot-high tower that, if built, would have been the tallest skyscraper in the history of the Twin Cities. A redesigned version, just shorter than the IDS Tower, was finally built.

UNION STATION
First Street and Hennepin Avenue, LeRoy Buffington, 1912. Illustrated in *Western Architect*,
February 1913.

CITY HOSPITAL
Park Avenue and Sixth Street South, Harry Wild Jones, 1898. Illustrated in *Inland Architect*,
October 1898.

THIRD STREET BRIDGE
Across Trout Brook-Phalen Creek valley,
Clarence Johnston, ca. 1917.

NORTHERN STATES POWER
COMPANY BUILDING
Southeast corner of Fifth and Wabasha streets,
Ellerbe Architects, ca. 1930. Illustrated in *St. Paul
Pioneer Press*. A smaller version of the building was
constructed on this site.

STATE CAPITOL
Site of present Capitol, Harry Wild Jones, 1895. Jones's design was one
of four runners-up to Cass Gilbert's winning entry. Illustrated in *Inland
Architect and News Record*, November 1895.

PUBLIC COURT
Seventh Street between
Cedar and Minnesota
streets, Altman-Saichek
Architects, Chicago,
1963.

SKY TOWER
Seven Corners area, architect
unknown, 1965. Illustrated in *St. Paul
Pioneer Press*. The tower would have
been more than nine hundred feet tall.

REFERENCE NOTES

INTRODUCTION

1. *Minneapolis Tribune*, March 3, 1935, p. 11.

2. *Minneapolis Journal*, May 31, 1890, p. 1; *St. Paul and Minneapolis Pioneer Press*, June 1, 1890, p. 7; *Minneapolis Tribune*, March 3, 1935, p. 11.

3. For a fascinating account of the rise and fall of the Gateway area, see David L. Rosheim, *The Other Minneapolis or the Rise and Fall of the Gateway, the Old Minneapolis Skid Row* (Maquoketa, Iowa: Andromeda Press, 1978).

4. Judith A. Martin and Antony Goddard, *Past Choices/Present Landscapes: The Impact of Urban Renewal on the Twin Cities* (Minneapolis: University of Minnesota, Center for Urban and Regional Affairs, 1989), 60–64. See also Linda Mack, "Gateways of Change," *Architecture Minnesota* 17, no. 3 (May–June 1991): 36.

5. The comment about local buildings being unworthy of preservation is in Donald Torbert, "Minneapolis Architecture and Architects, 1848–1908: A Study of Style Trends in Architecture in a Midwestern City Together with a Catalogue of Representative Buildings" (Ph.D. diss., University of Minnesota, 1951), 7. The attorney for the Minneapolis Housing and Redevelopment Authority was Ben W. Palmer, who not only called the Metropolitan Building a "monstrosity" but also claimed it was "a definite threat to the public safety" because of pieces of stone that occasionally fell from its walls and parapets. His remarks appeared in an article written for the *Minneapolis Star*, September 9, 1961, p. 6A. The Minnesota Supreme Court's decision is also quoted in this article. One of the surrounding properties the Metropolitan was said to threaten by its antiquated, unattractive presence was the new Sheraton Ritz Hotel, a lackluster building completed in 1963 and demolished, to no one's evident regret, just twenty-seven years later.

6. *Minneapolis Tribune*, December 17, 1961, Upper Midwest sec., p. 1, 6.

7. For a general discussion of panoramas, see John W. Reps, *Views and Viewmakers of Urban America: Lithographs of Towns and Cities in the United States and Canada, Notes on the Artists and Publishers, and a Union Catalog of Their Work, 1825–1925* (Columbia: University of Missouri Press, 1984).

8. *Atlas of the City of St. Paul, Minnesota* (Philadelphia: G. M. Hopkins Co., 1884); *A Complete Set of Surveys and Plats of Properties in the City of Minneapolis* (Philadelphia: G. M. Hopkins Co., 1885). St. Paul still has a substantial number of pre-1885 structures in and around the downtown area. The bulk of these are located in the Irvine Park Historic District, the West Seventh Street neighborhood, and the lower East Side. The oldest commercial structure in the city is the Coney Island Bar (1858) at 448 St. Peter Street. For an incomplete listing, see Patricia A. Murphy and Susan W. Granger, *Historic Sites Survey of Saint Paul and Ramsey County, 1980–1983, Final Report* (St. Paul: Saint Paul Heritage Preservation Commission and Ramsey County Historical Society, 1983), 344–45. In Minneapolis, most pre-1885 buildings are located in the warehouse district north of Hennepin, around St. Anthony Falls (especially on the east side) and on Nicollet Island. Two of the finest pre-Civil War commercial structures in Minneapolis are the Upton Block (1855) and the Morrison/Martin Block (1858), both on Main Street Southeast and now part of the St. Anthony Main retail complex. See James Berman, ed., *Saint Anthony Falls Rediscovered* (Minneapolis: Minneapolis Riverfront Development Coordination Board, 1980), 98–101.

9. John Ruskin, *The Seven Lamps of Architecture* (Kent, England: George Allen, 1880; Minneola, N.Y.: Dover, 1989), 178.

THE SHAPE OF THE PAST: LAND AND STREETS

1. *St. Paul and Minneapolis Pioneer Press*, October 14, 1883, p. 8.

2. George H. Herrold, "The Necessity for Coordinated Planning," *Civil Engineering* 1 (December 1931): 1328; Virginia Brainard Kunz, *St. Paul: Saga of an American City* (Woodland Hills, Calif.: Windsor Publications, 1977), 6–10.

3. Edmund C. Bray, *Billions of Years in Minnesota: The Geological Story of the State* (St. Paul: Science Museum of Minnesota, 1977).

4. Kunz, *St. Paul*, 10.

5. Kunz, *St. Paul*, 11; Thomas M. Newson, *Pen Pictures of St. Paul, Minnesota, and Biographical Sketches of Old Settlers, from the Earliest Settlement of the City, up to and Including the Year 1857* (St. Paul: The Author, 1886), 39; Henry A. Castle, *History of St. Paul and Vicinity: A Chronicle of Progress . . .* (Chicago and New York: Lewis Publishing Co., 1912), 1:2; J. Fletcher Williams, *A History of the City of Saint Paul to 1875* (St. Paul: Minnesota Historical Society, 1876; Borealis Books, 1983), 259.

6. Castle, *History of St. Paul*, 1:1; *St. Paul and Minneapolis Pioneer Press*, August 21, 1881, p. 3.

7. Josiah B. Chaney, "Early Bridges and Changes of the Land and Water Surface in the City of St. Paul," *Collections of the Minnesota Historical Society* 12 (1908): 136.

8. *St. Paul Pioneer Press*, August 11, 1907, editorial sec., p. 1, 4.

9. William W. Howard, "The City of St. Paul," *Harper's Weekly*, February 22, 1890, p. 149; Castle, *History of St. Paul*, 1:7; Paul Donald Hesterman, "Interests, Values and Public Policy for an Urban River: A History of Development along the Mississippi River in Saint Paul, Minnesota" (Ph.D. diss., University of Minnesota, 1985), 104.

10. Maria Rice Dawson, "A Letter to My Grandchildren About My Childhood Home 'Trout Brook,'" unpublished manuscript, Minnesota Historical Society.

11. *St. Paul Daily Globe*, June 23, 1889, p. 1.

12. Jonathan Carver, *Travels Through the Interior Parts of North America, in the Years 1766, 1767, and 1768* (London: N.p., 1781; Minneapolis: Ross and Haines, 1956), 63–64; Stephen H. Long, *The Northern Expeditions of Stephen H. Long: The Journals of 1817 and 1823 and Related Documents*, ed. Lucile M. Kane, June D. Holmquist, and Carolyn Gilman (St. Paul: Minnesota Historical Society Press, 1978), 67–68. For more on Carver's Cave, see *Minnesota Pioneer*, September 16, 1852, p. 1, and *St. Paul Pioneer Press*, May 30, 1892, p. 7. The *Pioneer* said in its 1852 article that the famous cave, which Carver had described in such magnificent terms, "now looks like a half dug cellar." The most recent exploration of the cave was undertaken in 1990 by a scuba diver, who reported that the underground lake extended about 120 feet back into the cliff; *St. Paul Pioneer Press*, July 29, 1991, p. 1D, 3D.

13. Charles T. Burnley, "Case of the Vanishing Historic Site or What Happened to Carver's Cave?" *Ramsey County History* 4, no. 2 (Fall 1967): 8–12; *St. Paul and Minneapolis Pioneer Press*, October 11, 1885, p. 8.

14. Long, *Expeditions of Stephen Long*, 68–69; Kunz, *St. Paul*, 6; Virginia Brainard Kunz, "Promoters Waxed Lyrical in 'Selling' St. Paul," *Ramsey County History* 11, no. 2 (Fall 1974): 21.

15. In 1891 a visitor to Fountain Cave wrote that "it contains several chambers, some of ample dimensions, and it is said that at 1,000 feet from the opening in the rock no termination has yet been discovered"; *St. Paul Dispatch*, December 8, 1959, East Area sec., p. 2. It is not clear exactly when the cave's entrance was closed by debris, but this appears to have occurred in the 1950s. The entrance was sealed off forever in 1960 when about 25,000 yards of fill were dumped into the ravine in front of the cave during construction of Shepard Road. See *St. Paul Dispatch*, August 2, 1960, p. 13, for a photograph of this work. A plaque placed along Shepard Road is the only reminder of the cave.

16. Mitchell E. Rubinstein and Alan R. Woolworth, "The Dakota and Ojibway," in *They Chose Minnesota: A Survey of the State's Ethnic Groups*, ed. June Drenning Holmquist (St. Paul: Minnesota Historical Society Press, 1981), 17–20.

17. Marion D. Shutter, ed., *History of Minneapolis, Gateway to the Northwest* (Chicago and Minneapolis: S. J. Clarke Publishing Co., 1923), 1:27–29.

18. Here and below, Lucile M. Kane, *The Falls of St. Anthony: The Waterfall That Built Minneapolis* (St. Paul: Minnesota Historical Society Press, 1966; rev. ed., 1987).

19. Shutter, ed., *History of Minneapolis*, 1:106.

20. E. V. Smalley, "Progressive Minneapolis," *Northwest Magazine*, February 1895, p. 21; John H. Stevens, *Personal Recollections of Minnesota and Its People, and Early History of Minneapolis* (Minneapolis: Privately published, 1890), 20–21. The regretful pioneer is quoted in Isaac Atwater, ed., *History of the City of Minneapolis, Minnesota* (New York: Munsell and Co., 1893), 1:69.

21. Bray, *Billions of Years*, 56; Thomas F. Waters, *The Streams and Rivers of Minnesota* (Minneapolis: University of Minnesota Press, 1977), 226–27. When the falls split at the Fort Snelling site, the segment on the Minnesota River receded about two miles upstream before losing its limestone cap and disappearing forever.

22. Long, *Expeditions of Stephen Long*, 70; Berman, ed., *Saint Anthony Falls*, 2.

23. Kane, *Falls of St. Anthony*, 2–5; Carver, *Travels*, 69; Scott F. Anfinson, *Archaeological Potentials on the West Side of the Central Minneapolis Waterfront* (St. Paul: Min-

nesota Historical Society, 1984), 21.

24. Anfinson, *Archaeological Potentials*, 30; Smalley, "Progressive Minneapolis," 21.

25. Kane, *Falls of St. Anthony*, 62–80; Anfinson, *Archaeological Potentials*, 12; Berman, ed., *Saint Anthony Falls*, 10–11. The concrete apron over the falls was installed in 1963. Spirit Island, located just below the cataract, was also removed at this time as part of the Upper Harbor Project. This project included construction of a lock—the highest on the Mississippi River—that allowed boats for the first time to navigate past the falls.

26. The destruction of Silver Cascade was noted in *St. Paul and Minneapolis Pioneer Press*, April 24, 1883, p. 3. For more on Wells's caper, see *St. Paul Pioneer Press*, April 24, 1949, sec. 4, p. 14; C. E. Van Cleve, "The Nesmith Cave Hoax: A Communication," *Minnesota History* 11 (March 1930): 74–75. Wells used the name "Nesmith" in an article about the cave he sent to an encyclopedia. Charon's activities were recounted in *St. Paul and Minneapolis Pioneer Press*, December 1, 1889, p. 13.

27. For the fate of Bassett's Creek, see *St. Paul and Minneapolis Pioneer Press*, November 23, 1884, p. 3. For the natural history of the Loring Park area, see Frank W. Wiltberger, "Some Facts and Fancies about Loring Park and the Adjoining Area," *Hennepin County History* 7, no. 2 (April 1947): 5–6. The swamps and ponds that once dotted Minneapolis were often filled with dirt and debris taken from downtown building sites. Hoag's Lake, for example, was filled in part with material excavated during construction of the New York Life Insurance Building (1890) at Fifth Street and Second Avenue South. The armory's settling problems are described in Jack El-Hai, "Lost Minnesota," *Architecture Minnesota* 16, no. 2 (March–April 1991): 68.

28. Wiltberger, "Facts and Fancies," 6.

29. *Minnesota Pioneer*, April 15, 1852, p. 1.

30. *Minnesota Weekly Democrat*, September 30, 1853, p. 1; Williams, *Saint Paul to 1875*, 314; *St. Paul and Minneapolis Pioneer Press*, November 26, 1882, p. 13; "St. Paul," *Northwest Magazine*, April 1886, p. 1.

31. All plats for St. Paul, beginning with St. Paul Proper, are on file at the Ramsey County Courthouse.

32. For more on street names and their changes over the years, see Donald Empson, *The Street Where You Live: A Guide to the Street Names of St. Paul* (St. Paul: Witsend Press, 1975).

33. Jeffrey A. Hess and Paul Clifford Larson, "An Architectural History of the City of St. Paul," manuscript prepared for the Heritage Preservation Commission, St. Paul, 1990–91, chap. 1, p. 11. Hess wrote the first chapter, Larson the second.

34. West Seventh Street is now also known as Fort Road.

35. Herrold, "Necessity," 1328.

36. "St. Paul in 1884," *Northwest Magazine*, June 1884, p. 1.

37. Information on Omaha's streets is from Leonard K. Eaton, *Gateway Cities and Other Essays* (Ames: Iowa State University Press, 1989), 61. For St. Paul's downtown street problem, see Edward H. Bennett, William E. Parsons, and George H. Herrold, *Plan of St. Paul: The Capital City of Minnesota* ([St. Paul]: Commissioner of Public Works, 1922), 30–34.

38. *St. Paul Pioneer Press*, January 13, 1878, p. 7.

39. Herrold, "Necessity," 1327–28; George Herrold, "City Planning in St. Paul," *City Planning* 7 (October 1931): 220.

40. The reference to "low river dives" is in [Alix J. Muller and Frank J. Mead, comps.], *History of the Police and Fire Departments of the Twin Cities* (Minneapolis and St. Paul: American Land & Title Register Assn., 1899), 55.

41. Seymour's comments are quoted in Williams, *Saint Paul to 1875*, 215. There were a number of early efforts to establish a park along Third Street, one of which was rejected by city voters in the early 1880s. In 1885 St. Paul businessman E. F. Drake resurrected the idea, proposing a plaza and fountain overlooking the river near Third and St. Peter. But nothing ever came of Drake's scheme, which is discussed in *St. Paul and Minneapolis Pioneer Press*, October 28, 1885, p. 8, November 1, 1885, p. 4. The Kellogg Boulevard project is described in Herrold, "City Planning," 220.

42. Judith Benton, "A History of Planning in St. Paul," in *A City Plan for Public Art* (St. Paul: Public Art St. Paul, 1989), 16.

43. Here and below, *St. Paul Daily Pioneer*, June 25, 1872, p. 2. A small park was later created at the intersection of Summit Avenue and Ramsey Street.

44. The area once occupied by Merriam's overlook later became Cass Gilbert Park. All of the great mansions that once lined Sherburne Avenue are long gone, and a rather forbidding concrete structure now serves as a modern overlook. Although the lookout is gone, part of the staircase leading up to it was still visible in 1991 on Robert Street just north of University.

45. *St. Paul Pioneer Press*, November 14, 1902, p. 2. For Gilbert's various plans, see Gary Phelps, *History of the*

Minnesota State Capitol Area (St. Paul: Capitol Area Architectural and Planning Board, 1985).

46. Phelps, State Capitol Area, 9–12. The quote from Gilbert can be found in Catherine Welsh, "A Capitol Place," unpublished manuscript, chap. 6, p. 10, private collection.

47. For the City Beautiful movement, see Marcus Whiffen and Frederick Koeper, American Architecture, 1607–1976 (Cambridge, Mass.: MIT Press, 1981, 1983), 1: 274–76, and Mark Girouard, Cities & People: A Social and Architectural History (New Haven: Yale University Press, 1985), 353–56. For the hiring of Nolen and Comer, see Phelps, State Capitol Area, 19, and Benton, "A History of Planning," 20–21. The Nolen-Comer plan, besides being largely ignored, was ultimately discarded. St. Paul City Planning Engineer George H. Herrold saved the document for posterity in the early 1930s when he rescued it from a trash can where it had been tossed prior to the move to a new city hall building. About the same time that Nolen and Comer prepared their plan, A. B. Stickney of the St. Paul Park Board published a plan of his own for the city park system. This plan, however, did not generally concern itself with downtown issues. See A. B. Stickney, A Comprehensive System of Parks for the City of St. Paul as Proposed by A. B. Stickney (St. Paul: The Author, 1910).

48. Bennett and Parsons, Plan of St. Paul.

49. For a detailed account of the planning of Interstate 94 through St. Paul, see Alan A. Altshuler, The City Planning Process: A Political Analysis (Ithaca, N.Y.: Cornell University Press, 1965), 17–83. The new highway proposed in 1920 along St. Anthony Avenue would have been a four-lane divided parkway, since the limited-access freeway was yet to be invented at that time. For the drawing of the proposed freeway in front of the State Capitol, see St. Paul Pioneer Press, November 4, 1945, Rotogravure sec., n.p.

50. Altshuler, City Planning, 40–48, 60–70. Herrold's comments are in Northwest Architect, September–October 1956, p. 47.

51. Ironically the decision to place Interstate 94 in front of the Capitol and link it there with Interstate 35 produced precisely the sort of traffic tangle—the infamous "Spaghetti Junction"—from which the freeways were supposed to rescue St. Paul.

52. Smalley, "Progressive Minneapolis," 21.

53. Stevens, Personal Recollections, 233–34. The actual survey work was done by Charles W. Christmas on Stevens's behalf.

54. The steamboat landing in Minneapolis, located near the foot of Hennepin Avenue, served boats going upriver as far as Sauk Rapids. The old territorial road is mentioned in one of the most valuable of all books about the physical and human history of the Twin Cities: Calvin F. Schmid, Social Saga of Two Cities: An Ecological and Statistical Study of Social Trends in Minneapolis and St. Paul (Minneapolis: Council of Social Agencies, Bureau of Social Research, 1937), 39. The idea of Hennepin Avenue as a hinge is suggested by Smalley, "Progressive Minneapolis," 21.

55. Streets in Minneapolis narrowed outside the historic downtown core. Seventh Street, for example, was eighty feet wide while Eighth, considered more residential, was platted at only sixty feet. St. Paul's original plat also paid no attention to the public realm, but adjoining plats soon provided open space in the form of Rice and Smith (later Mears) parks.

56. Stevens, Personal Recollections, 234–35; "Street Names: For St. Anthony and Minneapolis," Hennepin County History 18, no. 4 (Spring 1959): 8–10; Warren Upham, Minnesota Geographic Names (St. Paul: Minnesota Historical Society, 1920; rev. ed., 1969), 599–600; Smalley, "Progressive Minneapolis," 21.

57. There was, of course, some urban planning in Minneapolis in the nineteenth century, since such infrastructure elements as sewer and water lines had to be put in place. But even this work was often done on an ad hoc basis, particularly in the 1870s and 1880s. For more on Cleveland's park plans, see Shutter, ed., History of Minneapolis, 1:232–34, and Theodore Wirth, Minneapolis Park System, 1883–1944: Retrospective Glimpses into the History of the Board of Park Commissioners (Minneapolis: Board of Park Commissioners, 1946).

58. Horace B. Hudson, ed., A Half Century of Minneapolis (Minneapolis: Hudson Publishing Co., 1908), 67. Hudson also complained in his book about the failure of city voters to approve a plan for setting aside Nicollet Island as a park.

59. Here and below, see Minneapolis Journal, December 2, 1906, editorial sec., p. 1–2, where the Jager plan is presented in detail with a large map. Charles B. Stravs, C. E. Edwins, and F. E. Halden worked on the plan with Jager. The plan is also discussed in Official City Plan of the City of Minneapolis, Minnesota (Minneapolis: City Planning Commission, 1954). For more on Jager, a fascinating figure who was born in 1871 in what later became Yugoslavia, see Michael K. Garrity, "John Jager: An Unheralded Champion of Urban Planning," Architecture Minnesota 7, no. 3 (April–May 1981): 148–50. Jager's best known building in the Twin Cities is the Church of

St. Bernard (1907, extant) in St. Paul.

60. A number of the Gateway schemes were depicted in *Western Architect* 11 (December 1908): n.p. The comment on Minneapolis' lack of cleanliness is in the same issue (p. 64).

61. Edward [H.] Bennett, with Andrew Wright Crawford, *Plan of Minneapolis* (Minneapolis: Civic Commission, 1917). Beautifully printed and illustrated, this document remains an intriguing source of ideas. See also Vincent Oredson, "Planning a City: Minneapolis, 1907–17," *Minnesota History* 33 (Winter 1953): 332–34; Thomas Balcom, "Mills, Monuments and Malls," *Hennepin County History* 47, no. 2 (Spring 1988): 8–14; John R. Borchert, David Gebhard, David Lanegran, and Judith A. Martin, *Legacy of Minneapolis: Preservation amid Change* (Minneapolis: Voyageur Press, 1983), 32–37.

62. Bennett, *Plan of Minneapolis*, 193.

63. Some of the grand boulevards envisioned by Bennett were to be 250 feet wide. The general recommendation, however, was that all downtown streets should be at least 125 feet wide. See Bennett, *Plan of Minneapolis*, 54. See also Oredson, "Planning a City," 335–36.

64. Oredson, "Planning a City," 337, 339.

URBAN BEGINNINGS, 1840-1880

1. Upton's photographs can be seen in Lucile M. Kane and Alan Ominsky, *Twin Cities: A Pictorial History of Saint Paul and Minneapolis* (St. Paul: Minnesota Historical Society Press, 1983), 17–33.

2. Schmid, *Social Saga*, 5; Williams, *Saint Paul to 1875*, 376–77; Henry S. Fairchild, "Sketches of the Early History of Real Estate in St. Paul," in *Collections of the Minnesota Historical Society* 10 (1905): 417–43, especially page 420; Newson, *Pen Pictures*, 515.

3. Williams, *Saint Paul to 1875*, 380–81.

4. Newson, *Pen Pictures*, 38–39. Newson's obvious contempt for Native Americans and his racial arrogance were all too typical of the period. In fact, not all the early settlers of St. Paul were white. Among the city's pioneers was at least one black man, James Thompson, who settled around 1840 on what is now the West Side of St. Paul; Williams, *Saint Paul to 1875*, 46, 270. Population figures are taken from Kane and Ominsky, *Twin Cities*, 6.

5. Information on the early boundaries of St. Paul and Minneapolis comes from Schmid, *Social Saga*, 43,

387–88. Schmid's book includes a reproduction of the 1857 Minneapolis map, drawn by Orlando Talcott. See also David A. Lanegran and Ernest R. Sandeen, *The Lake District of Minneapolis: A History of the Calhoun-Isles Community* (St. Paul: Living Historical Museum, 1979), 19.

6. Schmid, *Social Saga*, 41; Atwater, ed., *City of Minneapolis*, 27, 31, 35; Hess, "Architectural History of St. Paul," 10.

7. Williams, *Saint Paul to 1875*, 396; Kane and Ominsky, *Twin Cities*, 47; Kunz, *St. Paul*, 43.

8. Ernest R. Sandeen, *St. Paul's Historic Summit Avenue* (St. Paul: Living Historical Museum, Macalester College, 1978), 108; Paul Clifford Larson, *Historic Dayton's Bluff Site Survey, Final Report* (St. Paul: Heritage Preservation Commission, 1989), 24.

9. J. G. Pyle, ed., *Picturesque St. Paul* (St. Paul: Northwestern Photo Co., [1888]), n.p. This delightful book depicts many of St. Paul's finest buildings of the 1880s.

10. The placement of houses in the nineteenth century was amazingly casual and sometimes downright dangerous. In the 1870s, for instance, a man identified only as a "Swedish laborer" erected a shanty for himself and his family directly below a huge wooden grain elevator built into the side of a steep bluff along Third Street in St. Paul. One day in 1876 part of the elevator collapsed, sending tons of grain down the bluff. The shanty was obliterated in an instant. Fortunately the laborer and his family were elsewhere at the time. See *St. Paul Dispatch*, May 19, 1876, p. 4.

11. Murphy and Granger, *Historic Sites Survey*, 344–45. St. Paul historian James Sazevich is the source of the estimate that at least one hundred 1850s-vintage structures survive in St. Paul. The oldest identified residential structure in St. Paul is the Charles Symonds house (1850) at 234 Ryan Street. Sazevich, based on his research, believes that a like number of pre-Civil War buildings survive in Minneapolis. The Ard Godfrey house (1848), moved to Chute Square in Minneapolis in 1909, may be the oldest surviving structure in either city.

12. Williams, *Saint Paul to 1875*, 216. It appears that the balloon frame method arrived in St. Paul by at least 1844, according to research by James Sazevich. For more on the invention of the balloon frame, see Carl W. Condit, *American Building: Materials and Techniques from the First Colonial Settlements to the Present* (Chicago: University of Chicago Press, 1968), 43–45.

13. W. B. Hennessy, *History of the Saint Paul Fire Department* (St. Paul: St. Paul Fire Department Relief Fund Assn., 1909), 12, 18, 22, 40, 45, 49; Williams, *Saint Paul to 1875*, 428. Among the St. Paul hotels destroyed

by fire during this period were the Sintomine, just before it was to open in 1854; the Rice House, 1856; the Galena House and Canada House, 1857; the Winslow House, 1862; the American House, 1863; the Cosmopolitan, 1866; and the Mansion House, 1867. Minneapolis, perhaps because most of its early hotels were built of brick, did not suffer nearly so many fires.

14. Hennessy, *Saint Paul Fire Department*, 34. See also Williams, *Saint Paul to 1875*, 392.

15. The account of the female fire fighter is in Rosheim, *The Other Minneapolis*, 17.

16. For the early use of brick in the Twin Cities, see Williams, *Saint Paul to 1875*, 233; Torbert, "Minneapolis Architecture," 22; Jean Anne Vincent, "Saint Paul Architecture, 1848–1906" (Master's thesis, University of Minnesota, 1944), plate no. 5.

17. The use of terra cotta from Red Wing on buildings in the Twin Cities is discussed in *St. Paul Daily Press*, August 6, 1874, p. 3.

18. Torbert, "Minneapolis Architecture," 20, 73; Murphy and Granger, *Historic Sites Survey*, 177. On January 1, 1869, St. Paul's black community gathered at Ingersoll Hall to celebrate an amendment to the Minnesota Constitution giving black men the right to vote in state and local elections; Williams, *Saint Paul to 1875*, 434. For more information on the history of cast-iron architecture in America, see Margot Gayle's introduction to Daniel D. Badger, *Badger's Illustrated Catalogue of Cast-iron Architecture* (New York: Baker & Godwin, 1865; New York: Dover Publications, 1981).

19. Warren Upham, "History of Mining and Quarrying in Minnesota," in *Collections of the Minnesota Historical Society* 8 (1898): 291–302; Vincent, "St. Paul Architecture," 9; Torbert, "Minneapolis Architecture," 23.

20. For a mention of an early "double tenement house," see *St. Paul Daily Press*, November 24, 1867, p. 2. A four-unit stone row house was built on Cliff Street in St. Paul in 1859, according to James Sazevich. This row house, possibly the city's first true multiple dwelling unit, was razed in the 1960s.

21. For general information on the Winslow House, see Kane and Ominsky, *Twin Cities*, 27, and Berman, ed., *Saint Anthony Falls*, 76. For more on the first State Capitol and the first Ramsey County Courthouse, see Hess, "Architectural History of St. Paul," 26–30. For the description of the Wabasha Bridge by James Caird, an English traveler, see Federal Writers' Project, *The WPA Guide to Minnesota* (New York: Viking, 1938; St. Paul: Minnesota Historical Society Press, Borealis Books, 1985), 221. The first Wabasha Street Bridge was, like the

suspension bridge in Minneapolis, originally a toll structure. It was rebuilt in 1872, and the tolls were abolished two years later. The bridge was again rebuilt about 1884 before being replaced by the present-day Wabasha Street Bridge, parts of which date from 1889.

22. Hess, "Architectural History of St. Paul," 28–30.

23. Howard F. Koeper, *Historic St. Paul Buildings: A Report of the Historic Sites Committee* (St. Paul: City Planning Board, 1964), 12; Torbert, "Minneapolis Architecture," 416–18; Hess, "Architectural History of St. Paul," 45; Larson, "Architectural History of St. Paul," chap. 2, p. 9–10, 17–18.

24. Andrew Jackson Downing, *Victorian Cottage Residences*, 5th ed. (New York: John Wiley and Son, 1873; New York: Dover Publications, 1981); Andrew Jackson Downing, *The Architecture of Country Houses* (New York: D. Appleton and Co., 1850; New York: Dover Publications, 1969). For Downing's influence on nineteenth century domestic architecture, see Clifford Edward Clark, Jr., *The American Family Home, 1800–1960* (Chapel Hill: University of North Carolina Press, 1986), 16–17. For Downing's and Vaux's influence in St. Paul, see *St. Paul Pioneer and Democrat*, November 25, 1860, p. 1. See also Vaux, *Villas and Cottages* (New York: Harper & Brothers, 1857).

25. Montgomery Schuyler, "Glimpses of Western Architecture: St. Paul and Minneapolis," *Harper's Magazine*, October 1891, reprinted in Montgomery Schuyler, *American Architecture and Other Writings*, ed. William H. Jordy and Ralph Coe (Cambridge, Mass.: Harvard University Press, Belknap Press, 1961), 308. Buffington's last major commission in St. Paul appears to have been the second State Capitol.

26. Kane and Ominsky, *Twin Cities*, 49; Schmid, *Social Saga*, 387–88; Williams, *Saint Paul to 1875*, 420.

27. For streetlights, see *100 Years in the St. Paul Pioneer Press, 1849–1949* (St. Paul: St. Paul Dispatch and Pioneer Press, 1949), 19; water system, Hesterman, "Interests, Values and Public Policy," 96; beginnings of sewer system, *St. Paul and Minneapolis Pioneer Press*, October 4, 1885, p. 8; problems with sewer system, *St. Paul Pioneer Press*, May 1, 1875, p. 4; paving of Third Street, "Kellogg Boulevard: The Story of Old Third Street," *Ramsey County History* 6, no. 2 (Fall 1969): 14.

28. For information on early sewer, water, gas, and telephone service in Minneapolis, see Shutter, ed., *History of Minneapolis*, 1:123, 155–56, 160, 174. For a complaint on mud in Minneapolis, see *St. Paul Pioneer*, December 28, 1866, p. 4. Mud was eighteen inches deep in some city streets, and this was the source of a memo-

rable incident in 1881. During construction of the Boston Block on Hennepin Avenue, a huge iron beam intended for the building mysteriously disappeared. No one could figure out how thieves might have made away with so massive a piece of iron. The answer, of course, was that it had sunk into the avenue's deep mire, where it was discovered the next spring.

29. Russell L. Olson, *The Electric Railways of Minnesota* (Hopkins, Minn.: Minnesota Transportation Museum, 1976), 13–15. There is some question as to when horse-cars first went into service in Minneapolis. Olson says it may have been as early as 1872, but most other sources say service started in 1875.

30. Figures on steamboat dockings are from Schmid, *Social Saga*, 7. The comment on "low river dives" is in [Muller and Mead], *Police and Fire Departments*, 55. Hill's account of his street fight is in Albro Martin, *James J. Hill and the Opening of the Northwest* (New York: Oxford University Press, 1976; St. Paul: Minnesota Historical Society Press, Borealis Books, 1991), 40–41.

31. Information on saloons in St. Paul is from Joel Best, "Keeping the Peace in St. Paul: Crime, Vice, and Police Work, 1869–74," *Minnesota History* 47 (Summer 1981): 242. See also two related articles by Best: "Looking Evil in the Face: Being an Examination of Vice and Respectability in St. Paul as Seen in the City's Press, 1865–83," *Minnesota History* 50 (Summer 1987): 241–51, and "Long Kate, Dutch Henriette, and Mother Robinson: Three Madams in Post-Civil War St. Paul," *Ramsey County History* 15, no. 2 (1979): 3–10. For more on Mary Robinson's house, see Best, "Long Kate," 7–8, and *St. Paul Daily Pioneer*, January 1, 1871, p. 4. The Minneapolis police chief's adventures in St. Paul are recounted in Lawrence James Hill, "A History of Variety-Vaudeville in Minneapolis, Minnesota, from Its Beginning to 1900" (Ph.D. diss., University of Minnesota, 1979), 93.

32. Best, "Keeping the Peace," 242. The best source of information about the Theater Comique is Hill, "Variety-Vaudeville in Minneapolis."

33. Schmid, *Social Saga*, 18–19; Anfinson, *Archaeological Potentials*, 23, 89, 98–99, 105.

34. Kane, *Falls of St. Anthony*, 102. For a typically overwrought account of the Washburn A disaster, see *Minneapolis Tribune*, May 3, 1878, p. 1, 4. Many national publications also gave extensive coverage to the explosion.

35. The influence of American grain elevators on modernist architecture in Europe is explored in Reyner Banham, *A Concrete Atlantis: U.S. Industrial Building and European Modern Architecture, 1900–1925* (Cambridge, Mass.: MIT Press, 1986). For early grain elevators in the Twin Cities, see Robert M. Frame III, *A Historic Context for Grain Elevators in Minnesota* (St. Paul: Minnesota Historical Society, 1989).

36. Henry Castle, author of a three-volume history of St. Paul published in 1912, was among those who tried to drum up support for calling St. Paul the "Terrace City."

37. For information on early rail connections to St. Paul, see *St. Paul Daily Pioneer*, April 1, 1871, p. 2, and Schmid, *Social Saga*, 22.

38. For a description of the Beaupre and Kelly store and the fire that destroyed the building, see *St. Paul and Minneapolis Pioneer Press*, August 24, 1880, p. 1.

39. For a general description of stone quarrying in the Midwest, see John C. Hudson, "The Midland Prairies: Natural Resources and Urban Settlement," in *The Spirit of H. H. Richardson on the Midland Prairies: Regional Transformations of an Architectural Style*, ed. Paul Clifford Larson with Susan M. Brown (Minneapolis and Ames, Iowa: University Art Museum, University of Minnesota, and Iowa State University Press, 1988), 123–37. The Kasota quarries were developed by Joseph W. Babcock in 1869, and the stone was used for bridge piers in St. Paul as early as 1870. The first major St. Paul building to be constructed of this stone apparently was the First Baptist Church (1875). St. Cloud granite first appeared in St. Paul in the early 1870s when it was used as trim on the U.S. Customs House. See *St. Paul Pioneer Press*, May 19, 1875, p. 4, for more information on the use of various building stones in the city.

40. *An Illustrated Historical Atlas of the State of Minnesota* (Chicago: A. T. Andreas, 1874; Evansville, Ind.: Unigraphic, Inc., 1976). The St. Paul building figures for 1872 are from Williams, *Saint Paul to 1875*, 444.

41. *St. Paul Dispatch*, January 12, 1876, p. 4.

42. The easiest way to appreciate how many buildings were once clustered around Bridge Square is to look at old insurance maps, such as *Insurance Maps of Minneapolis, Minnesota*, vol. 3 (New York: Sanborn Map Co., 1912), plates 231–33.

43. For more on Hill's house, see Robert M. Frame III, *James J. Hill's Saint Paul: A Guide to Historic Sites* (St. Paul: James Jerome Hill Reference Library, 1988), 3–5. For Irvine Park, see *A Brief History of the Irvine Park District: The People and Architecture of an Extraordinary Neighborhood* (St. Paul: Historic Irvine Park Assn., [1986]). It is interesting to note that only thirteen houses were built on Summit Avenue between 1865 and 1880. By contrast, the decade of the 1880s saw sixty new houses

go up on the avenue. See Sandeen, *Summit Avenue*, 108.

44. Lanegran and Sandeen, *Lake District*, 31.

45. For early tenements in St. Paul, see *St. Paul Daily Pioneer*, March 23, 1873, p. 4.

46. The Market House was built by Harlow Gale, one of the most prominent real estate dealers in Minneapolis. It quickly proved to be inadequate, and by 1885 Gale was looking for a new market site. See *Inland Architect and Builder*, August 1885, p. 10.

47. For a good account of the Pence, see Donald Z. Woods, "Playhouse for Pioneers: The Story of the Pence Opera House," *Minnesota History* 33 (Winter 1952): 169–78. See also J[oseph] W. Zalusky, "Early Theater, or the History of Entertainment in Minneapolis," *Hennepin County History* [19, no. 4] (Fall 1960): 3–7. The St. Paul Opera House is described in Frank M. Whiting, *Minnesota Theatre: From Old Fort Snelling to the Guthrie* (St. Paul: Pogo Press, 1988), 58–60.

48. Torbert, "Minneapolis Architecture," 421–24.

49. *American Architect and Building News*, June 29, 1878, p. 227, quoted in Torbert, "Minneapolis Architecture," 74–75. Torbert notes that of the twenty-three architects listed in Minneapolis city directories between 1865 and 1879, eight are listed only once or twice and five have no known buildings to their credit.

50. The best general source on these early architects remains Torbert, "Minneapolis Architecture," 416–63.

51. The most detailed study of nineteenth-century St. Paul architects, and the source of much of the information in this paragraph, is Larson, "Architectural History of St. Paul."

52. All of these outside architects, except for Dudley, are relatively well-known figures. For Dudley's role at St. Mark's, see Torbert, "Minneapolis Architecture," 149.

53. *American Architect and Building News*, June 29, 1878, p. 227, quoted in Torbert, "Minneapolis Architecture," 89.

Building Profiles

ST. PAUL HOUSE-MERCHANTS HOTEL: George E. Warner and Charles M. Foote, comps., *History of Ramsey County and the City of St. Paul, including the Explorers and Pioneers of Minnesota, by Rev. Edward D. Neill, and Outlines of the History of Minnesota, by J. Fletcher Williams* (Minneapolis: North Star Publishing Co., 1881), 439; Williams, *Saint Paul to 1875*, 165, 172–73; *100 Years in the Pioneer Press*, 8; Newson, *Pen Pictures*, 646–47 (it is Newson who attributes much of the design of the hotel to Knight); *St. Paul Pioneer*, March 31, 1870, p. 4, Decem-

ber 13, 1870, p. 4; *Northwest Magazine*, April 1886, p. 38; *St. Paul and Minneapolis Pioneer Press*, December 25, 1877, p. 7, March 6, 1882, p. 6, January 14, 1883, p. 10; *St. Paul Daily Press*, May 21, 1871, p. 4; *St. Paul Pioneer Press*, April 24, 1949, sec. 4, p. 2.

FIRST AND SECOND STATE CAPITOLS: William B. Dean, "A History of the Capitol Buildings of Minnesota with Some Account of the Struggles for Their Location," in *Collections of the Minnesota Historical Society* 12 (1908): 1–9, 18, 21, 23; Williams, *Saint Paul to 1875*, 143–44; *St. Paul City Directory, 1856–57*, 12; Eileen Michels, "Landscape of Government," in *Saint Paul Omnibus: Images of the Changing City*, ed. Bonnie Richter (St. Paul: Old Town Restorations, Inc., 1979), 23–27; Hess, "Architectural History of St. Paul," 27–29; *St. Paul Pioneer*, December 7, 1873, p. 4; "Burning of the First Capitol," *Gopher Historian* 23 (Fall 1968): 5–8; *St. Paul and Minneapolis Pioneer Press*, March 2, 1881, p. 1, April 21, 1881, p. 7, December 16, 1882, p. 12; *St. Paul Daily Globe*, December 31, 1883, p. 10; *St. Paul Daily News*, April 5, 1889, p. 1; *Northwest Magazine*, September 1896, p. 5; *St. Paul Dispatch*, February 13, 1893, p. 5; *Saturday Evening Spectator*, December 10, 1887, p. 1.

ALPHEUS FULLER-LAFAYETTE EMMETT HOUSE: Talbot Hamlin, *Greek Revival Architecture in America: Being an Account of Important Trends in American Architecture and American Life prior to the War Between the States* (New York: Oxford University Press, 1944; New York: Dover, 1964); Virginia McAlester and Lee McAlester, *A Field Guide to American Houses* (New York: Alfred A. Knopf, 1984), 179–80, 184; "Local History Items," *Minnesota History* 9 (June 1928): 200–201; Williams, *Saint Paul to 1875*, 357, 364, 365; *Minnesota Pioneer*, July 28, 1853, p. 2; *St. Paul Dispatch*, January 28, 1942, p. 17.

FIRST AND SECOND SUSPENSION BRIDGES: Condit, *American Building*, 104–10, 148–51; Anfinson, *Archaeological Potentials*, 80–84; *Bridges of Minneapolis and the State of Minnesota, Minneapolis Public Schools Bulletin No. 56* (Minneapolis: Minneapolis Board of Education with Works Projects Administration, [1942?]), 2; Stevens, *Personal Recollections*, 260; William E. Leonard, "Early Days in Minneapolis," in *Collections of the Minnesota Historical Society* 15 (May 1915): 501; "The First Suspension Bridge," *Hennepin County History* 12, no. 3 (July 1952): 2–3; Rosheim, *The Other Minneapolis*, 12; *St. Paul Pioneer*, February 2, 1871, p. 1, November 19, 1874, p. 3, April 1, 1875, p. 3, April 2, 1875, p. 3; Frederick Cappelen, "The Late Suspension Bridge of Minneapolis," in *Association of Engineering Societies Journal* 10 (August

1891): 400–426, cited in Kenneth Bjork, *Saga in Steel and Concrete: Norwegian Engineers in America* (Northfield, Minn.: Norwegian-American Historical Assn., 1947), 146; *St. Paul and Minneapolis Pioneer Press*, September 3, 1882, p. 10; Schuyler, "Western Architecture," 307–8; *St. Paul Pioneer Press*, July 13, 1988, p. 1C.

NICOLLET HOUSE: Joseph Zalusky, "Hotel Nicollet," *Hennepin County History* [27, no. 3] (Winter 1968): 9–13; *Minneapolis Journal*, September 26, 1903, p. 10; *St. Paul and Minneapolis Pioneer Press*, July 21, 1881, p. 6, March 16, 1882, p. 6.

THIRD ST. PAUL CATHEDRAL AND BISHOP'S RESIDENCE: Eric C. Hansen, *The Cathedral of Saint Paul: An Architectural Biography* (St. Paul: Cathedral of Saint Paul, 1990), 5, 12–14, 43; "Forgotten Pioneers, VIII: Bishop Joseph Cretin," *Ramsey County History* 6, no. 2 (Fall 1969): 16–17; James M. Reardon, *The Catholic Church in the Diocese of St. Paul from Earliest Origin to Centennial Achievement* (St. Paul: North Central Publishing Co., 1952), 77, 125, 152–53, 270, 372–80; *St. Paul Pioneer and Democrat*, November 25, 1860, p. 1. Note: The second St. Paul Cathedral, used as a school after 1858, was demolished in 1889 to make way for a new building that later became Schuneman and Evans department store; see *St. Paul Daily News*, August 5, 1889, p. 2. Historian James Sazevich says that some stone from the third cathedral may have been salvaged and used for the huge retaining wall around the Goodkind house at the crest of Oakland Hill on Grand Avenue in St. Paul.

WEST SIDE FLOUR MILLING DISTRICT: Kane, *Falls of St. Anthony*, 99–105, 172–73; Anfinson, *Archaeological Potentials*, 89–132, 175; Berman, ed., *Saint Anthony Falls*, 39–41; *St. Paul and Minneapolis Pioneer Press*, May 3, 1878, p. 1, March 12, 1880, p. 6; *Northwest Magazine*, November 1883, p. 13; *St. Paul Pioneer Press*, February 28, 1991, p. 1B.

HORACE THOMPSON HOUSE: Christopher C. Andrews, ed., *History of St. Paul, Minnesota, with Illustrations and Biographical Sketches of Some of Its Prominent Men and Pioneers* (Syracuse, N.Y.: D. Mason and Co., 1890), 2:122–24; Frank P. Donovan, Jr., and Cushing F. Wright, *The First through a Century, 1853–1953: A History of the First National Bank of Saint Paul* ([St. Paul]: Itasca Press, 1954), 15–24, 31; *St. Paul Pioneer and Democrat*, November 25, 1860, p. 1; Hess, "Architectural History of St. Paul," 42; Downing, *Cottage Residences*, 140–51; *St. Paul and Minneapolis Pioneer Press*, January 31, 1880, p. 1; Chaney, "Early Bridges and Changes," 138.

BOHEMIAN FLATS: Writers' Program, Works Projects Administration, *The Bohemian Flats* (Minneapolis:

University of Minnesota Press, 1941; reprint with new introduction by Thaddeus Radzilowski, St. Paul: Minnesota Historical Society Press, Borealis Books, 1986), xvii, xx, xxviii, 15, 19; Joel Benton, "The Wood Gatherers of St. Anthony's Falls," *Northwest Magazine*, July 1887, p. 16; O. E. Rølvaag, *The Boat of Longing* (New York: Harper, 1933; St. Paul: Minnesota Historical Society Press, Borealis Books, 1985), 108.

FIRST AND SECOND WASHINGTON SCHOOLS: Torbert, "Minneapolis Architecture," 417–18; Leonard, "Early Days," 509–10; Joseph Zalusky, "The Union School," *Hennepin County History* [23, no. 3] (Winter 1964): 17; *Minneapolis and St. Paul Pioneer Press*, April 8, 1888, p. 12; *Saturday Evening Spectator*, February 25, 1888, p. 2; *Minneapolis Star*, November 5, 1963, p. 4B, August 16, 1971, p. 9A.

ACADEMY OF MUSIC: Hill, "Variety-Vaudeville in Minneapolis," 70, 117; Goodrich Lowry, *Streetcar Man: Tom Lowry and the Twin City Rapid Transit Company* (Minneapolis: Lerner Publications Co., 1979), 26–27; Torbert, "Minneapolis Architecture," 115–16, 416; *Minneapolis Tribune*, December 31, 1871, p. 4; *St. Paul and Minneapolis Pioneer Press*, June 14, 1880, p. 6, June 18, 1880, p. 6, March 16, 1882, p. 6, November 21, 1883, p. 6, December 26, 1884, p. 6; Whiting, *Minnesota Theatre*, 43.

WILLIAM JUDD HOUSE: *Atlas of the State of Minnesota*, 77; Atwater, ed., *City of Minneapolis*, 242, 581; *Minneapolis Journal*, November 26, 1902, p. 7; *Minneapolis Tribune*, October 3, 1875, p. 2, September 16, 1934, sec. 3, p. 1; Torbert, "Minneapolis Architecture," 97–99, 424–25; *Notable Buildings of Minneapolis, Social Studies Bulletin No. 57* (Minneapolis: Minneapolis Board of Education with Works Projects Administration, 1942), 47; *St. Paul Pioneer and Democrat*, November 25, 1860, p. 1; George E. Warner and Charles M. Foote, comps., *History of Hennepin County and the City of Minneapolis, including the Explorers and Pioneers of Minnesota, by Rev. Edward D. Neill, and Outlines of the History of Minnesota, by J. Fletcher Williams* (Minneapolis: North Star Publishing Co., 1881), 449; Michael P. Conforti, "Orientalism on the Upper Mississippi: The Work of John S. Bradstreet," *Minneapolis Institute of Arts Bulletin* 65 (1981–82): 6.

MINNEAPOLIS CITY HALL: *Minneapolis Tribune*, October 23, 1873, p. 4, October 24, 1873, p. 4; Torbert, "Minneapolis Architecture," 117–18; Kane and Ominsky, *Twin Cities*, 62; *St. Paul and Minneapolis Pioneer Press*, January 31, 1882, p. 7, January 14, 1883, p. 10; Anfinson, *Archaeological Potentials*, 27; Rosheim, *The Other Minneapolis*, 71.

U.S. CUSTOMS HOUSE: Williams, *Saint Paul to 1875*, 445, 446; *Northwest Magazine*, July 1890, p. 15; Richter, ed., *Omnibus*, 26; Castle, *History of St. Paul*, 1:38, 42; Hess, "Architectural History of St. Paul," 35; *St. Paul and Minneapolis Pioneer Press*, January 26, 1882, p. 7.

PLYMOUTH CONGREGATIONAL CHURCH: Atwater, ed., *City of Minneapolis*, 189–90; Adolf K. Placzek, ed., *Macmillan Encyclopedia of Architects* (New York: Free Press, 1982), 4:150; Whiffen and Koeper, *American Architecture*, 1:218; Henry F. Withey and Elsie Rathburn Withey, *Biographical Dictionary of American Architects (Deceased)* (Los Angeles: Hennessy & Ingalls, Inc., 1970), 581–82; *Fifty Years of Plymouth Church* (Minneapolis: Plymouth Church, 1907), 75, 176; *Minneapolis Tribune*, October 10, 1875, p. 5; *American Architect and Building News*, June 29, 1878, p. 227; Shutter, ed., *History of Minneapolis*, 1:585–86.

EASTMAN FLATS: Berman, ed., *Saint Anthony Falls*, 60–62; *St. Paul Dispatch*, January 4, 1874, p. 4; *Minneapolis Tribune*, June 16, 1877, p. 4, March 13, 1878, p. 4; *Minneapolis, Minnesota* (New York: Sanborn Map Publishing Co., 1885), plate 56; Rosheim, *The Other Minneapolis*, 207. Note: City records indicate that a wrecking permit was issued for the last section of Eastman Flats on October 28, 1958.

MINNEAPOLIS AND ST. PAUL CENTRAL HIGH SCHOOLS: *St. Paul and Minneapolis Pioneer Press*, April 8, 1877, p. 6, April 28, 1882, p. 6, April 29, 1882, p. 6, March 7, 1883, p. 7, March 14, 1888, p. 6; Torbert, "Minneapolis Architecture," 137–39; "Tribute to Triumph: Central High School, 1860–1982," publication of students of Central High School, May 1982, p. 2–3, copy at Minneapolis Public Library; *Saturday Evening Spectator*, January 21, 1888, p. 9; *St. Paul Public Schools: A Century of Service, 1856–1956* (St. Paul: St. Paul Public Schools, 1956), n.p. Note: Information on Randall's career in Chicago was provided by Tim Samuelson of the Commission on Chicago Historical and Architectural Landmarks.

COMING OF AGE, 1880–1900

1. Mark Twain, *Life on the Mississippi* (Boston: James R. Osgood, 1883; New York: Penguin Books, 1986), 398. Twain spent a night in St. Paul during his stopover but apparently did not visit Minneapolis.

2. Schuyler, "Western Architecture," 293; Schmid, *Social Saga*, 6, 70. Minneapolis annexed its last property in 1927, taking 5.4 square miles from the town of Richfield.

3. *St. Paul and Minneapolis Pioneer Press*, October 14, 1883, p. 8. This story, quoting the annual Bradstreet Building Report, says construction totalled $8.3 million in Minneapolis for the year. Other cities posting large construction totals were Chicago with $12.7 million and Cincinnati, $11 million. See also *Inland Architect and Builder*, March 1883, p. 25. The names of prominent buildings of the era, such as the Boston Block (1881, 1887) in Minneapolis, often reflected the influence of eastern capital.

4. *St. Paul and Minneapolis Pioneer Press*, August 12, 1883, p. 8; Schuyler, "Western Architecture," 293.

5. *St. Paul and Minneapolis Pioneer Press*, May 7, 1882, p. 12, September 12, 1889, p. 5, October 31, 1889, p. 36. The comments on real estate speculation are from E. Dudley Parsons, *The Story of Minneapolis* (Minneapolis: Privately published, 1913), 97–98.

6. Buffington's proposed skyscraper is illustrated in *Inland Architect and News Record*, July 1888. It was to be 80 by 80 feet on the ground, 350 feet high (a height not reached in the Twin Cities until the construction of the Foshay Tower in 1929), and have 728 offices. The hotel designed by Long and Kees was to be called the Palisade. See *Saturday Evening Spectator*, January 15, 1887, p. 3–4.

7. *St. Paul Daily Globe*, December 25, 1886, p. 1. The elevated train proposal is described in *St. Paul and Minneapolis Pioneer Press*, May 13, 1888, p. 6. For the underground train in Lowertown, see *St. Paul and Minneapolis Pioneer Press*, July 1, 1890, p. 1.

8. Malodorous air was a particular problem in St. Paul. In June 1890, for example, a terrible stench literally drove people from their homes near the High Bridge. "Clothespins for Noses" advised the *St. Paul and Minneapolis Pioneer Press*, June 29, 1890, p. 5, in an article on the big stink. Nearby slaughterhouses and rendering plants, not to mention a large city dump along the river, may all have contributed to the aromatic quality of the air in this part of the city. Even the wealthy, high on their hills, were not immune from olfactory assaults. In 1887, for example, a newspaper headline reported in the deadpan style of the era: "Crocus Hill People Revel in an Odor That Doesn't Resemble Attar of Roses to any Particular Extent"; *St. Paul and Minneapolis Pioneer Press*, July 30, 1887, p. 5.

9. For the first paving project in Minneapolis, see *St. Paul and Minneapolis Pioneer Press*, December 24, 1882, p. 14. The *Pioneer Press* even sent a reporter around

the country in the 1880s to study paving in other cities. Wealthy neighborhoods received the best paving because residents were willing to foot the bill. Thus the first asphalt paving in St. Paul appeared on Summit Avenue about 1887. Summit's counterpart across the river, Park Avenue, was the first asphalt street in Minneapolis.

10. *St. Paul and Minneapolis Pioneer Press*, March 13, 1882, p. 6.

11. Joseph W. Zalusky, "Bridge Square: Going, Going, Gone," *Hennepin County History* 21, no. 1 (Summer 1961): 5–7; "Tablet Marks First Hydro-Electric Plant, St. Anthony Falls, 1882," *Hennepin County History* 29, no. 1 (Summer 1969): 17. See also Shutter, ed., *History of Minneapolis*, 1:163–64. St. Paul also had a light mast, which was located at Wabasha and Third streets.

12. *St. Paul and Minneapolis Pioneer Press*, December 3, 1883, p. 2.

13. Paul Larson, "Tall Tales: The Story of the Twin Cities' First Towers," *Architecture Minnesota* 15, no. 2 (March–April 1989): 44; *St. Paul and Minneapolis Pioneer Press*, December 18, 1879, p. 5.

14. For more on the Tribune Tower in New York, see Thomas A. P. van Leeuwen, *The Skyward Trend of Thought: The Metaphysics of the American Skyscraper* (Cambridge, Mass.: MIT Press, 1988), 94–99.

15. *St. Paul and Minneapolis Pioneer Press*, April 26, 1885, p. 3. There are at least two competing schools of thought among skyscraper historians. What might be called the Chicago School holds that technological advances, along with high land costs and other financial incentives, led to the development of the modern skyscraper in Chicago in the 1880s. See Sigfried Giedion, *Space, Time and Architecture: The Growth of a New Tradition* (Cambridge, Mass.: Harvard University Press, 1941), and Carl W. Condit, *The Chicago School of Architecture: A History of Commercial and Public Building in the Chicago Area, 1875–1925* (Chicago: University of Chicago Press, 1964). Another group of scholars, less technologically oriented, argues that the skyscraper was an essentially poetic creation, a striving toward height that expressed some of the deepest dreams and myths of American civilization. This school contends that the skyscraper actually came out of New York City, beginning in the 1870s. For two delightful, if not entirely convincing, presentations of the skyscraper-as-myth theory, see van Leeuwen, *Skyward Trend*, and Rem Koolhaas, *Delirious New York: A Retroactive Manifesto for Manhattan* (New York: Oxford University Press, 1978).

16. Schuyler, "Western Architecture," 294.

17. The tower was, in fact, extremely visible from various points along Nicollet Avenue and appears prominently in many photographs.

18. A writer for the *St. Paul and Minneapolis Pioneer Press*, January 2, 1887, p. 3, noted "dissatisfaction among some of the architects and builders with the provision of the new building ordinance which restricts the height of buildings to 125 feet." For passage of the 1890 ordinance, see *Minneapolis Tribune*, March 29, 1890, p. 6, March 30, 1890, p. 4. The *Tribune's* March 30 editorial prompted a strong reply several days later from Minneapolis architect Franklin Long, who argued in a letter to the editor (April 4, 1890, p. 4) that the ordinance might drive developers away. Height restrictions were established in many other cities at this time. In 1893, for example, Chicago imposed a 130-foot limit on office buildings.

19. Insurance maps indicate that the tallest non-church building in St. Paul before the late 1880s may actually have been the St. Paul Roller Mill, built in 1878–80 and located at the bottom of the bluff along Third Street near St. Peter. The mill was ten stories high.

20. Larson, "Tall Tales," 47.

21. *Northwest Magazine*, November 1894, p. 17.

22. *Saturday Evening Spectator*, June 11, 1887, p. 14.

23. *Minneapolis Industrial and Art Exposition Souvenir and Illustrated Hand Book* (Minneapolis: Baldwin, Brice, and Brundage, 1886), 49.

24. Schmid, *Social Saga*, 54.

25. *St. Paul and Minneapolis Pioneer Press*, May 10, 1885, p. 8, September 10, 1882, p. 6, April 13, 1884, p. 3.

26. Schmid, *Social Saga*, 77; *St. Paul and Minneapolis Pioneer Press*, March 12, 1882, p. 6. Harrison Salisbury, who was raised in Oak Lake, gave a fine description of the neighborhood in Chester G. Anderson, ed., *Growing Up in Minnesota: Ten Writers Remember Their Childhood* (Minneapolis: University of Minnesota Press, 1976), 53–54.

27. *Saturday Evening Spectator*, January 15, 1887, p. 8; *St. Paul and Minneapolis Pioneer Press*, September 10, 1889, p. 6.

28. Castle, *History of St. Paul*, 1:392.

29. *St. Paul and Minneapolis Pioneer Press*, April 22, 1881, p. 7; Sandeen, *Summit Avenue*, 9.

30. *St. Paul and Minneapolis Pioneer Press*, September 3, 1882, p. 5; *St. Paul Daily News*, March 30, 1889, p. 2.

31. [Muller and Mead], *Police and Fire Departments*, 280–81.

32. *St. Paul Pioneer Press*, May 23, 1886, p. 3.

33. *St. Paul Daily Globe*, May 1, 1889, p. 2.

34. New apartment buildings in the 1880s were often referred to as "French flats," either because they were

modeled on apartments found in France or simply to give them added cachet.

35. *Northwest Magazine,* April 1887, p. 7.

36. Smalley, "Progressive Minneapolis," 22.

37. *St. Paul and Minneapolis Pioneer Press,* February 22, 1885, p. 13.

38. For more on the dime museums, see Henry Broderick, "I Remember Minneapolis," unpublished manuscript, 1962, p. 10, Minneapolis Public Library and Minnesota Historical Society; Alice M. Dunn, "People and Places in Old St. Paul: Reminiscences of Alice Monfort Dunn," *Minnesota History* 33 (Spring 1952): 2–3; Hill, "Variety-Vaudeville in Minneapolis," 101, 130–31, 167, 181, 216 (quote from *Saturday Evening Spectator*), 253, 268; Max Winkel, "A Collection of One-Page Articles on the History of St. Paul," prepared for Junior Pioneer Association of St. Paul, mimeographed, 1955–61, Minnesota Historical Society.

39. For a brief description and drawings of the Felsenkeller, see *Northwest Magazine,* November 1886, p. 34–35. This peculiar establishment is also depicted in *Atlas of St. Paul,* vol. 4 (Chicago: Rascher Insurance Map Publishing Co., 1891), plate 340. Its exact address was 98 West Chicago (rear) (a street now vanished).

40. The *Journal* reporter's adventures are in Rosheim, *The Other Minneapolis,* 41.

41. Stew Thornley, *On to Nicollet: The Glory and Fame of the Minneapolis Millers* (Minneapolis: Nodin Press, 1988), 14, 19.

42. *St. Paul and Minneapolis Pioneer Press,* September 4, 1883, p. 2. St. Paul staged another giant celebration in June 1893 when the Great Northern Railway completed its transcontinental line. At least six large arches were constructed for this parade; see *St. Paul Pioneer Press,* June 8, 1893, p. 1, for details. For the Villard parade in Minneapolis, see Kane and Ominsky, *Twin Cities,* 90.

43. *St. Paul and Minneapolis Pioneer Press,* February 2, 1886, p. 1, February 2, 1888, p. 1.

44. There are good descriptions of St. Paul's early ice palaces in Fred Anderes and Ann Agranoff, *Ice Palaces* (New York: Abbeville Press, 1983), 47–66. For various features of the 1886 carnival, see *St. Paul and Minneapolis Pioneer Press,* January 31, 1886, carnival number, p. [1]–4.

45. Bookwalter's lament for profits lost is in *St. Paul and Minneapolis Pioneer Press,* January 21, 1890, p. 5. See also Anderes and Agranoff, *Ice Palaces,* 62–66.

46. *Minneapolis Tribune,* August 24, 1886, p. 1–2. Many other newspapers, as well as magazines and special pamphlets, trumpeted the opening of the exposition.

47. Atwater, ed., *City of Minneapolis,* 853–54; Shutter, ed., *History of Minneapolis,* 1:672–74; *Minneapolis Tribune,* September 24, 1891, p. 1.

48. *St. Paul and Minneapolis Pioneer Press,* August 22, 1881, p. 2, January 1, 1889, p. 10. Most of the depot's passengers, it should be noted, were daily commuters. Of the 220 trains said to use the depot on an average day, 164 were "locals" and only 56 were "through" trains.

49. Schmid, *Social Saga,* 61–62.

50. Wirth, *Park System,* 39.

51. Washburn's complaint is in *St. Paul and Minneapolis Pioneer Press,* February 23, 1886, p. 3. The "steam motor" ran along Marquette from First to Thirteenth streets, then down Nicollet to Thirty-first Street, across Thirty-first to Hennepin, and finally to Lake Calhoun. See "History of Minneapolis Street Railways—The Old 'Motor Line,'" *Hennepin County History* 11, no. 1 [1951]: 2–3, and no. 2 [1951]: 2–3.

52. Olson, *Electric Railways,* 17; Lowry, *Streetcar Man,* 102–3.

53. Karl Marx and Friedrich Engels, *The Communist Manifesto,* cited in Marshall Berman, *All That Is Solid Melts into Air: The Experience of Modernity* (New York: Simon and Schuster, 1982; New York: Penguin Books, 1988), 95. For a typical newspaper account of an industrial accident (involving a man whose feet were "pounded off" after he became caught in a rotating shaft at a Minneapolis box factory), see *St. Paul and Minneapolis Pioneer Press,* June 5, 1880, p. 6. No statistics are readily available for the number of fatal train accidents in the Twin Cities in the 1880s and 1890s. But in Chicago, which probably led the world in such accidents because of its flat terrain and extensive track system, as many as 430 people a year were killed by trains in the 1890s. See Ross Miller, *American Apocalypse: The Great Fire and the Myth of Chicago* (Chicago: University of Chicago Press, 1990), 243. Among the numerous examples of public suicide in the 1880s was the case of a sixteen-year-old boy who, after being spurned by his girlfriend (and attempting to kill her), put a forty-four caliber revolver to his forehead and fired as horrified witnesses looked on at the corner of Eighth and Broadway streets in downtown St. Paul; *St. Paul and Minneapolis Pioneer Press,* May 4, 1882, p. 7.

54. *Minneapolis Tribune,* March 30, 1890, p. 4.

55. *St. Paul and Minneapolis Pioneer Press,* February 6, 1882, p. 7.

56. For the introduction of Sioux quartzite (Jasper stone) in the Twin Cities, see *St. Paul and Minneapolis Pioneer Press,* December 2, 1883, p. 8.

57. The copper facade system is described in *Northwest Magazine,* August 1892, p. 34.

58. *St. Paul and Minneapolis Pioneer Press*, May 6, 1886, p. 5, May 11, 1886, p. 6; Winkel, "A Collection of One-Page Articles," [59].

59. *St. Paul Daily Globe*, December 2, 1889, p. 1; *St. Paul Dispatch*, November 12, 1948, p. 25.

60. *St. Paul and Minneapolis Pioneer Press*, May 27, 1883, p. 8.

61. *American Architect and Building News*, April 7, 1883, p. 166; Larson, "Architectural History of St. Paul," 25.

62. Larson, "Architectural History of St. Paul," 10, 38. See also Stevens's obituary in *St. Paul Dispatch*, April 27, 1937, p. 11.

63. Larson, "Architectural History of St. Paul," 26–31.

64. Patricia Anne Murphy, "The Early Career of Cass Gilbert: 1878 to 1895" (Master's thesis, University of Virginia, 1979), 6, 14, 16, 32–33. See also Larson, "Architectural History of St. Paul," 31–34.

65. Architects and contractors file, Historic Sites Survey of Saint Paul and Ramsey County, 1980–83, Ramsey County Historical Society, St. Paul; Larson, "Architectural History of St. Paul," 11, 34, 48, 50.

66. Here and below, the chief sources of information are Architects and contractors file, Historic Sites Survey, and Larson, "Architectural History of St. Paul."

67. For Charles Joy, see Anderes and Agranoff, *Ice Palaces*, 55–62. Here and below, see Ellen Threinen, "Harvey Ellis as Architect and Draftsman: A Clarification and Re-evaluation" (Master's thesis, University of New Mexico, 1976), 14; Eileen Manning [Michels], "The Architectural Designs of Harvey Ellis" (Master's thesis, University of Minnesota, 1953); Larson, "Architectural History of St. Paul," 11, 36, 48.

68. Here and below, see Torbert, "Minneapolis Architecture," 440–43.

69. For Jones, see Hudson, ed., *Half Century*, 132; *Minneapolis Journal*, September 26, 1935, p. 17; Torbert, "Minneapolis Architecture," 448–50.

70. John Burrows, "The Work of E. Townsend Mix: A Study of His Artistic Development and His Relationship with the Yankee Society of the City of Milwaukee" (Master's thesis, University of Virginia, 1980). See also Torbert, "Minneapolis Architecture," 452–53.

71. Brief biographies of most of the architects mentioned in this paragraph can be found in Torbert, "Minneapolis Architecture."

72. For more on the Northern Pacific building, see *St. Paul and Minneapolis Pioneer Press*, November 5, 1882, p. 7.

73. The most comprehensive work on the Chicago School remains Condit, *Chicago School*. For Sullivan, see Robert Twombly, *Louis Sullivan: His Life and Work* (New York: Viking, 1986). For Root, see Donald Hoffmann, *The Architecture of John Wellborn Root* (Baltimore: Johns Hopkins University Press, 1973; Chicago: University of Chicago Press, 1988). See also Robert Prestiano, *The Inland Architect: Chicago's Major Architectural Journal, 1893–1908* (Ann Arbor, Mich.: UMI Research Press, 1985).

74. Schuyler, "Western Architecture," 328.

75. *St. Paul and Minneapolis Pioneer Press*, November 23, 1884, p. 8.

76. *St. Paul and Minneapolis Pioneer Press*, April 9, 1882, p. 7.

77. The style's name is a misnomer because the kind of architecture that flourished in England during Queen Anne's reign (1702–14) was based on Renaissance models and was quite restrained. For the Watts Sherman house, see Henry-Russell Hitchcock, *The Architecture of H. H. Richardson and His Times* (New York: Museum of Modern Art, 1936; rev. ed., Cambridge, Mass.: MIT Press, 1966), 156–64, and Antoinette F. Downing and Vincent J. Scully, Jr., *The Architectural Heritage of Newport, Rhode Island: 1640–1915* (Cambridge, Mass.: Harvard University Press, 1942; rev. ed., New York: Clarkson N. Potter, 1967), 154–55.

78. *St. Paul and Minneapolis Pioneer Press*, November 23, 1884, p. 8; *Inland Architect and Builder*, January 1885, p. 6.

79. For more on Richardson and his influence both in Minnesota and nationally, see Paul Clifford Larson, "Curator's Introduction," in *Spirit of H. H. Richardson*, ed. Larson, 13–17. See also Hitchcock, *Architecture of H. H. Richardson*, and James F. O'Gorman, *H. H. Richardson: Architectural Forms for an American Society* (Chicago: University of Chicago Press, 1987).

80. Thomas J. Schlereth, "H. H. Richardson's Influence in Chicago's Midwest: 1872–1914," in *Spirit of H. H. Richardson*, ed. Larson, 44–65.

81. Here and two paragraphs below, see Paul Clifford Larson, "H. H. Richardson Goes West: The Rise and Fall of an Eastern Star," in *Spirit of H. H. Richardson*, ed. Larson, 18–43. For the McNair house, see Jack El-Hai, "Lost Minnesota," *Architecture Minnesota* 17, no. 4 (July–August 1991): 110.

82. *Northwest Magazine*, April 1887, p. 8.

83. The first Shingle Style house was built for Isaac Bell, Jr., in Newport, R.I., in 1883 and designed by McKim, Mead, and White. See Richard Guy Wilson, *McKim, Mead and White Architects* (New York: Rizzoli,

ساخ

1983), 78–83. The standard work on the Shingle Style is Vincent J. Scully, Jr., *The Shingle Style* (New Haven, Conn.: Yale University Press, 1955; rev. ed., *The Shingle Style and the Stick Style,* 1971).

84. Larson, "Architectural History of St. Paul," 43–45.

85. Paul Larson pointed out the Hinkle house as an early example of Colonial Revival in the Twin Cities.

86. Wilson, *McKim, Mead and White,* 95–99, 134–45. See also Richard Guy Wilson, Dianne Pilgrim, and Murray Richard, *The American Renaissance: 1876–1917* (Brooklyn and New York: Brooklyn Museum and Pantheon Press, 1979).

87. For Gilbert's involvement with the State Capitol, see Neil B. Thompson, *Minnesota's State Capitol: The Art and Politics of a Public Building* (St. Paul: Minnesota Historical Society, 1974), 5–23.

88. For the Partridge house, see Lanegran and Sandeen, *Lake District,* 71, and *Western Architect* 13 (March 1904): 25.

Building Profiles

ST. PAUL CITY RAILWAY COMPANY-DICKINSON'S DEPARTMENT STORE: *St. Paul and Minneapolis Pioneer Press,* January 23, 1880, p. 7, July 26, 1880, p. 7, May 17, 1885, p. 5; Olson, *Electric Railways,* 15; *St. Paul Pioneer Press,* February 19, 1893, p. 10.

MARKET HALL: *St. Paul Pioneer Press,* July 11, 1898, p. 4; Rosemary J. Palmer, "The St. Paul Farmer's Market—A 130-year-old Tradition," *Ramsey County History* 17, no. 2 (1982): 3–7; *St. Paul and Minneapolis Pioneer Press,* February 9, 1879, p. 7, January 15, 1882, p. 7, May 2, 1883, p. 7; George M. Brack, "Steamboats and Cable Cars—St. Paul's Gaslight Era," *Ramsey County History* 1, no. 2 (Fall 1964): 6; *St. Paul Daily Globe,* June 2, 1888, p. 1; Phelps, "St. Paul Public Library," 1–14.

UNION DEPOT: *St. Paul and Minneapolis Pioneer Press,* April 13, 1880, p. 1, April 26, 1880, p. 1, May 7, 1881, p. 2, April 18, 1883, p. 10, June 11, 1884, p. 3, June 19, 1884, p. 8, August 22, 1884, p. 2, September 28, 1884, p. 8, October 26, 1884, p. 10, March 29, 1889, p. 5; Castle, *History of St. Paul,* 1:230; Chaney, "Early Bridges and Changes," 137; *Northwest Magazine,* March 1885, p. 8, October 1887, p. 32; Condit, *American Building,* 131–38; *St. Paul Daily News,* March 29, 1889, p. 2; *St. Paul Pioneer Press,* April 30, 1904, p. 2, January 23, 1910, sec. 2, p. 1, October 4, 1913, p. 1.

BEARD'S BLOCK: Atwater, ed., *City of Minneapolis,* 419–20; Borchert et al., *Legacy of Minneapolis,* 66; *St. Paul and Minneapolis Pioneer Press,* December 31, 1880, p. 6; *Minneapolis Journal,* February 13, 1910, classified sec., p. 10; Carl G. O. Hansen, *My Minneapolis: A Chronicle . . .* (Minneapolis: Privately printed, 1956), 54.

SYNDICATE BLOCK AND GRAND OPERA HOUSE: *Minneapolis Tribune,* September 23, 1881, p. 7, October 7, 1881, p. 7, November 2, 1881, p. 7, January 1, 1882, p. 1; *St. Paul and Minneapolis Pioneer Press,* January 26, 1882, p. 6, April 24, 1882, p. 6, July 16, 1882, p. 6, December 16, 1882, p. 13, March 25, 1883, p. 9, April 3, 1883, p. 6, December 9, 1883, p. 12; *St. Paul Pioneer Press,* April 2, 1989, p. 2D; Withey and Withey, *Biographical Dictionary,* 129; *Minneapolis Journal,* December 12, 1882, p. [4]; Whiting, *Minnesota Theatre,* 44–45; Conforti, "John S. Bradstreet," 6; Hill, "Variety-Vaudeville in Minneapolis," 71, 81. Note: Tim Samuelson provided information about Oscar Cobb.

CENTRAL PARK AND CENTRAL PARK METHODIST EPISCOPAL CHURCH: E. C. Parish, *A Brief History of the Church Known as Market Street, Jackson Street, Central Park Through Eighty-five Years of Continuous Service in St. Paul, Minnesota* (St. Paul: Central Park Methodist Episcopal Church, 1933), 5–19; Lloyd Peabody, "History of the Parks and Public Grounds of St. Paul," in *Collections of the Minnesota Historical Society* 15 (May 1915): 613; *St. Paul and Minneapolis Pioneer Press,* June 20, 1886, p. 11, July 31, 1887, p. 9; *St. Paul Pioneer Press,* May 17, 1907, p. 2.

NORMAN KITTSON HOUSE: *St. Paul and Minneapolis Pioneer Press,* December 3, 1882, p. 12; *Northwestern Architect and Improvement Record* 5 (May 1887): 37; "Forgotten Pioneers, VIII: Norman Kittson and the Fur Trade," *Ramsey County History* 6, no. 2 (Fall 1969): 18–22; *Inland Architect and Builder,* March 1883, p. 35; Paul Clifford Larson, "Lost Minnesota," *Architecture Minnesota* 15, no. 3 (May–June 1989): 114; *St. Paul Daily Globe,* December 31, 1883, p. 14; Vincent, "St. Paul Architecture," plate 60; *St. Paul Pioneer Press,* May 1, 1904, p. 1; Reardon, *Diocese of St. Paul,* 374. Note: Much of the Kittson mansion's interior was salvaged. Several mantels and stained-glass windows found their way to the Wright-Prendergast house in Irvine Park, according to James Sazevich.

WEST HOTEL: Schuyler, "Western Architecture," 303–6; David Watkin, "The Grand Hotel Style," in David Watkin, Hugh Montgomery-Massingberd, Pierre-Jean Remey, and Frederic Grendel, *Grand Hotel: The Golden Age of the Palace Hotel: An Architectural and Social History* (New York and Paris: Vendome Press, 1984), 14; Loring M. Staples, *The West Hotel Story: 1884–1940:*

Memories of Past Splendor (Minneapolis: Carlson Printing Co., 1979), 9–33, 105–27; *Minneapolis Tribune*, July 6, 1884, p. 3, July 21, 1884, p. 1; Sandeen, *Summit Avenue*, 71; Charles W. Johnson, comp., *The West Hotel Tourists' Guide to Minneapolis and Its Suburbs* (Minneapolis: Johnson, Smith, and Harrison, Printers, 1886), 6; *Inland Architect and Builder*, December 1884, p. 71; Conforti, "John S. Bradstreet," 6.

WILLIAM WASHBURN HOUSE: *St. Paul Daily Globe*, January 27, 1889, p. 3; *Northwest Magazine*, January 1885, p. 4–5; Atwater, ed., *City of Minneapolis*, 545–50; Kane, *Falls of St. Anthony*, 50; Burrows, "Work of E. Townsend Mix," 51; *Minneapolis Tribune*, September 23, 1881, p. 7; *Saturday Evening Spectator*, January 15, 1887, p. 15; *Minneapolis Journal*, July 3, 1921, city life sec., p. 1; *Atlas of Minneapolis* (Chicago: Rascher Insurance Map Publishing Co., 1892), plate 240; *Washburn-Fair Oaks: A Study for Preservation* (Minneapolis: City Planning Department, 1976).

RYAN HOTEL: *St. Paul and Minneapolis Pioneer Press*, July 3, 1885, p. 1; Withey and Withey, *Biographical Dictionary*, 191–92; A. N. Waterman, ed., *Historical Review of Chicago and Cook County* (Chicago and New York: Lewis Publishing Co., 1908), 2:880; John Summerson, *Victorian Architecture in England: Four Studies in Evaluation* (New York: Columbia University Press, 1970; New York: Norton, 1971), 38–45; Schuyler, "Western Architecture," 137; *St. Paul Daily Globe*, June 21, 1885, p. 9; *St. Paul Dispatch*, December 29, 1961, p. 1.

MINNESOTA LOAN AND TRUST BUILDING: *Saturday Evening Spectator*, April 26, 1884, p. 1, January 9, 1886, p. 9–10; Torbert, "Minneapolis Architecture," 255–56; Larson, "Tall Tales," 44; van Leeuwen, *Skyward Trend*, 99; *Notable Buildings of Minneapolis*, 59.

NATIONAL GERMAN-AMERICAN BANK: Donovan and Wright, *First Through a Century*, 62–71; Larson, "Architectural History of St. Paul," 23–24; *St. Paul Daily Globe*, December 31, 1884, p. 9; *St. Paul and Minneapolis Pioneer Press*, April 12, 1885, p. 8; *American Architect and Building News*, July 12, 1884, p. 19; *National German American Bank of St. Paul*, booklet published by bank, 1885, copy in Minnesota Historical Society; *Northwest Magazine*, July 1890, p. 21.

TRIBUNE BUILDING: *Saturday Evening Spectator*, May 10, 1884, p. 4, November 14, 1885, p. 12; Bradley L. Morison, *Sunlight on Your Doorstep: The Minneapolis Tribune's First Hundred Years, 1867–1967* (Minneapolis: Ross and Haines, 1966), 1–14; *Minneapolis Tribune*, December 2, 1889, p. 1; *Minneapolis Journal*, December 2, 1889, p. 1; *St. Paul and Minneapolis Pioneer Press*, July 1,

1883, p. 5, December 2, 1889, p. 1–2; *St. Paul Daily Globe*, December 2, 1889, p. 1.

INDUSTRIAL EXPOSITION BUILDING: *Minneapolis Tribune*, September 14, 1885, p. 3, August 24, 1886, p. 2; *Northwest Magazine*, April 1887, p. 31; Atwater, ed., *City of Minneapolis*, 300, 303; *St. Paul and Minneapolis Pioneer Press*, February 9, 1886, p. 2, February 12, 1886, p. 2; *Saturday Evening Spectator*, May 29, 1886, p. 1, September 24, 1887, p. 1; *Notable Buildings of Minneapolis*, 67; June D. Holmquist, "Convention City: The Republicans in Minneapolis, 1892," *Minnesota History* 35 (June 1956): 64–76; *St. Paul Pioneer Press*, March 10, 1895, p. 6; Berman, ed., *Saint Anthony Falls*, 78–79.

MINNESOTA CLUB: Robert Orr Baker, "The Minnesota Club: St. Paul's Enterprising Leaders and Their 'Gentlemen's Social Club,'" *Ramsey County History* 19, no. 2 (1984): 3–15; *St. Paul and Minneapolis Pioneer Press*, August 29, 1884, p. 2, October 14, 1888, p. 15; *Inland Architect and Builder*, February 1883, p. 15; Larson, "Architectural History of St. Paul," 43; *Minneapolis Journal*, February 27, 1900, p. 6. Note: Paul Larson provided information about Cass Gilbert's involvement with the club.

PANORAMA BUILDINGS: Hill, "Variety-Vaudeville in Minneapolis," 50, 224, 227–28; Kane and Ominsky, *Twin Cities*, 41; *St. Paul and Minneapolis Pioneer Press*, May 1, 1886, p. 9, May 1, 1887, p. 17, April 20, 1889, p. 6; *Northwest Magazine*, April 1887, p. 25, February 1888, p. 34; *St. Paul Dispatch*, May 4, 1889, p. 2. Note: The building permit for the Minneapolis Panorama Building, dated July 21, 1884, lists the architects as George and Fremont Orff; however, *Inland Architect and Builder*, November 1885, p. 52, attributes the building to Long and Kees. One possible explanation for this discrepancy is that Long and Kees designed the building while the Orff brothers supervised construction.

FIRST UNITARIAN CHURCH: Atwater, ed., *City of Minneapolis*, 232; *Inland Architect and Builder*, May 1885, p. 70; *St. Paul Daily Globe*, March 4, 1889, p. 1; *Saturday Evening Spectator*, January 9, 1886, p. 1, January 15, 1887, p. 4; Schuyler, "Western Architecture," 302.

BANK OF MINNEAPOLIS: Paul Larson, "Lost Minnesota," *Architecture Minnesota* 15, no. 2 (March–April 1989): 72; *Real Estate Review* (Minneapolis), April 15, 1885, p. 4; *Saturday Evening Spectator*, January 15, 1887, p. 1; Gerald R. Larson, "The Iron Skeleton Frame: Interaction Between Europe and the United States," in *Chicago Architecture, 1872–1922: Birth of a Metropolis*, ed. John Zukowsky (Chicago and Munich: Art Institute of Chicago and Prestel-Verlag, 1987), 49–53.

ST. PAUL GLOBE BUILDING: Herbert Y. Weber, "The Story of the St. Paul Globe," *Minnesota History* 39 (Winter 1965): 327–34; Burrows, "Work of E. Townsend Mix," 55; *St. Paul Daily Globe*, May 1, 1887, p. 9. Note: Information on the Globe Building after 1930 is from the photography files of the *St. Paul Pioneer Press*.

JOHN MERRIAM HOUSE: Castle, *History of St. Paul*, 2:703–4; Andrews, *History of St. Paul, Minnesota*, 2:118; Merrill E. Jarchow, *Amherst H. Wilder and His Enduring Legacy to Saint Paul* (St. Paul: Amherst H. Wilder Foundation, 1981), 53; Threinen, "Harvey Ellis," 24; Larson, "Architectural History of St. Paul," 37; *St. Paul and Minneapolis Pioneer Press*, August 21, 1887, p. 10; Vincent, "St. Paul Architecture," plate 69; *St. Paul Dispatch*, January 15, 1964, p. 31.

AMHERST WILDER HOUSE: *St. Paul and Minneapolis Pioneer Press*, August 28, 1887, p. 13; Jarchow, *Amherst H. Wilder*; *Northwest Magazine*, April 1886, p. 18; Sandeen, *Summit Avenue*, 22, 42.

LA VETA TERRACE: *Minneapolis Tribune*, May 25, 1884, p. 6; "William A. Hunt," architects file, Northwest Architectural Archives, St. Paul; *Northwestern Builder, Decorator and Furnisher* 1 (November 1887): 16; James Allen Scott, *Architecture*, vol. 1 of *Duluth's Legacy* (Duluth: City of Duluth, 1974), 108; *Saturday Evening Spectator*, July 9, 1887, p. 3; *Minneapolis Journal*, July 17, 1932, sec. 1, p. 9.

THEODORE HAMM BREW HOUSE AND MANSION: Gary J. Brueggemann, "Beer Capital of the State: St. Paul's Historic Family Breweries," *Ramsey County History* 16, no. 2 (1980): 3–4; John T. Flanagan, *Theodore Hamm in Minnesota: His Family and His Brewery* (St. Paul: Pogo Press, 1989), 1–12, 25–28, 60–63, 68, 94–100; *Northwest Magazine*, November 1894, p. 26; Susan K. Appel, "Brewery Architecture in America from the Civil War to Prohibition," in *The Midwest in American Architecture*, ed. John S. Gardner (Urbana: University of Illinois Press, 1991), 205; *St. Paul Pioneer Press*, September 28, 1894, p. 5.

DONALDSON'S GLASS BLOCK: Spiro Kostof, *A History of Architecture: Settings and Rituals* (New York: Oxford University Press, 1985), 596–97; *St. Paul and Minneapolis Pioneer Press*, May 21, 1882, p. 6, August 26, 1888, p. 8; *Saturday Evening Spectator*, January 21, 1888, p. 9; Paul Larson, "Lost Minnesota," *Architecture Minnesota* 16, no. 1 (January–February 1990): 64; *Minneapolis Journal*, August 29, 1903, p. 6; *Minneapolis Star-Journal*, March 30, 1942, p. 1; *St. Paul Pioneer Press*, November 26, 1982, p. 1, August 28, 1987, p. 4.

MINNEAPOLIS GLOBE BUILDING: Schuyler, "Western Architecture," 313; *St. Paul Daily Globe*, May 1, 1889, p. 1; *Minneapolis Journal*, August 20, 1933, p. 5; *Hennepin County History* 11, no. 1 ([January 1951]): 2; *Minneapolis Daily Times*, September 23, 1942, p. 5.

SAMUEL GALE HOUSE: *St. Paul Daily Globe*, May 1, 1889, p. 8; Atwater, ed., *City of Minneapolis*, 234–37; *St. Paul and Minneapolis Pioneer Press*, September 16, 1888, p. 13; *Saturday Evening Spectator*, May 12, 1888, p. 1; *Northwestern Builder, Decorator and Furnisher* 1 (November 1887), which has a drawing of the Gale house by Harvey Ellis; *Minneapolis Journal*, March 6, 1933, p. 5. Note: Paul Larson provided information regarding the house's use as a nursing home.

MINNEAPOLIS PUBLIC LIBRARY: Bruce Weir Benidt, *The Library Book: Centennial History of the Minneapolis Public Library* (Minneapolis: Minneapolis Public Library and Information Center, 1984), 18–38, 109–13, 171–74; *St. Paul and Minneapolis Pioneer Press*, February 21, 1886, p. 14, August 19, 1888, p. 15; Schuyler, "Western Architecture," 132; *Building Budget* 6 (May 1890): 60, quoted in Larson, "Richardson Goes West," in *Spirit of H. H. Richardson*, ed. Larson, 23.

ST. PAUL CITY HALL AND RAMSEY COUNTY COURTHOUSE: Schuyler, "Western Architecture," 296; Howard, "The City of St. Paul," 149; Dane Smith, "The City Hall–County Courthouse and Its First Fifty Years," *Ramsey County History* 17, no. 1 (1981): 8; *St. Paul Daily Globe*, December 31, 1883, p. 10, May 7, 1889, p. 1; *St. Paul Daily News*, April 5, 1889, p. 1; *St. Paul and Minneapolis Pioneer Press*, April 28, 1889, p. 1.

PEOPLE'S CHURCH: *St. Paul Daily News*, April 13, 1889, p. 6; *St. Paul Daily Globe*, February 11, 1889, p. 1; *St. Paul and Minneapolis Pioneer Press*, April 14, 1889, p. 9; Schuyler, "Western Architecture," 301; "Rachmaninoff in Recital," program, concert at People's Church, March 9, 1925, copy in possession of author; *St. Paul Pioneer Press*, January 1, 1939, p. 3.

ABERDEEN HOTEL: *Northwest Magazine*, February 1889, p. 21; *St. Paul and Minneapolis Pioneer Press*, December 11, 1887, p. 9; *St. Paul Pioneer Press*, June 10, 1893, p. 1, July 16, 1963, Picture magazine sec.; Alan K. Lathrop, "A French Architect in Minnesota: Emmanuel L. Masqueray, 1861–1917," *Minnesota History* 47 (Summer 1980): 55.

NEW YORK LIFE INSURANCE BUILDINGS: Kenneth Turney Gibbs, *Business Architectural Imagery in America, 1870–1930* (Ann Arbor, Mich.: UMI Research Press, 1976, 1984), 89–90; *Northwestern Architect and Improvement Record* 6 (June 1888): 50; Schuyler, "Western Architecture," 318; *St. Paul and Minneapolis Pioneer*

Press, September 16, 1888, p. 11; *Office Buildings of New York Life Insurance Company* (New York: New York Life Insurance Co., 1890), n.p.; *St. Paul Dispatch*, June 6, 1967, p. 21; *St. Paul Pioneer Press*, June 29, 1967, p. 24; *Minneapolis Star*, April 7, 1958, p. 12A. Note: Schuyler, "Western Architecture," 320, suggests that the double staircase in the Minneapolis New York Life Building was inspired by the rood screen of St. Étienne du Mont in Paris, built around 1545. However, other than having a pair of spirals, the two staircases do not appear all that much alike. For an illustration of the staircase at St. Étienne du Mont, see *Sir Banister Fletcher's A History of Architecture*, 19th ed., ed. John Musgrove (London: Butterworths, 1987), 932.

GERMANIA LIFE BUILDING: *St. Paul Daily Globe*, January 20, 1888, p. 2; *Northwest Magazine*, July 1890; *St. Paul and Minneapolis Pioneer Press*, April 8, 1888, p. 15; *Minneapolis Journal*, April 26, 1901, p. 7; *St. Paul Pioneer Press*, March 3, 1918, p. 1.

ATHLETIC PARK AND DOWNTOWN BASEBALL PARK: "St. Paul in Organized Baseball," Annals of Minnesota, Writers' Project, Works Projects Administration, Minnesota Historical Society; Thornley, *On to Nicollet*, 13–14, 17; Broderick, "I Remember Minneapolis," 2–3; *St. Paul Daily Globe*, March 10, 1889, p. 6, March 24, 1889, p. 1; *Insurance Maps of Minneapolis, Minnesota* (New York: Sanborn Map Co., 1903), plate 457; *St. Paul Pioneer Press*, July 21, 1903, p. 4; Hennessy, *St. Paul Fire*, 104.

NORTHWESTERN GUARANTY LOAN BUILDING: *Minneapolis Journal*, May 31, 1890, p. 1; Schuyler, "Western Architecture," 318; Murphy, "Cass Gilbert," 31; Whiffen and Koeper, *American Architecture*, 2:252; Torbert, "Minneapolis Architecture," 452; *St. Paul and Minneapolis Pioneer Press*, June 1, 1890, p. 7; *Minneapolis Tribune*, March 3, 1935, p. 11, November 18, 1962, home and hobby sec., p. 1; *Minneapolis Star*, August 11, 1961, p. 11A, April 30, 1975, p. 1B.

METROPOLITAN OPERA HOUSE: *St. Paul and Minneapolis Pioneer Press*, March 25, 1883, p. 9, January 22, 1889, p. 1, March 29, 1889, p. 1, May 11, 1889, p. 1, November 27, 1889, p. 6, December 30, 1890, p. 1, 4; *St. Paul Daily Globe*, March 3, 1889, p. 2; *St. Paul Dispatch*, December 30, 1890, p. 1; Castle, *History of St. Paul*, 2:510; Whiting, *Minnesota Theatre*, 61; *100 Years in the Pioneer Press*, 52. Note: Whiting says the Metropolitan seated 1,576 people.

FREE WILL BAPTIST CHURCH: *Minneapolis Journal*, May 29, 1890, p. 6, June 27, 1891, p. 6; "First Free Baptist Church of Minneapolis, Minn., Fiftieth Anniver-

sary, October 26, 1901," souvenir pamphlet, 7–9, copy in Minnesota Historical Society; Isaac Atwater, ed., *History of Minneapolis . . . and Hennepin County*, ed. by Col. John H. Stevens (New York: Munsell Publishing Co., 1895), 1:209–10; Hitchcock, *Architecture of H. H. Richardson*, 215–16; *Views of the Principal Buildings in Minneapolis and Vicinity Designed by Long & Kees* (Minneapolis: Privately published, [1890?]), n.p.; *Insurance Maps of Minneapolis, Minnesota*, vol. 4 (New York: Sanborn Map Co., 1912), plate 301. Note: The so-called "Akron Plan," pioneered in Akron, Ohio, in 1868, involved a flexible church interior organized around a square auditorium, which could be enlarged for special occasions by opening movable partitions connecting to other rooms. This basic plan was used for innumerable Protestant churches in the late nineteenth century. See Torbert, "Minneapolis Architecture," 333–34.

VISIONS OF CHANGE: THE TWENTIETH CENTURY

1. Here and below, see *Minneapolis Journal*, May 31, 1904, p. 13.

2. *Minneapolis Journal*, May 31, 1904, p. 13; *St. Paul Pioneer Press*, January 1, 1900, p. 8.

3. *Minneapolis Journal*, May 31, 1904, p. 13.

4. There were, of course, instances of large-scale urban renewal in both cities before the 1950s, but none of these earlier projects matched the scope of the work done in the post-World War II era.

5. Kane and Ominsky, *Twin Cities*, 158, 231; Schmid, *Social Saga*, 6.

6. *St. Paul Pioneer Press*, January 1, 1895, p. 11; Schmid, *Social Saga*, 6–7; Kane and Ominsky, *Twin Cities*, 231.

7. Schmid, *Social Saga*, 38, 181.

8. Steve Trimble, "The First Hundred Years: Loring Legends and Landmarks," in Burt Berlowe et al, *Reflections in Loring Pond: A Minneapolis Neighborhood Examines Its First Century* (Minneapolis: Citizens for a Loring Park Community, 1986), 12; Rosheim, *The Other Minneapolis*, 55; Schmid, *Social Saga*, 38.

9. Judith A. Martin and David A. Lanegran, *Where We Live: The Residential Districts of Minneapolis and Saint Paul* (Minneapolis: University of Minnesota Press, 1983), 50–51; Schmid, *Social Saga*, 77–79.

10. Lincoln Steffens, "The Shame of Minneapolis,"

McClure's Magazine, January 1903, reprinted in Steffens, *The Shame of the Cities* (New York: McClure, Phillips and Co., 1904; New York: Hill and Wang, 1957), 43–44.

11. For the condition of the Ramsey County jail, see *St. Paul Dispatch,* January 4, 1900, p. 5. St. Paul's low levels of public spending are mentioned in Martin and Goddard, *Urban Renewal,* 56. In this regard it is interesting to note that as late as 1916 less than 14 percent of St. Paul's streets were paved or macadamized, according to the *St. Paul Dispatch and Pioneer Press Almanac and Year-Book* (St. Paul: Dispatch Printing Co., 1916), 633. As of 1992 some residential streets in St. Paul were still without true paving, curbs, or gutters. By contrast all Minneapolis streets have been paved.

12. A plan for renovating and restoring city hall was developed in 1983, but a limited amount of work has been done to date. For more on this plan, see Frederick Bentz/Milo Thompson/Robert Rietow, Inc., and Miller Dunwiddie Architects, Inc., *A Civic Place: The Comprehensive Plan for Revitalizing the City Hall Courthouse* (Minneapolis: City of Minneapolis, 1983). Plans for a new federal courthouse, being finalized in 1992, could eventually lead to the creation of a plaza or mall along the Fourth Street side of city hall, thereby fulfilling at last the dream of its architects.

13. Borchert et al., *Legacy of Minneapolis,* 30.

14. Larson, "Tall Tales," 48; Bennett, *Plan of Minneapolis,* 122.

15. The Manhattan Building referred to here should not be confused with a seven-story building nearby that once had the same name. This building was completed in 1891 at the southeast corner of Fifth and Robert streets. It still stood in 1991 and was known as the Empire Building.

16. Temple banks in America go back to 1824 when William Strickland's Second Bank of the United States was completed in Philadelphia. This bank, with its great Doric portico, was one of the first Greek Revival buildings in the country; see Whiffen and Koeper, *American Architecture,* 1:153–56.

17. For Dayton's, see *St. Paul Pioneer Press,* March 28, 1990, p. 1E. For Donaldson's, see Paul Larson, "Lost Minnesota," *Architecture Minnesota* 16, no. 1 (January–February 1990): 64. In St. Paul, both the Emporium and Golden Rule were enlarged over a period of years, but it was not until about 1915 that their buildings were extended to full block length.

18. Nineteenth-century arcades in Minneapolis included the Syndicate Arcade (part of the Syndicate Block on Nicollet Avenue), which opened in 1883, and the Times Arcade (1889) on Fourth Street South near Marquette Avenue. St. Paul had the Endicott Arcade (1890) between Fourth and Fifth streets near Robert Street, the Murray Arcade (ca. 1890) between Seventh and Eighth streets near Robert, and the Grand Arcade (1893) between Fourth and Fifth streets near St. Peter Street. All were gone in 1991 except for the Endicott.

19. For a good description of mill construction, see Eaton, *Gateway Cities,* 10–13.

20. Banham, *Concrete Atlantis,* 23–107; Condit, *American Building,* 243.

21. "A List of Tall Reinforced Concrete Buildings of Ten Stories or More," unpublished survey compiled by Portland Cement Assn., Skokie, Ill., October 1927, rev. January 1930. California at this time had eleven such buildings, Illinois only one, and Michigan none. The author is grateful to Robert Frame for providing a copy of this study.

22. *St. Paul Pioneer Press,* December 30, 1989, p. 9A.

23. Condit, *American Building,* 259.

24. Schmid, *Social Saga,* 12.

25. *Dispatch and Pioneer Press Almanac, 1916,* 603.

26. The State Theater, designed by Chicago architect J. E. O. Pridmore was restored in 1990–91 as part of the new La Salle Plaza shopping and office complex.

27. Linda Johnson, "A Place to Worship: The Churches of Loring," in *Reflections in Loring Pond,* 82–83, 86, 88–89.

28. For the first Swedish Tabernacle, see *St. Paul Pioneer Press,* August 12, 1903, p. 2. For the building's acoustics, see *The Book of Minnesota* (St. Paul: Pioneer Press Co., 1903), 107.

29. There is a discussion of the Wesley Temple Building in van Leeuwen, *Skyward Trend,* 71–78. See also Bill Scott, "A Place to Live: An Architectural History of Loring," in *Reflections in Loring Pond,* 67.

30. *St. Paul Pioneer Press,* October 31, 1907, special sec., n.p.

31. Scott, "A Place to Live," 57–58; Sandeen, *Summit Avenue,* 108.

32. Gary Phelps, "Aronovici's Campaign to Clean Up St. Paul," *Ramsey County History* 15, no. 2 (1980): 11–17; *Fortune Magazine,* April 1936, p. 118.

33. The information on architects here and three paragraphs below comes primarily from Torbert, "Minneapolis Architecture," 419–63, and Larson, "Architectural History of St. Paul," 47–72.

34. For Masqueray's life and career, see Lathrop, "Emmanuel L. Masqueray," 43-56; Larson, "Architectural History of St. Paul," 57–59; Hansen, *Cathedral of Saint*

Paul, 7–8, 21–25, 31–36, 46, 48.

35. The best introduction to the work of William Purcell and George Elmslie remains H. Allen Brooks, *The Prairie School: Frank Lloyd Wright and His Midwest Contemporaries* (Toronto: University of Toronto Press, 1972; New York: Norton, 1976). See also Larry Millett, *The Curve of the Arch: The Story of Louis Sullivan's Owatonna Bank* (St. Paul: Minnesota Historical Society Press, 1985), and Craig Zabel, "George Grant Elmslie and the Glory and Burden of the Sullivan Legacy," in *The Midwest in American Architecture,* ed. John S. Gardner (Urbana: University of Illinois Press, 1991). At least one other architect of note arrived in the Twin Cities shortly after the turn of the century. This was Franklin Ellerbe, who established a firm in St. Paul in 1909. Ellerbe was not especially significant as a designer, but the firm he founded later evolved into one of the nation's largest, known as Ellerbe Becket, Inc., and based in Minneapolis; see Bonnie Richter, ed., *The Ellerbe Tradition: Seventy Years of Architecture and Engineering* (Minneapolis: Ellerbe, Inc., 1980).

36. In many cases, outside architects won important commissions in the Twin Cities because of family or social connections. Litchfield, for example, was well known to the chief patron of the St. Paul Public Library, James J. Hill. Litchfield's father, W. B. Litchfield, had once been president of the St. Paul and Pacific Railway, predecessor to Hill's Great Northern. See Frame, *James J. Hill's St. Paul,* 30–31.

37. Kees and Colburn's largest work in St. Paul was the Lowry Medical Arts Building (1912, extant).

38. *Minneapolis Journal,* May 1, 1902, building and improvement edition, p. 5.

39. For more on the popularity of the bungalow, see Clark, *American Home,* 171–92. Louis Lockwood is often credited with introducing the bungalow style to the Twin Cities with his design for a house in St. Paul in 1899.

40. For Liebenberg and Kaplan, see *Marquee on Main Street: Jack Liebenberg's Movie Theaters, 1928–41* (Minneapolis: University of Minnesota Art Gallery, 1982). One of the firm's few downtown theaters was the Gopher (1938, gone) on Hennepin Avenue in Minneapolis.

41. The Forum and everything around it were swallowed up in 1979 by the huge City Center office-shopping-hotel complex, which opened three years later. Much of the Forum's interior was saved and later remounted in a new restaurant called the Paramount, but the old magic could not be restored. The Paramount closed in 1990, and the fate of the Forum interior remained uncertain.

42. *Fortune Magazine,* April 1936, p. 112–19. St. Paul was, as the magazine suggested, a noted gangster hangout in the 1930s. Bars along St. Peter Street were particularly favored by this clientele. *Fortune* claimed that "St. Peter Street is the toughest highway in the country" (p. 119) and "If you want somebody killed, inquire about St. Peter Street" (p. 112).

43. Lewis's comments are quoted in Eaton, *Gateway Cities,* 6.

44. For the Chapel of St. Paul, see Williams, *Saint Paul to 1875,* 113, and Ambrose McNulty, "The Chapel of St. Paul and the Beginnings of the Catholic Church in Minnesota," in *Collections of the Minnesota Historical Society* 10 (February 1905): 244–45.

45. Jane Jacobs, *The Death and Life of Great American Cities* (New York: Random House, 1961). Philadelphia's experience with urban renewal is discussed in Jon C. Teaford, *The Rough Road to Renaissance: Urban Revitalization in America, 1940–1985* (Baltimore: Johns Hopkins University Press, 1990), 151.

46. Bernard J. Frieden and Lynne B. Sagalyn, *Downtown, Inc.: How America Rebuilds Cities* (Cambridge, Mass.: MIT Press, 1989), 11–13; Martin and Goddard, *Urban Renewal,* 69–70.

47. Georges Eugene Haussmann's creation of new boulevards in Paris in the 1860s was one of the first modern examples of urban renewal. See Berman, *All That Is Solid,* 150–52. Skyways were one product of the modernist obsession with separating vehicles from pedestrians. Loewy's St. Paul plan was discussed in a series of articles in the *St. Paul Dispatch* in 1945. For his proposal for apartment buildings on Kellogg Boulevard, see *St. Paul Dispatch,* April 3, 1945, p. 16.

48. Nichols's comments are in *St. Paul Pioneer Press,* January 11, 1970, leisure sec., p. 1. The 1957 planning conference is mentioned in Frieden and Sagalyn, *Downtown,* 16. For Wright's remarks, see *Northwest Architect,* November–December 1956, p. 32–33. Wright's vision of a distinctly American mix of urban and suburban space, which he called "Broadacre City," seems to be coming true as suburbs continue to sprawl away from the old core cities. For fascinating discussions of this trend, see two works by Robert Fishman, *Bourgeois Utopias: The Rise and Fall of Suburbia* (New York: Basic Books, 1987), and "Megalopolis Unbound," *Wilson Quarterly,* Winter 1990. See also John Herbers, *The New Heartland: America's Flight Beyond the Suburbs and How It Is Changing Our Future* (New York: Times Books, 1986); Joel Garreau, *Edge City: Life on the New Frontier* (New York: Doubleday, 1991).

49. Frieden and Sagalyn, *Downtown*, 21–24.

50. Here and below, Martin and Goddard, *Urban Renewal*, 26–27, 48.

51. For a delightful account of life on the West Side flats in the early years of this century, see William Hoffman, *Those Were the Days* (Minneapolis: T. S. Denison and Co., 1957). See also Sara Bashefkin Ryder, *Of Thee I Write: I Am a Product of the St. Paul West Side Flats* ([St. Paul?]: The Author, 1989).

52. Sumner Field was the first true public housing project in the Twin Cities. Here and below, see Martin and Goddard, *Urban Renewal*, 32–41; Martin and Lanegran, *Where We Live*, 51–53.

53. Here and below, Rosheim, *The Other Minneapolis*, iii, 165–66, 174.

54. Mack, "Gateways of Change," 36–39.

55. Martin and Goddard, *Urban Renewal*, 60, 64–66.

56. Teaford, *Rough Road*, 214. About the only new works of real quality in the Gateway were Minoru Yamasaki's Northwestern National Life Insurance Building (1963) and Gunnar Birkerts's Federal Reserve Bank (1973). Birkerts's building, however, faced an uncertain future in 1991 after the bank announced plans to build a new structure.

57. Victor Gruen and Associates were the architects for Southdale and Dayton's St. Paul store. The firm also conducted a planning study of downtown St. Paul in 1958–59.

58. Robert Van Hoef, quoted in *St. Paul Pioneer Press*, August 10, 1986, p. 6C. The 1958 study is in Martin and Goddard, *Urban Renewal*, 69.

59. *Capital Centre: A Project for the Central Business District of Downtown St. Paul* ([St. Paul: Metropolitan Improvement Committee, 1962]).

60. In 1990 there was talk of moving the New York Life eagle to Mears Park, but as of 1992 the big bird remained on its perch by a parking ramp at Fourth and Jackson streets.

61. Frieden and Sagalyn, *Downtown*, 120.

62. Hugh Ferriss, *The Metropolis of Tomorrow* (New York: Ives Washburn, 1929; Princeton, N.J.: Princeton Architectural Press, 1986), 66–67. For Purcell's "highwalk" proposal, see *Northwest Architect*, March–April 1955, p. 58–60.

63. The first Minneapolis skyway is discussed in Bernard Jacob and Carol Morphew, *Pocket Architecture: A Walking Guide to the Architecture of Downtown Minneapolis and Downtown St. Paul* (Minneapolis: Minnesota Society, American Institute of Architects, 1984; 2d ed., rev., 1987), unpaginated. The first modern, glass-sided skyway

bridge actually appeared in downtown St. Paul in 1956. It was built by the Golden Rule Department Store to carry pedestrians across Eighth Street to a new parking ramp. But this rather crude, unheated bridge was never intended to be part of a larger system, as was the bridge built over Fourth Street in 1967. The St. Paul planner's comments are in *St. Paul Pioneer Press*, March 6, 1966, sec. 3, p. 6.

64. William H. Whyte, *City: Rediscovering the Center* (New York: Doubleday, 1988), 228.

65. Martin and Goddard, *Urban Renewal*, 77–78.

66. For a good description of the Loring Greenway project, see *Loring Park Development Progress Report* (Minneapolis: City of Minneapolis, 1975).

67. For Landmark Center, see Eileen Michels, with a chapter by Nate N. Bomberg, *A Landmark Reclaimed* (St. Paul: Minnesota Landmarks, 1977).

68. Another big improvement in downtown St. Paul—the rebuilding of Mears Park—began in 1990 and was to be finished in 1992. The park, buried in bricks during a misguided makeover in 1973, will have far more green space in its new form.

69. Block "E" is bounded by Sixth and Seventh streets, Hennepin Avenue, and First Avenue North. The block once offered an unsavory but lively mix of bars, bookstores, porno theaters, and entertainment arcades, all occupying a jumble of old brick buildings along Hennepin. Citing high crime statistics, fears of street violence, and a desire to create a more attractive setting for the new Minnesota Timberwolves arena (Target Center), the city of Minneapolis bought most of the buildings on Block "E" and tore them down. An upscale entertainment complex has been promised for the site, but as of 1992 most of the block was being used as a parking lot. Meanwhile the vigorous street life that was once attracted to this stretch of Hennepin has disappeared.

70. Architects in the 1980s began to move away from plazas, and a few—such as Pelli—made a genuine effort to relate their large new buildings to the street.

Building Profiles

CREAM OF WHEAT BUILDING: *Minneapolis Star*, June 17, 1947, p. 1; Mike Diamanti, "Great Milling Families of Minneapolis," Part 4, *Lake Area News* (Minneapolis), September 1988, p. 24; *Minneapolis Journal*, July 4, 1903, p. 11, November 19, 1904, p. 10; Howard S. Knowlton, "The New Building for the Cream of Wheat Company," *Engineering Record*, October 29, 1904, p. 513;

Notable Buildings of Minneapolis, 53; *Minneapolis Tribune*, November 8, 1939, p. 13.

BRADSTREET SHOP AND CRAFTHOUSE: "John Scott Bradstreet," memorial pamphlet, 1916, Minnesota Historical Society; Conforti, "John S. Bradstreet," 2–6, 10, 13, 16–21, 29; Schuyler, "Western Architecture," 306; *Northwest Magazine*, April 1887, p. 45; *Minneapolis Journal*, January 30, 1904, p. 5; "John S. Bradstreet & Co.," pamphlet, 1905, Minnesota Historical Society.

FREDERIC CLIFFORD HOUSE: Harry Jones Scrapbooks, Hennepin County Historical Society, Minneapolis; *Minneapolis Star*, June 17, 1947, p. 1; *Minneapolis Tribune*, May 23, 1968, p. 28. Note: Jones also designed a house in Minneapolis for Emery Mapes, who along with Clifford was one of the founders of the Cream of Wheat Company in North Dakota.

ST. PAUL AUDITORIUM: *St. Paul Pioneer Press*, May 9, 1893, p. 9, April 3, 1907, p. 1, 2, 4; "Report of the Board of Auditorium Commissioners," St. Paul, 1907, Minnesota Historical Society; *The Auditorium at St. Paul, Reed & Stem, Architects* (St. Paul: Midway Publishing Co., [1910?]), n.p. Note: The 1893 auditorium was on the north side of Eighth Street between Cedar and Minnesota streets.

SELBY AVENUE STREETCAR TUNNEL: Brian J. Cudahy, *Cash, Tokens, and Transfers: A History of Urban Mass Transit in North America* (New York: Fordham University Press, 1990), 27–34; *St. Paul Pioneer Press*, June 13, 1886, p. 15, May 28, 1887, p. 5, January 28, 1888, p. 1, August 11, 1907, sec. 2, p. 1, 4; *St. Paul Daily Globe*, January 22, 1888, p. 2; Olson, *Electric Railways*, 16; Brack, "Gaslight Era," 4–5. Note: The maximum grade for cable cars in San Francisco is 22 percent.

RADISSON HOTEL: *Minneapolis Journal*, December 12, 1909, part 10, Hotel Radisson sec., p. 2, 9; Torbert, "Minneapolis Architecture," 419–20; *Minneapolis Golden Jubilee, 1867–1917: A History of Fifty Years of Civic and Commercial Progress* (Minneapolis: [Tribune Job Printing Co.?], 1917), 84; Sharon S. Darling, with Richard Zakin, *Teco: Art Pottery of the Prairie School* (Erie, Penn.: Erie Art Museum, 1989), 60. Note: The Dyckman Hotel was the first in the city to offer a private bath with each room. The Radisson's claim to be the tallest concrete-frame building in the world in 1909 was not true. A sixteen-story concrete-frame office building had gone up in Cincinnati six years earlier; see *Architecture and Construction in Cincinnati: A Guide to Builders, Designers and Buildings* (Cincinnati: Architectural Foundation of Cincinnati, 1987), 54.

LOEB ARCADE: Johann Friedrich Geist, *Arcades: The History of a Building Type* (Cambridge, Mass.: MIT Press, 1985), 237–44, 371–401, 448–49, 539–42; Frank Lloyd Wright, *An Autobiography* (New York: Duell, Sloan & Pearce, 1943), 101; *Western Architect* 20 (December 1914): 128 (following). Note: Photographs at the Minnesota Historical Society show that the fifth floor was added to the Loeb Arcade no later than 1923.

GREAT NORTHERN STATION: *Western Architect* 19 (February 1913): 16 (following); Michael A. Diamanti, "Depot at the Crossroads," *Mpls.-St. Paul Magazine*, December 1988, p. 138; John A. Droege, *Passenger Terminals and Trains* (New York: McGraw-Hill, 1916; Milwaukee: Kalmbach Publishing Co., 1969), 99–103; John K. Sherman, "New Architecture Needs More Color and Variety," *Hennepin County History* [20, no. 3] (Winter 1961): 30; Rosheim, *The Other Minneapolis*, 162–63.

GATEWAY PARK AND PAVILION: Wirth, *Park System*, 180–84; *Western Architect* 12 (December 1908): 79 (following); Torbert, "Minneapolis Architecture," 459–61; Rosheim, *The Other Minneapolis*, 95, 168.

CAPITOL THEATRE: *St. Paul Pioneer Press*, September 3, 1920, p. 21, September 8, 1920, p. 12, 13, September 9, 1920, p. 1, 5; David Naylor, *American Picture Palaces: The Architecture of Fantasy* (New York: Van Nostrand Reinhold, 1981), 40; *St. Paul Dispatch*, September 8, 1920, p. 30, May 4, 1965, p. 19, June 16, 1965, p. 66.

MINNESOTA THEATER: James Zieba, "Minnesota Theatre, Minneapolis," *Marquee: The Journal of the Theatre Historical Society* 5 (First Quarter 1973): 12–15; Withey and Withey, *Biographical Dictionary*, 401–2; *Minneapolis Journal*, March 19, 1928, p. 11, March 23, 1928, p. 37, 39, 40; *Minneapolis Tribune*, March 24, 1928, p. 1, March 25, 1928, arts sec., p. 5; *Minneapolis Star*, October 9, 1958, sec. B., p. 2–Z1.

BIBLIOGRAPHY

NOTE: This bibliography is limited to works I found especially helpful in preparing this book. The footnotes contain references to many additional works dealing with specific people, places, and buildings in the Twin Cities.

Altshuler, Alan A. *The City Planning Process: A Political Analysis.* Ithaca, N.Y.: Cornell University Press, 1965.

Anfinson, Scott F. *Archaeological Potentials on the West Side of the Central Minneapolis Waterfront.* St. Paul: Minnesota Historical Society, 1984.

Atwater, Isaac, ed. *History of the City of Minneapolis, Minnesota.* New York: Munsell and Co., 1893.

Banham, Reyner. *A Concrete Atlantis: U.S. Industrial Building and European Modern Architecture, 1900–1925.* Cambridge, Mass.: MIT Press, 1986.

Bennett, Edward H., with Andrew Wright Crawford. *Plan of Minneapolis.* Minneapolis: Civic Commission, 1917.

———, William E. Parsons, and George H. Herrold. *Plan of Saint Paul: The Capital City of Minnesota.* [St. Paul]: Commissioner of Public Works, 1922.

Berlowe, Burt et al. *Reflections in Loring Pond: A Minneapolis Neighborhood Examines Its First Century.* Minneapolis: Citizens for a Loring Park Community, 1986.

Berman, James, ed. *Saint Anthony Falls Rediscovered.* Minneapolis: Minneapolis Riverfront Development Coordination Board, 1980.

Borchert, John R. *America's Northern Heartland.* Minneapolis: University of Minnesota Press, 1987.

———, David Gebhard, David Lanegran, and Judith A. Martin. *Legacy of Minneapolis: Preservation amid Change.* Minneapolis: Voyageur Press, 1983.

Bray, Edmund C. *Billions of Years in Minnesota: The Geological Story of the State.* St. Paul: Science Museum of Minnesota, 1977.

A Brief History of the Irvine Park District: The People and Architecture of an Extraordinary Neighborhood. St. Paul: Historic Irvine Park Assn., [1986].

Bromley, Edward A., comp. *Minneapolis Portrait of the Past: A Photographic History of the Early Days of Min-*

neapolis. Minneapolis: F. L. Thresher, 1890. Minneapolis: Voyageur Press, 1973.

Brooks, H. Allen. *The Prairie School: Frank Lloyd Wright and His Midwest Contemporaries.* Toronto: University of Toronto Press, 1972. New York: Norton, 1976.

Capital Centre: A Project for the Central Business District of Downtown St. Paul. St. Paul: Metropolitan Improvement Committee, 1962.

Castle, Henry A. *History of St. Paul and Vicinity: A Chronicle of Progress. . . .* 3 vols. Chicago and New York: Lewis Publishing Co., 1912.

Chaney, Josiah B. "Early Bridges and Changes of the Land and Water Surface in the City of St. Paul." *Collections of the Minnesota Historical Society* 12 (1908): 131–48.

Condit, Carl W. *American Building: Materials and Techniques from the First Colonial Settlements to the Present.* Chicago: University of Chicago Press, 1968.

Discover St. Paul: A Short History of Seven St. Paul Neighborhoods. St. Paul: Ramsey County Historical Society, 1979.

Donovan, Frank P., Jr., and Cushing F. Wright. *The First through a Century, 1853–1953: A History of the First National Bank of Saint Paul.* [St. Paul]: Itasca Press, Webb Publishing Co., 1954.

Eaton, Leonard K. *Gateway Cities and Other Essays.* Ames: Iowa State University Press, 1989.

Empson, Donald. *The Street Where You Live: A Guide to the Street Names of St. Paul.* St. Paul: Witsend Press, 1975.

Frame, Robert M., III. *James J. Hill's Saint Paul: A Guide to Historic Sites.* St. Paul: James Jerome Hill Reference Library, 1988.

Frieden, Bernard J., and Lynne B. Sagalyn. *Downtown, Inc.: How America Rebuilds Cities.* Cambridge, Mass.: MIT Press, 1989.

Gebhard, David, and Tom Martinson. *A Guide to the Architecture of Minnesota.* Minneapolis: University of Minnesota Press, 1977.

Gibbs, Kenneth Turney. *Business Architectural Imagery in America, 1870–1930.* Ann Arbor, Mich.: UMI Research Press, 1976, 1984.

Grossman, Audley. "The Professional Legitimate Theater in Minneapolis from 1890 to 1910." Ph.D. diss., University of Minnesota, 1957.

Hamlin, Talbot. *Greek Revival Architecture in America: Being an Account of Important Trends in American Architecture and American Life prior to the War Between the States.* New York: Oxford University Press, 1944. New York: Dover Publications, 1964.

Hansen, Eric C. *The Cathedral of Saint Paul: An Architectural Biography.* St. Paul: Cathedral of Saint Paul, 1990.

Hennessy, William B. *Past and Present of St. Paul, Min-*

nesota. Chicago: S. J. Clarke Publishing Co., 1906.

Herrold, George H. "City Planning in St. Paul." *City Planning* 7 (October 1931): 217–24.

Hess, Jeffrey A., and Paul Clifford Larson. "An Architectural History of the City of St. Paul," manuscript prepared for the Heritage Preservation Commission, St. Paul, 1990–91.

Hesterman, Paul Donald. "Interests, Values and Public Policy for an Urban River: A History of Development along the Mississippi River in Saint Paul, Minnesota." Ph.D. diss., University of Minnesota, 1985.

Hill, Lawrence James. "A History of Variety-Vaudeville in Minneapolis, Minnesota, from Its Beginning to 1900." Ph.D. diss., University of Minnesota, 1979.

Hitchcock, Henry-Russell. *The Architecture of H. H. Richardson and His Times*. New York: Museum of Modern Art, 1936. Rev. ed. Cambridge, Mass.: MIT Press, 1966.

Hoffmann, Donald. *The Architecture of John Wellborn Root*. Baltimore: Johns Hopkins University Press, 1973. Chicago: University of Chicago Press, 1988.

Hudson, Horace B., ed. *A Half Century of Minneapolis*. Minneapolis: Hudson Publishing Co., 1908.

Jacob, Bernard, and Carol Morphew. *Pocket Architecture: A Walking Guide to the Architecture of Downtown Minneapolis and Downtown St. Paul*. Minneapolis: Minnesota Society, American Institute of Architects, 1984; rev. ed., 1987.

Kane, Lucile M. *The Falls of St. Anthony: The Waterfall That Built Minneapolis*. St. Paul: Minnesota Historical Society Press, 1966; rev. ed., 1987.

———, and Alan Ominsky. *Twin Cities: A Pictorial History of Saint Paul and Minneapolis*. St. Paul: Minnesota Historical Society Press, 1983.

Koeper, Howard F. *Historic St. Paul Buildings: A Report of the Historic Sites Committee*. St. Paul: City Planning Board, 1964.

Kunz, Virginia Brainard. *The Mississippi and St. Paul: A Short History of the City's 150-Year Love Affair with Its River*. St. Paul: Ramsey County Historical Society, 1987.

———. *St. Paul: Saga of an American City*. Woodland Hills, Calif.: Windsor Publications, 1977.

Lanegran, David A., and Ernest R. Sandeen. *The Lake District of Minneapolis: A History of the Calhoun-Isles Community*. St. Paul: Living Historical Museum, 1979.

Larson, Paul Clifford. *Historic Dayton's Bluff Site Survey, Final Report*. St. Paul: Heritage Preservation Commission, 1989.

———. "Tall Tales: The Story of the Twin Cities' First Towers." *Architecture Minnesota* 15, no. 2 (March-April 1989): 44–49.

———, with Susan M. Brown, eds. *The Spirit of H. H.*

Richardson on the Midland Prairies: Regional Transformations of an Architectural Style. Minneapolis and Ames, Iowa: University Art Museum, University of Minnesota, and Iowa State University Press, 1988.

Martin, Albro. *James J. Hill and the Opening of the Northwest*. New York: Oxford University Press, 1976. St. Paul: Minnesota Historical Society Press, Borealis Books, 1991.

Martin, Judith A., and Antony Goddard. *Past Choices/Present Landscapes: The Impact of Urban Renewal on the Twin Cities*. Minneapolis: University of Minnesota, Center for Urban and Regional Affairs, 1989.

———, and David A. Lanegran. *Where We Live: The Residential Districts of Minneapolis and Saint Paul*. Minneapolis: University of Minnesota Press, 1983.

McAlester, Virginia, and Lee McAlester. *A Field Guide to American Houses*. New York: Alfred A. Knopf, 1984.

Michels, Eileen, with a chapter by Nate J. Bomberg. *A Landmark Reclaimed*. St. Paul: Minnesota Landmarks, 1977.

Morison, Bradley L. *Sunlight on Your Doorstep: The Minneapolis Tribune's First Hundred Years, 1867–1967*. Minneapolis: Ross and Haines, 1966.

Morrison, Andrew, comp. *The City of St. Paul and State of Minnesota*. St. Paul and Chicago: George W. Engelhardt & Co., [1888].

———. *Minneapolis: Metropolis of the Northwest*. Minneapolis: Star Publishing Co., 1887.

Murphy, Patricia A., and Susan W. Granger. *Historic Sites Survey of Saint Paul and Ramsey County, 1980–1983: Final Report*. St. Paul: Saint Paul Heritage Preservation Commission and Ramsey County Historical Society, 1983.

Newson, Thomas M. *Pen Pictures of St. Paul, Minnesota, and Biographical Sketches of Old Settlers, from the Earliest Settlement of the City, up to and including the Year 1857*. St. Paul: The Author, 1886.

O'Grady, Donald J. *The Pioneer Press and Dispatch: History at Your Door, 1849–1983*. St. Paul: Northwest Publications, Inc., 1983.

Olson, Russell L. *The Electric Railways of Minnesota*. Hopkins, Minn.: Minnesota Transportation Museum, 1976.

100 Years in the St. Paul Pioneer Press, 1849–1949. St. Paul: St. Paul Dispatch and Pioneer Press, 1949.

Oredson, Vincent. "Planning a City: Minneapolis, 1907–17." *Minnesota History* 33 (Winter 1953): 331–39.

Peabody, Lloyd. "History of the Parks and Public Grounds of St. Paul." *Collections of the Minnesota Historical Society* 15 (May 1915): 609–30.

Phelps, Gary. *History of the Minnesota State Capitol Area*. St. Paul: Capitol Area Architectural and Planning Board, 1985.

Pyle, J. G., ed. *Picturesque St. Paul*. St. Paul: Northwestern Photo Co., [1888].

Reardon, James M. *The Catholic Church in the Diocese of St. Paul from Earliest Origin to Centennial Achievement*. St. Paul: North Central Publishing Co., 1952.

Reps, John W. *Views and Viewmakers of Urban America: Lithographs of Towns and Cities in the United States and Canada, Notes on the Artists and Publishers, and a Union Catalog of Their Work, 1825–1925*. Columbia: University of Missouri Press, 1984.

Richter, Bonnie, ed. *Saint Paul Omnibus: Images of the Changing City*. St. Paul: Old Town Restorations, Inc., 1979.

Rosheim, David L. *The Other Minneapolis or the Rise and Fall of the Gateway, the Old Minneapolis Skid Row*. Maquoketa, Iowa: Andromeda Press, 1978.

Sandeen, Ernest R. *St. Paul's Historic Summit Avenue*. St. Paul: Living Historical Museum, Macalester College, 1978.

Schmid, Calvin F. *Social Saga of Two Cities: An Ecological and Statistical Study of Social Trends in Minneapolis and St. Paul*. Minneapolis: Council of Social Agencies, Bureau of Social Research, 1937.

Schuyler, Montgomery. *American Architecture and Other Writings*. Edited by William H. Jordy and Ralph Coe. Cambridge, Mass.: Harvard University Press, Belknap Press, 1961. Abridged ed. New York: Atheneum, 1964.

Shutter, Marion D., ed. *History of Minneapolis, Gateway to the Northwest*. 3 vols. Chicago and Minneapolis: S. J. Clarke Publishing Co., 1923.

Staples, Loring M. *The West Hotel Story, 1884–1940: Memories of Past Splendor*. Minneapolis: Carlson Printing Co., 1979.

Stevens, John H. *Personal Recollections of Minnesota and Its People, and Early History of Minneapolis*. Minneapolis: Privately published, 1890.

Stipanovich, Joseph. *City of Lakes: An Illustrated History of Minneapolis*. Woodland Hills, Calif.: Windsor Publications, 1982.

Thompson, Neil B. *Minnesota's State Capitol: The Art and Politics of a Public Building*. St. Paul: Minnesota Historical Society, 1974.

Torbert, Donald R. *A Century of Minnesota Architecture*. Minneapolis: Minneapolis Society of Fine Arts, 1958.

———. "Minneapolis Architecture and Architects, 1848–1908: A Study of Style Trends in Architecture in a Midwestern City Together with a Catalogue of Representative Buildings." Ph.D. diss., University of Minnesota, 1951.

———. *Significant Architecture in the History of Minneapolis*. Minneapolis: City Planning Commission, 1969.

Trimble, Steve. *In the Shadow of the City: A History of the Loring Park Neighborhood*. Minneapolis: Minneapolis Community College Foundation, 1989.

Vincent, Jean Anne. "Saint Paul Architecture, 1848–1906." Master's thesis, University of Minnesota, 1944.

Warner, George E., and Charles M. Foote, comps. *History of Ramsey County and the City of St. Paul, including the Explorers and Pioneers of Minnesota, by Rev. Edward D. Neill, and Outlines of the History of Minnesota, by J. Fletcher Williams*. Minneapolis: North Star Publishing Co., 1881.

Washburn-Fair Oaks: A Study for Preservation. Minneapolis: City Planning Department, 1976.

Westbrook, Nicholas, ed. *A Guide to the Industrial Archeology of the Twin Cities*. St. Paul and Minneapolis: Society for Industrial Archeology, 1983.

Whiffen, Marcus, and Frederick Koeper. *American Architecture, 1607–1976*. 2 vols. Cambridge, Mass.: MIT Press, 1981, 1983.

Whiting, Frank M. *Minnesota Theatre: From Old Fort Snelling to the Guthrie*. St. Paul: Pogo Press, 1988.

Williams, J. Fletcher. *A History of the City of Saint Paul to 1875*. St. Paul: Minnesota Historical Society, 1876; Borealis Books, 1983.

Wilson, Richard Guy. *McKim, Mead and White Architects*. New York: Rizzoli, 1983.

Wirth, Theodore. *Minneapolis Park System, 1883–1944: Retrospective Glimpses into the History of the Board of Park Commissioners*. Minneapolis: Board of Park Commissioners, 1946.

Woods, Donald Z. "A History of the Theater in Minneapolis, Minnesota from Its Beginnings to 1883." Ph.D. diss., University of Minnesota, 1950.

Writers' Program. *Minneapolis: The Story of a City*. Minneapolis: Minneapolis Board of Education and Minnesota Department of Education, 1940. New York: AMS Press, 1948.

Writers' Program, Works Projects Administration. *The Bohemian Flats*. Minneapolis: University of Minnesota Press, 1941. St. Paul: Minnesota Historical Society Press, Borealis Books, 1986.

Zieba, James. "Minnesota Theater, Minneapolis." *Marquee: The Journal of the Theatre Historical Society* 5 (First Quarter 1973): 12–15.

INDEX

NOTE: Numbers in italic refer to pages on which a picture appears.

PICTURE CREDITS

Photographs and other illustrations used in this
book appear through the courtesy of the institutions or persons listed below. The name of the photographer or artist, when known, is given in paren-
theses, as is additional information about the source
of the item.

Minnesota Historical Society collections, St. Paul—
    pages ix (Norton & Peel), **1** (Sweet Studios), **4
    top** (detail of W. V. Herancourt, *Minneapolis,
    Minnesota* [Minneapolis: I. Monasch, 1885]), **4
    bottom** (detail of Henry Wellge, *St. Paul: State
    Capital, County Seat of Ramsey Co., Minnesota*
    [Madison, Wis.: J. J. Stoner, 1883]), **6** *(St. Paul
    Dispatch)*, **9** (detail of George C. Nichols, *Map of
    the City of Saint Paul: Capital of Minnesota* [U.S.,
    1851?]), **11 top** (W. H. Illingworth), **11 bottom**
    (E. A. Bromley), **12, 13, 14** (Illingworth), **21
    bottom** (Illingworth), **24, 25, 29** (C. M. Foote
    & Co., *Atlas of the City of Minneapolis, Minnesota*
    [Minneapolis: The Co., 1892]), **30–31** (*Minnea-
    polis Journal*, Dec. 2, 1906), **33 top, 33 middle**
    (Robert O. Sweeny), **33 bottom, 34 middle, 34
    bottom** (Isaac Atwater, ed., *History of the City of
    Minneapolis, Minnesota* [New York: Munsell &
    Co., 1893]), **35 right, 38–39** (B. F. Upton), **41,
    42 bottom, 43 bottom, 45 top, 45 bottom**
    (Illingworth), **46 bottom, 46–47 top middle, 47
    bottom, 48, 50** (Dearborn Melvill; *Minneapolis
    Times*, Feb. 10, 1896), **52, 53 top, 53 bottom**
    (Illingworth), **54, 55** (Illingworth), **56, 58 bot-
    tom, 59 bottom** (Joel E. Whitney), **60 top**
    (Alonzo Phelps, *Biographical History of the North-
    west, Being Volume Four of American Biography of
    Representative Men* [Boston: Ticknor & Co.,
    1890]), **60 bottom, 61** (Lee Bros.), **62, 63 top,
    63 bottom** (C. P. Gibson), **64 bottom** (Upton),

64–65 *top* (Alfred Palmquist & Co.), **65** *bottom* (Illingworth), **67, 68, 69, 70, 72, 74, 75** *bottom, s*(R. W. Ransom), **77, 79** *left* (Farr), **79** *right* (William H. Jacoby), **80** *left* (Charles A. Zimmerman), **80–81, 82** (George E. Luxton for *Minneapolis Star*), **84** (Michael Nowack), **86** (Illingworth), **87, 88–89** (A. T. Andreas, *An Illustrated Historical Atlas of the State of Minnesota* [Chicago: The Author, 1874]), **89** *right*, **93, 94, 95, 97, 98, 100** (Gibson), **101, 102** *top*, **102** *bottom left*, **102** *bottom right* (Winfred C. Porter), **103** *top left*, **103** *bottom right*, **104** *top left* (Elmer & Tenney), **104** *top right* (Gibson), **104** *bottom* (Gibson), **105, 108** (*St. Paul Daily Globe*, Dec. 25, 1886), **111, 112** *top*, **112** *bottom* (Gibson), **113, 114, 115** (*Builder and Decorator* [Minneapolis & St. Paul], July 1893), **116** *top*, **118, 119** *bottom*, **120** *top*, **120** *bottom* (Gibson), **121** *top right* (*Annual Announcement: Young Men's Christian Association* [Minneapolis, 1907–08]), **121** *bottom* (*St. Paul Daily News*), **122** *bottom* (Rotograph Co., New York), **123** *top*, **123** *bottom* (William S. Horton; *Northwest Illustrated Monthly Magazine* [St. Paul], Nov. 1886), **124** (Illingworth), **125** *top* (North Western Photo Co.), **127** *top*, **127** *bottom* (F. Jay Haynes & Bro.), **128, 130, 133** *left*, **133** *top right* (Kenneth M. Wright Studios), **133** *bottom right*, **134** (Gibson), **135** *top* (Sweet), **135** *middle* (J. E. Barclay), **135** *bottom* (Sweet), **136, 137** *top*, **137** *bottom* (*Minneapolis Illustrated* [Minneapolis Board of Trade, 1889]), **139, 140** (Jacoby), **141** (Gordon Ray), **142** (Long & Kees, *Views of the Principal Buildings in Minneapolis and Vicinity Designed by and Erected under the Supervision of Long & Kees, Architects* [Minneapolis, 189-]), **143, 144** (*Baptist Greetings from Minneapolis* [Minneapolis: Harrison & Smith Co., 1902]), **145** *top left* (Haynes), **145** *top right* (Gibson), **145** *bottom* (Eugene D. Becker), **146, 147, 149** (*St. Paul and Minneapolis Pioneer Press*, May 17, 1885), **151, 152** (Nowack), **153, 154** *bottom* (Jacoby), **154–55, 155** *bottom* (*Insurance Maps of Minneapolis, Minnesota* [New York: Sanborn Map Co., 1912]), **156, 157** (Gibson), **158** (Jacoby), **159, 160** (Truman W. Ingersoll), **161, 162** (Wright), **163** (*St. Paul Dispatch-Pioneer Press*), **164** *bottom*, **164–65** (Ingersoll), **167** *bottom*, **168, 169** *top*, **170** (*St.*

Paul Dispatch), **172, 173, 174** (Gibson), **175** (*The National German American Bank of Saint Paul, Minnesota* [St. Paul: Pioneer Press Co., 1885?]), **176, 177** (Arthur B. Rugg), **178, 179** *bottom*, **180, 181** ("Dinger"), **182** (H. Anderson), **183** (detail of J. H. Mahler Co., *St. Paul, Minn., January 1888* [St. Paul: The Co., 1888]), **184–85, 189** *left* (*St. Paul Daily Globe*, May 1, 1887), **189** *right* (*St. Paul Dispatch-Pioneer Press*), **190, 191** *top* (Gibson), **191** *bottom*, **192** (Becker), **193** *left*, **194–95** (*Saturday Evening Spectator* [Minneapolis], Jan. 21, 1888), **195** *right* (*Minneapolis Journal*, July 17, 1932), **196, 197, 199, 200, 202, 203, 204, 205, 206, 207** *top*, **208, 209** *top* (Wright), **209** *bottom* (Gibson; Wright Studios), **210, 211, 212, 213, 216, 217, 218, 219, 220–21** (*Pioneer Press*, July 12, 1903), **221** *right* (*Pioneer Press*, July 21, 1903), **222** (Sweet), **223, 226** (Gibson), **227** *bottom* (*St. Paul Pioneer Press*, Dec. 30, 1890), **228, 229** (*Northwestern Architect and Building Budget* [Minneapolis], Sept. 1891), **230** *bottom*, **231** *top*, **232** *top* (*St. Paul Daily News*), **232** *bottom* (Gibson), **233** *top* (*St. Paul Daily News*), **233** *bottom* (Gibson), **235** (A. D. Roth), **238** (Gibson), **239, 240** *left* (Gibson), **240–41, 241** *right*, **242** (Gibson), **243** (Gibson), **245** (C. J. Hibbard), **247** *top* (Sweet), **247** *bottom*, **248** *top* (Norton & Peel), **249** (Gibson), **250** *top* (Carl O. Erickson), **251** *bottom* (Gibson), **252** (Albert H. Spahr; *American Architect and Building News* [Boston], Sept. 1, 1894, clipping in scrapbook, Harry Wild Jones Papers), **253, 254** (J. C. Strauss), **255** *bottom* (*Western Architect* [Minneapolis], Jan. 1915), **258, 259** *left* (Norton & Peel), **265** *bottom* (Gibson), **271** (Metropolitan Improvement Committee, *Capital Centre: A Project for the Central Business District of Downtown Saint Paul* [St. Paul: The Committee, 1962]), **278** (Sweet), **279** (Edmund A. Brush), **280, 281, 282, 284** (Ingersoll), **285** *top* (Reed & Stem, *St. Paul Auditorium* [St. Paul: Midway Pub. Co., 1907?]), **285** *bottom* (A. C. Bosselman & Co., New York), **286** (V. O. Hammon Pub. Co., Minneapolis & Chicago), **290 & 291** *top* (*Western Architect*, Dec. 1914), **291** *bottom* (Norton & Peel), **293** (*Minneapolis Star-Journal-Tribune*), **296, 297** *bottom*, **298** *bottom* (Gibson), **300** *top right* (*Western Architect*, June

1912), **301** *top* (*Western Architect*, Feb. 1913), **301** *bottom* (clipping in scrapbook, Jones Papers), **302** *top*, **302** *bottom left*

Cesar Pelli & Associates—**page 300** *bottom right* (Wolfgang Hoyt; composite)

Hennepin History Museum, Minneapolis—**page 283**

Robert Jacobson, photographer—**pages 224 & 225**

Paul Larson—**page 215**

Minneapolis Public Library, Minneapolis Collection—**pages 3** (Earl Chambers; Anthony Lane Studio), **15** (B. F. Upton), **32** (Jules Guerin), **34** *top*, **40, 44, 47** *top right*, **51, 58** *top*, **59** *top*, **71** (W. H. Illingworth), **73, 78, 83** (M. Eva McIntyre), **90, 91** (Arthur B. Rugg), **96, 99, 103** *top right*, **103** *bottom left*, **103** *bottom middle*, **109, 119** *top*, **121** *top left*, **122** *top* (C. J. Hibbard), **129** (E. T. Abbott), **166, 167** *top*, **169** *bottom*, **179** *top* (*Minneapolis Times-Tribune*), **186, 198** (John H. Kammerdiener), **201** ("C.B."), **214, 230** *top*, **231** *bottom*, **250** *bottom* (Norton & Peel), **251** *top* (*Minneapolis Tribune*), **288** (*Minneapolis Times*), **289** (Hibbard), **292, 294, 295** (*Minneapolis Star*), **298** *top* (Anthony Lane), **299** (Lane)

Northwest Architectural Archives, University of Minnesota Libraries, St. Paul—**pages 85, 255** *top* (John Jager), **300** *left*

Oberösterreichisches Landesmuseum, Linz, Austria—**page 46** *top left* (Johann Baptist Wengler)

Osmondson Collection, courtesy of Rosalind Coleman—**pages 35** *left* (St. Paul Souvenir Co.), **75** *top*, **248** *bottom* (Minneapolis Selling Co.)

Ramsey County Historical Society collections, St. Paul—**pages 21** *top*, **92, 116** *bottom*, **150, 171, 265** *top* (composite)

St. Paul Pioneer Press—**pages 2, 7** (Joe Oden), **23, 42** *top*, **43** *top*, **57, 66, 117, 125** *bottom*, **188, 193** *right* (Hi Paul), **207** *bottom*, **227** *top*, **236, 237, 259** *right* (Spence Hollstadt), **260, 261, 262, 264, 266, 267, 268, 269** (John Connelly), **270** (Don Spavin), **272, 273** (John Stewart), **274** (Oden), **275** (Scott Takushi), **276** (Hollstadt), **287, 297** *top* (Buzz Magnuson), **302** *bottom right*, **303**

Maps on **pages 18 & 27** by Alan Ominsky